Ethiopia Under Mussolini

Fascism and the Colonial Experience

Alberto Sbacchi

Zed Books Ltd.

Ethiopia Under Mussolini was first published by Zed Books Ltd., 57 Caledonian Road, London N1 9BU, in 1985.

Copyright © Alberto Sbacchi, 1985.

Cover designed by Andrew Corbett
Printed in Great Britain at
The Bath Press, Avon.

All rights reserved

> **British Library Cataloguing in Publication Data**
> Sbacchi, Alberto
>   Ethiopia under Mussolini : fascism and the colonial experience.
>   1. Ethiopia — Colonization   2. Ethiopia — History — 1889-1974
>   I. Title
>   963'.056   DT387.9
>   ISBN 0-86232-254-5
>   ISBN 0-86232-255-3 Pbk

US Distributor
Biblio Distribution Center, 81 Adams Drive,
Totowa, New Jersey 75012, USA.

Contents

Acknowledgements	vii
Glossary	ix
Abbreviations	xiii
Chronology	xv
Preface	xix

PART I: HISTORICAL PROLOGUE — 1

1. **European Encroachment in Ethiopia and the Rise of Shoa** — 3
2. **The Drift Toward War** — 7
   - Military Preparations — 8
   - The Laval-Mussolini Accords — 8
   - The Stresa Meeting — 11
   - The Maffey Report — 12
   - Eden in Rome — 13
   - Italian Plans for a Protectorate/Mandate in Ethiopia — 14
   - The Hoare-Laval Plan — 17
3. **The Invasion and the War** — 24
   - Italo-Ethiopian Secret Negotiations — 27
4. **The Italian Occupation and After** — 32
   - The Flight of Haile Selassie — 32
   - A New Generation of Ethiopians — 34
   - Ethiopian Collaborators — 35
   - Italian Colonial Policy — 37
   - British-Patriot Collaboration — 38

PART II: ITALIAN ADMINISTRATION AND COLONIZATION OF ETHIOPIA — 41

5. **The Constitution of the Italian Empire** — 43
6. **Colonial Rulers: Jealousies and Antagonisms, 1936-37** — 46
   - Badoglio: The First Viceroy — 46
   - Graziani: A Neurotic Viceroy — 48
   - Graziani and the Duke of Aosta — 50
   - The Controversy over Article 12 — 51
   - The Removal of Lessona — 52
7. **Colonial Rulers: Jealousies and Antagonisms, 1938-40** — 55
   - The Duke of Aosta as Viceroy of Ethiopia — 55

	Reign and Rule Controversy	58
	Teruzzi: Mediocre but Faithful	61
8.	**The Powers of the Viceroy**	66
	The Governor-General as Inspector-General	66
	The General Council	68
	Ministerial Bureaucratic Interference	69
9.	**The Finances of Italian East Africa**	71
	The Financial Organization of AOI	73
	The Cost of Empire	74
10.	**The Administrative Personnel**	78
	The Colonial Personnel	78
	Lack of Preparation of Colonial Officials	80
	The Enthusiasm for Colonies Wanes: 1938 and After	81
11.	**Local Administration**	85
	The Residency System	86
	The Resident and the Ethiopians	89
	Addis Ababa's Military Sectors	91
	The Governorship of Amhara	91
	Governorship of Oromo-Sidamo	92
12.	**Italian Colonization**	95
	Colonization Projects	95
	Military Colonization	97
	The Battle for Bread	99
	Italo-Ethiopian Share-Cropping Agreements	100
	Land-grabbing	101
	The Policy of Limited Colonization: 1938	106
	The Investment in Colonization	107
	PART III: VICTOR AND VANQUISHED	119
13.	Italy and Haile Selassie	121
	Secret Negotiations Between Haile Selassie and Italy	121
	Negotiations for the Submission of Asfaw Wassen	124
14.	**Italy and the Ethiopian Nobility**	129
	Italian Policy Toward the Ethiopian Aristocracy	129
	No Power-Sharing with the Rases	133
	The Rases	135
	Exiled Nobles to Italy	137
	The Rases and the Council of the Empire	139
	The Rases and the Second World War	141
15.	**The Lesser Chiefs**	146
	The Local Chief: Italian Government Spokesman	146
	The Chiefs of Amhara	148
	Nasi and the Lesser Chiefs	148
	Honorary Titles	149
	The Chief: A State Employee	150

16. Divide and Rule: Italian Policy Toward Amhara, Oromo and Muslims	157
The Amhara	157
The Oromo	160
The Muslims	161
17. Racism Italian Style	167
Italian Apartheid Policy	167
Madamismo	170
The "Half-Caste" Children	172
Toward a Special Citizenship for Colonial Subjects	173
18. Ethiopia After the Occupation of Addis Ababa	176
The Massacre of Lekept	181
Addis Ababa: a Beleaguered City	182
The Attack on the Ministerial Train	183
The First Ethiopian Martyrs	184
The Defeat and Execution of *Ras*Desta	186
The Attempt on Graziani's Life	189
The Massacre of Debra Libanos	194
The Italian Abuses and Cruelties	196
The Beginning of the Revolt	197
Stalemate in Patriotic Activities	198
Negotiations for the Submission of Abebe Aragai	201
The Results of Four Years of Opposition	204
19. The Return of Haile Selassie	211
The Internal Conditions of Italian East Africa	211
The Return of Haile Selassie: National Concerns vs. Military Strategy	212
The Italian Problem	215
Haile Selassie and the British Authorities	217
Haile Selassie and the Ethiopian Chiefs	219
The Italian Underground Movement	220
Haile Selassie's Negotiations with Italy	221
Conclusion	224
20. An Epilogue	229
Bibliography	245
Index	259

Tables

10.1 Colonial Positions 1935-39	78
10.2 Colonial Positions Filled	79
10.3 Positions for Colonial Technical Services	79
10.4 Colonial Officials Living in AOI with their Families	82
11.1 Fluctuations in the number of District Commissioners, Residencies and Vice-Residencies from 1936-1940	87
11.2 Military Personnel Employed in Ethiopia: Early 1938	88
12.1 Farmers Settled in Ethiopia 1936-1940	109
12.2 Hectares of Land Reserved for Demographic Colonization	110
12.3 Cost for the Settlement of a Farming Family	113
14.1 Ethiopian Nobles Who Received Salaries From the Italian Colonial Government	137
15.1 The Best Paid Chiefs of Amhara	153
15.2 Best Paid Chiefs of Harar	154
18.1 Estimated Ethiopian Rebel Forces 1937-38	177
18.2 Italian Armed Forces in East Africa 1936-40	178
18.3 Military and Political Expenditures of Italian East Africa, 1937-40	178
18.4 Weapons Surrendered by the Ethiopians from 10 October 1935 to 14 April 1940	180

Maps

Project for the partition of Ethiopia — April 1936	xxiv
Italian occupation of Ethiopia — May 1936	xxv

Acknowledgements

My research in Italy, Great Britain, Sweden, and Ethiopia was made possible by the generous financial support of governments, educational institutions, and private foundations. I express my deep gratitude to the University of Illinois at Chicago for a research grant and a fellowship; to the Italian Ministry of Foreign Affairs for a two-year research grant; to the American Council of Learned Societies; to the American Philosophical Society and the America-Italy Society for grant-in-aid; to the Fulbright-Hays Commission for a one-year research fellowship; to Atlantic Union College for Faculty Research Grants.

I also acknowledge with gratitude the Hoover Institution Press's permission to quote from G. Baer, *Test Case: Italy, Ethiopia and the League of Nations* (1976), pages 217-221; and Norman Bennett, Editor of the *International Journal of African Historical Studies* for permission to republish here my article 'Secret Talks for the Submission of Haile Selassie...' (1974).

This study could not have been brought to a successful conclusion without the moral support, continuous encouragement, daily inspiration of many people, and for putting at my disposal documentation, oral information and for allowing me to consult personal papers. Here are the names of friends, colleagues, and critics who have helped me: Richard K. Pankhurst, the late Giuseppe Costanzo-Beccaria, the Duke Amedeo of Aosta, (the nephew of the former Viceroy of Ethiopia), Paolo di Revel, Alessandro Lessona, Attilio Scaglione, Giuseppe Puglisi, Guglielmo Guglielmi, Armando Maugini, Arturo Marazzi, Giuseppe Rochetti, G. Mariottini, G. Giannini, the late Eric Palm, Giuseppe Cupertino, the late Alberto Viterbo, the late Jole Zambon, the late Gustav Von Rosen, Emilio Spada, Edoardo Borra, George Baer, Giorgio Rochat, Franco Valsecchi, Renato Mori, Gaspare Ambrosini, Mario Gazzini, A. D'Amato, Leopoldo Sandri, Renato Grispo, C. Casucci, Giuseppe Carbone, Armando Cepollaro, Luigi Firpo, Marina Soraci, Dolores Weinberger, Marion Miller, Renzo De Felice, Enrico Serra, Teobaldo Filesi, Romain Rainero, Angelo Del Boca, A. Triulzi, J. Smoot, W. Utt, B. Beach, L. Goglia, R. Greenfield, Claudio Segre, John Spencer, W. Shorroch, Harold Marcus, Wison Bishai, A. Fraser, M. Wehtje, Larry Lewis, Seifu Abba Wollo, Tadesse Zwolde, Jonathan Girma, Joseph Saboka, Donald Crummey, Rolf and Eva Hellgren, Mike Kelley, Giovanni and Lena Valcarenghi, G. Shadel and Brenda Wright.

Above all I owe the completion of this research to the unfailing attention, aid, and assistance of the late Carlo Giglio during my stay in Italy, and to Professor Robert L. Hess for being a continuous inspiration, a patient listener, and for his indispensable criticisms and advice. He has been to me a master, friend and mentor.

And lastly a heartfelt thank you to Robert Molteno, editor of Zed Books for his patience, encouragement and advice in revising this manuscript.

To my wife Margaret and our children, Ingrid and Paul, I dedicate this study.

Glossary

Abagas: A war leader, mostly used in Wollo Amhara. In Gurage it simply means a leader. During the Italian administration it connoted a chief of regions.

Abba: Honorary title for a priest. It has the meaning of father. In Oromo it also means owner.

Abba Burka: Chief of a region.

Abbakoro: Chief of a district.

Abuna: Literally means 'our father'. It is used in reference to bishop and archbishop in the Ethiopian Orthodox Church.

Afanegus: The literal translation is the 'mouth of the king' or the king's spokesman or chief judicial magistrate.

Afagesar: Italian-introduced word to replace the Amharic Afanegus.

Aleka: An Amharic term meaning chief or leader. It was used by the Ethiopian administration to refer to a traditional teacher of the Orthodox Church.

Askari: In Amharic it simply means 'servant', but it is better known as Italian colonial soldier.

Amhara: This term refers to the Amhara people, one of the two dominant nationalities (Tigre being the second) of Ethiopia. The Amharas reside mostly in the northern provinces of Begemder and Gojam, but in Shoa and Wollo they are a minority. The Amharas colonized Tigre, Eritrea and the southern provinces.

Arbagnoch: Ethiopian Patriot. Name given to those Ethiopians who fought the Italians for the independence of Ethiopia.

Asrat: An Amharic term that means 'one tenth'. In the feudal system the people were taxed one tenth of their agricultural crops, therefore the word became synonymous with tax.

Ballabat: A landlord. In the south this title was given to local leaders together with some land. Ballabats are also referred to in the south as 'middlemen' for the Ethiopian

	colonial administration. The Fascist government maintained this title allocating to the holder the meaning of a chief in charge of a group of districts.
Ballabat-el Kebir:	Chief of a region used during the Italian occupation of Ethiopia.
Balambara:	Title given to a civilian local leader. It also refers to a commander of a fort.
Bitwodded:	It is a rank title given to a trusted individual in feudal Ethiopia. Literally 'beloved', it refers to the position of first councillor.
Blata:	Literally 'youth', it is a title implying learning and given to civilians connected with the imperial Ethiopian court.
Blattengeta:	Is an even higher title than Blata and it literally means 'Master of youths' usually bestowed on learned men.
Bekerod:	The treasurer or chief accountant.
Burka:	Is an Oromo term that means 'spring' or water. The Italians used the title too in Harar for local chief.
Cadi:	Moslem judge.
Ciqa-shum:	Local headman; chief of village; widely used during the Italian administration.
Dagna:	A judge.
Damina:	In Oromo it is a chief who presides in the process of reconciliation involving murder. The Italian administration used this title with the connotation of chief of a district.
Dejaz:	Abbreviation of Dejazmatch.
Dejazmatch:	Means 'the one who in the war camp resides near the door of the emperor's tent', or Marshall of provincial headquarters, equivalent to a count. Under the Italian administration the title was stripped of all its authority and prestige.
Dug:	Chief of a circuit, assisting a vice-resident in the Italian administration system.
Etchege:	Traditional title of administrative head of the Ethiopian Orthodox Church.
Fitaurari:	Commander of the advance guard, similar to a knight. In the civilian context the title was given to persons loyal to the emperor.
Galla:	A term used by the Amhara to refer to the Oromo people with derogatory connotations similar to 'Nigger' or 'slave'.
Galla Sidamo:	One of the six administrative divisions under the Italian administration. It included all territories south of Addis Ababa.
Garad:	Local chief in Harar.
Gebbar:	In Amhara speaking territories it meant 'one who pays

Glossary

	tribute'. In the south it implied exploitation and a form of forced labour.
Grazmatch:	He who leads the left wing of the army. In the civilian context this title was given to high ranking government personalities.
Gult:	Conditional land given to peasants provided that tribute was paid and corvée labour rendered.
Lij:	Literally 'boy' used as an honorific for the sons of noble houses.
Kagnazmatch:	Commander of the right wing of the army, or major. In civil life the title was bestowed on governors of districts during the Ethiopian imperial government.
Kao:	It literally means 'luck' but the Italians used it to denote the position of chief in Oromo Sidamo.
Kantiba:	Mayor.
Kenazmatch:	The same as Kagnazmatch.
Maderiya:	A temporary land concession given as a form of payment by the Ethiopian government to civil or military servants.
Malkagna:	Administrator of a small territory under the Ethiopian government and retained by the Fascist administration.
Mesfin:	Prince. The term implies 'high', often in social position or power.
Meslanie:	Traditional Amharic title for regional governors. In the Italian administration it was equivalent to chief of a district.
Negradas:	Chief of merchants or trade commissioner.
Negus:	King.
Oromo:	Is the name of the Hamitic people who live in Ethiopia, Somalia and Kenya.
Oromo Sidamo:	*see* Galla Sidamo.
Ras:	Literally 'head'; a title conferred on heads of important houses, provincial governors, ministers and high officials. It is equivalent to a duke. During the Italian occupation the rases lost all their privileges.
Rist:	Hereditary rights to the use of land.
Sangadogna:	Chief of sub-district, or village chief used by the Italian administration.
Shoa:	The south central province of Ethiopia. Although the majority of the people in the province are Oromo, Shoa is the home of the prominent Ethiopian rulers, such as king Sahle Selassie (1813-1847), Emperor Menelik II and Haile Selassie.
Shoan:	A person of Amhara background residing in Shoa, but includes also sociological Amhara such as Oromo and Gurages.

Shaik-el Mashaik:	An Arab term meaning teacher. The Italians used this title to imply chief of chiefs.
Shifta:	Bandit, rebel, outlaw.
Taq lai Endersalassie:	A governor of a province, representing the emperor.
Teff:	An indigenous grass cultivated in Ethiopia as a cereal grain.
Zapatie:	Italian colonial policeman.
Waraba:	Chief of a district during the Italian administration.
Woizero:	Amharic term to designate the status of a married woman, or mistress, lady.

Abbreviations

ACS	*Archivio Centrale dello Stato, Rome*
ACS/CP	*Fondo Ministero della Propaganda e Cultura Popolare*
ACS/EB	*Diari Emilio De Bono*
ACS/FB	*Carte Francesco Barracu*
ACS/INT-CM	*Fondo Ministero dell'Interno: Conflitto Mondiale Serie A-5-G*
ACS/INT-P	*Fondo Ministero dell' Interno: Polizia Politica*
ACS/MA	*Fondo Ministero dell'Aeronautica*
ACS/MAI	*Fondo Ministero dell' Africa Italiana*
ACS/MM	*Carte Manlio Morgagni*
ACS/MMM	*Fondo Ministero della Marina Militare*
ACS/PAR	*Fondo Primo Aiutante di Campo del Re*
ACS/PB	*Carte Pietro Badoglio*
ACS/PCM	*Carte della Presidenza del Consiglio dei Ministri*
ACS/PCM-B	*Carte della Presidenza del Consiglio dei Ministri, Governo Italiano a Brindisi-Salerno*
ACS/RG	*Fondo Rodolfo Graziani*
ACS/SPD-O	*Segreteria Particolare del Duce, Carteggio Ordinario*
ACS/SPD-R	*Segreteria Particolare del Duce, Carteggio Riservato*
ACS/SPD-RS	*Segreteria Particolore del Duce, Carteggio Riservato, Repubblica Sociale di Salo'*
ACS/TS	*Carte Tommaso Sillani*
ADG	*Archivio Dino Grandi, c/o Renzo De Felice, Rome*
AOI	*Africa Orientale Italiana*
ATR	*Archivio Paolo Thaon di Revel, Fondazione Einaudi, Turin*
CC	Great Britain, Public Record Office, London, Cabinet Conclusions
CSC	*Consiglio Superiore Coloniale*
FO	Great Britain, Public Record Office, Foreign Office Archives, London. Correspondence respecting Abyssinia
GGAOI	*Governorato Generale dell' Africa Orientale Italiana*
IAA	*Archivio dell' Instituto Agronomo d'Oltre mare, Florence*
MAE	*Ministero degli Affari Esteri, Rome*
MAI	*Ministero dell' Africa Italiana, Rome*

MAI/AS	*Archivio Storico del Ministero dell' Africa Italiana*
MAI/AS-N	*Archivio Storico Documentario della Repubblica Sociale di Salo', Italia del Nord*
MAI/AV	*Carte Adolfo Vitale*
MAI/CSC	*Documenti Del Consiglio Superiore Coloniale*
MAI/EF	*Direzione Affari Economici e Finanziari*
MAI/FC	*Carte Froncesco Caroselli*
MAI/GAB	*Archivio Segreto di Gabinetto*
MAI/MC	*Carte Massimo Colucci*
MAI/POL	*Direzione Affari Politici*
ONC	*Opera Nazionale Combattenti*
ONCA	*Archivio Opera Nazionale Combattenti, Rome*
PCM	*Presidenza del Consiglio dei Ministri*
UP/FG	*University of Palermo, Faculty of Jurisprudence, Doctoral thesis of Amedeo Duke of Aosta:* "*I Concetti Informatori dei Rapporti Giuridici fra Stati Moderni e le Popolazioni Indigene nelle Colonie.*"
USNA/ICD	United States National Archives, Washington, D.C., Italian Captured Documents, 1922-1943

Chronology

1855: Coronation of Emperor Theodore II
1867: Sir Robert Napier's rescuing mission
1869: Italians acquire Assab
1872: Coronation of Emperor Johannes IV
1885: Italians occupy Massawa
1887: Italian defeat at Dogali
1889: Coronation of Emperor Menelik II
1896: Italian defeat at Adowa
1906: Anglo-French-Italian Tripartite Agreement on Ethiopia
1913: Death of Emperor Menelik II, succeeded by grandson, *Lij* Yasu
1916: *Lij* Yasu deposed; succeeded by Empress Zauditu; *Ras* Tafari (later Emperor Haile Selassie) becomes Regent
1922: The Fascist take-over in Italy
1923: Ethiopia becomes a member of the League of Nations
1925: Mussolini prepares for war against Ethiopia
1928: Italo-Ethiopian Treaty of Friendship
1929: A-Lessona Undersecretary at the Ministry of Colonies
1930: Death of Empress Zauditu; creation of the Ethiopian State Bank; Haile Selassie becomes Emperor
1931: Haile Selassie grants Ethiopia a constitution

1934: Mussolini and De Bono make military plans for the take-over of Ethiopia

1935:
7 January, Laval-Mussolini Agreements
11-14 April, Stresa Conference
18 June, Maffey Committee Reports
24-25 June, Eden's conversations with Mussolini in Rome
27 June, Peace Ballot's results
15-18 August, Anglo-French-Italian conference in Paris: Italy rejects Anglo-French Plan
24 August-17 September, British Fleet movement in the Mediterranean
22 September, Italy rejects report of Committee of Five
23 September, Ethiopia accepts Committee of Five's report
3 October, Italy invades Ethiopia
14 November, British general elections
17 November, DeBono replaced by Badoglio as Commander-in-Chief of Italian forces in East Africa

7–8 December, Hoare-Laval Peace Plan
15 December, Ethiopian war offensive
18 December, Hoare resigns
December, Graziani defeats *Ras* Desta at Dolo: use of poison gas reported for the first time in the Italo-Ethiopian War

1936:
21–24 January, Italians resist Ethiopian offensive at Wariew Pass
22 January, Laval resigns
10–19 February, Italian counter-offensive; Badoglio defeats *Ras* Mulugeta's army at Amba Aradam
15 February, Chukry Jacir Bey attempts to kidnap Haile Selassie
20–24 February, Haile Selassie requests a British Protectorate for Ethiopia
27 February, *Ras* Kassa and *Ras* Seyum defeated at Tembien
3 March, Badoglio defeats *Ras* Imru
31 March, Haile Selassie defeated at Mai Cew and his army routed at Lake Ashangi
March-April, Various Italian attempts to negotiate a secret peace settlement with Haile Selassie
14–16 April, Italian troops enter Dessie
22 April, British Cabinet permits Ethiopian Imperial family to go in exile in Jerusalem
2 May, Haile Selassie leaves Ethiopia
5 May, Italian troops enter Addis Ababa
7 May, *Ras* Seyum submits to Badoglio
9 May, Italy proclaims annexation of Ethiopia; King of Italy declared its Emperor
28 May, Badoglio returns to Italy
1 June, *Legge Organica* (Imperial Constitution); Graziani becomes Viceroy of Ethiopia
3 June, Haile Selassie arrives in London
11 June, A-Lessona Minister of Colonies
26 June, The massacre of Lekept
28 July, Ethiopian Patriots besiege and attack Addis Ababa
30 July, Abuna Petros executed for his participation in the siege of Addis Ababa
12 October, Patriots attack the ministerial train at Akaki
21 December, Aberra and Asfaw Kassa executed; Ethiopian opposition to Italian rule disintegrates

1937:
7 January, Racial legislation prohibits mixed marriages
19 February, Attempt on Graziani's life
21 February, End of Addis Ababa massacre
24 February, *Ras* Desta captured and executed
March, The Corvo mass executions at Lake Tana; the beginning of Ethiopian rebellion
8 April, Ministry of Colonies changes title to Ministry of Italian Africa
21–26 May, The massacre of Debra Libanos
July, Ethiopian Patriots organize the revolt
August, Italian positions attacked

June, Secret negotiations for Haile Selassies's submission
June, Ethiopian nobles exiled to Italy
November, Attilio Teruzzi undersecretary at the Ministry of Italian Africa
10 November, Mussolini informs Graziani that his term as Viceroy was to be terminated
15 November, New imperial charter: *Ordinamento Politico Amministrativo*
21 December, Amedeo Duke of Aosta, Viceroy of Ethiopia
December, Lessona requested to resign from the Ministry of Africa
December, Formation of colonizing agencies, *Ente Nazionale Combattenti, Ente Romagna d'Etiopia, Ente Veneto d'Etiopia, Ente Puglia d'Etiopia*

1938: Ethiopian nobles (collaborators) visit Italy.
   first budget for Ethiopia prepared
1 January, General Audit office set up in Ethiopia
March–May, General Cavallero attacks Ethiopian Patriots' strongholds
April, Asfaw Wassen negotiates with Italy for his return to Ethiopia
August, Duke of Aosta attempts to persuade *Ras* Abebe Aragai to submit

1939: Stalemate in Patriot activities
June, Racial legislation imposes heavy penalties on Italians found guilty of undermining the Italian race
3 September, Britain and France declare war on Germany
October, A. Teruzzi becomes Minister of Africa

1940: Racial legislation debases mixed race (Italian-Ethiopian) children to the status of colonial subjects
12 February, Alleged date of *Ras* Abebe Aragai's submission
March-June, Italy invests great *rases* with military power
14 March, Abebe Aregai refuses to submit
10 June, Italy declares war on Britain and France
24 June, Churchill invites Haile Selassie to stir up the revolt in Ethiopia
3 July, Haile Selassie reaches Khartoum
July, Journalist George Steer prepares propaganda campaign in favour of Haile Selassie
November, British plan to retake Kassala with the help of Ethiopian Patriots

1941: British authorities propose a separate peace to the Duke of Aosta
20 January, Haile Selassie enters Ethiopia; asks his people to forgive the Italians
6 April, *Ras* Hailu submits to Haile Selassie
5 May, Haile Selassie enters Addis Ababa
May, Duke of Aosta defeated at Amba Alagi; taken prisoner to Kenya
27 November, Fall of Gondar
December, British authorities reiterate proposal for an autonomous Italian Empire under the Duke of Aosta

1942:
31 January, Anglo-Ethiopian agreement
1 May, Italo-Ethiopian plan for co-operation after the victory of the Axis powers
June-July, Lorenzo Taezaz plans to discuss peace with Italian officials in Egypt

1943:
  January, Duke of Aosta dies in Nairobi
  25 July, Mussolini removed
  3 September, Teruzzi removed as Minister of Africa

1944:
  19 December, Anglo-Ethiopian Treaty

1947: Italo-Ethiopian Peace Treaty

1952: Italy and Ethiopia resume diplomatic relations

1956: Italo-Ethiopian agreement on war reparations to be paid to Ethiopia

Preface

When I began to research the Italian presence in Ethiopia during the Fascist period, I realized to my surprise that I was pioneering a period relatively neglected by historians due to the scarcity of source materials, and that people involved in the conquest, occupation, and administration of Ethiopia were still alive. Another impediment to progress was that publications of the 1930s are propagandist and misrepresent Italian colonialism in Ethiopia. There are many studies on British and French colonialism in Africa, and fewer on German, Belgian, and Portuguese, but virtually none on the history of Italian colonialism in Africa. With the exception of R. L. Hess's *Italian Colonialism in Somalia*, C. Segrè's, *Libya: Fourth Shore*, the journalist-historian Del Boca's three volumes *Gli Italiani in Africa Orientale* and Mokler's *Il Mito dell'Impero: Storia delle Guerre Italiane in Abbissinia e in Etiopia* little has been published that deals in depth with what happened in Ethiopia after Badoglio entered Addis Ababa in 1936. Most other accounts are concerned only with the military, political, or diplomatic events of the Italo-Ethiopian War, and their Eurocentric viewpoint reduces them simply to an extension of European history.

I was, however, privileged to consult the archives of the former Ministry of Italian Africa, and other state and privately owned archives in Italy and other parts of Europe. Consequently, most of the information here is derived from unpublished archival evidence. From cabinet papers, the political office correspondence of the Italian Ministry of Africa, and Mussolini's private records among others, an amazingly unvarnished, uncensored picture of Italian colonial rule in Ethiopia emerges. This book is, therefore, part of an ongoing process of remaking colonial history, taking as the basic reference point the impact of the Italian occupation on the indigenous population.

No work can ever be truly definitive, and this study does not purport to be a comprehensive history of Italian colonialism, but rather an indepth study of some special aspects of the Italian presence in Ethiopia from 1935–41. It does, however, treat three main issues not yet faced elsewhere: 1) the Italian administration of Ethiopia; 2) the implantation of settlers in Ethiopia; and 3) the relationship of the Italians with the Ethiopians.

The day-to-day Italo-Ethiopian relations are difficult to reconstruct for lack of data. While British residents and commissioners have left to posterity their memoirs and recollections, their Italian counterparts have been hesitant and far less generous. Of the several hundred Italian colonial officials, only five have written about their Ethiopian colonial experiences.[1]

I hope this study will demonstrate how much remains to be done, and will stimulate further research towards a fuller view of the Italian period in Ethiopia.

When Mussolini decided to invade Ethiopia, it was, with the exception of Liberia, the only independent African country, and a member of the League of Nations. The Italian invasion took place just as nationalist forces in West Africa, South Africa, and Egypt had begun to gather momentum, and colonialism had started its downward trend. The Fascist conquest, therefore, startled the world and was a blow to liberal minded colonial authorities. The anachronistic development of events has baffled scholars who have tried to explain the Italian dictator's reasons for the occupation of Ethiopia.

Recent research questions notions such as whether Mussolini's decision to occupy Ethiopia was to divert the attention of the Italians from internal problems; or that the regime wanted to avenge Adowa; or that Italy needed more land for settling its excess population; and that the Duce, to make Italy a first-class power, created an empire. But although such issues, and others subject to speculation by historians, make a contribution, none in itself provides the answers.

As early as 1928, Mussolini began to cultivate friendships with the French, culminating in the Laval-Mussolini Agreements of 1935. Although Laval insisted that he had given Mussolini an economic free hand in Ethiopia, corroborating documents and eyewitness accounts led to the conclusion that the Franco-Italian Accords went further. A document published by R. De Felice provides evidence that Laval agreed that in case of political change in Ethiopia, France would not claim any compensation except respect for French economic interests. Likewise, when Mussolini went to Stresa, he did not raise the issue of Ethiopia with Sir John Simon of Great Britain, because he knew Britain opposed Italian aims in Ethiopia. By discounting the possibility that Italy would use force against Ethiopia, Britain did not take Italian threats seriously. Junior Italian and British diplomatic officials at Stresa did, however, discuss Ethiopia, and both sides made their position clear: if Italy waged war on Ethiopia, Anglo-Italian relations would suffer. Nevertheless, Mussolini concluded that Great Britain would not go to war for Ethiopia. The result of Stresa was British efforts to appease Mussolini with various territorial exchanges, always upholding Ethiopia's independence and maintaining the principles of the League of Nations.

Although Mussolini failed to get what he wanted from Great Britain, namely, a protectorate over the non-Amhara territories, Italian archival documentation strongly suggests that Italy planned to use diplomatic means, force and bribes to achieve its aims of controlling those parts of Ethiopia accorded to Italy in the 1906 Tripartite Agreement. In Europe, Mussolini used the threat of Germany to extract concessions from Great Britain and France. In this he was successful, with the aid of the diplomatic skills of

Preface

Dino Grandi, Ambassador to London, and the pro-Italian R. Vansittart, head of the Foreign Office. These two men, in an effort to further good Anglo-Italian relations, worked out a compromise, at the expense of Ethiopia, whereby Italy would receive a League of Nations economic monopoly in the southern regions of Ethiopia, Italy could annex most of the conquered Tigre, and receive advantageous boundary rectifications. These proposals, known as the Hoare-Laval Plan of December 1935, were accepted by Mussolini because, although the plan did not recognize the Italian authority, it made Ethiopia a *de facto* protectorate. The Plan failed, owing to British public opinion opposing rewarding the invader with a piece of land. Mussolini then intensified his military action in Ethiopia. Italian and British archives reconfirm that Mussolini did not anticipate a complete conquest of Ethiopia, that he used force to extract concessions from London and Addis Ababa.

Although in December 1934, and in his speeches, Mussolini claimed he would destroy Ethiopia, this was largely propaganda; realistically, he knew that the military conquest of Ethiopia would be costly, but used military threats to back up his diplomacy. In real terms, the 1934 military preparation must be seen as a contingency plan to be put to use in case diplomacy or other means failed.

The East African military campaign became full-fledged war after the debacle of the Hoare-Laval Plan. Up to December 1935, the Italian advance into Ethiopia was limited to a few square miles. It was the arrival of Pietro Badoglio as the new commander-in-chief of the Italian army in Africa that transformed a colonial campaign into a war of invasion with use of massive artillery fire, the employment of the air force, and gas. Italy's military superiority made it possible to win the war against the poorly equipped and badly led Ethiopian army. In spite of military victories and the failure of European diplomacy to bring about a negotiated compromise, Mussolini continued to seek secret negotiations with Haile Selassie. To the very last, he requested concessions in the lands conquered by Menelik II, which were not part of historic Ethiopia, agreed to recognize Haile Selassie and his dynasty as rulers of Amharic-speaking territories and offered Italian financial and technical assistance to the Ethiopian government. Haile Selassie realized that if he acceded to Italian requests, sooner or later Mussolini would find ways to swallow Ethiopia whole; thus after his defeat, he decided to go into exile. In so doing, he made the task of direct Italian rule in Ethiopia easier, as there was no one with whom to negotiate peace terms.

The short period of Italian administration of Ethiopia was difficult because, anticipating a peaceful assumption of a mandate/protectorate type government, and convinced that to reach a diplomatic agreement would take time, Mussolini had made no plans for the administration and organization of Ethiopia. Once his efforts at peaceful negotiations failed to have the anticipated results, his attention was absorbed in diplomatic and military matters to solve the Ethiopian question, and again, no steps were taken to prepare for the administration of Ethiopia. When the Italians entered Addis Ababa in 1936, they had no contingency plans ready as they took on the awesome task of governing their new empire.

The Fascist colonial administration was based on direct rule because they mistrusted the Ethiopians. Possibly, too, they were afraid that by sharing power, the Ethiopians would, in turn, challenge Italian authority. Hence the reason for the Italian use of military government during the five years of administration. Racism was another factor motivating harsh, Fascist rule; the Ethiopians were considered to be inferior to the Italians. This also provided a peculiar justification for continued European colonial domination. The ultimate significance of the Italian case exploded once and for all the ideological legitimizing notion of the European civilizing mission.

Once Ethiopia was defeated, high-ranking colonial administrators could not agree on the type of colonial policy appropriate for the Fascist Empire of Ethiopia. Personality conflicts made a bad situation worse. A crippling bureaucracy required the Viceroy of Italian East Africa to obtain orders from Rome before he could use his administrative and fiscal powers. Initially, no consensus could be reached on the role of Ethiopians within the Italian colonial framework. Moreover, despite a half-century or more of contact with Ethiopia, the Italian government was woefully ignorant of the local situation within the various provinces of their new empire.

Faced with complicated problems that varied from region to region, instead of retaining local chiefs to help Italian colonial officials administer Ethiopia, young and inexperienced army officers were appointed as Residents. Unaware of local traditions and anxious to introduce sweeping changes, they abused their authority and provoked the defiance and antagonism of the Ethiopian population. In some parts of Ethiopia, however, Ethiopian Muslims and part of the Oromo people were favourably inclined towards the Italians because they had freed them from the yoke of Amhara domination. But because the Italians mistreated and alienated the Amhara chiefs, the development of a means to gain favour with the Ethiopian people on behalf of Italian rule was lost. Subsequently, Ethiopian guerrilla resistance and great military expenditure to pacify the countryside made Italian colonization of Ethiopia impossible.

Although the Fascists claimed that the conquest of Ethiopia was necessary to give land and bread to the Italian people, Ethiopia did not produce enough food to feed the invading army, let alone peninsular Italy. Ethiopian farmers did not collaborate with the colonial authorities. Attempts were made to introduce mechanized agriculture and to settle Italian farmers in Ethiopia, but they did not have the time to solve tropical agricultural problems. Farm machinery was expensive, good land hard to obtain, and capital to sponsor colonization programmes was difficult to raise. Moreover, time was too short to experiment with new crops. Italian colonizing attempts produced none of the beneficial results anticipated by the Italians.

Italian failures in Ethiopia can be attributed to lack of preparation on the part of colonial administrators and to limited funds, but above all to the strong desire for independence by Ethiopians and their willingness to continue to fight for it.

Notes

1. Luigi Pignatelli, *Africa Amica*; Pier Marcello Masotti, *Ricordi d'Etiopia . . .*; Alberto Denti di Pirajno, *A Cure for Serpents*; Vincenzo Ambrosio, *Tre Anni Fra i Galla-Sidama*; Teobaldo filesi, "Morte d'uomini" in Fabio Roversi Monaco, *Africa come un Mattino*.

Project for the partition of Ethiopia — April 1936

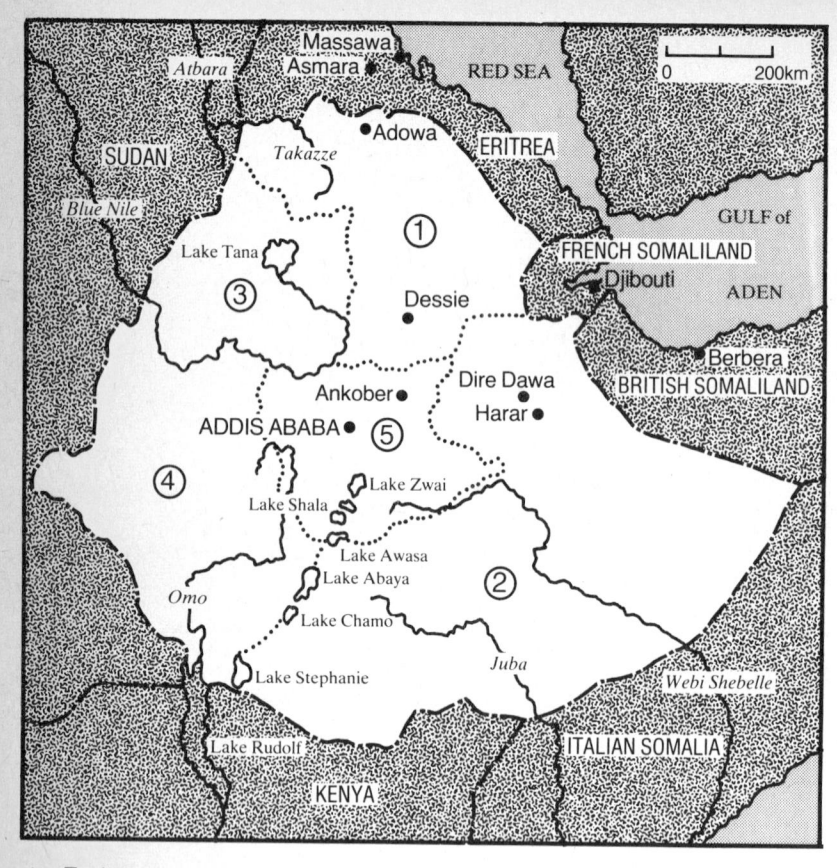

1. Territory to be annexed to Eritrea
2. Territory to be annexed to Italian Somalia/Somaliland
3. Territory to become Italian protectorate
4. Territory to become Italian mandate
5. Kingdom of Shoa under the military and political control of Italy

Source: ACS/RG 57/173-3

Italian occupation of Ethiopia — May 1936

Only one third of Ethiopia had been occupied by the Italians at the time when P. Badoglio entered Addis Ababa in May 1936.

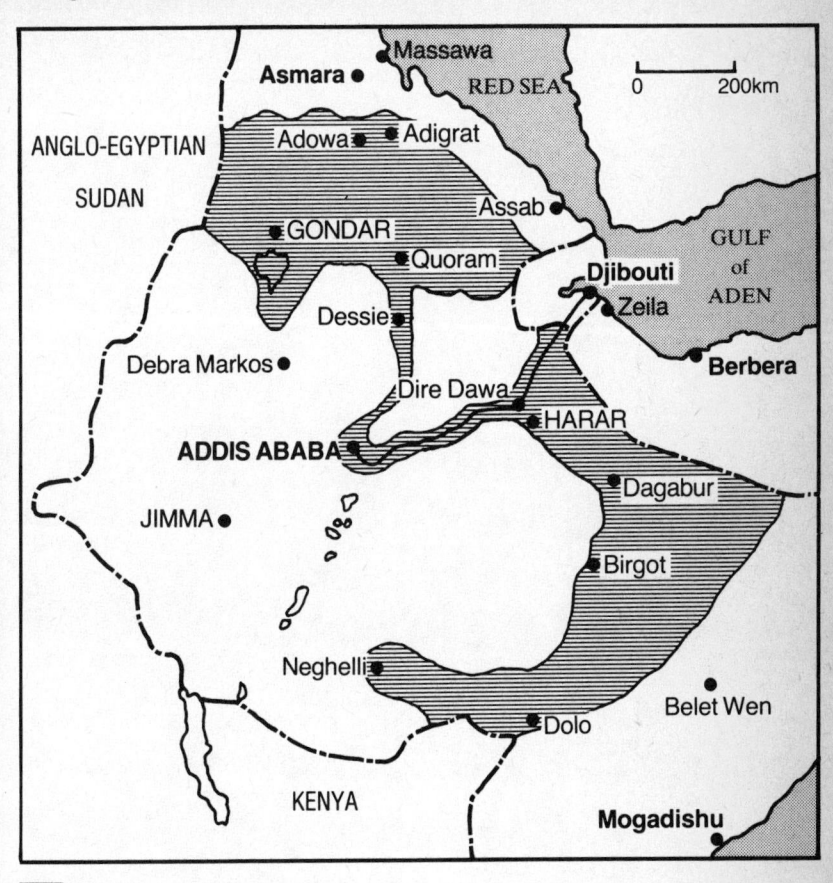

Italian-occupied Ethiopia

Dejaz Gerasu Duki (sitting) and a group of Patriots, operating in Mecha, Shoa.

Part I: Historical Prologue

1. European Encroachment in Ethiopia and the Rise of Shoa

From the late 18th to the mid-19th Centuries Ethiopia was divided into a number of small kingdoms, of which the most important were Gojam, Tigre, Begemder-Amhara and Shoa. The ruling families of these kingdoms all at one time or another aspired to the imperial crown. Outside interferences, quarrels among the nobility, and incompetent kings were responsible for the disappearance of central power, that is, the Ethiopian empire. Power devolved to the nobles, regional rulers and governors who converted their offices into hereditary positions. This time of trouble is known in Ethiopian history as the "Era of judges". Shoa, an independent kingdom, governed by hereditary governors, was detached by natural boundaries from the rest of northern Ethiopia, and thus partially spared the civil turmoil in the Empire. Shoan rulers were able men and it is from them that the former Emperor, Haile Selassie, descended.

With the dissolution of law and order in the early 19th century, bandits or *shifta* appeared in the central highlands; in 1855 one of them became Emperor Theodore II. He defeated the local rulers of Gojam and Begemder but still had to contend with Tigre and Shoa. Military victories eliminated Shoa as an enemy, and Menelik II, the young king of Shoa, was taken prisoner. In his attempt to modernize Ethiopia, Theodore solicited the help of foreigners, but a series of errors led to a British punitive expedition in 1867, which defeated Emperor Theodore's army and he shot himself. With the death of the Emperor civil war once again rent Ethiopia until 1871 when the *ras* of Tigre, who had superior fire-power, was crowned Emperor Yohannes IV. Like Theodore, Yohannes continued a policy of restricting the power of the nobles and laying the basis for a modern state, but struggles with regional lords, French, Italian and British colonial encroachments during the scramble for Africa, and Sudanese Muslims, prevented him from achieving his goals. Yohannes died at Matemma defending his country from a Sudanese invasion. The only real rival for Yohannes' throne was Menelik.

Menelik's claim to the throne was as good as Yohannes', both could claim Solomonid descent and the loyalty of a large segment of the population. But while Yohannes was fighting Ethiopia's enemies, Menelik, with modern French and Italian weapons, methodically set about conquering Oromo-

Historical Prologue

Sidamo, Borana, Harar, and Kaffa in southern Ethiopia. Menelik maintained his rule in the subjugated regions through garrisoned towns, and spared the lives of the conquered people in return for payment of tribute and military service. Yohannes, fearing Menelik's power, came to terms with him; in 1882 they agreed on respective territories. Menelik was recognized as the sovereign over southern Ethiopia, and Yohannes over the north. The contract was sealed by a political marriage between the Emperor's twelve-year-old son, and Zauditu, Menelik's daughter, aged seven. At Yohannes' death Menelik was to succeed him as Emperor. Although just before his death in 1889 Yohannes reneged on this understanding by nominating his son, *Ras* Mangasha of Tigre as his heir, Menelik was so strong that Mangasha could not but acknowledge him as Emperor of Ethiopia. Thus the Shoan branch of the Solomonid dynasty began its rule over Ethiopia.

During the reign of Yohannes the Italians acquired Assab in 1869 and in 1885 occupied Massawa. They soon expanded their coastal beach-heads to the borders of Tigre. *Ras* Alula, Yohannes' general, defeated the Italians in 1887 at Dogali; the first major setback received by any European power at the hands of an African army. The Italians then resorted to diplomacy and, in an attempt to make Ethiopia an Italian protectorate, tried to exploit Tigrean-Shoan rivalry. A Shoan-Italian treaty of commerce and friendship, providing the king of Shoa with arms and ammunition to be used against Yohannes, was proposed. This treaty illustrates the extent of Menelik's power and independence and Yohannes' failure to create a unified Ethiopian state.

Upon becoming Emperor, Menelik concluded the treaty of Wichale with Italy in order to gain European support and consolidate his rule. The Italians construed the treaty as transforming Ethiopia into an Italian protectorate. Menelik's refusal to accept this interpretation led to the battle of Adowa, in 1896 in which the Ethiopians were victorious — a victory attributed to Ethiopian nationalism, the contributions of *Ras* Makkonen (cousin of Menelik and governor of Harar), and the ineptness of the Italian general Oreste Barattieri. Ethiopian independence was assured; but the Italians never forgot the ignominy of defeat which the Fascist government later set out to expunge.

With the military success of Adowa, Menelik had not only forestalled Italian colonial encroachment, but also controlled the northern kingdoms of Gojam, Tigre and Begemder-Amhara. Ethiopia under Shoan rule had reached its present territorial extent (except for Eritrea) and given the Empire a centrally located capital at Addis Ababa.

After his experience with the Italians, Menelik exercised extreme caution in foreign policy. Both *Ras* Mangasha of Tigre and *Ras* Makkonen died in 1906, and Menelik's health became poor; in 1908 a stroke left him paralysed. In 1906, Italy, Great Britain and France, anxious to ensure protection of their interests in case of the Emperor's death, concluded a Tripartite Treaty. While acknowledging the independence of Ethiopia, they pledged to recognize their mutual rights and to take action to protect their citizens in the event of changes in Ethiopia. Lake Tana and the river Nile were recognized as the British sphere of influence, the area around the Djibouti-Addis Ababa railway that of the French, and Italy's over a crescent-shaped strip linking Eritrea and Somalia and running through to the west of Addis Ababa.

When Menelik was informed of the Treaty he was incensed and, in 1907, countered by appointing his nephew, *Lij* Yasu, aged 12, as his successor.

Like other Emperors, Menelik had also to deal with rival authorities at home. He created many *rases* thus augmenting imperial power. He purposely ignored those who, on the basis of heredity, claimed titles of nobility, and instead surrounded himself with men from the conquered Oromo regions. Menelik also employed traditional marriage connections with the Ethiopian aristocracy to strengthen his political position. His fourth wife, Taitu, was of Oromo origin, and one of his daughters married the powerful *Ras* Michael of Wollo.

Menelik died in 1913. Yasu who succeeded him — and ruled from 1913-16 — was clever, but dissolute and irresponsible, and lost his throne by accepting the Muslim faith. In 1921 he was imprisoned in care of *Ras* Kassa. The Shoan nobles offered the crown to Zauditu, Menelik's daughter, and made *Ras* Makkonen's son, *Ras* Tafari, regent and heir to the throne. Tafari wanted to westernize Ethiopia; he was patient, and gradually introduced innovations with the help of foreigners. Tafari also began to concentrate power by gathering a large body of loyal troops. In 1923 Ethiopia became a member of the League of Nations and Tafari visited Europe in 1924. In 1928 Mussolini and Tafari signed the Italo-Ethiopian Pact for economic co-operation providing Ethiopia with a free zone at the Italian port of Assab, connected by road to Dessie. The Ethiopian army was trained by Belgian and Swedish officials, and in 1930, Ethiopia was provided with a state bank. Tafari also attempted to introduce compulsory education for all, but it remained a dead letter outside Addis Ababa. Students were, however, sent abroad to study. When Zauditu died in 1930, Tafari became Emperor with the throne name of Haile Selassie. Now he was free to Westernize Ethiopia, but above all he had to ensure that the country was secure against sedition and secession. He appointed governors in the provinces who were loyal to him. By 1932 *Ras* Kassa was the only powerful member of the old school to remain at his post.

In 1924 the first law to abolish slavery was passed. In 1931 the Emperor followed it up with a radical decree which provided for the emancipation of the children of slaves, and of all slaves upon their owner's death. In spite of these efforts, immediate results were negligible. In 1931 Haile Selassie granted Ethiopia a constitution, but Ethiopia was far from a constitutional monarchy. By 1934 the governors of provinces such as Shoa, Amhara, Gojam, Sidamo, Kaffa, were Western-trained. The frontier areas of Ogaden, Danakil, Aussa, Wallega and other Oromo southern territories were less likely to be loyal to the Shoan dynasty.

Haile Selassie's reforms were interrupted by the Italian invasion. Ethiopia had no effective allies, and with military supremacy in the air, and poison gas, the Italians overran the country. Dissident Ethiopians, who looked upon the departure of the Emperor as their opportunity to re-establish regional family interests, aided the invaders.[1]

Notes

1. A. Marcus, *The Life and Times of Menelik II*, chapters 4 and 5; R.L. Hess, *Ethiopia: The Modernization of Autocracy*, pp 45-7; R. Greenfield, *Ethiopia: A New Political History*, pp. 67-165; and A. H. Jones and E. Monroe, *A History of Ethiopia*, pp. 127-59.

2. The Drift Toward War

Italy's ambitions in Ethiopia resurfaced during the Paris peace treaty negotiations after the First World War. Italian claims then presented were for exclusive economic monopoly and the privilege of using Ethiopian territory to unite Italian Somalia with Italian Eritrea by means of a railway.[1] Fire still smouldered under the ashes of Italian imperialism when Mussolini came to power in 1922.

As early as 1925, Mussolini gave orders for military preparation with a view to waging war against Ethiopia,[2] but not until 1934 did plans for the conquest of Ethiopia receive his full attention. There is no doubt that Mussolini wanted Ethiopia as a colony for Italian emigration. It has been suggested that he invaded Ethiopia to distract attention from economic problems and Fascism's failure to introduce social reforms, or that Adowa was still an open wound and, to enhance his prestige, Mussolini needed to create an empire making Italy a first-class colonial power. Although valid, these suggested motives are not sufficient explanation of the colonial adventure; victory over Ethiopia could exalt Mussolini at home, but defeat could precipitate his downfall and reduce Italy to a third-rate power. Italy's war with Ethiopia was not only in response to internal pressures but also rather a matter of foreign policy.

Mussolini was convinced that Britain and France would not oppose Italian expansion in Ethiopia. His decision to go ahead with the 30 December 1934 military plan against Ethiopia derived firstly from the 1935 Mussolini-Laval Agreements, in which France agreed to favour Italian plans in Ethiopia. Secondly, he estimated that Germany was too weak to endanger the peace of Europe at the time Italy would be engaged in Africa, but would be strong enough by 1937 when Italy would be free to help contain any threats from Germany. For these reasons Mussolini expected that British reaction to Italy's occupation of Ethiopia would be negative, and thus, to gain time, was reluctant to inform London of his military plans. The Italian dictator foresaw a serious crisis with London for which he had to take a calculated risk: to make a show of force and resolve.

Military preparation must be seen as applying pressure on Great Britain to come to a compromise, meeting Italy's wishes. Once this was accomplished, Italy was willing to partition Ethiopia with Great Britain and France. As a contingency measure, Italy prepared for war.[3]

Military Preparations

The years following the introduction of Fascism in Italy, Italian resources were concentrated on the reconquest of Libya. Under Governor Cesare De Vecchi, Italian dominion was expanded in Somalia in the 1920s, but financial restrictions prevented Italy from reinforcing the defences of Eritrea and Somalia. Following the failure of the 1928 Italo-Ethiopian Pact for economic co-operation, Italian policy toward Ethiopia in the 1930s turned from collaboration to antagonism.

In 1932, Emilio De Bono, the Minister of Colonies, began a programme of militarization of the colonies with a view to war on Ethiopia. In 1934 Mussolini decided to hasten military plans for the occupation of Ethiopia. The preparation involved huge sums of money, and quantities of trucks, tanks, artillery, aeroplanes, and stockpiling of poison gas, to ensure Italy's military superiority.

Despite these preparations, as late as December 1934 Italy had no clear view of its political and strategic priorities. De Bono, who represented the Fascist regime, opted for a limited war with limited territorial objectives, while the military, headed by Chief of the General Staff Badoglio, advocated total military action to defeat the Ethiopian army. Mussolini himself did not plan for the immediate execution of a military solution of the Ethiopian question. He anticipated the war in two years since first he had to make diplomatic preparations. He surmised that if the war was brief and Anglo-French interests were upheld according to the 1906 Tripartite Agreement, there would be no interference. He estimated that London and Paris were more interested in friendship with Italy and the maintenance of peace in Europe than in keeping Ethiopia. As the major bulwark against potential German aggression Italy was too strategically important to be offended.

Although Italy was confident that France and Britain would not oppose its planned colonization of Ethiopia and despite it having been the object of intensive study, Italy had no plans for dealing with the situation once Ethiopia was defeated.[4] This may infer either that the complete disappearance of the Ethiopian state was not anticipated, or that Italy assumed that it would receive parts of Ethiopia as protectorate territory or that its objectives would be fulfilled through diplomatic negotiation.

The Laval-Mussolini Accords

Italian diplomacy, on the basis of French sympathy for the Italian colonial demands, proposed the resolution of the Ethiopian problem with an agreement first with France and then with Great Britain.

The Laval-Mussolini Agreements of January 1935 were instrumental in encouraging Mussolini to go to war with Ethiopia. The Italians made it clear that they coveted Ethiopia as the natural territorial extension to Eritrea and Somalia. In 1932, Dino Grandi, then Italy's Minister of Foreign Affairs, met the French Prime Minister Laval who suggested that Italian colonial aspirations could be fulfilled, because Ethiopia was the ideal place for Italian expansion and emigration in the context of the 1906 Tripartite Agreement. This meant that France was prepared to allow Italy a free hand in the zones of Italian influence as demarcated in 1906.

French politicians favoured a *rapprochement* with Italy, not only to solve the outstanding colonial problems, but also to link Italy to the French security alliances against Germany. France had supported Haile Selassie because a stable government was essential to protect French economic interests; but the Ethiopian Emperor's difficulty in controlling "the feudal anarchy" of his administration encouraged the French to consider the prospect of making a deal with the Italians more seriously.

Any understanding with Italy prejudicial to Ethiopian sovereignty would, therefore, have to be made in secret and also to recognize French economic interests.

This change of attitude of France toward Ethiopia explains why, in 1932, the French turned down the Ethiopian government's request for a loan to purchase weapons and to pursue a road-building project. Fearing political isolation, Haile Selassie then asked for a secret treaty guaranteeing Ethiopia's independence, which the Quai d'Orsay refused. Hence it can be surmised that by 1932 France had virtually abandoned Ethiopia to the Italians.[5]

The settlement of the "Ethiopian question" did not come until January 1935, during Laval's visit to Rome. In short order, France and Italy agreed upon the special status of Italians in Tunisia, cession of small territories along the boundaries between Eritrea and French Somaliland and between Tunisia and Libya, and a pact of non-aggression with all states bordering Austria. Other articles remained secret, including possible joint Franco-Italian action against Germany, a protocol which would maintain the status quo in the Red Sea, and two letters in which the French disavowed their interest in the economy of Ethiopia and allowed Italian participation in the strategic railway from Addis Ababa to Djibouti.

Mussolini's main purpose in reaching a Franco-Italian agreement was to obtain French assurances that Italy would be given freedom of action in Ethiopia. Only this could justify Italian concessions to France in North Africa. In return for French political disinterest in Ethiopia, Mussolini was willing to guarantee the security of French economic interests along the Djibouti railway and to make commitments in Europe.

Furthermore, the 4 January 1935 text of the talks, including the Italian interpretation of France's *desistement* (waiver of any claim), was accepted by Laval. Article 2 states: "Le Gouvernement Français s'engage . . . dans le cas de modifications du *status quo* dans la region en question, a ne rechercher aucun advantage en Ethiopie autre que ceux d'ordre economique". Laval anticipated a change of the political status of Ethiopia and thought to secure French economic interests.[6]

Although Mussolini thus received approval for a free hand or an assurance of non-intervention, from France, Laval later defended himself, saying that he had made Mussolini aware that he (Mussolini) had "two strong hands" and that a "free hand" referred to taking and not to strangling. He apparently sought a formula that would present the French attitude as correct even when the accords became public. On 6 January 1935, Mussolini emphasized to Laval the importance to Italy of French non-intervention in Ethiopia, and Laval confirmed that he understood the Italian interpretation of this concept.[7]

At Laval's request, French political and territorial disinterest in Ethiopia was not mentioned in the letters he and Mussolini exchanged lest they become public. Rather, a negative formula was adopted. Thus, when the French government renounced its territorial claims in the Harar region (as stated in Article I of the Tripartite Treaty of 1906), this in fact was in favour of any political-territorial claim in Ethiopia by Italy.

On 7 January 1935, it was agreed that Italy would recognize the rights of French subjects in Ethiopia, based on the treaty of Klobukowski (negotiated in 1908 between France and Emperor Menelik II in which French subjects were granted the rights of extra-territoriality) including the liberty of commerce, and special jurisdiction. This agreement strongly suggests that a change in Ethiopia's political, territorial and juridical status quo was already foreseen, that is, Italian sovereignty would replace the Ethiopian. Talking with Vittorio Cerutti, Italian Ambassador in Paris, Laval realized (but disagreed) that Mussolini maintained war was a necessary evil and even, in some instances, indispensable. Laval, in his letter of 7 January 1935, sought to clarify his understanding of non-intervention: he suggested that Italy could ask and obtain from Haile Selassie concessions in Ethiopia for the economic exploitation of the country with necessary guarantees, including the right to keep Italian garrisons and an Italian police force to protect Italian interests. This means that France was aware of Italy's military plans, and in May 1935, the then French Prime Minister, Flandin, suggested to Galeazzo Ciano, Mussolini's son-in-law and Minister of Propaganda, that Italy provoke a revolt of the *rases* (Ethiopian feudal lords) against Haile Selassie as a means of giving Italy an opportunity to intervene militarily.[8]

Furthermore, during the Rome talks at Palazzo Farnese, Laval gave "adherence and sympathy" to the principle of Italian political and economic predominance in Ethiopia, and gave some advice on obtaining a "free hand" in Ethiopia. Laval hoped Mussolini would follow the example of Marshall Hubert Lyautey in Morocco, that is once the economic tasks were fulfilled, leaving Ethiopia's independence intact, he would then be able to develop political influence. Laval never admitted he had given a free political hand to Mussolini because this meant that Italian military resources — which France wanted for protection against Germany — would be absent from the European continent. Statesmen of the time, however, admit that Mussolini was convinced he had obtained acquiescence for his Ethiopian venture and acted accordingly. He could draw the equally correct conclusion that Italy had France's adherence and sympathy because the Franco-Italian security alliance had to be maintained at any cost.[9]

Scholars agree that in spite of the ambiguous language of the "free hand", Laval handed over Ethiopia as a price he was willing to pay for an entente with Italy. Laval did not care much about Ethiopia, as far as he was concerned, it was a purely African matter.[10]

The Stresa Meeting

With his newly won French assurance of a free hand, Mussolini assumed other governments would act as unscrupulously, regardless of Ethiopia's independence. He turned next to London, informing the British Foreign Office of his intentions to solve the Ethiopian problem by installing Italian rule while at the same time safeguarding British interests. Receiving no response, he assumed silence to be consent to the conquest of Ethiopia, and that Great Britain would not go to war to save Ethiopia.[11]

The best place to solve the Ethiopian question would have been at the Stresa meeting 11-14 April 1935, where the British, the French, and the Italians met to create a common front against Hitler's rearmament plans. Mussolini was supposed to discuss the Ethiopian problem there with John Simon, British Foreign Secretary. No ministerial consultations took place, instead they were carried out at a lower level, between Geoffrey Thompson, an expert on Egyptian affairs, Leonardo Vitetti, counsellor to the Italian Embassy in London, and Giovan Battista Guarnaschelli, head of the African desk at Palazzo Chigi.

At four informal meetings, the Italians made it plain that Italy could not exclude the possibility of solving the Ethiopian crisis by war. The British reaction was that such a war would have a negative effect on Anglo-Italian relations. Thompson immediately informed Simon of the Italians' real intentions in Ethiopia; why did Simon not talk with Mussolini? Was he still convinced that Mussolini was bluffing, after having received reports from the British Embassy in Rome and the British Intelligence Service that Italy was determined to use force in Ethiopia? Or did he believe that by side-stepping the Ethiopian issue he could avoid estranging Great Britain from Italy?

Although Ethiopia was not officially discussed at Stresa, the Italians felt reassured that London would simply regulate its foreign policy according to developments; but nothing transpired to suggest that Britain would go to war to defend Ethiopia. But, once Mussolini was informed of Britain's negative reaction to Italian plans, why did he not discuss Ethiopia? Possibly he decided that he could not ask the British for a free hand in Ethiopia because he anticipated a refusal, that in turn would jeopardize the future of his African policy. Hence, he preferred silence to devising new ways to overcome British opposition.

The conference closed with a commitment to protect the independence of Austria. In the final session of the Stresa meeting, Mussolini asked that the words "in Europe" should be inserted. In so doing, he gave an opportunity to the French and British delegates to aid Ethiopia — but they were silent on this issue. The Italians concluded that the British government had given its tacit agreement to their ambitions in Ethiopia. In retrospect, however, perhaps Great Britain did not take Italian military preparation seriously at the time, and were sceptical of Mussolini's threats to annex Ethiopia.[12]

The Maffey Report

During the summer of 1935, Italian troop-transports were on their way to the Red Sea, and Italy was preparing for war against Ethiopia. Samuel Hoare, the new British Foreign Secretary and a friend of Mussolini, informed the cabinet that "Italy would have to be bought off, otherwise Ethiopia was going to perish and so would the League". Bu then proposing ceding Zeila to Ethiopia, with a corridor to British Somaliland, in exchange for which Italy would receive a large part of the Ogaden from Ethiopia, the British government took its first step in appeasing Italy.

Meantime, on 18 June 1935, John Maffey, former Governor of the Sudan, and now Permanent Under-Secretary of the Colonial Office, presented the results of a study of British interests in Ethiopia, known as the Maffey Report. It stated that Italy would have the advantage over Britain in securing Sudanese frontiers and increasing trade. No vital British interests existed in Ethiopia to oblige the British government to resist Italy's conquest there. The only British concerns in Ethiopia were the Lake Tana waters and the Nile basin. If Ethiopia ceased to be an independent country, Great Britain would make provisions to ensure British control over these territories, as well as some grazing rights. The report was clear: Britain's interests in Ethiopia were compatible with Italy's domination of the country.[13] This is the original interpretation of the report. Additional research, however, reveals, that the Maffey Commission had not been invited to state its views of the effect Italian expansion would have on imperial defence. A further reading of the document clearly implied that an Italian presence in East Africa would weaken the British security system in the Mediterranean and the Red Sea area. From the point of view of imperial defence, therefore, it was preferable for Ethiopia to remain independent. Once in possession of Ethiopia the Italian colonial appetite might not be satisfied and the Italian military forces could push toward the Sudan, menacing vital British interests on Lake Tana, the Nile, their dependencies in the Mediterranean and the Red Sea. Italian colonial forces would be a potential danger for British possessions in East Africa. Italy's plan to unify all its colonial possessions in North Africa with East Africa, would have serious repercussions for the Sudan and Egypt. The increased Italian presence in the Mediterranean with its extended interests in the Red Sea, through the conquest of Ethiopia, and the policy of penetration in Yemen and in the Near East, compelled Great Britain to re-evaluate the Italian military factor.*[14]

But the British mood was not for war, as was revealed in the results of the Peace Ballot of 1935. To the question of whether economic sanctions should be imposed upon a would-be aggressor the response was: affirmative, 10,027,608; negative, 635,072; abstentions, 855,074. To the question of whether, should it prove necessary, military measures should be taken against an aggressor the response was: affirmative 6,784, 368; negative 2,351,981; abstentions, 2,364,411. The reliability of the Peace Ballot is questionable but the outcome strengthened the British Cabinet's intention to steer a middle course between upholding the principles of the League of Nations and giving satisfaction to Italy's ambitions in Ethiopia. Hence the British government policy was for delays. In June 1935, it did, however, send Antony Eden, Under-Secretary for the League of Nations affairs, to Rome to offer Zeila to Ethiopia in exchange for the secession of the Ogaden to Italy.[15]

Eden In Rome

Although, in public, Mussolini took an intransigent position *vis-à-vis* Ethiopia, diplomatically his stand was less demanding. In May-June 1935, he had suggested to France and Great Britain the dismemberment of Ethiopia and the partition of the country on the basis of the 1906 Treaty, allowing Haile Selassie to maintain his throne. Specifically, Mussolini solicited French and British assistance for generous boundary rectification at Ethiopia's expense. He justified this concession as improving the security of Somalia and Eritrea from Ethiopian aggression and allowing Italy to link its colonies

---

*Because at the Paris Peace Treaty the Italians were cheated out of the war booty in the Middle East, it was Italy's right to be dominant in the Mediterranean. Under Fascism Italy insisted on the right to a great imperial destiny and territorial expansion. Mussolini backed his colonial claims by a forward policy in the Middle East. Fascist aims in the Middle East were to make trouble such as supporting – with little success – patriotic forces in India and Egypt to undermine the status quo of the British Empire. In Yemen, where from 1923 onward arms and money sustained conflict against the British, Mussolini was more successful. In 1926 Italy concluded a ten year Treaty of Commerce and Friendship in the expectation that the Red Sea would become an Italian zone of influence.

Italian policy in the Middle East aimed to make Italy a preponderant power from the Mediterranean to Persian Gulf, but Italy's policy of support for nationalist forces against Great Britain was aimed at compelling London to recognize Rome's special position in the Mediterranean and that Great Britain should share parity of influence in the Red Sea area. After the occupation of Ethiopia, Great Britain recognized Italy's new political and strategic position in the Mediterranean and Red Sea, by subscribing to the January 1937 Anglo-Italian Agreement in which both parties agreed to respect their reciprocal interests in the area.

through Ethiopian territory. Mussolini had, therefore, presented his minimum request to Paris and London before Eden's visit to Rome. What Eden offered was not enough to appease the Duce's colonial appetite, short of the drastic reduction of Ethiopia's territory and its status as a political entity.[16]

Eden's proposals to Mussolini on 24-25 June 1935 were to give Ethiopia sea access through the port of Zeila; in return Italy would receive the Ogaden and other economic advantages to be determined at a later date. Mussolini replied that Italy should receive all non-Amhara territories (the territories conquered by Menelik II) under direct administration. Eden was shown Italy's demands on the map: all of Ethiopia except the regions of Gojam, Tigre, and Shoa, for which Italy requested a mandate similar to Morocco or Egypt.[17] Furthermore, the Zeila/Ogaden exchange would bring economic competition to the Djibouti railway; also it was contrary to the Treaty of 1906. In 1931, Italy had already refused a secret proposal from Haile Selassie to exchange Ogaden for an outlet to the sea at Assab. This proposal would have been more advantageous to Italy than Eden's, because Ethiopian maritime trade would have passed through Italian territory and not be in British hands.[18]

The British insisted that they could not accede to Italian requests for a protectorate over Ethiopia because Italy did not want to work through the League of Nations, and because an Anglo-Italian pact would not be accepted by the British public.[19]

Italian Plans for a Protectorate/Mandate in Ethiopia

Before another attempt was made to conciliate Mussolini at the Tripartite Meeting in Paris in August 1935, the Italian Colonial Ministry drew up three projects for a protectorate in Ethiopia. It is important to note that these plans assumed British and French co-operation. The first called for vesting authority in those Ethiopian chiefs who were willing to co-operate with the Italians, leaving them their land. In the Muslim areas like Harar, a personal fiefdom of Haile Selassie, Italy could continue a pro-Islam policy. Southwest Ethiopia would become an Italian mandate. The province of Tigre would be governed by Italy as a protectorate; *Dejaz* Haile Selassie Gugsa, the ruler of that region was already favourably inclined to Italy and would be given the title of *ras*. The Italians believed that after Haile Selassie Gugsa's submission, other chiefs from nearby regions would follow, attracted by high salaries and honours.

It was in Italy's interest to be able to document the defections of chiefs, to show Europe that Italy was not *occupying* Ethiopia, but *liberating* it from feudalism, and eliminating slavery. Italian influence would be maintained through the presence of an Italian High Commissioner in Addis Ababa, supported by an Italian military corps, including the air force. Italian officers would command Ethiopian troops and the colonial police. Italian advisers would be introduced in all Ethiopian ministries and various regional governments.[20]

A second study envisioned a Moroccan type of protectorate over Ethiopia.* Accordingly, Italian advisers would have veto powers. If Italy could not have direct rule over the non-Amhara regions and could obtain a generous revision of boundaries only along Somalia and Eritrea, then the governors of Ethiopia's peripheral regions bordering the Sudan, Kenya, British and French Somaliland should be Italian, even if nominated by Haile Selassie. As in India, the indigenous nobility would be allowed to retain their titles. The *rases* would be given power over their regions, more independence from Addis Ababa, and some would also have the title of *negus* over their traditional areas. The title of Emperor would be given to the king of Italy, and Haile Selassie would be given the title of Regent for the Empire.

The third plan provided for Italy to build a railway from Eritrea to Somalia. The rail route would follow a central direction from Eritrea to Addis Ababa, via Adigrat, Makale, Lake Ashangi, and Dessie, and continue to Somalia through Arussi and Ogaden. An alternative direction would be the western route, which implied the annexation to Italy of those territories, depriving Ethiopia of three-quarters of its territory.[21]

Italy's minimum programme called for direct rule over the non-Amhara-speaking lands and tight control over the rest of Ethiopia, even though retaining Haile Selassie as the country's figurehead. The maximum programme involved a protectorate similar to that of Morocco, including the presence of Haile Selassie.

Italy would accept a protectorate or a mandate without interference from the League of Nations. Laval and Eden, however, proposed plans in which the League of Nations was a part; this was unacceptable to Mussolini because he was not willing to share his power with the international organization.

In view of the projected Tripartite powers meeting in Paris in August 1935, Sir Sidney Barton, British Minister in Addis Ababa, had tested Haile Selassie to see how far he would go in terms of concessions to Italy. The Emperor had considered the British proposals of exchange of territories between Zeila and Ogaden and would allow Italy to have Aussa, to reopen talks of the 1928 Assab-Dessie road project and to permit the construction of a motor road from Asmara to Gondar. In return for these concessions Haile Selassie asked to be provided with an international loan for public works and administrative reforms, with the help of foreign nationals chosen by the League of Nations. He also requested that the Tripartite Agreement of

---

*In 1912 Morocco became a French protectorate. The Sultan, Mulay Yusef, was vested with complete authority in religious affairs and encouraged to have pomp and splendour in his court. But the French Resident-General made the important decisions, and a staff of French officials supervised the nation. The *Council of Viziers* was given considerable authority in internal civil government; traditional officials, the *Caids* or tribal leaders, the *Pachas* or town leaders, and the *Cadis* or judges were retained. French officials supervised, in an unobtrusive manner, but French control was real and included power to initiate and direct.

1906 be revised to include Ethiopia.[22]

Paolo Aloisi, Italian Ambassador at the League of Nations, reiterated Italian demands for a Class "C" mandate; that is, territory assigned by the League of Nations to more advanced powers. The mandate "C" territory was administered under the laws of the mandatory power as an integral part of its territory, but was required to guarantee freedom of conscience and religion, to prohibit traffic in liquor, arms or slaves, prevent military training of the local people, and secure, for other League of Nations members, equal opportunities for trade and commerce. There was scant hope for independence of a "C" mandated territory. Laval instead proposed to give Italy economic concessions, the right to technical assistance, the Ogaden, the possibility of settling Italians in Ethiopia and of building a railway between Eritrea and Somalia, on the condition that Ethiopian independence be respected and the co-operation of the Tripartite powers in the technical development of Ethiopia. Aloisi explained to Laval and Eden that economic concessions without Italian military garrisons were useless. Nevertheless, the French and British suggestions amounted to an Italian protectorate and an economic condominium between the signatory powers of the 1906 Agreement.[23] This was precisely the interference Mussolini did not want.

The talks for a compromise failed even before they started, because Mussolini insisted on a protectorate – which France and Great Britain could not concede. By the time Italy rejected the Anglo-French proposals, Italy had a 280,000-strong military force in East Africa and had spent over two billion lire. Italy, Mussolini stated, would not retreat and would not sacrifice its prestige! In a private letter to Laval, Mussolini explained that the economic concessions could not satisfy Italian demands. He also rejected the point that the 1906 Agreement should also include Ethiopia, as this would increase the prestige of the very country he proposed to conquer.

With the approach of war, Laval, Eden, Salvador de Madariaga of Spain, Joseph Beck of Poland, and Rustu Aras of Turkey worked out the so-called "compromise" of the League of Nations Council of Five, but Italy was not represented. Aloisi privately informed the Council that Ethiopia must be disarmed and that Great Britain and France must accept the concept that barbaric Ethiopia was not a state, but territorially, politically and ethnically divided, and did not belong in the League of Nations.[24] In short, Italy would not accept any of the programmes suggested by the League of Nations.

On 19 September 1935, the programme of the Council of Five was sent to Rome. It was an international mandate, with the independence and integrity of Ethiopia to be assured by the League. The plan included social, public administration and economic reforms with the aid of foreign specialists. With the agreement of the Emperor, the principal advisers were to be appointed by the Council of the League. In order to help resolve the Italo-Ethiopian dispute, France and Great Britain were willing to facilitate territorial adjustments in the Somalilands, and to uphold Italian economic interests.

Mussolini found the proposals unacceptable. In reality, little progress had been made from the proposals put forward in August. In Paris, the agreement would have been worked out between the three powers, but now the League was called upon to participate, and this would make it more difficult for Mussolini to have a free hand. The League, not Italy, would make the reforms in Ethiopia.[25] This interference on the part of the League would prevent Mussolini from avenging Adowa and getting the satisfaction of conquering an empire.

Ethiopia accepted the proposals of the Council of Five, but Italy officially rejected them on 22 September 1935. Soon after, Mussolini submitted a list of his demands to Laval: a) annexation of Tigre; b) a mandate on the non-Amharic regions; c) boundary rectification in favour of Italy along the Danakil and Ogaden; d) Italian participation in a League of Nations mandate in Amharic regions; e) the League's control of Ethiopian armament, and f) Ethiopia's access to the sea at Assab.[26]

Although Mussolini attempted to justify his request, he was prepared to bargain, realizing that the very most he could expect to obtain was sixty to seventy per cent of his demands.[27]

The Hoare-Laval Plan

During the Italo-Ethiopian crisis, the great powers used Ethiopia as a pawn in the game of European politics; without scruples, without any consideration for its interests, desires, and destiny. British appeasement policy was to find a compromise satisfying to Mussolini's prestige, to protect the Anglo-Franco-Italian co-operation, to prevent a possible Italo-German rapprochement and to save the League system. As a show of force, in September 1935, the British government sent the Home Fleet into the Mediterranean. At the same time, Hoare informed Mussolini that in sending its navy into the Mediterranean, Great Britain had no aggressive intentions, that the Suez Canal would not be closed to Italian shipping, and that the British government had no desire to humiliate Italy. Simultaneously Hoare and Laval resolved that a war against Italy was too risky, and also excluded military sanctions or military blockade; Mussolini was duly informed of these decisions. Knowing that his potential antagonists had decided against preventing his African adventure, it can be concluded that the British establishment tacitly endorsed Mussolini's military solution to the Ethiopian crisis.

Owing to the German and Japanese threats, Great Britain had no plans to go to war over Ethiopia. The British Cabinet was apprehensive of the possibility of rash and suicidal actions by Mussolini, fearing attacks on the fleet or aerial bombardment of London, although the Italian air force was overrated and inferior to Great Britain's. The real reason for dispatching the fleet was then to attempt to induce Mussolini to accept a compromise.[28] To defuse the tension, the British reassured Rome that naval deployments were not meant to menace Italy, and two battle cruisers were recalled to home waters.

Great Britain would not go to war, but economic sanctions against the aggressor were contemplated in order to uphold British prestige, and to weaken the Italian economy, and thus enable a diplomatic settlement to be made. To France the economic sanctions were means to prevent Italian military action against Ethiopia, or an oil boycott against Italy.

Laval thought the economic sanctions would give Mussolini the time and the opportunity to compel Haile Selassie to accept Italy's demands for a protectorate. Mussolini realized the risk of a war but before Italian troops began the invasion of Ethiopia by crossing the Mareb River on 3 October 1935 – without a declaration of war – he reiterated that the crisis would be solved if Italy received the non-Amhara territories. But unless her hand was forced Great Britain would not concede; hence, the reason for Mussolini's insistence on a quick war. For this he needed a large army, a huge arsenal of war material, use of all available means, gas, corruption of the Ethiopian chiefs, and indiscriminate air bombing. Although the 30 December 1934 military plan and Mussolini's statement to Eden when he visited Rome in June 1935 suggest that Italy planned to occupy Ethiopia, Mussolini realized that the disintegration of Ethiopia would humiliate Great Britain and make friendly relations between the two powers difficult. With the armed intervention in Africa, he really aimed at forcing Haile Selassie, Britain and the League of Nations to come to a compromise and to accept his demands, that is: direct rule over the non-Amhara regions.

Because Italy could obtain only what it conquered De Bono was urged to occupy Tigre up to Makale by November. Mussolini used military force and diplomacy to ensure success and, at all costs, attain a rapid conclusion to his objectives.[29]

Although the sanction created difficulties for the Italian economy, Italy had taken precautions to resist it for a two year period. Moreover, Italy received sympathetic co-operation and aid both from members of the League of Nations and non-members such as Austria, Albania, Germany, USA, Brazil, and Japan.[30] Even the Baldwin administration was not fully committed to economic sanctions. In reality, their application was a façade to hide British hypocrisy, because the government knew they were unlikely to be effective.[31]

Italy also had a major supporter in the person of Robert Vansittart, Permanent Under-Secretary of State and head of the British Foreign Office. He felt that to direct its aggressive energy into productive channels Italy's ambitions in Africa had to be satisfied. Anglo-Italian friendship was indispensable to contain Germany, and Italy should thus be paid the right price in the form of concessions in Africa, long overdue since 1915.[32]

To demonstrate the British government's serious intentions to negotiate a peaceful settlement, Maurice Peterson, head of the Ethiopian Department at the Foreign Office and René Saint-Quentin, a French Africa expert, met in Paris in October 1935 to modify the League Council of Five plan of 18 September, in order to find a formula that might be acceptable to Italy and to incorporate Mussolini's requests. This was the first serious attempt to resolve the crisis in Italy's favour, stop the war, cool passions, and shape a settlement.

Under French pressure, Peterson and Saint-Quentin examined the possibility of awarding Italy a mandate south of the 8th parallel and, in exchange, grant Ethiopia access to the sea at Assab. Haile Selassie was unlikely to accept this as by the end of October neither side had sustained a military defeat. Furthermore, if the Emperor accepted the plan, the *rases* would dethrone him upon an accusation of cowardice in surrendering part of Ethiopia to the enemy.

Peterson and Saint-Quentin reported that it was impossible to incorporate Tigre with Eritrea as the Italians had requested, because it was part of historic Ethiopia; neither could Harar be detached from Ethiopia because it was Haile Selassie's hereditary fief. The two specialists found that boundary corrections along the Ogaden and Danakil in Italy's favour to be a workable solution.[33] Meanwhile, Mussolini continued to use force, since without it he would have lost credibility and because force would induce London and Addis Ababa to make concessions.[34] Simultaneously the Duce maintained secret communication channels with London for a negotiable solution on his own terms!

In November, Mussolini sent Ezio Garibaldi to London on a secret mission reiterating the Italian maximum terms of 16 October: direct control over Tigre already conquered, rectification of boundaries in the Danakil and Ogaden, a mandate in non-Amharic regions, a preponderance of Italian influence in Amhara territories under a League of Nation Commission, disarmament of Ethiopia, and a sea port at Assab for Ethiopia. These proposals were presented to Vansittart and Hoare. Almost at the same time as the Garibaldi mission, Grandi, acting on his own initiative, but with Mussolini's blessing, visited Vansittart on 26 November to add his support to Garibaldi's terms. The Hoare-Laval plan, which in reality was the result of continued Italian initiations to reach a compromise, originated from this initiative. Garibaldi's presence in London and Grandi's diplomatic contacts with Vansittart meant that Rome would welcome British counter-proposals, even if they were below the minimum of Italian requests. Concomitantly, Grandi, acting on a personal basis, signified that if the negotiations failed the Italian government could disclaim its involvement and be free to continue with the military operations in Africa in order to safeguard the regime's prestige.

The Grandi-Vansittart conversations took place on 26 and 29 November and from 3 to 5 December 1935, at which time Vansittart gave in to Italian demands: Mussolini did not receive what he had requested on 16 October, but it was a reconciliation of his desires. The fate of Tigre was to be considered later, but would eventually become Italian, using the self-determination formula. Italy would receive cession of territory in Danakil and Ogaden in exchange for Ethiopia's access to the sea. Exclusive economic monopoly by Italy of the territories south of the 8th parallel was the main concession to Mussolini. Territorial unification of Eritrea and Somalia east of Addis

Ababa, with the possible cession to Italy of Aussa and Harar was considered. Vansittart also accepted Italy's request to limit the League's interference, and to allow assistance (limited to technical development co-operation and capital investment) to Ethiopia by the Tripartite powers, with Italy in the preponderant position. The rapid and complete British capitulation to Italian requests and the hasty preparation of the plan was due to Vansittart's concern with British military deficiencies and the potential danger presented by Germany.[35]

For Mussolini the compromise was of less value than the defeat of Ethiopia would have been; but it would be advantageous for saving the lives of many men and spending less money. Mussolini's willingness to submit to a negotiated deal corroborates the fact that he did not expect the total conquest of Ethiopia. Once the historic battle places were conquered, Mussolini intensified his negotiations, assured that he had saved Italian honour by the conquest of those few square miles of territory in Tigre.

Before the Hoare-Laval Plan was completed, Mussolini further modified his requests. For example, he would not give up Tigre, but was unequivocal in terms of allowing an Amhara state under Haile Selassie, and also in permitting the continuation of the Emperor's sovereignty over the non-Amhara territories under an Italian mandate.[36]

On 8-9 December 1935, with the Cabinet's approval, Vansittart took the plan to Hoare and Laval in Paris. The British government was now committed to making sweeping concessions to Italy at Ethiopia's expense. The British Cabinet had fully grasped the essential features of a large-scale Italian economic and military penetration of Ethiopia; Laval and Hoare had accepted the fact that Ethiopia would fall under some form of Italian domination. While Mussolini was kept informed of the progress of the talks, Ethiopia was not consulted beforehand about the Hoare-Laval Plan, allegedly in order not to compromise the Emperor's position *vis-à-vis* his chiefs, which would jeopardize his leadership.[37]

The final draft of the Hoare-Laval plan gave Mussolini part of Tigre, including Adowa, Adigrat, and Makale excluding Axum. Ethiopia was compensated by Italy with the cession of Assab and a corridor to the sea held in full Ethiopian sovereignty. Italy would further obtain frontier rectification along Ogaden and Danakil. Hoare thought that since the area in the south would not be a cession but an economic monopoly, the bigger the area the better, extending from the 8th parallel west to the 35th meridian. The administration was not solely Italian but a League-appointed non-Italian adviser was situated in Addis Ababa. An Italian might be his delegate, but sovereignty would remain Ethiopian. This brought the League to the forefront of any settlement. Laval informed the British government that if Ethiopia rejected the Plan, France could not continue to support the sanctions.

Likewise, the British Cabinet decided that in the event of Ethiopia refusing the terms, Great Britain would neither propose nor support further sanctions. On 18 December, the Ethiopian government rejected the plan because it interpreted the terms as improving conditions under which Italy could at a later date attack again. Once it had signed away Ethiopia's claims under the Hoare-Laval Plan, the rights to territorial integrity, no further appeal could be made to Europe when the Italians came again to absorb the land.

Mussolini submitted the Hoare-Laval Plan to the Grand Council of the Fascist Party, which means he had accepted it as a base for further negotiations. The Council was to meet on 18 December and all evidence points to the fact that Mussolini was in favour of adopting the Plan, as were the majority of the Grand Council members. Mussolini had also to consider the international situation: the League of Nations threatened Italy with an oil boycott. He realized that the Plan offered half of Ethiopia and the rest could be absorbed later. The press leaks in December, however, limited Mussolini's liberty to negotiate, putting him in the position of acting under an ultimatum. It was Hoare's 18 December resignation, meaning British repudiation of the Plan, that provoked Mussolini to adjourn the meeting of the Council without taking a vote.[38]

Laval was disappointed that Mussolini had not replied with immediate acceptance of the Paris Plan. Frenchmen supported Laval's prudent course to conciliate Mussolini, his proclaimed intent. By January 1936, Laval too resigned.

Mussolini had counted on the Hoare-Laval Plan to end the Ethiopian crisis. Now that resources of diplomacy were brought to a halt, the only thing left to resolve the crisis was the use of force. By the end of December, Italian military reports were not good. It was only toward mid-January 1936 that Graziani reported a decisive military action on the southern front, while Badoglio's victories were not heard of until February at the battles of Tembien and Amba Alagi.[39]

Notes

1. For a description of the Italian aims in Ethiopia at the end of the First World War, see the secret edition of the Ministero delle Colonie, Direzione Generale degli Affari Politici. . . *Africa Italiana: Programma Massimo e Programma Minimo di Sistemazione dei Possedimenti Italiani nell'Affrica Orientale e Settentrionale*, Rome, 1917-20, 4 volumes.

2. Hess, "Italy and Africa: Colonial Ambitions in the First World War", pp. 107-13; *Messaggero*, 29 November 1938; Lloyd George, *Memoirs of the Peace Conference*, 2, p. 583; Baer, *The Coming of the Italian-Ethiopian War*, p. 12; MAI/GAB 322 Government of Asmara to De Bono: Preparation of Abbyssinia for War, n.d.

3. De Felice, *Mussolini il Duce: Gli Anni del Consenso*, pp. 609-16; Baer, *Test Case: Italy, Ethiopia and the League of Nations*, p. 13; Quartararo, *Roma tra Londra e Berlino*, p. 91.

4. ACS/PB 4/13 Baistrocchi to De Bono 15 September 1933; ACS/PB

4/20 Badoglio to Mussolini 20 January 1934; ACS/PB 4/127 Mussolini to Badoglio 30 December 1934; ACS/PB 4/6 De Bono to Gazzera 29 April 1932; Rochat, *Militari e Politici nella Preparazione della Campagna d'Etiopia*, pp. 95-105.

5. F. Perfetti, "Alle Origini degli Accordi Laval-Mussolini. . ."; pp. 688-705; W. Shorrock, "The Jouvenel Mission to Rome. . .", quoted with permission of the author; J. Spencer, communication, 15 July 1983.

6. Miège, *L'Imperialisme Colonial Italien*, p. 211; France also ceded Italy 2,500 shares of the Djibouti Railway or 7%; MAI/GAB 306I-1-C Mussolini to Italian Embassies in Paris and London, 17 January 1936; Baer, *The Coming*, p. 78; De Felice, *Gli Anni*, p. 532; Askew, "The Secret Agreement Between France and Italy on Ethiopia"; Watt, 'The Secret Laval-Mussolini Agreement of 1935 on Ethiopia"; USMA/ICD T-586/1291 Ministero delgi Affari Esteri; "Francia: Situazione Politica, 1935 and 1936".

7. Askew, "The Secret Agreement", p. 47; Miège, *L'Imperialisme* p. 212; Lagardelle *Missionà Rome: Mussolini*, pp. 273-87, Appendix; Laval, *The Diary of Pierre Laval*, p. 20; Harris, *The United States and the Italo-Ethiopian War*, p. 8.

8. MAI/GAB 306/I-1-C Mussolini to Italian Embassies in Paris and London, 17 January 1936; Jones and Monroe, *A History of Ethiopia*, p. 154; MAI/GAB 306/I-1-C MAE to MAI 13 January 1936; Ciano, *Diario 1937-1938*, p. 313.

9. Baer, *The Coming*, pp. 79, 83; Harris, *The United States*, p. 9; Vansittart, *The Mist Procession: Autobiography of Lord Vansittart*, pp. 515-16; Guariglia, *Ricordi: 1922-1946*, pp. 220-21; Roatta, *Processo Roatta*, p. 18.

10. De Felice, *Gli Anni*, p. 531; Baer *Test Case*, p. 2; Quartararo, *Roma*, p. 96; ADG 44/108/1 MAE to MAI, 21 January 1936; MackSmith, *Mussolini's Roman Empire*, pp. 65-6; Milza "Le Voyage de Pierre Laval à Rome en Janvier 1935", in J.B. Duroselle et al., *Italia e Francia*, pp. 219-42.

11. Quartararo, *Roma*, p. 111; Mack Smith, *Mussolini's Roman Empire*, p. 66.

12. Baer, *The Coming*, pp. 119-22; A. Lessona, *Verso L'Impero*, pp. 91-7; Guariglia, *Ricordi*, pp. 226-7, 781-2; Thompson, *Front Line Diplomat*, pp. 96-8; Flandin, *Politique Française 1919-1940*, p. 178; Serra, "La Questione Italo-Etiopica alla Conferenza di Stresa"; Robertson, *Mussolini as Empire Builder*, pp. 128-38.

13. Robertson, *Mussolini*, p. 144; Lessona, *Verso l'Impero*, pp. 91-5; Lagardelle, *Mission*, pp. 128-31; Harris, *The United States*, p. 10; Baer, *The Coming*, pp. 188-9.

14. Quartararo, *Roma*, pp. 115, 126, 131, chs. 4 and 5; Robertson, *Mussolini*, pp. 143-5; Mack Smith, *Mussolini's Roman Empire*, pp. 33-4; Mack Smith, *Mussolini, A Biography*, pp. 33, 99, 153; Rava, *Nel Cuore*, pp. 8-9.

15. Robertson, *Mussolini*, pp. 146-7; De Felice, *Gli Anni*, p. 672; Baer, *The Coming*, p. 204.

16. M. Toscano, "Eden a Roma alla Vigilia del Conflitto Italo-Etiopico," in *Pagine di Storia Diplomatica*, p. 137; Bova Scopa to Mussolini, 21 June 1935 in Toscano, *Pagine*, p. 139; De Felice, *Gli Anni*, p. 664.

17. Pignatti to Mussolini, in Toscano, *Pagine*, pp. 140, 144, 147; Baer, *The Coming*, p. 189; ADG 42/103/1 Suvich to Grandi, 19, 24 25

June 1935; Drummond to Mussolini, 24 July 1935; Mussolini to Drummond, 31 July 1935.

18. "Eden a Roma" in Toscano, *Pagine*, pp. 151, 152, 154.

19. Aloisi, *Journal: 1932-1936*, p. 294.

20. MAI/GAB 160/XI Ministry of Colonies: Directions for a Possible Protectorate in Ethiopia, July 1935.

21. MAI/GAB 160/XI Ministry of Colonies: Ethiopian Protectorate, 18 July 1935; Ibid., Ministry of Colonies: Possible Protectorate over Ethiopia, 19 July 1935; The 1906 Tripartite Agreement permitted Italy to build the railway west of Addis Ababa. This route had the inconvenience of not touching Addis Ababa, the political and commercial centre of Ethiopia. It also was the longest way to connect the two Italian colonies.

22. Virgin, *The Abyssinia I Knew*, pp. 159-60; Baer, *The Coming*, pp. 261-2.

23. Villari, *Storia Diplomatica del Conflitto Italo-Etiopico*, pp. 184-5; Baer, *The Coming*, p. 263; Aloisi, *Journal*, p. 295; Villari *Storia*, pp. 123-4; Miège, *Imperialisme*, p. 223.

24. Mussolini to Laval, 25 December 1935 in Lagardelle, *Mission*, pp. 146, 203-205; Aloisi, *Journal*, p. 302; Villari, *Storia*, pp. 132-5; Baer, *The Coming*, p. 343; Mori "Come Mussolini Giustificò l'Azione Armata contro l'Etiopia", pp. 217-220.

25. Baer, *The Coming*, pp. 343-4; League of Nations, *Official Journal* 1935, N. 1620-1627; Guariglia, *Ricordi*, pp. 266-8; Villari, *Storia*, p. 146; Mussolini to Laval, 25 December 1935, in Lagardelle, *Mission*, p. 208, Appendix.

26. Lagardelle, *Mission*, p. 183; De Felice, *Gli Anni* pp. 681-8.

27. ADG 44/108/1 Suvich to Grandi, 17 October 1935; ADG 42/103/1 Mussolini to Cerruti, 17 October 1935; ADG 44/108/1 Guariglia: Notes for Suvich, 24 October 1935; ADG 44/108/1 Mussolini: Information about Tigre, 27 October 1935; ADG 44/108/1 MAE to Grandi, 27 November 1935.

28. Mori, "Come Mussolini Giustificò l'Azione . . ." p. 223; ADG 42/103/1 Gasparini to Grandi, 3 October 1935; Baer, *Test Case*, pp. 80-5, 91-6; Mack Smith, *Mussolini's Roman Empire*, p. 69; De Felice, *Gli Anni*, pp. 648, 675-7, 681; Robertson, "The British General Elections of 1935", pp. 157-9.

29. De Felice, *Gli Anni*, pp. 681-8; ADG 42/103/1 Cerruti to MAE, 15 and 17 August 1935; Baer, *Test Case*, pp. 46-111.

30. Mori, "Come Mussolini Giustificò l'Azione", p. 221; De Felice, *Gli Anni*, pp. 687-701.

31. Robertson, "The British General Elections", pp. 149-64.

32. Goldman, "Sir Robert Vanisttart's Search for Italian Cooperation Against Hitler", pp. 95, 108, 114-5.

33. Baer, *Test Case*, pp. 46, 52, 111; De Felice, *Gli Anni*, p. 714; ADG 44/108/1 Guariglia to Grandi, 5 and 9 November 1935.

34. Baer, *Test Case*, p. 35; Quartararo, "Le Origini del Piano Hoare-Laval", pp. 756, 759.

35. Quartararo, "Le Origini", pp. 758-65; Baer, *Test Case*, pp. 114-18; De Felice, *Gli Anni*, pp. 715-17.

36. ADG 44/108/1 Mussolini to Grandi, 4 December 1935.

37. Robertson, "The Hoare-Laval Plan", pp. 440-41, 445.

38. De Felice, *Gli Anni*, pp. 720-22; Baer, *Test Case*, pp. 124-7, 135, 141.

39. Robertson, "The Hoare-Laval Plan", p. 447; Baer, *Test Case*, pp. 136-144.

3. The Invasion and the War

Mussolini admitted that the Ethiopian War was not popular in Italy. Public opinion expressed fear of defeat. The bureaucracy, the aristocracy, and the leaders of the armed forces were against the war; even some leading Fascists were for peace. Fascist propaganda, however, declared that the war of Ethiopia would test Italy's greatness, and its capabilities as a civilizing and liberating mission. Italy was determined to emerge from its poverty and sense of inferiority. But it was not rhetoric that changed the people's mood toward the conflict; the war became popular only after Italy reported victories such as the one at Mai Cew when Haile Selassie's army was smashed.[1]

Mussolini did not believe in a quick war because his military advisers, and Badoglio, expected at least two years of war, as did most European military experts. Although the Ethiopian War is usually referred to as the war of "seven months", it must be pointed out that when Badoglio entered Addis Ababa in May 1936, Italy controlled only one-third of the country and that another year was required to extend Italian rule to the remainder of the country. In order to appease home fears and for reasons of foreign policy, Mussolini, hard pressed for military victories and territorial conquest, became impatient with De Bono's cautious colonial war strategy of slow advance at a time when he needed the annexation of Tigre in case of a negotiated European settlement. Nevertheless, only one soldier died in avenging Adowa! The occupation of Tigre was a tonic for Italy, wiping out the humiliating memory of the 1896 defeat. But instead of advancing further De Bono stopped. That in the absence of resistance a great army did not go further made it easier for Geneva to argue that sanctions could work. Mussolini's position was weak as long as his troops were only 30 kilometres beyond the frontier. On 17 October the northern front lay close to the Adigrat-Adowa-Axum line. Under Mussolini's pressure De Bono eventually took Makale on 8 November, but following this there was no Italian advance for two months. On 11 November, Mussolini ordered De Bono to advance to Amba Alagi. De Bono refused. On the following day Mussolini replaced him with Badoglio as military field commander of Italian East Africa.

Badoglio, a prominent soldier and Marshal of Italy, was well supported by the Crown and popular with the people. He gave better technical guarantees for the swift military victories needed to free Mussolini from diplomatic troubles. With Badoglio in East Africa, the Ethiopian War escalated from a Fascist to a national war. In December, when the Hoare-Laval Plan was being considered, Mussolini insisted that Badoglio should take Amba Alagi, because an additional territorial conquest might push the Ethiopians into accepting the Plan. The decision to mount a full-scale offensive was, however, taken only in January 1936 when the Hoare-Laval Plan had failed. After that, Mussolini no longer opposed Badoglio's war strategy of using all available means, including gas.[2]

Three months after the invasion, the League of Nations' oil boycott was still being debated; further sanctions and the spring rains loomed ahead, but operations in Ethiopia were at a standstill. There had been no victories of any strategic importance, instead, on 15 December, a counter-offensive mounted by Ethiopia to split the Italian armies almost cut through the right flanks of the Italian line. The Ethiopian objective was to isolate Makale. *Ras* Imru on the left flank crossed the Takkaze River, forcing the Italians to retreat 12 miles to the Dambeguina Pass. In the centre, *Ras* Kassa linked up with *Ras* Seyum's troops in Tembien. On 22 December 1935, Seyum retook Abbi Addi and moved to Wariew Pass. On the right, *Ras* Mulugeta advanced on Makale, threatening the Italians' most advanced post. The last two weeks in December were the darkest period of the war for the Italians, and Mussolini was compelled to accept the Hoare-Laval Plan.

The Ethiopian counter-offensive was turned back at the first battle of Tembien in January 1936 when the Italian army was held at Wariew Pass from 21 to 24 January. This was the most anxious period of the war. Relief was possible with the use of mustard gas, which became the conclusive retaliatory weapon. After the battle of Tembien, Badoglio realized that Ethiopia could not carry through an offensive to crush the Italian army.

On the southern front, General R. Graziani's strategy was to attack Harar and bomb the Djibouti railway in order to cut Ethiopia's main supply and ammunition line. His first war objective was Gorrahei, occupied in October. In December, Graziani defeated *Ras* Desta at the battle of Dolo, when, contrary to Italy's adherence to the gas protocol of 1925 gas was used for the first time. Graziani's occupation of Neghelli at about the same time that Badoglio was resisting the Ethiopians at Wariew Pass, gave Mussolini the first major victory, lifting the depressed spirit of Italy. Graziani's victory at the battle of Neghelli cut off the route for Ethiopia to get supplies from Kenya, and put Italy 400 kilometres deep into Ethiopia.

Between February and March 1936 in a series of battles on the northern front Badoglio defeated the Ethiopians, routing their forces and making it impossible for them to regroup. Badoglio was quick to learn that he could halt the Ethiopian impetus with heavy artillery fire and the intensive use of the air force. By the second week in February, Badoglio was ready to advance to Addis Ababa. From 10 to 19 February, at Amba Aradam, he defeated Mulugeta's army with overwhelming artillery power. Whoever was left of

Mulugeta's 50,000 men were pursued and dispersed by the air force. In this battle of annihilation, Badoglio destroyed both the Ethiopian will to fight and the will to live. In addition, the effect of the aerial bombardment destroyed the Ethiopians' traditional response to their leader, and demolished the aristocracy which was the core of the military organization. Mulugeta had the best troops, and his defeat dealt a crushing blow to Ethiopian morale. Badoglio then turned to *Rases* Kassa and Seyum at the second battle of Tembien where they were defeated on 27 February, trapped by two arms of the Italian army. Only *Ras* Imru remained in the north in Shire, where Badoglio attacked on 29 February and encountered the most determined opposition yet; the battle of Shire saw the bitterest fighting of the campaign. By 3 March, Imru was in retreat, his men victims of gas bombing, or deserters. The Gojami troops refused to fight; defeatism and regionalism prevailed. In March Gojam was in revolt against Haile Selassie. By 7 March, Badoglio had broken the Ethiopian northern front. Should there be a settlement, at least Italy would have the north under control.

During his march south, Badoglio occupied Sardo and made an agreement with the Sultan of Aussa near French Somaliland. Badoglio also sent a mechanized column to Gondar, 300 kilometres south-west, thereby opening the road to Debra Markos, the capital of Gojam, taken in April, thus threatening Addis Ababa. The Italians occupied Sardo and Gondar without incident and controlled 166,000 square kilometres of Ethiopian territory. The only obstacle to Badoglio's occupation of Addis Ababa was Haile Selassie's army at Mai Cew. The Emperor disregarded advice not to fight the Italians in the open field, but doubtless felt he must take the risk or retire in dishonour. His offensive was thus a political act in order to maintain his authority. On 31 March he attacked, and at dawn next day, ordered the retreat. The battle of Mai Cew was over; the Ethiopians were hunted down to Lake Ashangi to Quoram. The retreat, which began in disorder, ended in disintegration. Unprecedented quantities of bombs and gas deluged the survivors of Mai Cew trapped at Lake Ashangi. On 14 April 1936 Dessie was in Italian hands. Italian field victories meant the end of the war and that the oil sanction would be a useless provocation.[3]

The Italian army owed its victory to their superior weaponry, and the employment — for the first time in a colonial war — of aerial bombardment and gas. The Ethiopians, with their aristocratic military leadership, not only lacked sophisticated armaments, but fought a conventional war of pitched battles with frontal assault, using mostly horse-mounted soldiers armed with a sword or spear, reminiscent of medieval war strategy.

By spring 1936, Italian troops were at the gates of Addis Ababa, but Hitler's occupation of the Rhineland, on 7 March 1936, shifted the League's attention from Africa to Europe. London and Paris, faced by the German danger, were compelled to abandon the Ethiopian crisis quickly in order to restore the Stresa front.[4]

Italo-Ethiopian Secret Negotiations

Incredible as it may seem, Mussolini was determined to use every means to achieve his aim of conquering Ethiopia. He used both diplomacy and force and at the same time opened secret negotiations with Haile Selassie himself. Available information leads to the conclusion that the Italian dictator sought a territorial agreement with the Emperor at this time because politically and militarily the realization of his plan to acquire Ethiopia was far from certain and, therefore, it was in Italy's interest to grab Ethiopian territory at minimum cost. Haile Selassie, apparently abandoned by the European powers, seems to have given at least some thought to arriving at a compromise with Mussolini and, for all practical purposes, co-operating with the Italians in exploiting his people for a price.

One of the most bizarre arrangements was a contract between General Mario Roatta, Chief of Italian Military Intelligence, and Chukry Jacir Bey, a Palestinian. Jacir Bey was willing to attempt to persuade Haile Selassie to reach an agreement with Italy, by 15 February 1936; for these services he received 100,000,000 lire [US $ 1.00 = 5.6 lire] from Roatta.[5] Jacir Bey claimed to be a good friend of *Ras* Mulugeta, and of *Abuna* Kirillos V, spiritual chief of the Ethiopian Orthodox Church.

The terms provided for Ethiopia to receive a sea outlet at Assab, a corridor of 20 kilometres, and Italian recognition of Ethiopian independence. In return, Italy would receive Tigre, Danakil and Aussa, Ethiopia would give up Borana, Sidamo, Bale, Arussi and Harar in the south and Haile Selassie would accept Italian advisers. If the Emperor refused to comply with these peaceful terms, Jacir Bey would kidnap him and deliver him to the Italian military authorities in East Africa. As might be expected, this plan failed.

A second meeting to work out a possible solution for peace took place in Amsterdam, where Enrico Cerulli, Director of the Ministry of Colonies, met the Ethiopian Minister of Foreign Affairs, *Blattengeta* Heruy Wolde Selassie. The Ethiopian terms consisted of a guarantee of safety for Haile Selassie and his dynasty, a compensation of three hundred million lire, participation in the Italian companies which would exploit Ethiopia, and a treaty of alliance. This direct Italo-Ethiopian meeting brought no peaceful results as both sides were concerned to assess each other's intentions, and thus was conducted in an atmosphere of mutual suspicion. In the end, Mussolini found the Ethiopian terms unacceptable.

By March 1936, with successive Italian victories, it was evident that Ethiopia could not hold out much longer. One explanation for Ethiopia's willingness to have secret talks with the Italians was to gain time in the hope of a rescue forthcoming.[6]

While Haile Selassie negotiated with the Italians, he exchanged notes with Britain seeking a possible British protectorate for a specific number of years in order to avoid complete annexation of Ethiopia by Italy. In 1935, before the Italo-Ethiopian war had started, Colonel E.H.M. Clifford, leader of the British boundary dispute at Wal-Wal, revealed to the press that Ethiopia had asked to become a British protectorate for 25 years.[7]

In early 1936, Haile Selassie asked the British Minister in Addis Ababa, to send a message to King Edward VIII expressing the wish for Great Britain to accept Ethiopia as a protectorate, but leaving its independence intact. British government policy was, however, to avoid war with Italy even at the cost of Ethiopia's independence.[8] Nevertheless, Haile Selassie planned to ask Great Britain to take the Amhara provinces, the Lake Tana region and Wallega under its protection.

Talks between Rome and Addis Ababa continued between the former Ethiopian Minister in Rome, Afework Gebre Jesus (who had married an Italian lady) and Captain Stefano Micciche; Afework travelled between Addis Ababa and Djibouti three times for this purpose. Ethiopian requests included recognition of Haile Selassie's sovereignty over all non-occupied Ethiopia, in return for which Italy would receive a mandate over Tigre and the lands north of Somalia. Italy would also nominate advisers to the Emperor, and establish a corporation to exploit Ethiopia's riches. For these concessions, Ethiopia requested the port of Assab, 1.5 billion lire for war damages and a pact of mutual assistance between Italy and Ethiopia.[9]

It seems that both parties were interested to parley, though for different reasons. Mussolini was still hoping to work out an agreement with Ethiopia as he did not anticipate occupying the whole of Ethiopia. The absence of a programme for administering and governing Ethiopia after its occupation, thus delaying its political and economic development, substantiates this. Ethiopia's willingness to negotiate with Italy was seemingly to bring an end to Italian air raids.

The Italians sent their counter-proposal through Afework's wife who went to Djibouti to meet her husband. Italy would respect Ethiopian independence and the Emperor could retain his title. Italy claimed the territories conquered by Menelik II as a Moroccan-type protectorate, and would recognize one of the Emperor's sons as King of these regions; Haile Selassie would receive 1.2 billion lire to be distributed among his chiefs.[10] Furthermore, the Italians were prepared to give up Assab and Axum, but would request territorial concessions. Another Italian proposal was to keep Ethiopia intact, and give Italy a Moroccan-type mandate. Italy would receive Oromo-speaking territories for 20 years, during which time they would be considered Italian. At the end of this period the local population would be asked to decide whether they wished to remain under Italian rule or that the territory should revert to Ethiopia. Italy would be responsible for Ethiopian diplomatic relations with the rest of the world.

Contacts continued to be maintained. Italy's main theme was still a Moroccan-type mandate, direct rule over the lands conquered by Menelik II, and recognition of Haile Selassie as head of the Amhara provinces. Another proposal was brought by Adrien Zervos, Haile Selassie's personal physician. Zervos contacted Cerulli in Athens in late March 1936. He asked guarantees for Haile Selassie's dynasty, compensation of 300,000,000 lire, financial aid, technical help to develop the country, and a treaty of alliance.

Italy was willing to take into account the needs of Haile Selassie's family and the great lords. They suggested an appearance of Ethiopian independence could be maintained, but with state power in Italian hands. Haile Selassie could have one-third of the Ethiopian territory and Italy would give him 150 million lire. His sons, Asfaw Wassen and Makonnen, would also receive positions in the northern Ethiopian territories.[11]

The most complete plan is revealed by Belgian Colonel Leopold Reul, Chief of Staff of the Ethiopian Army. According to his statements, Haile Selassie realized that while Ethiopia had no more funds to finance the war, Italy still had billions of lire available to obtain a military victory and buy Ethiopia's submission and as a result he and his dynasty would disappear.

Allegedly, Haile Selassie was willing to retain nominal sovereignty over Ethiopia. He would preside over a council of ministers made up entirely of Italians and would need only to sign their legislative bills in order to satisfy the Ethiopian people that he was still their Emperor. To ensure the execution of orders, Ethiopia would have an army of 40,000 men – trained by Italian officers. The word "protectorate" was not to be used. It would be preferable to emulate a relationship such as that of Egypt's with Great Britain, or a perpetual Italo-Ethiopian alliance. Italy would have to provide 1,000,000,000 lire annually for public works, and allow Ethiopia a sea outlet at Assab.[12] This plan, if applied, would be a face-saving arrangement for both countries.

But would Italy accept such terms after it had defeated the Emperor and when there were no forces capable of preventing Badoglio reaching Addis Ababa? Just before Badoglio entered Dessie in April 1936, Asfaw Wassen, heir to the throne of Ethiopia, indicated that he would send messengers to discuss peace. For this reason, Badoglio asked Alessandro Lessona, Under-Secretary at the Ministry of Colonies, to come to East Africa to work out a solution with his aide, General Melchiade Gabba. Badoglio had already planned his march on Addis Ababa, with 1,700 trucks, in the second part of March 1936. Italian victory was in sight, but negotiations were continued. Gabba's plan envisioned the Italian claim on Tigre up to Lake Ashangi, Danakil, Begemder, and the Lake Tana region, and Italy's annexation of Sidamo, Borana, Bale, Ogaden, and Harar in the southern regions. This would prevent Shoa having an outlet to the sea, and give Italy control of the Djibouti railway. Gojam would be ruled by its royal family (*Ras* Hailu Tekle Haymanot) but under Italian protection. The south-western regions, such as Beni Shangul, Wallega, Jimma, Gherar, Limma, and Kaffa were to become Italian "C" Mandates.[13] Haile Selassie would rule Shoa but under Italian control. The negotiations failed because with the wet season imminent it was not advisable to stop military operations, and the Ethiopians could not be prevented from regrouping. Moreover, Haile Selassie, still hoping for aid from the League of Nations, rejected the Italian proposals. In addition, international public opinion believed Italy would be unable to complete the Ethiopian campaign. Mussolini was concerned about extension of the League's sanctions and feared the possible closing of the Suez Canal and the deterioration of Anglo-Italian relations. For reasons of expediency, he preferred that Graziani and Badoglio should take Addis Ababa as soon as possible.

On 16 April 1936, a day after the occupation of Dessie, Badoglio, together with Lessona, composed a letter to Haile Selassie manifesting his desire to prevent any further Christian bloodshed and to enter into direct peace talks. The idea was ingenious: it was to Italy's advantage to have the Emperor concede before the final blow; guerrilla warfare would be reduced and the government's move to the provinces thwarted. In return, Badoglio would march on Addis Ababa in order to guarantee His Imperial Majesty's person and to maintain order in the capital. Haile Selassie did not reply because these talks were not in the spirit of the League of Nations Covenant.

It is important to note that although the main trend in the Italian demands was for a mandate of the Oromo regions, Italy was prepared to allow Haile Selassie to remain with his family and rule over a limited territory on the central plateau. The French diplomat and confidant of Mussolini, Lagardelle confirms this in his memoirs in which he states that Haile Selassie would have had the honours of his rank. Rachele, Mussolini's wife, recalls that her husband told her that if the *negus* had not fled, he would have been nominated head of Ethiopia or at least of Shoa, with the co-operation of an Italian governor.[14]

In the long run, however, that Haile Selassie's parley with the Italians was conducted to assess Italian intentions, to gain time and to delay air bombing must also be taken into account. As long as he was convinced that Great Britain was the sole guardian of Ethiopia's independence, and the more London supported the sanctions – at least publicly – the firmer the Emperor's resolve, and the harder it was for the Italians to move him toward compromise. In the end, he preferred the humiliation and the discomfort of exile in England to submission.

Notes

1. Mack Smith, *Mussolini's Roman Empire*, p. 70; G. Baer, *Test Case: Italy, Ethiopia and the League of Nations*, p. 159.
2. De Felice, *Gli Anni*, pp. 707-10; Baer, *Test Case*, pp. 172-3; Mack Smith, *Mussolini's Roman Empire*, p. 77.
3. Baer has the best, concise presentation of the Italo-Ethiopian War in *Test Case*, pp. 159, 217-21; see also Del Boca, *The Ethiopian War*, pp.70-189; Barker, *The Rape of Ethiopia*, pp. 44-133; Haile Selassie, *My Life and Ethiopia's Progress*, pp. 256-85.
4. Robertson, "Hitler and Sanctions: Mussolini and the Rhineland", pp. 429 ff.
5. Perria, *Impero Mod. 91*, p. 216.
6. Roatta, *Processo Roatta*, pp. 57, 103, 258-61; Bandini, *Gli Italiani in Africa*, pp. 531-66; Del Boca, *La Guerra D'Abissinia*, p. 101; Faldella "La Campagna d'Etiopia", p. 623; Puglisi, *Chi è Dell.Eretrea*, p. 79; Canevari,

La Guerra Italiana, p. 375; MAI/GAB 281 Blattengeta Heruy to Haile Selassie, 6 March 1936 and Makkonen Apte Wolde to Haile Selassie, 6 March 1936; MAI/AV 112 Wolde Mariam to Ethiopian Ministry of Foreign Affairs, 18 February 1936. The telegrams were intercepted by the Italian Intelligence Service.

7. *The Times* (London) 5 June 1935.

8. CC 9/36 and 23/83 and Appendix 24, February 1936; FO 371/20173 Barton to Eden; 20 February 1936; CC 9/36 and 28/83 24 February 1936; FO 371/20173/84 Eden to Barton, 24 February 1936 quoted from Baer "Haile Selassie's Appeal to Edward VIII", p. 310; MAI/POL 15/24 MAE to MAI, 20 April 1936.

9. MAI/GAB 204/28 Makkonen Apte Wolde to Haile Selassie, 11 March 1936; MAI/GAB 281 Makkonen Apte Wolde to Haile Selassie, 30 March 1936; Haile Selassie to Ethiopian Ministry of Foreign Affairs, 27 March 1936; Interview with G. Puglisi, 17 April 1972; ACS/MMM 168 S. Micciche to Ministry of Marine, 7 October 1936; Blattengeta Heruy to Emperor, 8 March 1936; Baer, *Test Case*, p. 251; ACS/RG 12 Badoglio to MAE, 2 March 1936.

10. MAI/GAB 11/II-2 Makkonen Apte Wolde to Haile Selassie, 29 March 1936; Badoglio to Mussolini, 28 March 1936; MAI/AV 112 Afework Gebre Jesus to Ethiopian Military Headquarters, 25 March 1936; MAI/GAB 281 Ethiopian Ministry of Foreign Affairs to Emperor, 5 March 1936.

11. MAI/GAB 281 Ethiopian Ministry of Foreign Affairs to Emperor, 30 March 1936; Baer. *Test Case*, pp. 251-3; Rouaud, "Les Contacts Secrets Italo-Ethiopiens", p. 409.

12. ACS/MM 7/18 Rinaldini to Morgagni: Interview with Colonel Reul, 19 March 1936; Bernoville, *Monseigneur Jaroseau et la Mission des Gallas*, p. 336.

13. Lessona, *Verso l' Impero*, pp. 212-15; Lessona, *Memorie*, p. 252; ACS/RG 12 Badoglio to Lessona, 6 March 1936; Badoglio to Capo del Governo, 8 March 1936.

14. MAI/AV 112 Lessona to Mussolini, 14 April 1936; MAI/GAB 12 Graziani to Lessona, 10 March 1936; Mussolini to Badoglio, n.d; Baer, *Test Case*, p. 254; De Felice, *Gli Anni*, p. 747; Mussolini, *La Mia Vita con Benito*, p. 130; Lagardelle, *Mission à Rome*, p. 168; Lessona, *Verso l'Impero*, pp. 216-17.

4. The Italian Occupation and After

The Flight of Haile Selassie

Haile Selassie left Addis Ababa on 2 May 1936. Already on 22 April, the British Cabinet had decided to allow members of the imperial family to go to Jerusalem; this implies that Haile Selassie had planned to leave Ethiopia long before May. British press communications from Addis Ababa to London had anticipated the imperial family's departure since 26 April 1936, before the capital was occupied by the Italian army. The day before the royal exodus, a British news release reported that the Emperor and his family would depart for Jerusalem, but that Asfaw Wassen would take refuge to the west of Addis Ababa. Conversely the Emperor, in a press conference, said he would never leave Ethiopia. Furthermore, it seems strange that while the British Cabinet had been contacted in spring 1936 and the press had predicted the departure of Haile Selassie in April, Barton, the British representative to Ethiopia, questioned by the House of Commons at the time of the departure of the imperial family, said that he had known only a few hours before. Instead, it can be implied that he was instrumental in advising the Emperor to leave Ethiopia. Other sources said that *Ras* Kassa suggested Haile Selassie should go into exile.

While there is no conclusive evidence that Haile Selassie planned his departure from Ethiopia well in advance, he was influenced by Empress Menen, *Ras* Kassa, and by the Council of Ministers' allegedly favourable vote of 21 to 3, for him to go to Geneva to inform the League personally of the violence perpetrated by Italy against Ethiopia. Another, immediate reason for Haile Selassie's departure was that guerrilla warfare was difficult and dangerous owing to the hostility of the people of south-western Ethiopia. Haile Selassie also realized he had been deserted by his people and that his life was in danger. He could find no troops to defend Addis Ababa and only then did he decide to go into exile.[1]

Not all Ethiopians shared the idea that the Emperor would serve his country better by going abroad. An anonymous "Young Ethiopian", who had been educated in Europe and America, would have killed Haile Selassie for his departure because it was in Ethiopia that his people needed him the most. On discovering that the Emperor had fled, one patriot exclaimed

"My country, there is no one to defend your cause!"

When Graziani was informed about the flight of the imperial family, he wanted to bomb the train on its way to Djibouti, but was forbidden to do so by Mussolini. At this point, one must suggest that the Italians saw a greater advantage in having no one share their power and thus be able to impose direct control over Ethiopia. It is also possible that they did not expect the Emperor himself was on the train — only members of his family — so it would be worthless to massacre them and arouse public opinion against Italy.

Once the Emperor had gone, Addis Ababa was sacked by its inhabitants. It is alleged that Haile Selassie ordered the destruction of Addis Ababa in order to leave nothing to the Italians, and that under cover of the subsequent chaos he escaped to safety.[2] This order does not seem consistent with his personality, despite the fact that in such moments of desperation it is difficult to establish how even great men react. It is also possible that the Patriot, Tekle Wolde Haywariat, the mayor of the capital, the only authority left, suggested burning the city before it fell into the hands of the Italians. Together with Abebe Aragai, Chief of the Police of Addis Ababa, they were seen by European diplomats leading the systematic sacking of the capital.

Ironically, this reign of terror made the Italian invaders welcome in Addis Ababa as the saviours of the local population and the Europeans. Once Addis Ababa was under Italian control, for political and psychological reasons, Mussolini decided to annex Ethiopia, eliminating any possibility of a negotiated settlement. Not to have proclaimed Victor Emmanuel Emperor of Ethiopia, would have meant a long bureaucratic negotiation with Geneva which would have made victorious Italy a defendant. Politically, since negotiations with the Emperor were impossible, and owing to Britain's policy of dealing through the League of Nations, and fearing a change of French policy, to prolong the annexation process was futile. Mussolini preferred to face the world with the *fait accompli* of the occupation of Ethiopia; at last he had his empire, but at a very high cost. Between 1934 and 1937 the cost of the African adventure was about 40,000,000,000 lire. From 1936 to 1940 one US dollar averaged 5.60 lire, consequently the price of the Italian conquest of Ethiopia was equivalent to US $7,142,857,142. If the Italian dictator were to conquer Ethiopia today he would have to spend close to $40 billion.

In the Ethiopian war almost 15,000 Italians died and over 200,000 were crippled and wounded. Ethiopian sources estimate their war losses at 275,000 dead.[3] From a moral standpoint the Italian conquest of Ethiopia was not justified then, nor is it today, in view of the great expenditure in lives and lire involved.

Italy was determined to annex Ethiopia. France and Great Britain, hoping to induce Mussolini to accept their proposals of worthless land concessions — as had been done on previous occasions — failed to realize that there was an end "to collecting sand boxes", as when Eden proposed the cession to Italy of Ogaden. The European powers failed to understand that Mussolini could have been accommodated with a mandate, gaining international recognition as a world statesman, with Italy becoming a world power. He was willing to obtain Ethiopia by land compensation negotiations with France and Great Britain, thus maintaining the spirit of the Tripartite Agreement and a common front against Germany. But world powers could not hand over to Italy a territory that did not belong to them: Ethiopia was an independent nation and a member of the League of Nations. In spite of overt military preparation it is also possible that Italy hoped to secure Ethiopia peacefully. Examination of the diplomatic plans, the secret negotiations between the two parties, the absence of any plan to organize, administer and exploit Ethiopia all substantiate this. Italy's immediate plan permitted the continuation of local administration under the Ethiopian nobility and Haile Selassie. Ironically, in 1935, the Hoare-Laval plan would have awarded Italy about half of Ethiopia, while in 1936, five months after the defeat of Haile Selassie, Badoglio and Graziani controlled only one-third of the country when Italy declared Ethiopia part of the Italian Empire. Thus, Ethiopia was brought under the Italian fasces for five years because of Mussolini's determination to conquer an empire, and because the European powers had little desire to take up arms to protect Ethiopia, and limited diplomatic determination to defend the independence of the last free African nation.

A New Generation of Ethiopians

With the departure of Haile Selassie for Europe, Ethiopia experienced a vacuum and lack of direction. The ineffective Ethiopian government at Gore, western Ethiopia, under the old *Bitwodded* Wolde Tzadik, did not have the trust of the new Ethiopian generation.

As the traditional feudal rulers of Ethiopia had failed in the battles of Tembien and Mai Cew there arose a new generation of Ethiopians drawn chiefly from local country *ballabats*. Several were graduates of Holetta Military College and a few had attended courses at St Cyr in France. Among them there were also members of the noble families, but more significantly included several with at least a rudimentary knowledge of modern warfare and the conviction that feudal organization was quite inadequate. This group held the traditional respect for strong men who would sacrifice their lives for personal honour and national pride. They also searched for reasons that might explain why a proud nation had collapsed before the Italian invading armies. These Ethiopians are generally known as Patriots or *arbagnoch* who opposed the Italian administration and fought to liberate Ethiopia from foreign rule.

After Badoglio entered Addis Ababa the Patriots dispersed throughout Shoa and south-western Ethiopia. Yohannes Saomerjibashian started the underground paper *Pillar of Light of Ethiopia*. *Blatta* Kidane Mariam chose to stay in Addis Ababa where he organized the Ethiopian Youth Movement and a women's movement. Another newly formed Patriot group, the Black Lions, comprised mostly of Holetta graduates, asked *Ras* Imru to become their leader. This group is important because not only were they disenchanted with the failure of the feudal armies, but also because they now began to think in terms of a more modern and democratic government and leadership. Their leaders were Dr Alemwork, the sons of Dr Workne Martin, the Ethiopian Minister in London, the Oromo Yilma Deressa, a graduate of the London School of Economics. The Black Lions had several engagements with Italian forces and their ranks swelled, but in the end in front of Oromo hostility encouraged by the Italians and Italian military superiority, the Black Lions disbanded, only to resurface after the attempt on Viceroy R. Graziani's life in February 1937.

1937 was a period of optimism for the Italians, but for the few Patriots it was a time of desperation. The Holetta graduates had lost all hope of victory. Some went to Djibouti, others to the Sudan, Kenya, and Uganda. A number of them entered Addis Ababa by night, like Haile Mariam Mammo, camouflaged as *askari* organizing hit-and-run attacks, while others without plans went to Marabatie simply to evade the Italians and avoid capture. Perhaps they hoped to open talks with *Ras* Hailu of Gojam, whom they hoped would lead them if given the title of *negus*. But this hope was never realized.[4]

Ethiopian Collaborators

A year after the conquest many members of the Ethiopian nobility and the intelligentsia were liquidated or imprisoned, and their army defeated. Peace, except for a few rebellious centres in Shoa, was general. There was some co-operation with the Italian conquerors out of greed, deference, and for political survival.

Until the end of the Italian presence in Ethiopia, Araya, Yejju and Azebu Oromo continued to collaborate with the Italians against the Patriots. Their reasons were rooted in both religious discrimination and high taxation in the past. Likewise the pagan and Muslim people in southern Ethiopia, and the Oromo of Wollo succumbed to Italian bribery and continued to be loyal to *Lij* Yasu. Furthermore, Shoan mistreatment increased the hostility of the non-Amhara-speaking peoples to Haile Selassie's government. When *Ras* Mulugeta, Minister of War, arrived in Wollo, he destroyed Kobbo, the main centre of Azebu Oromo and ordered floggings; those who survived, he gave the choice of death or military service. When Haile Selassie was defeated by the Italians at the battle of Mai Cew in March 1936, he telegraphed his wife, Empress Menen, "the Oromo helped us only with shouts not with their strong right arm". The Azebu Oromo were bribed both by the Italians and the Ethiopian government. The Italians used the Azebu hatred for the Shoan-Amhara rule for their own military and political aims. The Oromo eagerly accepted money and weapons from the Italians. Reacting to Italian bribes Haile Selassie tried to make counter-offers of silver dollars to the Oromo to help him combat the Italians. In the end the Azebu took bribes from both sides but the majority of them fought against Haile Selassie's army.

The collaboration of the Oromo made the Italian occupation of Ethiopia easier. Asfaw Wassen barely escaped alive from Dessie, where the Wollo chiefs planned to capture him. The Wollo leaders, *Dejaz* Abauko and *Dejaz* Belai Kebbede betrayed Haile Selassie, who, on his way from the northern front to Addis Ababa, had to fight his way against Oromo attacks.

One after the other following the example of *Ras* Seyum and *Dejaz* Ayalu Burru, members of the Ethiopian aristocracy capitulated to the Italians. *Ras* Hailu, one of Haile Selassie's chief enemies, collaborated with the Italians. *Ras* Imru, one of those who had led the Ethiopian resistance, was imprisoned in Italy. *Dejaz* Balcha and *Gebre* Mariam and the three sons of *Ras* Kassa, were killed when trying to negotiate their surrender; *Ras* Desta was defeated and shot by the conquerors. A *Pax Romana* had been imposed. The advantages of civilization and colonization, of which the road network is the most important evidence, were appreciated even by the neighbouring colonial powers.

Among the great nobles who took the oath of allegiance to Italy when the Italians entered Addis Ababa were *Ras* Hailu, *Abuna* Kirillos, and a myriad of smaller chiefs. At a second ceremony, on 9 June 1936, *Ras* Gebre Haiwot Michael, *Dejaz* Amde Ali, Ayalu Burru, Hapte Michael, Mangasha Wube, and Afework, Ethiopian Ambassador in Rome, paid allegiance to Rome. Two weeks later at another ceremony, *Ras* Kebbede Mangasha Atikim, *Abba* Jobir, *Fitaurari* Kenfi, took the oath of loyalty to Italy.

Relations with the Ethiopian Orthodox church were not good. *Abuna* Kirillos, who represented the old regime, returned to his native Egypt instead of co-operating with the Italian authorities. This facilitated the Italian pro-Islamic policy which made Mussolini the champion of Islam. The Ethiopian clergy was accordingly hostile to Italy, and in turn the Italian authorities kept the clergy in contempt for its venality and ignorance.[5]

Graziani did not trust the Ethiopian nobles: their titles carried no power; their influence had gone. What their thoughts, their actions, their sentiments, were, no one knows. To conspire against the Italians was futile and their submission failed to provide the remuneration they had hoped for — only that they were spared their life! They were forgotten by the people and by relatives.

Divided by feudal, territorial and hereditary feuds, unable to withstand the overwhelming Italian military machinery, the aristocracy had no alternative but to surrender. The people too, after the defeat of the imperial army, lost their will to fight. The debacle had also undermined the authority of their feudal chiefs. The average Ethiopian still under shock, did not at first oppose the Italians but maintained an attitude of suspicion and wait-and-see. The urban population stood to gain the most from the invasion. In direct contact with their conquerors, they were hired by the Italian businesses and the various branches of government, with higher wages than they had received under the former Ethiopian government; their salaries were of little benefit, however, because Italian imported goods and food prices skyrocketed. Others were hired as soldiers. Most colonial operations used Eritrean battalions, or irregular Ethiopian troops. The latter served only because of the pay and loot, and were usually led by collaborating chiefs and did not exceed 1,200 men. Regular colonial troops, organized and led by Italian officials, were given the name of the region in which they operated, such as Wollo Yejju, or of the official who commanded them, one of the most famous being the *Banda* Rolle.[6]

Italian Colonial Policy

Graziani replaced Badoglio as Viceroy. Mussolini, knowing Graziani, should have advised him to act with moderation, instead he cabled him "all nobles captured to be shot", thus authorizing Graziani to carry out mass executions and to terrorize the population of entire regions with gas attacks. This type of policy was far from the civilizing mission, the alleged reason for which the Italians had gone to Ethiopia. Italian colonial policy was not only cruel but inconsistent. First Badoglio had flirted with indirect rule, this was reversed by Graziani. Under the third Viceroy, the Duke of Aosta, colonial administration was paternalistic and more humane. Rome, however, had a tight control over the affairs of Ethiopia and imposed stringent racial legislation which the more relaxed of Italian colonialists found difficult to apply.

By its militaristic and racial policy Italian Fascist rule alienated the Ethiopians who demonstrated their opposition to Italian rule, first with isolated acts of sabotage, and then an attempt to assassinate the Viceroy. Ironically, the rebellion started in Gojam, Begemder and Amhara, which had been easily conquered and, up to 1937, peaceful. The rebellion was spontaneous, with local uprisings led by local chiefs unknown outside their regions. In Bircutan, *Fitaurari* Mesfin Redda deserted with 40 men to attack an Italian column. Elsewhere, Ethiopian chiefs who had collaborated with the Italians, such as Iman Meshasha and *Dejaz* Mangasha Jamberie of Faguta, fled to the mountains with their following. In Ermachew the rebellion was sparked off when the elders challenged a group of young people at a wedding feast, to live as proud warriors. In Gojam the news of Italian massacres turned the thoughts of the people toward rebellion. The countryside was generally unsafe, and Addis Ababa and the main urban centres remained fortified military garrisons throughout the period of Italian occupation.

In late 1937, Fascist Italy embarked upon an expensive campaign to develop its new African Empire. Millions of lire were invested to build a network of superb roads across the rugged Ethiopian terrain. For the first time in Ethiopian history the main regions were linked by motor roads.

Mussolini hoped to develop Ethiopia as a granary for Italy, a source of raw materials and a colony of settlement, but in the years of occupation the Italians became disillusioned with their conquest of a land whose inhabitants they could not subdue. Italian colonialists were reluctant to move to Ethiopia, no profits were possible in the new empire to justify the great expenditures in naval bases, and in underwriting the cost of expensive military campaigns. The countryside was unpacified. Trade had been disrupted. No foreign capital was attracted, no minerals, petroleum in particular, were discovered in commercial quantities. The long-term development was established, but impatient Italy had little to show for it by 1940.

British-Patriot Collaboration

When Italy entered the Second World War in 1940, the British feared an Italian invasion of the Sudan from Ethiopia. Fascist propaganda concealed the true situation in Ethiopia from the Allies: that Ethiopia was ripe for rebellion. Not only did internal insecurity prevent the Italians from invading the Sudan, but more importantly, despite Italian denials, there was a great spirit of resistance and patriotism in Ethiopia.

The British-trained Ethiopian refugees in Khartoum, made contacts with Ethiopian Patriots in Gojam – who, although divided among themselves, were still loyal to the Emperor – and planned a three-pronged attack on Ethiopia.[7]

British forces from Kenya invaded Somalia and headed toward Harar and Addis Ababa; British Sudanese troops moved from the Sudan to Eritrea; and a third, small force, composed of English, Sudanese and Ethiopian troops from the Sudan, entered Gojam in January 1941. Poorly informed Italian authorities in Gojam assumed the British and the Ethiopians were an invading force and retreated. By March, victory was recorded on all those fronts and in May 1941 Haile Selassie re-entered Addis Ababa! The Patriots tied down a considerable number of Italian troops when they were needed on the battle front. Likewise the Italians could never be certain of the loyalty of their colonial troops. Hence the Ethiopian contribution to the overall war effort is greater than recorded.

Notes

1. ACS/RG 19; intercepted telephone call from Addis Ababa to Press Telenews in London, 26 April 1936; Greenfield, *Ethiopia: A New Political History*, pp. 222-3; Mokler, *Il Mito dell'Impero*, pp. 150-51; Perria, *Impero Mod. 91*, pp. 278-83; MAI/GAB 28: intercepted telegram: 1) from Addis Ababa to Reuters, London, 1 May 1936; 2) to AMUNIP, London, 1 May 1936; 3) to Internews, London, 1 May 1936; Baer, *Test Case*, p. 271; Haile Selassie, *My Life and Ethiopia's Progress*, pp. 290-91.

2. F.O. 401/1936/XXVIII/61; Greenfield, *Ethiopia*, p. 223.

3. Mokler, *Il Mito*, p. 153; ATR 1/127 E. Cambi: Notes on the Military Expenditure in Ethiopia, 16 November 1936. 38,851,000,000 lire was expended for the conquest of Ethiopia. Sbacchi, "The Price of Empire",

pp. 35–46; Del Boca, *The Ethiopian War*, p. 275.
   4. Greenfield, *Ethiopia*, pp. 224–46.
   5. Greenfield, p. 206; Mokler, *Il Mito*, pp. 165-74, 231–6.
   6. Mokler, pp. 234–41.
   7. Hess, *Ethiopia*, pp. 67–72.

Part II: Italian Administration and Colonization of Ethiopia

5. The Constitution of the Italian Empire

Italian sovereignty over Ethiopia became legal on 9 May 1936. The King of Italy became the Emperor of Ethiopia, and was represented in Ethiopia by a Viceroy or Governor-General.

Italy's claim to the acquisition of Ethiopia was based on the theory of *de bellatio*: military conquest. With the military defeat the Ethiopian government in effect disappeared and Italy acquired the right to rule over Ethiopia. Furthermore, Italy was able to impose its dominion owing to the absence of any form of government to negotiate a peace treaty.[1]

Ethiopia, with Italian Somalia and Eritrea, was referred to as *Africa Orientale Italiana* (AOI), with the status of colony. Ethiopia was divided into four governorships: Amhara, Harar, Oromo-Sidamo, and Shoa. The governors were given wide financial, juridical and administrative autonomy. Each governorship had its local executive council and each governor could correspond directly with the Ministry of Africa, and with other ministries upon the authorization of the Minister of Africa. The Governors' wide powers were recognized as necessary in view of local language, religious, political and ethnic differences, and expedient for speedy handling of local situations to meet their territories' needs.

Although jurists fought on paper to decide what really was the Italian Empire of East Africa, those who lived on the spot or visited Ethiopia gained a completely different opinion of the status of Ethiopia. Vice-Governor-General Arnaldo Petretti, for example, admitted that it was difficult to secure a police permit before undertaking a journey from one region to another. This implied that Ethiopia was a state within a state. Paolo Thaon Di Revel, Minister of Finance, who visited Ethiopia in 1938, reported that it was really a disunited federal state. Each governorship was in essence a separate entity; each region was an independent republic and acted autonomously. Individual governors ignored the problems of the neighbouring governors and had no interest in co-operating with them, fearing that their difficulties would cross governorate boundaries.

This division existed not only in the economic and administrative fields, but also in the military sector. General Ugo Cavallero, sent to Ethiopia as Commander-in-Chief of the Italian troops, found that troops were dependent on each governor, who acted within his own territory with his own troops when and where he decided.[2]

The difficulties encountered in the administration and attempted co-ordination of Ethiopia can also be attributed to the way the constitution was set up. Until 20 April 1936, it was not known whether Ethiopia would be completely occupied and directly ruled by Italy, or whether a defeated Haile Selassie would surrender, in which case Italy would receive Ethiopia as a mandate or a protectorate.[3] There were, therefore, no plans on how to rule or administer Ethiopia, and no colonial personnel ready to face and solve the problems of an immense, newly-conquered country. Nor were Italians expecting Haile Selassie to flee, leaving them the entire country in disorder and torn by war. Only when Badoglio was about to start his march from Dessie to Addis Ababa — after Haile Selassie's final defeat at Lake Ashangi — did Mussolini give orders to work out a charter constitution for AOI.

It is important to note that the administrative division of Ethiopia began before the whole country had been conquered; roughly only one-third was actually under Italian occupation. It was necessary for Italy first to claim its sovereignty over Ethiopia with the law of 9 May 1936, and then to provide new legislation, the *Legge Organica* of 1 June 1936. Absence of these laws would have hamstrung the administration and created disorder in commercial and political life.

When the 1 June 1936 law became effective, the Governorships of Amhara and Shoa were created, and the Governorship of Harar was formed soon after, but the Governorship of Oromo-Sidamo had to wait several months until that part of Ethiopia was conquered. Likewise owing to the wet season, the unsettled military situation and the lack of transport, many months had to elapse after the occupation of Addis Ababa before Italian political and administrative action was extended into the countryside.[4]

The organic law had been compiled soon after the proclamation of the Italian Empire, in response to the international situation. Italy was still under economic siege by the League of Nations and it had to show that all the territory was under effective Italian political and administrative rule. The new Charter of the *Ordinamento Politico Amministrativo* of 15 November 1937, was supposed to be an improvement on the organic law, but it was largely based on the older legislation of the first two Italian colonies of Eritrea and Somalia and applied, with little transformation, to meet the needs of Ethiopia.[5]

The Viceroy and the Ministry of Africa had different interpretations of the colonial legislation. In 1940, when Italy was engaged in the Second World War, in order to resolve this discord, a commission was set up to revise the basic laws of the Italian colonies based on a study of foreign colonial legislative experience. This task was given to two eminent Italian scholars with deep knowledge of Ethiopian problems, Enrico Cerulli and Martino Mario Moreno. Unfortunately, this attempt was too late to solve the constitutional problems of the empire.

Notes

1. Bertola, *Storia e istituzioni dei paesi afro-asiatici* p. 256; Ambrosini, *Impero d'Etiopia*, pp. 3-6.
2. ACS/RG 30/5 Petretti to Graziani, 13 May 1937; MAI/GAB 322 Thaon di Revel, Voyage in AOI, 1938; Canevari, *La Guerra Italiana*, II, p. 378.
3. MAI/GAB 160/XI Lessona: Memorandum to Mussolini, 20 April 1936.
4. MAI/GAB 160/XI Lessona to Graziani, 2 June 1936.
5. MAI/GAB 160/XI Lessona to Graziani, 9 June 1936; MAI/FC 170 Commissione per le modifiche dell'Ordinamanto Fondamentale dell'AOI to Teruzzi, 14 November 1940; MAI/GAB 330 Barracu to Mussolini, March 1943.

6. Colonial Rulers: Jealousies and Antagonisms, 1936-37

Badoglio: The First Viceroy

After the victory over Ethiopia, Italian officials vied for honours, titles and economic compensation for having collaborated in the making of the Italian Empire. The King offered Mussolini the title of prince, and public opinion insisted that he be invested with the Military Order of Savoy with the citation "Mussolini prepared, conducted and won the greatest colonial war that history remembers".

Although Mussolini received only one decoration, he liked to be called the "Founder of the Empire", and was extremely jealous of this position, and did not allow himself to be overshadowed by any of his collaborators who had become popular during the Ethiopian War. De Bono, at his own request had been sent as High Commissioner to East Africa in 1935, to supervise preparations for the first phase of the invasion of Ethiopia. But distrusting his strategic and military skills, Mussolini then sent Alessandro Lessona* and Badoglio to Eritrea, each to file a report on the preparation and conduct of the war; both reports were critical of De Bono's capabilities.

---

*Lessona was one of Mussolini's closest collaborators during the preparation for the occupation of Ethiopia. From 1918 to 1919 he served as personal secretary to General Armando Diaz; he then became head of the War Ministry. In 1922 he joined the Fascist Party and in 1924 was elected to Parliament; he also held important positions in Liguria and Tuscany. He became National Economy Under-Secretary in 1928, and Colonial Under-Secretary under the Minister of Colonies (Mussolini) on 12 September 1929. Lessona endorsed Graziani's Somali offensive. After visiting Eritrea he supported De Bono's replacement in November 1935. In March 1936 he returned to Ethiopia to unsuccessfully negotiate with Haile Selassie; he entered Addis Ababa with Badoglio. Named Minister of Colonies on 11 June 1936, he instructed the reluctant Graziani to enforce racial legislation and to impose a strong colonial policy. Lessona bypassed Graziani and dealt directly with the provincial governors. Graziani complained to Mussolini, whose respect for Lessona diminished as he schemed with Italo Balbo, Governor of Libya, against Ciano and Achille Starace, the Fascist Party secretary, and feuded publicly with De Bono. In summer 1937, after Italian cruelties sparked the revolt in Ethiopia, Graziani and Lessona exchanged recriminations. Lessona facilitated the substitution of Graziani with the Duke of Aosta before losing his post in November 1937.

Fearing that De Bono would be unable to handle any major battles, Mussolini sent Badoglio back to Eritrea to replace him. De Bono, realizing that he was about to be recalled, requested that on his return to Italy he be made Marshal and provided Lessona with a long list of merits to justify such promotion. He was made Marshal and also inspector for the colonial army that was to be formed in Ethiopia with Amharic *askaris*.

Nevertheless, De Bono was clearly no longer in Mussolini's good graces. He was aware of this and noted in his diaries that while he received only 250,000 lire each year, Badoglio received honorary citizenship of the city of Rome and 1,000,000 lire per year.[1]

Badoglio, who was invested with the highest powers in the war against Ethiopia, and became the first Viceroy of Ethiopia was not a Fascist. Mussolini preferred him to De Bono and others because he trusted his military skills. Upon arrival in Eritrea, Badoglio had to reorganize the Italian positions and bring to the front 200 cannons De Bono had left behind, which proved to be essential to Italy's war effort. This massive reorganization delayed the Italian advance for two months, and the impatient Mussolini considered removing Badoglio from his command, but his initial trust in Badoglio was vindicated. After the defeat of Haile Selassie at Lake Ashangi, Badoglio planned and carried out a master raid from Dessie to Addis Ababa, occupied the capital in less time than anyone expected and thus gave Mussolini the empire. In Rome there were champagne toasts for the proclamation of the Empire; in Addis Ababa Badoglio dined on overcooked spaghetti and Lessona on two fried eggs!

Badoglio was both very ambitious and avaricious; aware that he had accomplished a great military feat he wanted to be fully compensated.[2] When Lessona went to Ethiopia on 12 April 1936, Badoglio told him that he wished to return to Italy as soon as Addis Ababa was occupied. After a week in the capital, Badoglio told Mussolini that his heart trouble had become more serious and he was unable to remain as Viceroy of Ethiopia. Mussolini gave him permission to return to Italy. Graziani, Commander-in-Chief of the southern front sarcastically insinuated that Badoglio was going home to collect his honours and enjoy his triumphs. For his return to Italy Badoglio requested a whole ship for himself, the *Arborea*, which left Massawa on 28 May 1936, and upon his arrival he was given the title of Duke of Addis Ababa. In addition, he requested to be given all the money in the Bank of Ethiopia in Addis Ababa; a request based on the tradition that "to the victor belong the spoils".[3] His victory had made him popular, but his greed aroused the hostility of the people and the jealousy of the Fascists. The amount found in the Bank of Ethiopia was 1,700,000 Maria Teresa dollars, half of which went to Badoglio. With this money he built himself a villa in Rome and furnished it with 300 cases of war booty and gifts flown from Ethiopia by the air force. As if honours, gifts and salaries were not enough, the University of Pavia granted him an honorary degree. Roberto Farinacci, one of the Fascist leaders, commented that the only honour not bestowed upon Badoglio was that of Cardinal!

Badoglio was but one example of the high-ranking personalities who took advantage of their position to improve their financial situation. With the Italian Empire proclaimed, Ethiopia became El Dorado. Careers could be made very fast. People took upon themselves titles of dukes, marquises and princes; soon the so-called "Nobility of the Red Sea" was formed in the main Ethiopian centres. With the same facility, house-painters promoted themselves to master-painters; hack journalists became political counsellors, and masons, engineers. The army was no exception; a colonel referred to himself as general because he was sure his promotion would come soon.[4] This was the situation Graziani found when he replaced Badoglio as the Viceroy of Ethiopia.

Graziani: A Neurotic Viceroy

Graziani learned of Badoglio's departure on 14 May, when Badoglio called him to Addis Ababa. He did not realize that he had to go on to conquer Ethiopia, an effort which absorbed all his energy and health. The appointment of Graziani as Viceroy was also unfortunate for Italy, inasmuch as he was a good soldier, he carried out orders from Rome to the point of fanaticism. His reign of terror made him unpopular in Ethiopia and abroad and led to an attempt on his life in February 1937.

Mussolini nominated Graziani Viceroy on 1 June 1936 without consulting Lessona, who opposed it. It is not clear why the Duce made this decision; possibly being aware of the hostility between Graziani and Lessona he preferred not to discuss his choice. Lessona's antagonism discouraged Graziani to the point that he requested to be repatriated. He felt that he lacked enough authority, that Lessona was criticizing his policy and treating him as a "corporal". Graziani's eventual recall, however, resulted from a nervous breakdown he suffered after would-be assassins threw bombs at him on 19 February 1937. From then on Graziani suffered from a persecution complex and a desire for revenge against the Ethiopians, and his administrative and political effectiveness suffered as a result. It was, therefore, decided to replace him. On his return to Italy Graziani was made Marshal and *Marchese di Neghelli*, with a salary of 500,000 lire per year.[5] In many ways this was well-earned. During his 18 months' stay in Ethiopia he not only had to deal with Ethiopian Patriot attacks but the opposition and jealousy of Fascist Party members and Lessona.

Graziani had always feared that Lessona did not present Mussolini with the reality of the Empire's condition, and that his own communications to the Ministry of Africa did not reach Mussolini's desk. Farinacci informed Mussolini that Lessona was deliberately omitting the presentation of important Ethiopian issues. De Bono felt that only Graziani could explain to the Duce the real situation in Ethiopia. Instead of writing to him via the Ministry of Africa, Graziani corresponded directly with Mussolini, bombarding him with piles of documents. Irritated, the Duce ordered Graziani to stop sending him so many letters. To remove the tension between Addis and Rome in 1937 Lessona asked that Petretti, Vice-Governor-General, be sent to Rome to discuss Ethiopia's problems. Petretti's trip to Rome did not eliminate the irregularities and the sense of mistrust between Graziani and Lessona. Therefore, Graziani planned to go personally to Rome by December 1937 and meet Mussolini.[6] The meeting never took place, but Graziani's persistence and hysterical behaviour influenced Mussolini against him; the Italian public felt that Graziani was no longer qualified to rule. Mussolini was informed that Graziani was neurotic, that he harassed his subordinates, making their lives unbearable.[7]

Rumours of Graziani's ill health persisted. He received a great number of letters from well-wishers, to whom his responses were invariably hostile, even when inquiries were well-meant. After serving in East Africa, he complained that he was recompensed only with traps and bombs from the Ethiopians and attacks from the Italians. Graziani insisted that of the 350 small wounds he had suffered, only his right foot was permanently affected and needed surgery.[8]

Because of the Amhara rebellion Mussolini found it difficult to replace Graziani. The changeover thus dragged on for months because of Ethiopia's precarious military situation. In early October 1937 the international news media announced the removal of Graziani. The *Daily Telegraph* wrote that Graziani had been replaced by the Duke of Aosta.[9]

As early as 1936, Mussolini had sent Lessona, the Minister for Africa, to Addis Ababa, to obtain first-hand information on the Viceroy. Lessona reported only that Graziani was tired and seemed nervous. Mussolini saw no reason to remove him then, since he had suffered no military setbacks. Graziani's loyal friends informed him that the Duce supported him and held him in high esteem. Some of this trust remained even after Graziani's official substitution by the Duke of Aosta, as, instead of being recalled, Graziani was allowed to remain for a time as Commander-in-Chief of the Italian troops in AOI, but eventually he did leave Ethiopia.

Ciano noted in his diary on 26 February 1938 that, "although Mussolini had gone to meet Graziani at the station and had embraced him, the Duce said that Graziani had fought well, but governed badly". Mussolini ignored him and, although he was made Marshal, Mussolini did not keep his promise to make him senator, although generals like Nasi and Mezzetti, who had been under Graziani, had risen to that rank.[10] Graziani did not receive any position except that of honorary Governor-General of AOI; he doubtless felt ostracized, and retired to private life as a farmer at Arcinazzo.

As Viceroy, Graziani's time and attention had been divided between defending the Empire from the Ethiopian Patriots, and defending himself from his enemies in Italy and in Ethiopia. He did not have the peace of mind to devote himself fully to solving either the military situation in Ethiopia or the new Empire's many economic problems. He made errors — especially in regard to the treatment of the Ethiopian people — that culminated in the massacre of Addis Ababa after the February 1937 attempt on his life, and

Administration and Colonization

in the pogrom of Debra Libanos monastery. Mussolini and his collaborators had known of Graziani's cruelties in Libya* but did nothing to stop him. When he applied these tactics in Ethiopia, he continued to receive pressing messages and orders to be "tough" with the Ethiopian Patriots. If the first year and a half of the Italian Empire were the worst in colonial history, the responsibility lay not only with Graziani, but also with his superiors. De Bono said that Mussolini had too much on his mind (i.e., the Spanish War), and Lessona, during the same period, stated that Mussolini had lost interest in the colonies.[11]

Graziani and the Duke of Aosta

On 10 November 1937 Mussolini informed Graziani that his duties in Ethiopia were terminated; that same day Graziani reported Amhara's serious military situation to the Duce. According to Graziani, the rebellion occurred because De Feo and Pirzio Biroli, the Governors of Eritrea and Amhara respectively, had not fully co-operated with the Viceroy. He suggested that until the rebellion was put down, he should remain as Commander-in-Chief of the army. He would also act as military adviser to the new Viceroy and brief him on the problems of the empire.[12] He warned that his departure would demoralize the indigenous troops and that his presence alongside the Duke of Aosta was necessary.

Although Graziani's proposals apparently arose out of a genuine desire to ensure the success of the Italian Empire, General Soddu of the Army Headquarters felt that he was pushing too hard to remain in Ethiopia. In his diary the Duke of Aosta noted that Graziani's offer was a good gesture, but he disliked the idea of having him in Ethiopia. Mussolini was, however, receptive to Graziani's proposals, especially after hearing that 18 Italian officers had been killed in Amhara. Thus, Graziani was to remain until the military situation became clear.[13]

On learning that General Ugo Cavallero would arrive shortly in Ethiopia as Commander-in-Chief of AOI troops (as the Duke of Aosta and Mussolini had originally planned) Graziani wrote to the new Viceroy expressing his disapproval. The presence of two Commanders-in-Chief would destroy the unity of the army by allowing officers and troops to take sides. Graziani proposed that he remain as sole Commander until September 1938 – by which time the rebellion would be under control – and then return to Italy and report to Mussolini on the military situation; Cavallero would then assume

---

*In August 1921, in Tripolitania, Graziani distinguished himself in the savage war with the Arabs. In 1930, he became Vice-Governor of Cyrenaica and launched a brutal campaign against the Senusi. He imprisoned the nomad population in camps, in which 60,000 died; sealed the Egyptian border and relentlessly hunted rebels.

command. Meanwhile, Cavallero's presence in Ethiopia could be explained as a reconnaissance; but this meant that Graziani would remain longer than expected and that the Empire would not be administered under a single colonial policy, as the Duke of Aosta had intended.

The Duke reminded Mussolini of their conversations in Rome in December 1937, in which he had expressed his opposition to Graziani remaining as Commander of the Italian troops. He referred to the time when he had been in Libya with Graziani and witnessed Graziani disobey his superiors. The Duke was afraid that Graziani might be disloyal to him too.[14] Upon receiving these reports, Mussolini decided to recall Graziani immediately, since his position in the Empire would only create further complications.

The Controversy over Article 12

This discord among the Italian high-ranking personalities benefited the Patriots. The inadequately co-ordinated administration of Ethiopia failed to make the Italian presence felt. According to Lessona, colonial policy moved from weak, to too strong and cruel.

The interpretation of Article 12 of the *Legge Organica** had been a major source of friction between Graziani and Lessona. According to Graziani the Viceroy was responsible for all AOI policy and Governors were under him. He wanted them to inform him before they communicated with the Ministry of Africa, in order to provide a unitary form of government which would allow him to confirm Italian rule in Ethiopia. He claimed that he had insufficient liberty of action to achieve this aim. Lessona and Thaon Di Revel later admitted they were unwilling to give him a free hand as they were afraid he would misuse his powers, as he had done in Libya, and that the Ministry of Africa used the Governors to limit Graziani's powers.

Lessona did not conceal the fact that he had formulated Article 12 in such a way as to limit the powers of the Viceroy, believing that too much power would make the Viceroy unapproachable and inhibit any initiative on the part of the Governors. Lessona could impose his point of view as long as he received support from Mussolini and could send telegrams to Graziani in his name. Furthermore, Lessona had formed a "family government" in Ethiopia; his two cousins, who were Governors in Ethiopia, Pirzio Biroli of Amhara and De Feo of Eritrea, kept him informed.[15] In addition he had a number of relatives in high positions in Ethiopia, and a host of protégés.

---

*According to Article 12 (which had been formulated by Lessona) the Governors were subordinate to the Viceroy and implemented the Minister of Africa's political, administrative and military orders through the Viceroy. For routine administrative affairs they corresponded directly with the Minister of Africa.

Lessona's ambitions went further than just removing Graziani. He wanted to take his place, or failing that for Pirzio Biroli (Governor of Amhara) to be in charge of Ethiopia.[16]

The Removal of Lessona

A sign of the continued feud between Lessona and Graziani was the incident of Graziani's luggage. When 79 suitcases belonging to the returning Viceroy arrived in Naples, Lessona refused to allow them to pass duty-free, pointing out that there were 79 too many and implying that the Viceroy was taking advantage of his position.[17] Graziani's luggage was as nothing compared to Badoglio's 300 cases, and the truck loads of luggage of Teruzzi, who replaced Lessona as Minister of Africa. Behind the feud lay not only a clash of personalities, but two radically different approaches to solving the problems of the Empire. Graziani was the epitome of fanatic militarism, lacking imagination, and serving Mussolini blindly. Lessona was basically a civilian who viewed the Empire's problems from that angle but was unable to fully realize their complexities because he was too far away. Soon Lessona was to be far away not only from Ethiopia but also from the Ministry of Africa.

It is not clear why Mussolini removed Lessona, but there are many possible explanations. Once Mussolini's collaborators became too popular or too influential and self-reliant, he saw them as a threat to him; he manoeuvred his men to clash with one another. Possibly Mussolini used the Lessona-Graziani feud to destroy both men, by engineering their unpopularity with the Italian public and tiring them to the point that they would give up and resign. An example of official in-fighting was the lawsuit which Lessona as Minister of Africa brought against the Scalera brothers. Lessona accused them of defrauding the government of 50,000,000 lire with the connivance of De Bono. The Scalera Society was able to win all road-building tenders in AOI because they were tipped off to propose minimum prices on the understanding that once the contract had been signed the government would raise the prices. Badoglio, whose son, Paolo, was one of the presidents of the Scalera Society was also implicated. Mussolini did not want to make the Scalera scandal public, so he appointed a commission of five trusted men to settle the dispute and advise him if the Scaleras were guilty or not. Four out of five decided against Lessona. The only one to sustain Lessona's charges was Italo Balbo, the Governor of Libya. On the other side, De Bono was demanding the head of Lessona from the Duce and would not stop until he was satisfied.[18] A report by the Carabinieri in Ethiopia accused Lessona of being responsible for the rebellion of Amhara because he had aided and encouraged his cousins, Pirzio Biroli, and De Feo, in maintaining their independence from Graziani.

Lessona had alienated the Carabinieri by creating another corps to police Ethiopia, the *Polizia Africa Italiana* (PAI) Colonial Police, depriving the Carabinieri of that honour. Colonel Azolino Hazon of the Carabinieri was a close ally of Graziani, while Colonel Maraffa of the PAI, was a faithful supporter of Lessona. Thus, the Lessona-Graziani feud widened to include segments of political life in Ethiopia and Italy. The Carabinieri kept informing the Duce about Lessona, implying that Lessona was no longer an asset at the Ministry of Africa. According to Lessona, the Carabinieri had made a report to the Duce which precipitated his removal as Minister of Africa. The Carabinieri reported that Lessona was preparing a *coup d'etat* with the help of Balbo with Libyan troops, and Pirzio Biroli with his Amhara *askaris*. They would march on Rome and take over power from Mussolini, just as General Franco had seized power in Spain with the help of Moroccan soldiers. Ciano noted in his diary that when Lessona told him about his resignation, the man was very sad; Ciano added that because Lessona had never been sincere or friendly no one would help him.[19]

In retrospect, it seems that Lessona came to realize that the Fascist leaders had become jealous of his position and feared that he would use his power against them. Lessona had contributed toward the conquest of Ethiopia and been instrumental in the return of De Bono and Graziani from Africa. He was too powerful and had Mussolini's ear. In the end, however, Mussolini must have realized it was time to put an end to Lessona's ambitions.

Before leaving the Ministry of Africa, Lessona requested financial aid. Since Badoglio and Graziani had been granted titles, his release from the Ministry of Africa without compensation would make his departure look like disgrace. He asked to be made Marquess of Valmareb, and appointed an honorary colonial Governor-General or to be nominated professor at the University of Rome, holding the chair of Colonial History. He was granted the professorship and received 100,000 lire as compensation from the Duce.[20] Thus ended Lessona's career.

The years of turmoil and personal antagonism between these two men had delayed the proper development of the newly-conquered empire. They had different approaches to the problems of Ethiopia, and neither was willing to submit to the other, or even to concede that proposals put forward by the other might have merit. The personalities of high-ranking officials had been put above the well-being of millions of people, both Ethiopian and Italian. Graziani might have been right to disagree with Lessona's proposals for civil administration because the empire had not yet been conquered, and Lessona was correct when he argued that Graziani was treating Ethiopia as his military playground and disposing of it as a dictator.

Notes

1. Interview with A. Lessona, 27 October 1972; ACS/EB 41, 8 July 1936.
2. Interview with Lessona.
3. ACS/RG 69 Graziani's *Diary*, 20 May 1936; ACS/PAR 811 Fedele

to Asinari Rossillon, 19 June 1936.
    4. ACS/PCM 3/2/2/6947 the Prefect of Rome to the PCM, 31 July 1936; Bandini, *Italiani in Africa*, pp. 436, 438; ACS/SPD-R 63/389-R/2 Vinassa de Regny to Badoglio, 19 January 1937.
    5. ACS/RG 23 Mussolini to Graziani, 7 December 1937; MAI/GAB 294/2 Lessona to Graziani, 15 September 1936.
    6. ACS/SPD-R 41/242-R-C Farinacci to Duce, 13 May 1937; ACS/RG 40/3 De Bono to Graziani, 11 September 1937; ACS/RG 40/2 Fossa to Mazzi, 30 October 1937.
    7. ACS/SPD-RS 25/193-R/1-C Ruggeri to Duce, 1937.
    8. ACS/RG 28 Graziani to MAI, 20 May 1937; Ibid., Graziani to Aymonio, 20 May 1937.
    9. *Daily Telegraph*, 4 October 1937; *La Bourse Egyptienne*, 27 November 1937.
    10. ACS/RG 40/4 Piacentini to Di Stasio, 25 October 1936; Ibid., Fossa to Mazzi, 22 June 1936; Ciano, *Diario 1937-1938*, p. 122; Augenti, Martino, et al, *Il Dramma di Graziani*, p. 180.
    11. ACS/RG 40/3 De Bono to Graziani, 11 September 1937.
    12. ACS/RG 30/3 Mussolini to Graziani, 10 November 1937; Ibid., Graziani to Duce, 12 November 1937; MAI/GAB 261/83 Graziani to Duce, 27 December 1937.
    13. ACS/RG 37/10 Di Stasio to Graziani, 3 December 1937; Duke of Aosta, Diary 13 December 1937 in *Gente* 2 February 1969; MAI/GAB 294/5 Mussolini to Graziani, 10 December 1937.
    14. ACS/RG 40-A/102 Graziani to the Duke of Aosta, 31 December 1937; Lessona, *Memorie*, p. 316; Interview with Lessona, 27 October 1972.
    15. Graziani to Lessona, 20 June 1936 in Ethiopia; Ministry of Justice, *Documents on Italian War Crimes*, Doc. No. 8; Lessona, *Memorie*, pp. 290-3, 310; MAI/GAB 22/XI Lessona to Graziani, 8 September 1937; Canevari, *La Guerra Italiana*, I, p. 379.
    16. ACS/RG 40-A/105 Cerica to Graziani, 3 November 1937; ACS/RG 40-A/100 Puccinelli to Graziani, 16 September 1937.
    17. ACS/RG 30/3 Graziani to Teruzzi, 2 December 1937; ACS/SPD-RS 25/193 Graziani to Sebastiani, 21 November 1937.
    18. Interview with Lessona, 27 October 1972; ACS/RG 53/17-7 Piccioli to Graziani, 10 July 1937; ACS/EB 42, 12 May and 4 November 1937; ACS/SPD-RS 3/31-R/9 Secret information on De Bono, 15 May 1937.
    19. ACS/RG 40-A/112 Cerica to Hazon, 24 November 1937; ACS/SPD-RS 69/525-R Notes from the Carabinieri, 1937; Interview with Lessona, 27 October 1972; Lessona, *Memorie*, p. 334; Ciano, *Diario*, 19 November 1937.
    20. ACS/SPD-R 83/W-R Memorandum for Mussolini, 19 November 1937; Ibid., Bottai to Duce, 19 November 1937; Ibid., Ricci: Registration of Donation No. 61, 1 December 1937.

7. Colonial Rulers: Jealousies

Besides Patriot resistance to Italian rule, Italian administration in East Africa, between 1937 and 1940, suffered chronically from lack of competent colonial civil servants. In Italy there was no institute that prepared Italians for colonial service as there was in France, nor did Italian colonial administrators receive training for overseas assignments. Italian civil servants generally were not motivated by the sense of mission to the "less civilized" people of Africa that was peculiar to British colonial servants. With the coming of Fascism, whatever philanthropic ideals existed were replaced by racial prejudice and the feeling that Italians were superior to Africans.

Duke Amedeo of Aosta, Viceroy of Ethiopia between 1937 and 1941, had travelled widely in Africa and observed at first hand the colonial policies of the various colonial powers; he was a great admirer of the British colonial system. In colonial policy he was also influenced by his uncle, the Duke of Abruzzi, a pioneer in the colonization of Somalia. He believed in the gradual improvement of the people Italy administered, respect for their chiefs and traditions, and a paternalistic system. These ideals are described in his doctoral thesis at the University of Palermo written in 1925. Hence, when the Duke of Aosta became Viceroy of Ethiopia, he brought with him liberal colonial ideas, a sincere desire to improve the condition of the colonial people, and a keen interest in working with Ethiopians and sharing with them the burden of colonial administration.

The Duke received little support from the colonial officials he found in Addis Ababa, and no co-operation in Rome, in implementing such policies. He complained that the majority of officials at the lower echelons of the colonial administration were corrupt and inept. In many ways his situation was made worse by the Fascist system which appointed officials on the basis of loyalty to the party rather than ability to be good colonial officials. Despite all these problems, the Duke, in a spurt of enthusiasm, agreed to go to Ethiopia at the end of 1937.

The Duke of Aosta as Viceroy of Ethiopia

During the second phase of Italian administration in Ethiopia, the period of the Duke of Aosta's vice-royalty, conditions in the Empire began to improve. This was a result not only of the Duke's overall humanitarian outlook but also of his desire for co-operation between Italians and Ethiopians. On 25 October 1936, it was rumoured that the new Viceroy would be a prince of the House of Savoy. In his memoirs, Lessona makes it clear that he had opposed Graziani as Viceroy from the very start and that after the February 1937 attempt on Graziani's life Mussolini was determined to remove him. Lessona mentioned the Duke's name to the Duce as the next Viceroy of Ethiopia. On 9 September 1937, the Duke wrote in his private diary that Mussolini told him he would shortly be sent to Ethiopia to relieve Graziani. This would appear to be the first time that the Duke had heard that he was being considered for the position, but he was deeply gratified by the prospect. King Victor Emmanuel was originally opposed to the idea because he feared the task would prove too much for the prince and if he failed it might even discredit the House of Savoy. Mussolini acknowledged that his position in Ethiopia would not be an easy one but he had confidence in the Duke of Aosta and assured the King that the Duke *non sbaglierà* (would not make mistakes).

The Duke himself had a lengthy talk with Mussolini on 13 November in which the Duce outlined his five-point plan of action for Ethiopia. The first point concerned the problem of the racial dignity of the Italians. Mussolini felt that they had behaved so badly in Italian East Africa that they had given the nation a bad name: to rectify this he now ordered that some Italians be executed to show that justice would prevail. The second point was the need for an accurate military assessment. The Duce suspected that the Ministry of War had deliberately exaggerated the desperateness of the situation in Ethiopia so as to increase the number of troops assigned to the war — and incidentally, the number of promotions as well. The third point was the immediate need for Ethiopia to be economically and financially autonomous; otherwise, the colony would consume the Fatherland. Fourth was the need to solve the religious problem. Priests of all religions would be paid by the state, and thus become state employees, so that they would be favourable to the Italian government. Muslims should be treated on a par with the Copts, but "not a centimetre above". Finally, Mussolini wanted to give autonomy to the Governorships and ensure the independence of the Governors so that power would not be concentrated in the hands of any one person.[1]

The selection of the Duke of Aosta as Viceroy was a good choice in many respects, but one that was also motivated by political considerations. As a symbol of royalty, he was expected to create a favourable impression on Italy's Ethiopian subjects, who were, after all, accustomed to being ruled by an Emperor. And his acceptance by the Ethiopians would of course facilitate Italian political penetration. It was hoped that by putting into effect his philosophy of treating the native population kindly, he would pacify those regions which had rebelled against Italy as a result of Graziani's harsh treatment and Mussolini's inadequate knowledge of colonial policy.

On the other hand, in keeping with Machiavellian precepts, the young prince had been chosen so as to end competition for the office of Viceroy among other candidates who could not match the Duke's noble qualifications. His youth and relative lack of administrative experience would, it was felt, enable Rome to control and manoeuvre him easily. His health, however, was not good: he had already contracted, and been cured of, tuberculosis: as it turned out, the altitude at which he had to live and the pressures of his office meant that his health did not improve while in Ethiopia.

He reached Massawa on 21 December 1937. Mussolini wanted the arrival of the prince to receive the widest publicity in Ethiopia, and all means were used: newspapers, radio, proclamations, and loudspeakers. The festivities in honour of the new Viceroy lived up to expectations. He received a tumultous, though planned, welcome in the larger cities, but was unable to continue the journey to Addis Ababa by car because the roads were unsafe and the military situation critical. On 26 December he arrived by air in the capital.[2]

Reports on the Duke of Aosta as Viceroy were usually favourable. The Viceroy's personal prestige and activity restored calm and distension to both Ethiopians and Italians. He restored the Ethiopians' confidence in Italian justice, a confidence they had lost during the Graziani administration. The Duke's only liability was that he lacked the strength to impose his will over his immediate collaborators. Graziani for his part characterized the Duke as a person who knew what he wanted, and worked hard and with dedication, but who needed to be more forceful in order to carry his decisions through.

Farinacci declared that the Duke was a very nice man, *simpaticissimo*, full of enthusiasm and good will, but unfortunately lacking in a sound political and economic preparation, so that his decisions tended to bear the imprint of the last person to whom he had spoken. Others saw the Duke in a more negative light. For instance, General Ugo Cavallero, in charge of Italian troops in Italian East Africa, judged him to be lacking the maturity to govern such a large Empire effectively and claimed that he did not comprehend the precariousness of the Ethiopian military situation. De Bono, who was a friend of the Duke, doubted whether he would be able to pacify Gojam or restore peace in Amhara.[3]

On balance, the evidence concerning the Duke is more positive than negative. Teruzzi reported that the Viceroy seemed well informed about the problems of the Empire and that the longer he was there, the more political sensitivity he developed. The people in Ethiopia liked him and described him as *in gamba*, expressing the general feeling that he was efficient and clever. Similar comments came from the British consul in Addis Ababa, in whose opinion the Viceroy possessed a lively political aptitude and intelligence. And even Farinacci admitted that the Duke was the object of unanimous sympathy throughout the Empire.[4] Perhaps the most flattering appraisal of the Viceroy was expressed retrospectively by Abebe Aragai, the Patriot leader from 1937 to 1941, who saw the Duke as the greatest of Ethiopia's enemies whose good government came close to extinguishing the Ethiopians'

Administration and Colonization

desire for freedom and independence. Even Haile Selassie paid homage to the Duke as a man to whom Ethiopia had to be grateful.[5]

On 7 April 1938, the Duke underwent an emergency operation for a perforated appendix. Post-operative complications kept him away from his office for several months. Because of his precarious health, the doctors forbade the Viceroy to resume a full-time schedule, and advised rest in Italy. Three months after the operation the wound had still not healed and in Naples he again required surgery. He returned to Addis Ababa only in August 1938.[6]

This was not to be the Viceroy's only visit home. He visited Italy frequently for political and health reasons. In June 1939 he absented himself from Ethiopia ostensibly to attend his brother's wedding, in reality to take more time out to convalesce. But his heart remained in Ethiopia, and he always used these visits to talk at length with the Duce on the various problems of Italian East Africa.

On the eve of the Second World War, the Duke, fearing that the Empire would be sacrificed to Mussolini's world ambitions, tried to impress on the Duce that Ethiopia was unprepared for a role in the conflict. He flew to Rome several times in 1939 and 1940 to do so, his last visit being in June 1940, only a few days before Italy's declaration of war on 10 June. The Duke realized that the only way to convince Mussolini and bring him up to date on the many problems facing the Empire was by his personal intervention. But though he always won verbal assurances from the Duce on these occasions, he received little actual help, which only further discouraged him and added to the difficulty of his task. It was brought home to him that the leadership in Italy actually accorded a very low priority to their possessions in East Africa. On the outbreak of the Second World War, De Bono urged on Mussolini and the Duke himself that the latter should return to Italy. But the Duke felt obliged to fulfill his duty as a leader of the Italian Empire, and wanted to set an example to his men in an attempt to pin down as many British troops as possible in Ethiopia, with the object of allowing the Italo-German troops in Egypt to win there and then come to the rescue of Ethiopia (see chapter 19). However, he was taken prisoner following the battle of Amba Alagi in May 1941, and died in Nairobi in January 1943, of complications stemming from tuberculosis, amoebic dysentery, typhus and malaria. According to De Bono, most of the blame for the Duke's premature death could be attributed to the Duce (who would not allow him to come back while there was still a chance), the rest to the King of Italy. De Bono believed that for political reasons they both wanted to keep the Duke as far away from Italy as possible.[7]

Reign and Rule Controversy

While Viceroy, the Duke also had to contend with the hostility of some of his immediate associates: this was particularly true of the Vice-Governor-

General, Enrico Cerulli, an eminent scholar of Ethiopian studies and former Director of Political Affairs at the Ministry of Africa. The Duke and Cerulli were often at odds, thus further weakening the administrative machinery of Italian East Africa at the very top, where there should have been the greatest co-operation and unity. This contributed to the delay in rationalizing the administration in Ethiopia.

The fundamental cause of the conflict between the two men had to do with their differing conceptions of the Viceroy's role. Even before the Duke of Aosta had been appointed Viceroy, it had been predicted that a prince of the House of Savoy would be simply a figurehead, ruling in name only. Cerulli came to Ethiopia sharing this view: the Duke of Aosta was a symbol of authority, he believed, but should leave the actual government of Ethiopia to the Vice-Governor-General. But the Duke, desiring to be Viceroy in every sense of the word, wanted both to reign and to rule. This set the stage for administrative confusion in Ethiopia because under the circumstances no one knew whom to obey.

Cerulli, as a scholar and theoretician, saw and wanted to solve the problems of the Empire from a civilian point of view. The balance of power between the two personalities at first swung back and forth, but when the Viceroy was ill or away in Italy, Cerulli was in clear control and would brook no interference. Opinion in Italian East Africa in fact held Cerulli largely responsible for the administrative confusion, which sometimes even the timely intervention of the Viceroy could not cure.

According to Farinacci, Cerulli had a poor reputation in Ethiopia. The majority of those who knew him felt that he was unable to carry out the responsibilities of such a high office and lacked political experience. The Duke's opinion of Cerulli was similar. Cerulli was a highly cultured person, but he did nothing to win the sympathy of the different peoples of Ethiopia or of the foreign representatives there: he was slow in taking decisions and he was rude. He openly favoured and made use of Somalis in the government, over and above any other ethnic group, and he was reluctant to receive visitors in his office.

Yet, despite his defects, Cerulli was one of very few high colonial officials who had extensive colonial experience and was knowledgeable about the environment. It is possible that the Duce wanted to run Ethiopia through Cerulli. The British consul surmised that Cerulli had been sent to East Africa to do the bidding of Rome.[8] Although the Duke of Aosta wanted Cerulli removed, Teruzzi's view that the government could not be deprived of Cerulli's experience prevailed. In this way, instead of eliminating the cause of friction, Teruzzi imposed his will on the Duke and indefinitely postponed Cerulli's departure. Thus, the artificial administrative structure was allowed to go on. The Duke was left not only with an immense volume of work but also with the difficult situation bequeathed by Graziani, now made worse by the presence of Cerulli. Mussolini, still favourable to Cerulli, thereupon decided to give him the Governorship of Harar, and to make Guglielmo Nasi, then Governor of Harar, Vice-Governor-General of Italian East Africa.

Administration and Colonization

The Duke's troubles did not end with the departure of Cerulli, however. He also faced the opposition of General Cavallero. It was thought that Cavallero's presence in Ethiopia would reduce the Viceroy's work load: while the Viceroy was the supreme authority in Ethiopia, he would not take an active part in military affairs. Cavallero believed that the Viceroy was too young and inexperienced where colonial military matters were concerned and proposed that he should limit his duties exclusively to representing the Empire, at least until such a time as Ethiopia was pacified. The General wanted all military power in his hands so as to be able to carry out a unified military policy.[9] The Duke did not share this conception of either his own or Cavallero's role, and the stage was thus set for yet another conflict of wills.

Cavallero had been sent to Ethiopia in the first place chiefly because of his friendship with Lessona, even though he lacked adequate colonial experience and was not suitable for the task, which placed him in a disadvantageous position to wage this particular contest. Cavallero was not lacking in detractors. The Duke criticized him for his handling of the rebellion in Gojam: he felt his methods against the Patriots were disproportionate to the needs of the situation (Cavallero had resorted to the use of gas), and had failed to give the results predicted. Going on the offensive in self-protection, Cavallero blamed the military authorities of other territories. Cavallero also had a strong supporter in Farinacci, who reported to the Duce that Cavallero enjoyed great prestige in Ethiopia. His military failures in Gojam were due to Governor of Amhara Mezzetti's jealousy.[10] But Cavallero was unquestionably careless and over-optimistic in his appraisal of the military situation in Ethiopia, purposely making it look rosier than it was in order to fulfil his great ambition of being promoted supreme army commander. In defence of his record Cavallero drafted a twenty-page report for the Duce, but this the Viceroy declined to forward to Rome.[11] On 10 April 1939, Mussolini, under pressure from the Duke of Aosta, removed Cavallero from his post.

His successor in May 1940 was not much of an improvement. General Claudio Trezzani was a man of culture and a master strategist; however, he was completely devoid of any practical experience of fighting conditions in Africa. The choice of military men more interested in carving out careers for themselves or in theoretical solutions to military problems thus did nothing to alleviate the always precarious situation in Ethiopia, where only the boldest — or the subtlest — methods might have succeeded. The result was continued defeat or stalemate, with their inevitably demoralizing effects on both Italian and colonial troops as well as on the civilian population which could place little trust in the Italian government's promises of a better life and more efficient administration to come.

The Duke's experience with his new Vice-Governor-General was a much happier one. Not only was General Nasi content to execute the orders of his superior, the Viceroy, but he contributed to raising the moral and political status of the Italians. He took up his post on 6 May 1939, in promising circumstances. His Governorship of Harar had been a model for the rest of Italian East Africa, for here he had succeeded in winning the Ethiopians over to Italy. If peace and prosperity were achieved anywhere in Ethiopia during the period 1937-40, it was in Harar. As it turned out, Nasi became the most valued of the Duke of Aosta's collaborators, both in military matters and with respect to native policy. Even foreign authorities admired the skill Nasi had shown both in subduing rebellion in the territory and in protecting the Ethiopians from Italian abuses. Some Italians, on the other hand, complained that Nasi was too soft toward the Amhara and Shoans, whom he valued so highly that he was instrumental in giving back to the great *rases* their traditional military and political command at the beginning of the Second World War, in exchange for their willingness to collaborate in opposing the return of Haile Selassie.[12]

Teruzzi: Mediocre but Faithful

Nasi was an exception to the rule. In addition to difficulties with many of his closest associates in the government of Italian East Africa, the Viceroy was also plagued by differences of opinion and personality with a key figure in the home government. When he became Viceroy and was informed that Teruzzi had been appointed Minister of Africa, the Duke considered resigning. His objections to Teruzzi only increased with further contact, whether in Rome or in Ethiopia, for he considered Teruzzi's presence not only useless, but positively damaging to the cause of good government in Ethiopia.

Attilio Teruzzi was a professional military man. In 1921 Mussolini made him a Party Vice-Secretary because he trusted him for his stupidity and lack of an independent power base. Teruzzi crushed the 1922 Milan strike and prepared the march on Rome. Rewarded by appointment to high Fascist positions, he was also elected a deputy in 1924, a seat he retained until 1943. He became Governor of Cyrenaica in 1926, defeating the Senusi and clearing the area by 1928. In 1929 he became the Fascist Militia Chief-of-Staff and member of the Fascist Grand Council. Teruzzi organized six Black Shirt divisions for the Ethiopian campaign, assuming the command of one himself in 1935. During the Spanish Civil War he was sent to Spain as Inspector-General and Commander of the Black Shirts. In November 1937 Teruzzi became Under-Secretary of the Ministry of Africa. His rapaciousness, arrogance and disregard for the Duke of Aosta's authority retarded the development of Ethiopia. Teruzzi prepared the colonies for war poorly even after he became Minister of Africa in October 1939.

Each time Teruzzi visited Ethiopia he imposed his will on his host, showing little or no respect for his royal person or even for common decency. In 1938, though aware that the Duke was still suffering from complications arising from his April surgery he insisted on coming on his first visit to Italian East Africa anyway. Once in Ethiopia Teruzzi proposed an intensive schedule of work.[13] Teruzzi displayed similar discourtesy toward the Duke on his second visit to Ethiopia in 1939. For his last visit in 1940 it was hoped that some of the problems that had marred the previous two trips could be avoided by careful preparation. The effort was apparently wasted, however, for Teruzzi's behaviour once in the capital was, if possible, even more scandalous than on the previous visits. He first of all claimed the right to stay in the Viceregal palace, which would have meant the Duke and his wife moving out — though he ended by making do with the Villa Italia, the former residence of the Italian Legation, where he promptly surrounded himself with women of a questionable sort. He also transferred a troupe of dancing girls from Asmara to the capital, forcing the municipality of Addis Ababa to pay 50,000 lire to cover their expenses.[14]

De Bono noted that Teruzzi brought 38 people with him on this trip to Ethiopia, as if he were going forth to conquer the Empire. It was this exaggerated entourage, together with the bombastic quality of his very presence in Ethiopia, that made his relations with the Viceroy especially tense, for it seemed obvious that he was more concerned with satisfying his thirst for adulation than with serving the state in any useful manner. His mind was absorbed by frivolities, and he seemed intent on looking after his own personal economic interests. Nor surprisingly, after his visits to Ethiopia he was not able to give an accurate and objective picture of the problems of the Empire. In a report he submitted to Mussolini in 1939, he pictured the situation in Ethiopia quite optimistically, as being serene and calm. He failed completely to consider the major changes taking place: the culture-shock the Ethiopians were experiencing as a result of the Italian presence or the ravages brought on by the invasion of 1935-6, and the subsequent continuing guerrilla warfare waged by the Ethiopian insurgents.

Mussolini was aware that the reports of his ministers and officials were not always accurate and that they tended to bring to his attention only those things they wanted him to notice. It was, however, the Duce's fault if this happened, because in appointing men to key positions—as was the case with Teruzzi — he considered loyalty to himself more important than intelligence. Teruzzi, for instance, was called to the Ministry of Africa only because he was a good and faithful soldier. Ciano, however, reported that Teruzzi was a faithful but mediocre executor of orders, or rather, "more faithful than mediocre".[15] An unprepared, overbearing man like Teruzzi could obviously not solve the complex problems of the Empire, especially when he found it hard even to get on with those who were responsible for the day-to-day conduct of the administration of Ethiopia. According to De Bono, he was a man of weak character, open to influence from almost every quarter. In other words, he had neither the moral fibre nor the mind to organize and command at the ministry with which he was charged.

Teruzzi officially remained Minister of Africa until 3 September 1943, when he was arrested along with Ciano and Farinacci, betrayed to the police by a lover. On 29 September 1944, he was tried and condemned, accused of having taking possession of objects of value which had been donated to the state.[16]

It was customary for any personality who went to Ethiopia to receive gifts. De Bono brought back several cases of presents for himself, Graziani, 79 and Badoglio some 300! From his 1939 visit alone Teruzzi brought back goods from Ethiopia that required four trucks! But there was something special about Teruzzi: he was hated in Ethiopia. Nothing changed after his visits: he was accused of ignoring the welfare of Italians and of going there primarily to further the interests of the great industrial and financial companies (as well as his own), especially in the roadbuilding company, and the hotel industry. The people in Africa felt that Teruzzi was a speculator and feared that, since the Duce accepted him, his example would be imitated by others with impunity: people concluded that the Duce had become weak and soft and that he was morally, and perhaps even materially, associated with Teruzzi.[17] How, then, could the efforts of the Viceroy be fruitful, if the very man who was supposed to be his most intimate collaborator in the home government showed every sign of being intellectually and morally incapable of lending him support? He also could not count on Cerulli, who wanted more power for himself in the civil administration, while Cavallero sought the same thing in the military sphere. Only Nasi gave him his full support, but he had arrived too late, because the Second World War started soon after and thus there was no time to work toward pacification of Ethiopia.

Hampered by delicate health, the Duke could not dedicate all of his time to the administration of Ethiopia. The weight of the task was too much for his limited experience, and this, added to psychological differences with his immediate collaborators, made success almost impossible to achieve. Thus, Italian unpreparedness to govern was made worse by personal rivalries and self-interest which took priority over the well-being of the Empire and retarded the co-ordination of Italian rule in Ethiopia.

It may be argued that someone else with more experience and authority should have been put in command in Ethiopia, but, regardless of Mussolini's opportunistic motivation for the appointment of the Duke of Aosta as Viceroy, it can be concluded that in spite of his alleged weaknesses he was a wise choice. Had he received the necessary support and attention in Rome, rather than lip service, from a volatile Mussolini or from his ministers and colonial administration the Viceroy would have been able to restore prestige and trust in the Italian government among the Ethiopians by giving them humane treatment and administrative positions and gradually restoring them to their former positions. He fought corruption and incompetence at all levels, but was unable to eradicate abuses and racism because his collaborators were loyal to the Fascist tenet that Ethiopians were to be treated as inferior subjects. The Duke of Aosta's opposition to prejudice against the Ethiopians and ill-treatment of them brought out starkly the conflict of opinions and the antagonisms between the Fascist hierarchy and the Viceroy and his small group of progressive liberal supporters. Conflicts and disputes on colonial policy and personal rivalries eroded the power of the colonial rulers from

Administration and Colonization

within, and the Ethiopians in turn took advantage of the power struggle at government level to foster their own interests and remained suspicious and largely unconcerned about government advocated policies and promises.

Notes

1. Lessona, *Memorie*, pp. 312-15; Duke of Aosta, *Diary*, 9 September 1937 in *Gente*, 19 February 1969.
2. MAI/GAB 261/88 Mussolini to Graziani, 13 December 1937; ACS/RG 30 Teruzzi to Graziani, 29 November 1937.
3. MAI/GAB 278/483 Teruzzi: Report on the visit to AOI, 1938; ACS/RG 17 Graziani's Diary, 7 January 1938; ACS/SPD-R 41/242-R/39-D Farinacci to Duce, 25 December 1938; Canevari, *La Guerra Italiana*, II, p. 378; ACS/EB 43, 10 January 1939.
4. MAI/GAB 281 Teruzzi to Duce, 4 June 1938; MAI/GAB 75/5 Letter to Edda Ciano, October 1939; ACS/MAI 15 Maraffa to MAI Confidential information, September 1939.
5. *Gente*, 19 February 1969.
6. MAI/GAB 251/16 Duke of Aosta to Teruzzi, 27 May 1938; Ciano, *Diario 1937-1938*, 23 June 1938; Duke of Aosta, Diary in *Gente*, 12 March 1969.
7. MAI/GAB 261/82 Teruzzi: Notes for the Duce, 2 March 1940; Ibid., Teruzzi to Duke of Aosta, 3 March and 6 May 1940; ACS/EB 43: 1, 5, 8 April 1940; Ibid., 45: 24 and 25 February 1942.
8. ACS/RG 40/4 Piacentini to Di Stasio, 25 October 1936; Ibid., 40-B/45 Memorandum for Graziani, Summer 1938; MAI/GAB 287/2 Teruzzi to Duce, 4 June 1938; FO 371/22021/240 Stonehewer-Bird to FO, 25 March 1938 in Pankhurst "Italian Fascist Occupation . . ." pp. 71-4.
9. MAI/GAB 286/XV Teruzzi: Memorandum for Mussolini, 31 March 1939; Ibid., 278/483 Teruzzi: Report of the voyage in AOI 1939; Ibid., 251/16 Meregazzi to Teruzzi, 16 June 1938; Duke of Aosta, Diary in *Gente*, 12 March 1969; Canevari, *La Guerra Italiana*, II p. 378.
10. Lessona, *Memorie*, pp. 316-25.
11. ACS/SPD-R 257/63 Teruzzi to Duce, 18 January 1939; MAI/GAB 265/169 Teruzzi to Meregazzi, 19 January 1939.
12. ACS/MAI 1/5 Maraffa to MAI: Confidential information on the British Consul in Addis Ababa, 15 September 1939; MAI/GAB 307/A Meregazzi to Teruzzi: Information from *Dejaz* Hosanna Jiotte, 1938.
13. Interview with Lessona, 27 October 1972; Duke of Aosta Diary in *Gente*, 12 March 1969; MAI/GAB 278/483 Teruzzi to Viceroy, 29 April 1938.
14. Interview with Lessona, 27 October 1972; Un Emigrato in AOI, *Lettera Aperta*.
15. MAI/GAB 251/16 Meregazzi to Piccioni, 27 May 1938; Mussolini, *La Mia Vita con Benito*, p. 113; Ciano, *Diario*, pp. 33, 53.
16. Interview with Lessona, 27 October 1972; ACS/EB 42: 24 November 1937; Ibid., 43: 12 November and 7 May 1938; Ibid., 47: 3 September 1943; Ibid., 46: 3 June 1943; ACS/SPD-RS 14/64-R/10 Teruzzi, Process in absentia, 12 December 1944; MAI/GAB 256/166 Teruzzi to

Tecchio, 9 February 1939.

17. Interview with Mrs J. Zambon, 4 May 1972; Interview with G. Puglisi, 15 April 1972; Un Emigrato in AOI, *Lettera Aperta*.

8. The Powers of the Viceroy

The Governor-General as Inspector General

The Viceroy was in charge of the civil and military affairs of the Italian Empire but he had to account to the Minister of Africa.

To co-ordinate all the services of Italian East Africa, seven directorates were formed in Addis Ababa to perform colonial administrative tasks.[1] This replication of the office organization of the Minister of Africa was technically absurd. The Ministry of Africa did not realize that, besides the onerous expense of reproducing the Ministry's bureaucracy in Ethiopia in its smallest details, local conditions were unsuited for it. Moreover, the fundamental laws of June 1936 and November 1937 were vague on the powers of the Viceroy, the prerogatives of the Governors, and the real functions of the Ministry of Africa. The Ministry interfered with the government of East Africa because it believed itself to be the only organ responsible to the Italian government; this was true, but not practical, because problems seen from 5,000 kilometres' distance appeared out of perspective.

With the proclamation of the Italian Empire, the territory of East Africa was organized into six Governorships, (Eritrea, Somalia, Amhara, Harar, Shoa and Oromo-Sidamo) each Governor being responsible for the administration of his territory, but remaining subordinate to the Viceroy. The Viceroy became the intermediary between the Ministry of Africa and the Governors, taking away the vital direct contact between the Ministry and the Governors.

Graziani defended his prerogatives as Viceroy in relation to the powers of the Governors. He interpreted Article 12 (see footnote p. 51) of the June 1936 law as anti-hierarchical. The conflict over Article 12 began when Lessona ruled that Governors depended directly on the Ministry of Africa because they had been chosen and appointed by the Ministry. The Governors could correspond directly with the Minister of Africa, thus by-passing the Viceroy, who would not be able to express his opinion on colonial matters. Graziani argued that Governors should pass the orders given to them through the Viceroy, who in turn, received them from the Ministry of Africa. The Ministry of Africa reiterated that the Governors were to execute orders;

the Viceroy had to pass them on and the Ministry would formulate them. But how could the Viceroy see that orders were executed if he were kept ignorant of the problems of the local Governorships? Article 12 said that Governors could correspond with the Ministry of Africa directly for "routine administrative matters". We may deduce, therefore, that the term referred to secondary matters of everyday administration, whereas major issues were to be submitted to the attention of the Viceroy. Graziani rightly lamented that Governors were corresponding with the Minister for matters of ordinary *and* extraordinary administration, purposely ignoring the Viceroy. He believed that Article 12 was written in an ambiguous way and that it followed the principle of "divide and rule", which curtailed the position of the Viceroy and concentrated all power in the Ministry of Africa.[2]

Graziani, however, was quite meticulous in keeping the Ministry informed of all that was going on and transmitting all communications received from the various Governorships *verbatim*. Lessona suspected Graziani might not be informing him fully and above all wanted to retain a check on both the Governors and the Viceroy. Furthermore, Lessona admitted that the relationship of the Viceroy and Governors was an experiment in Italian colonial administration, and that Article 12 was ambiguous. The Ministry of Africa saw the Viceroy as a distributor of orders: management was left to the individual Governors.[3] The Viceroy was someone who would *co-ordinate* the administrative activities of Italian East Africa, *executive* tasks were reserved for the Governors. The committee for the reform of the *Legge Organica* concluded that the duty of the Viceroy was only to ensure the execution of orders given by the Ministry of Africa and did not include the power of direct management. The Governor, "the man on the spot" who knew his territory, could adapt orders to meet his local needs. If all powers were concentrated in the Viceroy, the functions of local government would come to a standstill and this would delay development of the Empire – instead Graziani meddled in the affairs of the Governors and put the latter in the humiliating position of simple commissioners. This interference delayed the solution to important problems which could have been solved directly and quickly between the Governors and the Ministry. As a result of intervening in the internal affairs of the territories, Addis Ababa came to have a superior bureaucracy of mammoth proportions and sedentary tendencies. The office of the Viceroy neglected to perform inspection functions, its only duty according to the *Legge Organica*. Furthermore, the Viceroy tended to substitute for the Ministry of Africa in its functions and by-passed it by corresponding in an offensive and critical way directly with Mussolini.[4]

Graziani was not the only Viceroy who was jealous of his prerogatives. The Duke of Aosta also wanted to reign and to rule, although he was more democratic and less authoritarian than Graziani. He found it difficult to decide where his jurisdiction ended and where the power of the Governors began. Mussolini reaffirmed his desire to give autonomy to the Governors to prevent the concentration of too much power in the hands of the Viceroy. In the Duce's opinion the Viceroy had to co-ordinate the action of the Governors but had to leave them autonomy of action and responsibility. In many ways, Mussolini accepted Lessona's point of view without having visited Ethiopia to realize the difficulties on the ground.

In the end Graziani and the Duke of Aosta's policy transformed the Governors into regional functionaries. This created more work for the Viceroy who found that instead of being able to dedicate his time to the defence of the Empire and economic and agricultural development, he was engulfed in bureaucratic work. The over-centralization took away the Governors' incentive. It would have been best to concede the Governors some autonomy permitting a certain elasticity within the various branches of government, in order to reach rapid conclusions to local problems.[5]

The devolution of power to the Governors in a rational way was justified, but it would have been hard to apply because of the local conditions. Governors could have been fully autonomous if Ethiopia had been completely conquered and pacified, if a civil administration had been functioning and the country had been developing economically and industrially. However, the most serious Italian problems were security and lack of transportation; the Governorships of Amhara and Oromo-Sidamo, which had the greatest share of these difficulties, were, at times, cut off from contact with Addis Ababa. What use would it have been for the Govenor of Amhara to have the privilege of corresponding directly with Rome when he was besieged by the Ethiopian Patriots! His immediate safety lay with the Viceroy who had the army to rescue him at his disposal. The *Legge Organica* had been framed for Eritrea or Somalia – where Italian rule had been established for several decades – but not for a country like Ethiopia, where war was an everyday occurrence.

The General Council

At the same time provisions were made to strengthen the position of the Viceroy who had at his disposal a General Council. It was composed of the Viceroy, the Governors, the highest personalities of the armed forces, and the Fascist Party and a representative of each of the various Ministries with branch offices in Ethiopia. The General Council was consulted on the budget, the programme of public works, agricultural, economic and industrial development, taxes and tributes. The Governors had a deliberate vote and, in case of emergency, the Viceroy could make decisions without the consent of the Council.

The General Council was designed to give advice to the Viceroy. Graziani however, made it clear to the Governors that he would call them only when strictly necessary. In order to save time he declared he would make decisions by himself.[6] Therefore, Graziani ruled without opposition because he was feared by his officials and imposed his will as a dictator.

Not so with the Duke of Aosta, who was more liberal. During his administration, he often convened the Council, which proved to be helpful because it prevailed in an atmosphere of general reciprocal confidence and trust. The meetings were irregular because of the great distances involved, or because the agenda was not full enough, or because there were no important matters to be discussed. Under the Duke of Aosta, the Council became the most important legislative body of Ethiopia. Reading the surviving minutes* gives the impression that discussions were carried on in a smooth and conciliatory manner and that the Governors and the Viceroy submitted to the majority vote in a democratic spirit of co-operation. The Council became the body where plans for the organization of all areas of the life of the Empire were made. In this body new resolutions were deliberated on, the Governors brought their territorial problems, the Viceroy was informed of the conditions of the various territories and all worked to co-operate in solving each other's problems. This was perhaps the most positive contribution of the Italian administration of Ethiopia.

Ministerial Bureaucratic Interference

The administration of Ethiopia was complicated by a number of provisions that were not always useful to its smooth running. To the personality differences between the Viceroy and the Ministers of Africa and their interpretations of their powers and prerogatives under the ambiguous colonial legislation, one must add the office controversy between the Ministry of Africa and Governor-Generalship of Italian East Africa.

Both Graziani and the Duke of Aosta felt the pressure exercised upon the affairs of Ethiopia by the Ministry of Africa. The smallest decision had to be made by Rome. At a time when the Empire needed unity of command to solve the military problems of the conquest, occupation and pacification, there was none. It was not only the Minister and the Viceroy who had administrative and personal differences. The crisis was made more acute by the attitude of the officials of the Ministry of Africa, who were indifferent to the needs of the Empire and affected by unwarranted optimism over the problems of Ethiopia. Furthermore, other Ministries interfered in the administration of Ethiopia by giving unsolicited advice and declaring their presence in Ethiopia indispensable.[7] The intrusion of seven ministries (the Ministries of Foreign Affairs, Agriculture, Foreign Currency Bureau, Public Works, Corporations, Finance, and Propaganda) and the Fascist Party was especially noticed. Their position had become so entrenched that they

---

*The first minutes of the General Council are dated 1938. By this time Cavallero and Cerulli were no longer a problem for the Viceroy. All the Governors were, by then, willing to co-operate with the Duke.

exercised veto powers over legislation regarding the colonies. A typical example of negative ministerial influence was the Ministry of Foreign Affairs, which, while dealing with Great Britain for the *de jure* recognition of the Italian Empire in 1938, failed to inform the Viceroy about the negotiations.[8] Thus it seems that if the Italian government was willing, at least in theory, to give power and authority to the Viceroy, in reality it did not work. The Ministries of Africa and Finance were the ones most strongly resisting release of their authority over the colonial government of Ethiopia. At first, the powers of the Viceroy were limited because of the distrust of Graziani's policies, but the Duke of Aosta too had to fight for his independence from the Ministry of Africa, although he realized that as long as Ethiopia was dependent upon financial support from Italy, he had to acknowledge the interference of the Ministry of Finance in Italian East Africa, and was willing to collaborate with it.

Notes

1. The General Directorates of the Government of AOI were: a) Superior Command of the Armed Forces; b) Political Affairs; c) Civilian Affairs; d) Economic and Financial Affairs; e) Demographic Colonization and Labour; f) Personnel and General Affairs; g) Accounting and Bookkeeping. The same arrangement was reproduced in every Governorship of AOI.

2. MAI/FC 170 Committee for the Reform of the Fundamental Laws of the Empire to Teruzzi, 14 November 1940; ACS/RG 36 Graziani to Lessona, 14 July 1937; Folchi, *La Figura del Governatore Generale*, p. 12; MAI/GAB 160 Lessona to GGAOI, 3 July 1937; Meregazzi, *Lineamenti*, p. 32; MAI/GAB 272/327 Petretti to Duce, February 1938; MAI/AS 181/47-222 Graziani to Lessona, 5 April 1937; MAI/GAB 18/XI-A Graziani to Lessona, 18 September 1936.

3. MAI/AS 181/60-306 Lessona to Graziani, 8 September 1936; Meregazzi, *Lineamenti*, p. 32.

4. MAI/GAB 256/53 Siniscalchi to Meregazzi, 18 February 1940; MAI/FC 170 Committee for the Reform . . . to Teruzzi, 14 November 1940; ACS/SPD-R 83/W-R, Lessona to Fossa, 16 September 1937; MAI/GAB 31/XI-II Lessona: Memorandum for Mussolini, 1937.

5. Duke of Aosta, Diary in *Gente*, 19 February 1969; MAI/GAB 160/XI Lessona to Mussolini, 1937; MAI/CSC 22/125 Resolution of the CSC, 17 November 1936.

6. Meregazzi, *Lineamenti*, pp. 46-7; Mondaini, *Legislazione Coloniale Italiana*, II pp. 421-2; MAI/GAB 18/XI-A Graziani to Lessona, 18 September 1936.

7. ACS/RG 40/2 De Bordonari to Ciano, 5 August 1936; Ibid., Fossa to Mazzi, 22 June 1936; ACS/INT-P 9-B--97/14 Confidential information, 2 October 1937; Lessona, *Memorie*, p. 272.

8. ACS/INT-P 9-B-97/12 Notes on AOI, 1 May 1937; MAI/GAB 179/4 Lessona to PCM, 28 June 1937; ACS/PCM 1937-39, 17/7/6643/7-13 Medici to all Ministries, 17 November 1937; ACS/MAI 21/23 Moreno to Buti, 25 April 1938.

9. The Finances of Italian East Africa

In matters of financial administration, the Viceroy of Italian East Africa also had restricted powers. He had to receive the approval of at least three administrative bodies – the Ministry of Africa, the Colonial Superior Council and the Ministry of Finance – before spending any funds. This lengthy procedure was especially sought by the Ministry of Finance in order to restrict all expenditures after the great financial drain that had bled Italy during the Ethiopian campaign of 1935-7.

Graziani was not a good administrator; moreover, he had inherited a very critical situation. Ethiopia had been only partially occupied; the country did not produce enough to feed Ethiopians and Europeans; food had to be imported from Italy, as did all other goods to which the Italians were accustomed. The war was going on and the army continued to be furnished from home. Forts and roads had to be built to complete the conquest of Ethiopia; airports had to be constructed to facilitate Italian expansion inland. These expenditures had not been anticipated by the Italian financial authorities because they had not conceived that Italy would have to fight to win Ethiopia. Rather they had foreseen a mandate; this would have meant, in principle, the maintenance of Ethiopian political and economic organization, which would take care of the needs of both the local population and the Italians. Italians and Ethiopians would co-operate in improving and increasing agricultural output. Moreover, if there were not a complete military conquest, they thought that Italians and Ethiopians would rapidly come to an agreement and Italy would have a firm foothold in Ethiopia without spending too much money.

In 1935 De Bono felt that, in order to prepare for war against Ethiopia, the High Commissioner should have wide administrative and financial powers. Because of the great distance and the time taken by the various branches of government, De Bono estimated that 50 days were necessary to secure approval of a financial bill. De Bono could not afford delay and so he and his collaborators made their purchases without first requesting estimates, whether it was for horses or for road-building.[1] The Ministry of Finance was thus compelled to pay whatever price the High Commissioner requested. This was, in large part, the cause of the great financial chaos that reigned in colonial finances from 1935 to 1937. This helps explain why the Ministry of Finance was even more reluctant to give financial autonomy to the Viceroy, an attitude which in many ways retarded the economic development of Ethiopia.

The *Legge Organica* stipulated that the Viceroy should prepare the budget for AOI for presentation to the Ministry of Africa, which ultimately transmitted it to the Ministry of Finance for final approval. The first budget was not prepared until 1938, and in 1936 and 1937 the Viceroy had the discretionary power to approve public projects up to 5,000,000 lire [US$1.00 = 5.6 lire] with Governors receiving 2,000,000 lire for emergency projects. When the Duke of Aosta came to Ethiopia and the AOI budget was under better control, he asked to be allowed discretionary expenditure on public projects up to 10,000,000 lire, but the Ministry of Finance conceded only 8,000,000 lire. Moreover, the Duke of Aosta could transfer funds from one budgetary category to another with the permission of the Ministry of Africa and the Ministry of Finance.

The Ministry of Finance, in an attempt to determine the needs of the Empire, requested economic information from the various Governorships. Their financial requests increased astronomically almost daily. For the first quarter of 1936-7, expenditure had been estimated at 5,000,000,000 lire; for the second quarter it reached 5,926,000,000 lire, and for the third quarter 8,210,000,000 lire. This made a total of 19,136,000,000 lire requested by the East Africa government, as against an estimate given by the Ministry of Africa of 5,000,000,000 lire.

The economy of Italy could not bear such expenditure. Italy's total government revenue for the same period was estimated at 18,581,000,000 lire, which meant that Ethiopia, alone, would absorb all Italian revenues! For this reason the Ministry of Finance demanded that the colonial administration reduce expenditure and that once its budget had been approved, it receive no extra funds, except for the military. With time however, it became obvious that most of the budget for Ethiopia would be used up by the military and that the civil administration would suffer. The military had been promised that they would be provided funds, and the Ministry of Finance sought to economize on items – like civil administration – regarded as less important. Thus, although the Viceroy was given responsibility for the budget, he had no choice but to spend it all for military and related purposes.

On the other hand, Graziani felt that he could not reduce expenditure because he was not aware of what the Governors had requested from the Ministry of Africa. As long as Article 12 gave them the privilege of corresponding directly with the Ministry, his power over the Governors would be minimal and he could not co-ordinate the efforts for the economic planning.[2] Thus, direct interference by the Ministry of Africa and the Ministry of Finance, led to the continuance of economic chaos in Italian East Africa. The Ministry of Finance explained that the presence of these two Ministries kept the rapport with the colonies alive and subordinated to the Fatherland: knowledge of the presence of the Ministries in the life of the colonies inspired confidence in Italian businessmen and contractors, who would then be more willing to invest in Ethiopia.

The Ministry of Finance's intransigence must be seen in the light of the fact that it did not have confidence in Graziani and that, while Italy was still bleeding from the financial wounds of the Ethiopian War, another military involvement in Spain was draining Italian finances.

The Financial Organization of AOI

In order to be fully informed of Ethiopian conditions, Paolo Thaon Di Revel, Minister of Finance, paid an extended visit to Ethiopia in 1938. He found a confused economic and financial situation that needed radical changes. The Ministry of Finance therefore installed branches of the General Accounting Office in Addis Ababa and in each of the Governorships. The Office's main duties were to ensure proper financial administration and accounting of the revenues of the Governor-Generalship, and of the local Governorships. It also had the duty of protecting state property, ascertaining the exact amount of revenues and ensuring the regular use and distribution of the budget. The Accounting Office exercised its duties independently of the colonial authorities: its members were appointed by the Ministry of Finance and corresponded directly with the Ministry. This meant that on colonial matters accountants had the same right as Governors to correspond directly with the Ministry of Africa, the Ministry of Finance and other Ministries. It was embarrassing to see a Governor's subordinates discussing internal affairs of his Governorship with other administrators without his knowledge. This undermined the Governor's prestige and the Viceroy's as well. It also created disunity because different Ministries tended to see things in a different way and occasionally issued orders different from those given by the Ministry of Africa.

In addition to their independence from local colonial authorities, the accountants compiled the proposed budget. (Colonial legislation also empowered the Viceroy to prepare the budget; but the Ministry of Finance instructed the Governor-Generalship and its accountants to prepare also a budget to check against the Viceroy's.) This created further confusion, since the Governor-Generalship of AOI, with the agreement of the Minister of Finance, had already created an economic and financial directorate in every Governorship for this very purpose. Another form of control over the finances of AOI, which constituted a further limitation on the powers of the Viceroy and the Governors, was that the Ministry of Africa and the Ministry of Finance could order inspections in offices with financial and economic responsibilities at any time. The General Audit Office began its work in AOI on 1 January 1938. Each Governorship was assigned an audit office which controlled all expenditures, assessed public debt, and registered Viceregal decrees. In short, all that had to do with the economy and finances of the Empire had to go through this special office, which was also an independent institution.

Having established this restrictive and limiting set-up in Ethiopia, the Ministry of Finance was faced with the storage of personnel and lack of technical preparation for the task of back-tracing accounts from 1937. The auditors were chosen among army officers who were only waiting to reach the age limit to retire; they had no interest in proceeding rapidly with the review of accounts. At the General Accounting Office in Addis Ababa, the personnel was numerically adequate but only a small percentage of them were professionally qualified. All this caused additional financial disorder. State payments for public works and goods bought for the various Government organizations could not be made rapidly enough; many contractors went out of business or lost faith in the ability to pay of the Government of Italian East Africa.[3]

The Cost of Empire

Given this state of financial anarchy, it is difficult to ascertain the amount spent for the Ethiopian campaign of 1935–36 and for the years of the Italian occupation of Ethiopia mainly because Mussolini prohibited the publication of the statistics of the Ministry of Finance and the Bank of Italy. The Ministry of Africa budget officially never exceeded two billion lire, when in reality it was three or four times as much. Di Revel stated in Parliament in June 1936 that "he could not give too many details on the real expenditure of the Ethiopian War, but that it had been estimated at 12,000,000,000 lire".

Ascertaining the cost of the Ethiopian War is further complicated by the fact that High Commissioners De Bono and Badoglio were permitted to draw funds without going through bureaucratic channels; thus, the records of those accounts are not always accurate or available. Mussolini, too, by a decree of 1 October 1936, received permission to sign bills for the Ministry of Africa and the Ministry of Public Works in order to concentrate in one single person the execution of war.

A memorandum of the Director of the General Accounting Office calculated the cost of the Ethiopian War at 38,851,000,000 lire (about US$ 7.2 billion) from 1934 to 1937. Monthly expenditure for East Africa reached 1,530,000,000 lire per month in January 1936,[4] well above the estimated expenditure of 1,000,000,000 lire per month. The Italian economy was prostrate! Not even the Ministry of Finance had definite information on expenditure and was never able to ascertain it for lack of data. The military expenditures of the seven months' war were higher than expected because at first Italy hoped for territorial compensations in Ethiopia with the help of France and Great Britain. When the Italian colonial demands were not met Mussolini conquered Ethiopia by force. This may explain why there were only 250,000 Italian troops in East Africa at first; later they reached about 500,000. This number of troops, enormous by colonial standards, is explained by the Duce's determination to acquire Ethiopia and prevent the repetition of another Adowa.

Their number, according to Lessona, was to be reduced after the conquest of Addis Ababa; he envisaged an army of 68,000, consisting of 25,000 metropolitan and 43,000 colonial troops. But Graziani maintained 240,000 troops, to combat the Patriotic resistance. This excessive number of troops cost Italy a billion lire per year in addition to the regular military budget of more than a billion lire per year. Lessona attributed the presence of 240,000 men under arms in Ethiopia to the fact that Graziani was obsessed with the internal security of Ethiopia. But even after the change of Viceroy, the Duke of Aosta confirmed that the number of men under arms could not be reduced for at least four more years. Military expenditures for the years 1938 and 1939 remained high, always above the four billion lire per year provided by the regular extraordinary budgets. To economize, reducing the army pay and expenses for military supplies was considered, but this was not realistic because the only way Italy could rule Ethiopia was by a well-paid army. For about 100,000 colonial troops, Italy spent more than 750 million lire per year in salaries and services. To this must be added another 250 million lire per year for counter-guerrilla warfare.[5]

Thus, even after Graziani had left Ethiopia, there was need for a large army to ensure the Italian presence there. Since most of the colonial budget was absorbed by the armed forces, little was left for public administration and public works, except roads, which were necessary for military penetration. Toward the end of 1939, there was a possibility of reducing the number of soldiers, as well as the military budget, but because of rumours of war in Europe, the number of men under arms was maintained at about the 200,000 mark. In order to continue financing the high military expenditures, the Italian East Africa budget for public works was reduced from one billion to half a billion lire per year. Colonial administrators did nothing to limit military and civilian expenditures. Every year new debts were accumulated and passed on to the next year's budget, allowing a chronic deficit to increase every year.[6]

To add to the cost of the empire, there were expenditures for the acquisition of imports from third countries which had to be paid for in hard currency. Mussolini pointed out to Graziani that Ethiopia was costing Italy over 100 million lire a month in foreign currency; if this continued, the economic life of the country would be crippled. Although the consumption of foreign currency decreased by 1938, Italy was using 850 million lire a year of its foreign exchange for the Empire. With its exports, Ethiopia provided only 100 million lire in foreign currency per year, which meant that Italy had to foot the balance. The Ethiopians paid almost nothing toward these expenditures because for reasons of political expediency, Italian colonial policy did not make the newly-conquered Ethiopia pay any tribute. But more and more people saw the necessity of taxing the colonial subjects. On 27 September 1937, Graziani decreed the Ethiopians had to pay a tithe of their agricultural products to the Italian government.

An annual tax was also assessed at 1/30 of the value per head of stock.[7] For the years 1937-8, it was estimated that 12 million lire would be collected; in 1938-9, 55 million lire and in 1939-40, 70 million lire. These, however, were only approximate figures; no one really believed that the tribute would amount to that much. They were written in the budget, but their value was purely hypothetical. Tax collection was organized for the fiscal year 1938-9 only for those territories where the political and military situation allowed it: Harar was such a place, but even here a lack of trained personnel and equipment meant that the taxes collected amounted to a mere 194,237 lire.[8]

In an attempt to secure better co-ordination of the finances of the Empire the Duke of Aosta requested more financial autonomy without the interference of either the Ministry of Africa or the Ministry of Finance. The increased financial power granted to the Viceroy in the autumn of 1939 was too little and too late. In 1939, anticipating the outbreak of the war, the Viceroy submitted a programme to prepare Ethiopia for the coming conflict, and a request of 48 billion lire a year. Owing to the unhealthy financial situation, the Italian government deferred the allotment of necessary funds for AOI. Instead 1,371,080,892 lire were first proposed, of which only 900 million lire were finally assigned for the military defence of Ethiopia.[9] Thus, even if the Viceroy had been given authority over the budget, the Ministry of Finance and the Ministry of Africa had the authority to accept, reduce or reject his proposals. Mussolini entered the war in June 1940, against the wishes of the Italian people. Once war came, the administration of Ethiopia, which had staggered from one difficulty to another, could not last long.

Notes

1. MAI/AS 181/10-46 De Bono to Mussolini, 5 April 1935; Ibid., De Bono to Superior Military Command, 4 July 1935.

2. MAI/CSC 25/119 CSC: Resolution, 17 December 1937; MAI/CSC 25/118 Teruzzi to CSC, 15 December 1937; MAI/AS 181/55-255 Meregazzi to Teruzzi, 24 June 1938; Mondaini, *Legislazione Coloniale Italiana*, II, p. 85; ACS/PCM 1937-1939 1/1.27/195 General State Accountant Office, Memorandum: Expenditures of the MAI and GGAOI, 24 March 1937; ATR 24/78 Cambi Expenditures for AOI, 24 March 1937; ATR 1/217 Cambi: Notes on the Military Expenditures for AOI, 16 November 1936; MAI/GAB 150/IX Lessona to GGAOI 5 April 1937.

3. Meregazzi, *Lineamenti*, p. 86; Mondaini, *Legislazione*, II pp. 472-3; ATR 24/151 Daodiace to GGAOI, 21 March 1938; Ibid., Pisano: Memorandum for the Minister of Finance, 8 April 1938; MAI/GAB 150/IX Teruzzi to Cambi, 6 April 1938; MAI/GAB 322 Di Revel: Diary: Visit in AOI, 1938.

4. ACS/PCM 1934-1936 17/1/3422/54 Mussolini: Decree, 22 November 1935; MAI/EF C/4-8 Teruzzi: Suspension order to publish

Finances

statistics on AOI, 3 October 1939; ATR 18/135 Di Revel: Presentation of the budget to the House of Deputies, June 1936; ACS/PCM 1937-1939 1/1.27/260/1-2 (this folder originally containing documents on the cost of the Ethiopian War is now empty!); ATR/1/127 Cambi: Notes on the military expenditure in Ethiopia, 16 November 1936. Major Fund Assignment for AOI, January 1936: Ministry of Africa 400,000,000 lire, Ministry of War 500,000,000, Ministry of Marine 200,000,000, Ministry of Aeronautics 350,000,000, Ministry of Interior 80,000,000.

5. ATR 24/80 Lessona: Memorandum for the Duce, 30 June 1937; MAI/GAB 150/IX MAI Military Office to the Duce, 1939; Ibid., Teruzzi to Minister of Finance, 12 June 1938; MAI/GAB 160/XI Cambi to Meregazzi, 3 February 1938; Ibid., MAI/EF Arguments presented to the Duke of Aosta, March 1938.

6. MAI/GAB 160/IX Viceroy: Military Expenditures in AOI, 21 October 1939; Ibid., Teruzzi to Duce, 24 January 1938; MAI/GAB 160/IX Teruzzi to Viceroy, 7 February 1938.

7. MAI/GAB 150/IX MAI/EF: Expenses for AOI, 25 May 1939; Ibid., Pisano to Cabinet of the Minister of Africa, 24 July 1939; ACS/RG 17 Mussolini to Graziani, 11 September 1937; MAI/GAB 152/IX MAI/EF Notes on foreign currency for AOI, 1939; MAI/GAB 52 MAI: Data for Parliamentary discussion-Budget 1939-1940.

8. MAI/GAB 52 Italy: Camera dei Deputati, *Atti Parlamentari*, Legislatura XXIX, "Disegno di Legge: Stato di Previsione della Spesa del Ministero delle Colonie 1937-1938", No. 1554, 20 January 1937; MAI/EF C/4-8 Cancellieri: Economic activity of Harar to December 1939.

9. MAI/GAB 250/13 Meregazzi to Teruzzi, 25 June 1938; D'Eramo, *Amministrazione delle Forze Militari . . . dell AOI*, pp. 42-59; MAI/GAB 304/4 Teruzzi to Duce, 7 October 1939; MAI/GAB 286 Commission for the Supreme Defence, February 1940.

10. The Administrative Personnel

The Colonial Personnel

The abysmal lack of education and trained colonial personnel to administer the new Italian Empire was due to Italy's unpreparedness for taking over the task of ruling Ethiopia. It was not expected that Ethiopia would be defeated as quickly as it was. To provide the necessary staff it was decided to borrow personnel from other state agencies, to lure new university graduates into entering the colonial service, or to use military officers already in Ethiopia. The 2 June 1936 law authorized an increase in the number of permanent colonial personnel by 94, from 256 to 350; in the auxiliary personnel, by 150, from 100 to 250; and in the ordinary personnel, by 155, from 245 to 405. Thus in 1936 colonial personnel almost doubled from 601 to 1000. Their number, however, was not enough for the activities they had to carry out.

A decree of 7 October 1937 allowed a further increase of 300 officials for service in Ethiopia. With the gradual settling down and partial pacification of the country, further needs arose. The law of 10 February 1938 permitted 420 more posts to be added to those existing. The forecast was that for 1939-40 there would be a further increase of 450 colonial posts, thus bringing the total available positions to approximately 2,470. Their distribution is shown in Table 10.1.

Table 10.1
Colonial Positions 1935-39

Category	1935	1936	1937	1938	1939 (estimate)
Permanent	256	350	450	520	1,070
Auxiliary	100	250	350	450	550
Ordinary	245	400	500	750	850
Total	601	1,000	1,300	1,720	2,470

This did not mean that all positions were filled. An in-depth study reveals that in 1940 of 2,700 positions available only 1,350 were occupied (see Table 10.2).

Table 10.2
Colonial Positions Filled

Category	Positions Available	Positions Ready to be Occupied	Positions Actually Occupied
Permanent	1,070	800	500
Auxiliary	555	463	350
Ordinary	850	660	550
Total	2,700	1,923	1,350

Besides colonial officials in the service for the civil and political administration of Ethiopia there was also a corps of colonial officials for technical services. Recruitment of these specialists was also a difficult problem. Many were on loan to the Ministry of Africa from other Ministries and the armed forces (See Table 10.3).

Table 10.3
Positions for Colonial Technical Services[1]

		Positions Available	Occupied
PAI:			
Colonial Police	a) High-ranking officers	200	NA
	b) Officers	650	NA
Public Health	a) Doctors	183	131
	b) Veterinarians	50	34
	c) Lab Technicians and Dentists	16	10
Mines	a) Engineers	28	10
	b) Assistant Engineers	31	9
Agriculture	a) Directors	36	18
	b) Inspectors	62	49
	c) Specialists	120	84
Translators	a) Translators	60	NA
	b) Temporary translators	11	22
Post-Telegraphic	a) Directors	45	25
	b) Officers	400	372
Corporations	a) Directors	45	30
	b) Officers	26	20
School Teachers		380	NA
Totals		2,517	2,140

Moreover, no qualified person, with a good job in Italy, would give up his employment to go to Ethiopia. Although remuneration was good, life was expensive in AOI; very few could save money.

Graziani and the Duke of Aosta found it difficult to administer Ethiopia without dependable colonial personnel. Although the *Ordinamento Politico Amministrativo* of 15 November 1937 gave the Viceroy the right to nominate directors of the main departments of the Governorship-General, the Ministry of Africa continued to appoint the personnel. Therefore, the Viceroy had to deal with people he might not know or might not trust. It is not clear, however, how many colonial personnel were in Ethiopia. Teruzzi refers to a total of 6,943. To pay the salaries of army officers used as civil servants cost Italy 16 million lire a year.[2] It is estimated that about 10,000 colonial employees were hired for clerical work to meet the requests of the Ministry of Africa for reports, statistics, projects and memoranda, which could not be done by the directors of the administrative offices and commissioners because they had too many political problems to solve. In main urban centres like Addis Ababa, Harar and Asmara colonial officials had little to do, particularly in the Office of Labour and Colonization. The Duke of Aosta proposed eliminating administrative organizations in areas where the Italian presence was not necessary, and instead establishing a smaller core of better colonial administrators with greater opportunity for creative initiative. The Viceroy was fully cognizant of the need to study and understand the problems of Ethiopia before reaching definite solutions.

Lack of Preparation of Colonial Officials

The Duke, like Graziani, had realistically presented the problem of colonial officials as people who had little desire to work. Patrick Roberts, the British Charge d'Affaires in Addis Ababa, described Italian colonial administrators as ignorant, insolent, overbearing and arbitrary. These officers had come to Ethiopia in order to make a career. The result was a heavy bureaucracy which paralysed the administration of the colony simply because there was interference by the various branches of government and consequent disorganization. Sixty per cent of the bureaucratic machinery was working in AOI to administer itself. There was a tendency to create committees and commissions to solve simple problems because no one wanted to take responsibility for decisions or was capable of deciding. Colonial officials were allegedly lacking in initiative and a pioneering spirit.[3] There were jealousies, antagonisms, competition and discord among colonial offices; these were known to the Ethiopians and undermined Italian authority. Moreover, the economic-agricultural exploitation and the political-administrative organization of the country were set up with too much haste. The economic development and organization of Ethiopia should have come at a later time; instead, in areas where Italian authority was not yet established, the government invested large sums of money with little economic and political success. These negative experiences were responsible for Italian mistrust and pessimism toward the possibilities of the Empire.

It was known that the majority of the colonial personnel were not qualified for their work – a problem that had long been present in the colonial history of Italy. In the past, inept colonial personnel had been sent to Somalia. During the 1930s they reached seniority; therefore, they occupied the highest colonial positions, despite their inefficiency. The highest ranking colonial officers came to Ethiopia from Somalia, Eritrea and Libya. They brought with them, besides little preparation, a limited mentality schooled in the vestiges of old colonial policy. Instead of improving colonial administration by training a new class of colonial officials, they added more men from other administrations, especially men from the military who had no experience in the art of dealing with colonized people. They were also found to be mediocre and incompetent.

Proposals were made to solve these shortcomings through the formation of a Fascist Colonial Academy to train colonial officials. Meanwhile, General Arcovaldo Bonaccorsi of the Black Shirts suggested that the colonial government be organized and function under the authority of the army. His proposal had some merits in that Ethiopia was still the scene of warfare. To introduce civil administration was to act against reality; the civilian colonial authorities were not qualified to face the responsibility of governing, or defending the Empire against Patriot attacks. Bonaccorsi argued that the army should administer Ethiopia for at least ten years. In that period colonial officials could be trained, who would gradually replace the military personnel.

Another way to train colonial officials would have been to associate them with colonial specialists acting as advisers and guides. But these proposals remained in the pages of reports and were never implemented. No one had foreseen that the formation of such a large Empire as Ethiopia – four times the size of Italy – would bring such a multitude of problems.[4] It had been believed that after the conquest of Ethiopia colonial problems would be identical to the ones Italy had experienced in Somalia and Eritrea, different in scale but not in kind. It was not appreciated that Italy had conquered new peoples with different problems and needs involving all spheres of civil, military and political life.

The Enthusiasm for Colonies Wanes: 1938 and After

It was also noticed that colonial officials, instead of staying for their normal tour of duty, were very anxious to return home. Under the pretext of bad health, Badoglio requested a leave which became a permanent return. Others, like the Governor of Amhara, Pirzio Biroli, or the first secretary of the Governorship of Oromo-Sidamo, requested permission to go home. There was little spirit of sacrifice, Graziani complained, and among other colonial officers there was the same attitude: everyone wanted to go home! Soon after the conquest of Ethiopia it was obvious that the enthusiasm for colonies that Mussolini had been able to kindle in the hearts of Italians was waning at the first difficulties.

Recruitment of good colonial officers was made difficult by the knowledge that life in Ethiopia was full of hardship and discomfort. The rebellion and tropical diseases endangered life. Officials from other Ministries were not willing to go to East Africa because the Ministry of Africa had a bad reputation for confused administration; the best men did not enter the competitive examinations organized by the Ministry of Africa to recruit colonial officers.[5] Those who successfully passed the examination begged the government to pressure the Ministry of Africa to allow them to remain in Italy; those who were directed to go to Ethiopia and did not immediately depart were disqualified. Officials already employed by the Ministry of Africa who would not go overseas were denied promotion. Typical was the case of Raffaele Di Lauro, a colonial official in the Governorship of Oromo-Sidamo and one-time Consul in Gondar. He had just arrived in Italy on leave when Teruzzi threatened to demote him. Again, when Giuseppe Daodiace, acting Vice-Governor-General, asked Di Lauro to be Commissioner of Lasta, he complained that he would rather receive a post as director of a Governorship, than go to the small town of Waldia. Other administrators already in Ethiopia were not willing to move from one place to another and claimed to suffer from all kinds of real and imaginary physical discomforts and diseases. The Viceroy then decided to repatriate anyone affected by "stomach-aches"![6]

Contributing to this reluctance to move from one Governorship to another was the knowledge that in Ethiopia housing was limited and furniture was extremely expensive. In 1937 only a fraction of the colonial officials brought their families with them, as shown in Table 10.4.

Table 10.4
Colonial Officials Living in AOI with their Families

	Officials Living with Families	Percentage of Officials Living with Their Families
Eritrea	350	44
Somalia	131	16.5
Harar	34	8
Amhara	14	1.5
Oromo-Sidamo	1	NA
Addis Ababa	244	NA
Total	744	

Housing conditions were critical everywhere, but in Gondar and Oromo-Sidamo colonial administrators had to live in tents and space was so limited that many of them resided in Asmara. Beside material sacrifices on the part of colonial personnel, quite a number of them were affected by tropical diseases and mental illnesses.[7] All these difficulties made it hard for anyone to consider joining the colonial service. By the time attempts were made to recruit better civil servants by giving promotions and higher salaries, it was 1939 and war in Europe was imminent and the Empire swarming with incompetent colonials.

Both foreign sources and Italian published information attest to the corruption of Italian colonial personnel. The Duke of Aosta declared that 50% of them were inept and 25% thieves. If true, this leaves only 25% of colonial officials who were honest and efficient in their work. Under the Duke's paternalistic rule life began to improve and many saw the Empire as a springboard to improve their financial position. Colonial employees came to Ethiopia to have their travel expenses paid by the government but, once there, they sought employment with other companies where the pay was better. Others simply engaged in commercial and economic activities while at the same time remaining on the state payroll.[8] General Nasi realized corruption was more widespread than it appeared: "there was a gold rush for speculative deals".

The bad example of corruption came from above and did not affect public servants only: it spread from the Ministry of Africa to Governors. Around them were a number of unscrupulous businessmen who received business deals from the Governors. In return these businessmen built luxurious villas for their patrons. It was widely known that the director of the Office of Political Affairs at Jimma was greedy and obliged the Ethiopian chiefs to give him presents of gold, ivory, skins and silver. The same problem of corruption was found in the Governorship of Amhara, where General Mezzetti, the Governor, denounced a number of colonial personnel. Some of them were involved in the sale of beer, land speculation, falsification of government records, and unlawful appropriation of government funds.[9] Although some colonial officials were found guilty of fraud, many were acquitted and repatriated without court action. The Duke of Aosta hoped in this way to get rid of undesirable personnel quickly, but this only added to the crisis of the administration of Ethiopia. Important posts such as the directorships of government offices were left vacant for months or filled by junior officials of limited experience.

To ensure that colonial officers behaved properly and carried out their duties, it was decided that each Governorship should have a special inspector,[10] but this, too, came too late and did not prove to be effective.

Notes

1. Meregazzi, *Lineamenti*, pp. 157–8; Italy: Ministero degli Affari Esteri, *Il Governo dei Territori d'Oltremare*, pp. 285–303; MAI/GAB 218 Lessona: Report to the Chamber of Deputies; Budget 1936–1937; ACS/PCM 1934–1936 17/7/6643/32 Mussolini to Ministeries of Public Works, Finance, and Africa, 26 October 1936; MAI/GAB 74/XI-V Lessona: Memorandum for Mussolini 7 August 1936; MAI/GAB 52 MAI: Data for parliamentary

discussion, Budget 1939–1940.

2. MAI/GAB 74/XI-V Teruzzi to MAI, 2 June 1939; Ministero degli Affari Esteri, *Il Governo*, p. 371; MAI/GAB 285/15 Duke of Aosta to MAI, 2 October 1939; Ibid., Minutes of the V Council of Governors, 11 December 1939.

3. MAI/AV 2 Duke of Aosta to Teruzzi, 1 and 18 January 1940; ACS/RG 19 Roberts: General Examination of the Ethiopian Situation under Italian Administration, 16 December 1936; ACS/INT-P 9/B–97/14 Confidential information, 8 March 1937.

4. MAI/GAB 160/XI Teruzzi to Duke Aosta, 28 April 1938; ACS/RG 40-B/100–14 Appelius: Report to the Duce, 1938; MAI/GAB 272/327 Petretti: Report to Mussolini, February 1938; MAI/GAB 288/XIII-II Bonaccorsi: Impressions to the Duke of Aosta, 30 April 1940.

5. MAI/AV 2 Duke Aosta to Teruzzi, 18 January 1940; MAI/GAB 72/XI-VIII Graziani to Lessona, 16 April & 13 May 1937; ACS/MMM 174 Graziani to Ministry of Marine, 26 November 1936; MAI/GAB 74/XI-V Teruzzi to di Revel, 28 February 1938.

6. MAI/GAB 265/171 Meregazzi to Teruzzi, 28 January 1939; Ibid., Meregazzi to Teruzzi 2 January 1938; MAI/GAB 74/XI–V Columbano to all MAI Directorates, 10 February 1939; MAI/GAB 265/170 Cerri to Ferlesh, 13 December 1938; ACS/FB 1822 Daodiace to Di Lauro, 5 March 1941.

7. MAI/GAB 70/XI-V MAI-Cabinet: Notes for the Chief of the Government, 1937; Ibid., MAI: Memorandum for Mussolini, 22 December 1939; MAI/GAB 31/XI-C Mezzetti to Teruzzi, 27 December 1937; MAI/GAB 72/XI-VIII Cerulli to MAI, 21 May 1938.

8. MAI/GAB 160/XI Mussolini to Teruzzi, 3 April 1939; Ciano *Diario 1937–1938*, p. 194; *Ordre*, (Paris), 9–15 August 1939; ACS/RG 37 Tharaud to *Paris Soir*, 24 January 1939; ACS/RG 19 Roberts to Eden, 16 December 1936; MAI/GAB 277 this folder is filled with petitions and letters of thanks; ACS/RG 57/184 Don Peppino to Mazzi, October 1937; MAI/AS 181/47–221 Nasi: Foglio D'Ordine, 19 July 1938; MAI/GAB 250/3 Meregazzi to Teruzzi, 24 June 1938.

9. MAI/GAB 75/5–C Nasi to all Colonial Officials, 5 September 1938; ACS/INT-P 9-B/97/12 Confidential information, 26 August 1937; ACS/CP 7/74 Intercepted radio information from *Radio Italia*, 9 May 1943; MAI/GAB 288/XIII-II Bonaccorsi, Impressions for the Duke of Aosta, 30 April 1940; MAI/GAB 75/5-C Meregazzi to Teruzzi, 1938; MAI/GAB 74/XI-V Mezzetti to Teruzzi, 19 July 1939.

10. MAI/GAB 250/13 Meregazzi to Teruzzi, 22 June 1938; MAI/GAB 160/XI Teruzzi to Duke Aosta, 28 April 1938.

11. Local Administration

The Italian Empire of East Africa, covering 1,725,330 square kilometres was organized into six territorial Governorships. The Governorship of Amhara, with its capital at Gondar, included the Amhara-speaking people, the majority of whom belonged to the Ethiopian Orthodox Church. The Governorship of Oromo-Sidamo with its administrative centre at Jimma, incorporated Oromo, Sidamo, and the Borana people. The Governorship of Harar, with the seat of government at Harar, was composed of the Ethiopian territories of the south-east, populated mostly by Muslims and the Harari and Arussi ethnic groups. After the conquest of Ethiopia, Ethiopian territories were added to the older Italian colonies. Eritrea received the region inhabited by Tigreans and Danakils, and Somalia added to its territory all the Somali ethnic groups of Ogaden. The sixth territorial division was the Governorship of Addis Ababa, replaced in 1938 with the Governorship of Shoa, with most of its traditional territories. A Governor was appointed in each Governorship, nominated by the Italian government. The Governor of Addis Ababa was also Vice-Governor-General. Governors carried out orders from the Viceroy and were responsible for all aspects of colonial administration including the military defence of their territories.

Although the powers of the Governor were intended to be broad, they were limited in reality by bureaucracy and by interference from the Viceroy, the Ministry of Africa and other agencies, such as the Ministry of Finance, the Armed Forces and the Fascist Party. In other instances, their powers were curtailed because the Governor was not able to act independently and solve colonial problems of his territory without external help. The greatest drawback was that Governors were always military careermen; they were thus not fully prepared to perform colonial administrative duties. The continuous harassment by the Ethiopian Patriots further limited the administrative functions of Governors. Thus, the administration of Ethiopia was never civilian and maintained at all times a huge military apparatus.

The *Legge Organica* and the *Ordinamento Amministrativo* provided for the division of the Governorships into districts with commissioners, which in turn were subdivided into residencies and vice-residencies. Ethnic principles were applied in dividing the territory. Traditional laws, customs, religion, and language were taken into consideration. This was difficult to achieve because Ethiopia was, in Lessona's words, a "museum of peoples". The principle of providing unitary ethnic local government was no doubt an ideal conception, but in practice it proved to be unworkable. Administrative boundary lines cut across ethnic groups.

Next to the ethnic principle, the geographical criterion was adopted, followed by economic interests. For all practical purposes, however, in territorial division, the principle of political opportunism prevailed, rather than the ethnic one, although the latter was followed when possible in order to maintain the ethnic unity of the most important peoples. The Duke of Aosta thought that the internal division of Ethiopia would be improved if people in each area were organized not on an ethnic basis but rather on the basis of already established economic and commercial ties.[1]

The Residency System

The *Legge Organica* was framed in Italy by people who could theorize over the organization of Ethiopia but did not grasp the practical problems. They set up a large number of residencies. Their number fluctuated from month to month according to the military situation. When isolated residencies were attacked by the Patriots, residents would withdraw to the seat of the commissioner. Thus the number of residencies shrank markedly, especially in Amhara where the Italian presence was resented. In other Governorships residencies were eliminated because they were not economical and were politically inconvenient or, as in many instances, there were no colonial personnel to fill the post. Often residencies were established only because the location seemed strategically important on the map, although the place might be scarcely inhabited and of little political value. There is no document giving the exact number of the internal divisions of the Empire. A recent study gives an average number of about 60 district commissionerships and about 300 residencies and vice-residencies.

The same could be said about how many people lived in Ethiopia. Plans to take a census in 1941 did not materialize because of the war. The Italians thought of using Ethiopian Orthodox priests to carry out a census, but since the enumerator had to receive a pecuniary compensation from each person counted, the Ethiopian people were not willing to co-operate. Furthermore, suspicious people associated the census with taxation and refused to give information. Besides popular resentment, the census-takers were handicapped by limited means of communications, an illiterate population and the small number of specialized personnel available to carry out the census.

The major obstacle to the counting of the population of Ethiopia was the unstable political and military situation, particularly in Amhara, where one could only guess the number of inhabitants. At Mussolini's insistence, the military, in co-operation with colonial personnel, undertook a population survey using empirical methods. Their efforts were mostly futile. Ethiopia

Table 11.1
Fluctuation in the number of District Commissioners,
Residencies and Vice-Residencies from 1936–1940

Governorships	Minimum Number District Commissionerships	Maximum Number	Minimum Number Residencies	Maximum Number	Minimum Number Vice-Residencies	Maximum Number
Addis Ababa and Shoa	3	13	2	47	3	19
Amhara	5	12	21	40	5	67
Harar	7	10	19	36	21	43
Oromo-Sidamo	10	14	35	58	3	30
Eritrea	11	18	16	34	11	20
Somalia	9	13	2	49	0	47

was estimated to possess between 6 million and 15 million inhabitants. The Duke of Aosta complained that the data were unreliable and that a full-scale census was necessary.

Regardless of the scanty knowledge of the country the Ministry of Africa showed a great desire to staff AOI with as many residents as possible.[2] This inflation in the number of residents can be attributed to the form of colonial government Italy imposed in Ethiopia. A process of direct rule was devised to eliminate the Ethiopian chiefs from their positions. By removing the traditional form of government, Italy hoped to bring modern ways of life to Ethiopia, but the social revolution, together with the abolition of slavery, would need several generations before it could bring positive results. Against expert advice, Rome eliminiated the power of the former Ethiopian chiefs. Shoans and Amhara were supposed to be contained in one Governorship alone, and *rases*, *dejazes*, and *balambaras* were replaced by Italian residents. Not all chieftainships were removed. Lower chiefs like *meslanie*, chief of a district and the *chiqa-shum*, chief of a village, were retained, but often not even those were available, so that in many instances *askaris* from Eritrea or Somalia were put in charge of a village only because they were faithful to Italy, regardless of their attitude and ability to govern or what consequence their presence among a different ethnic group might bring.

It was Italian colonial policy to establish numerous residencies so that there would be an Italian presence at all times among the Ethiopians. The resident was the main tool of Italian political penetration. His presence was supposed to win over the people and create trust in Italian justice and good administration. The residents had to give the people the impression that the Italian government was interested in them, by giving assistance, in time of famine and drought; educating the children; bringing relief to the poor; and protecting the rights of Muslims. The resident was also charged with bringing sanitary and health reforms and fostering trade and commerce. The resident had to visit his territory and local chiefs often, giving them advice and listening to their requests. Only by listening and observing the people would it become easier to govern.[3]

Because of the variety of responsibilities imposed on the residencies, they were organized into miniature ministries, with wide powers and much authority in their territory. If they came to fulfill their duties properly, the residents needed to be well-prepared and to possess qualities of versatility and political sensitivity. But the figure of the representative of the Italian government was painted too idealistically and failed to live up to expectations. According to colonial legislation, commissioners, residents and vice-residents were nominated by the Governor-General from among tenured colonial personnel. However, such personnel were not available, and they tended to be drawn from the officers of the armed forces. As it turned out, the entire Italian Empire was run by the military. In 1936, of the 2,000 Italian army officers, over 1,570 (about 79% of all officers) requested assignment as residents, of whom 502 had university degrees.

Although at first military personnel were used because of the urgency of the situation, it was hoped to replace them at a later date with colonial career people. Army officers however remained in administrative posts to the end of the Italian occupation of Ethiopia. In the early part of 1938 military personnel accounted for the bulk of personnel employed in the various residencies and without them the Italian administration of Ethiopia would have ground to a stop.[4]

Table 11.2
Military Personnel Employed in Ethiopia: Early 1938

Governorships	*% Military Personnel (Approximate)*
Amhara	90
Harar	80
Oromo-Sidamo	90
Addis Ababa/Shoa	33
Eritrea	70
Somalia	20

Somalia was the only Governorship with an almost wholly civilian administrative organization, except for Ethiopian regions attached to Somalia. Eritrea had the problem of a high percentage of military officers in its administration. After the conquest of Ethiopia it inherited Ethiopian territories which had to be guarded by military garrisons. Most of the remaining governorships were almost totally administered by the military.

In Harar too, most holders of administrative positions were military — that is, over the 90% mark. The Governors of Amhara and Oromo-Sidamo reported that military officers in their administrative divisions accounted for 98% and 94% respectively of all their government employees.

Not everybody believed that the military administration of Ethiopia was a disadvantage. Fascist supporters of military administration put forward some practical reasons to sustain their view. Since the conquest of Ethiopia had been achieved militarily, its initial organization had to be military, at least until such time as the people had been disarmed and pacified. A military government was the best guarantee against any rebellion and ensured protection of Italian interests. A gradual change of government could come with the co-operation of civilian and military authorities in matters of justice, commerce and the study of the needs of the various ethnic groups. A strong government supported by the military was the answer in the Ethiopian situation since there were large quantities of hidden weapons; while the Ethiopians still retained their traditional boldness and familiarity with the art of war, Italy's position in Ethiopia was secure only with the armed forces ever ready to intervene. Raiding was an Ethiopian custom, and it was certainly not possible for a civilian resident to stop or eliminate it: the proud Ethiopians, the Fascists insisted, needed to be ruled by force. And how could people who had enjoyed independence for centuries be reduced to humble and law-abiding subjects? Since Fascism called for the rule of force and racial policy advocated the inferiority of the colonial people, it is not surprising that a military role was advocated in the administration of Ethiopia.

The Resident and the Ethiopians

Italy failed to attract professional people to the colony because conditions were poor. Furthermore residents could not receive salary increases because after 1938, in order to economize, residents and commissioners were paid according to the military wage scale. This alone lowered the morale of the residents. In addition, after many months of service in remote, isolated and unhealthy places, residents had to wait their turn for their three months' home leave; indeed, lack of personnel to replace them often meant that they would not be able to go home. The leave system was in chaos. Residents served more than their established tours of two years and, when their turn for leave came, would discouragedly ask for permanent repatriation. Moreover, their working conditions were not pleasant. They had to deal with the Patriots, but also had many other duties. They had to visit the districts, conduct investigations, collect data, explore, make reports of all kinds and furnish statistics that only well-prepared specialized colonial officials could produce. Residents and commissioners were loaded with tasks and consequently their work and reports were superficial.[5] The quality as well as the quantity left much to be desired. Residents were too far away from each other and their isolation was increased by poor communications. Given the absence of supervision and the inconsistency of colonial policy, residents acted independently and behaved like little tsars in their areas of jurisdiction. Some residents acted unreasonably toward the people, often using brute force and imposing flogging, fines and insults with impunity. *Ballabats*, Ethiopian regional chiefs who had co-operated with the Italian authorities, left their territories to take refuge in Addis Ababa. These chiefs complained that they had beguiled themselves into believing they had found a better government in the Italians; instead it was proving to be worse than Haile Selassie's.

The resident's inexperience gave Ethiopians the impression that he lacked strength and was moved by juvenile impulses, rather than by a wise, considered attitude. Ethiopians complained that young residents sent to East Africa had wide powers given them. *Dejaz* Hasanna Jiotte of Dembidollo reported that officials administered justice as soon as they reached their destination, without first acquainting themselves with local law. It did not matter that some of them had a university degree in political science or in business administration. Their colonial inexperience exasperated the local people, and vast regions, led by their traditional chiefs, rebelled against Italian rule.

Di Revel reported that young residents were still filled with the spirit of war and not of conciliation. The bold residents were daring, but had not yet developed the sense of justice which matures with age. The inexperienced colonial official may have been a valorous soldier, but he did not know people and things. He had conquered an empire, but his excessive authority provoked revolt. He used his power without restraint, occasionally encouraged by self-serving Ethiopian interpreters who did not always translate faithfully.[6] They did not correctly translate Italian information or orders to the Ethiopians — telling them instead that if they gave them certain compensations they need not comply with Italian demands. Some were nationalists and used their position to encourage resistance to the Italian colonial power. Those who attempted to assassinate Graziani were translators at the Political Office in Addis Ababa. See also the example of Zerai Derres on p. 138.

Lack of knowledge of the local language (Amharic, Oromonya or Arabic) was also a drawback in the colonial administration, further evidence that Italy had not prepared itself to administer a conquered empire. Very few residents could speak Amharic. Ethiopians who knew Italian received advantageous positions with good salaries working for the Italian government as interpreters. Over 200 Eritreans were at the disposal of the Carabinieri and other government offices, regardless of their educational background, simply because they knew Italian. The psychological and cultural isolation of the resident from his subjects was encouraged by the interpreters who would act as a screen between the resident and the population for their own ulterior motives. Interpreters became influential and could delay or prevent people having access to the resident. The Duke of Aosta realized the importance of direct communication between colonial officers and the people and the psychological impact he could make upon Ethiopians if a resident could speak their language, so special funds were set aside to encourage colonial and military personnel to study Amharic, Oromonya or Arabic. A proposal was made to give a 4,000 lire per year increase in salary to those who knew at least one local language. The sum of 5 million lire was set aside to establish a Colonial Academy, to train residents and teach the languages used in Italian East Africa.[7] The academy however, never functioned and very few colonial officials learned to speak the languages of AOI.

Thus the administration of Italian East Africa was entrusted to unprepared people who committed many errors in colonial policy. Instead of winning over the people to Italy, residents antagonized them. The failure to win over the Ethiopians to Italy was perhaps the greatest failure in Italian colonial history; the failure was exacerbated by the issue of racial policy.

Addis Ababa's Military Sectors

The military domination of Italian administration became a permanent feature especially in the Amhara and Shoa Governorships,* which were in truth military sectors. Each sector had its commanding officer and an army to be used against the Ethiopian Patriots.

The colonial laws of 1 June 1936 and 11 November 1937 provided for the constitution of a Governorship of Addis Ababa covering 14,000 square kilometres of territory. Its first Governor was Alfredo Siniscalchi. Colonial legislation was designed to dismember the territory of Shoa, since the Shoans had been the ruling class before the Italian occupation. By dividing Shoa among the other Governorships, Italy sought to divide its people and eliminate any source of opposition. To better defend the capital from Patriot attack, in 1936 the traditional territories of Shoa were organized into three military sectors, sub-divided into six residencies and 17 vice-residencies. The generals of the three military sectors in Shoa (Western, North-Eastern and Eastern) were given wide administrative powers and were directly dependent on the Viceroy.

The dismemberment of Shoa did not give good results; the territory would have been better governed by only one authority. This would have allowed better political control of the hinterland of Addis Ababa and made the population realize that Italian policy was conciliatory, aimed at erasing the mistakes of the past and reaching a definite pacification. The first move toward the reconstruction of Shoa was made by the Duke of Aosta in 1938. However, it was soon discovered that colonial officials were unable to handle the rebellion in Shoa, and military sectors were reinstated. The presence of military sectors with both military and civilian functions was still necessary to pacify the population.[8] Eventually the decree of 1939 made it possible for areas around Addis Ababa to receive civil administration.

The Governorship of Amhara

The difficulties of dividing Shoa to meet military and security needs were also faced in the Governorship of Amhara. Lessona insisted that Amhara include only territories of Amharic-speaking people. The region of Tzellemt, though a Tigrean-speaking area, was annexed to Amhara to secure a well-defined frontier of that Governorship, alone the Takaze River.

Other regions like Wolkait, Woldebba, Tzeggede, Semien, Woggerat, and Belesa were inhabited by Tigrean-speaking people rather than Amhara. Before the Italian occupation of Ethiopia, all these regions south of the Setit River gravitated economically toward Asmara and not toward Gondar. Moreover, the Governorship of Amhara had poor communications, was too vast and, therefore, difficult to govern. Eventually in 1939 the territories between the Setit and Angareb Rivers were placed under the administration of Eritrea because the Governorship of Amhara could not protect these regions from Patriot incursions.

Lasta was another territorial change made in the Governorship of Amhara. Although ethnically Amhara, for political-military reasons in 1937 it was placed under Eritrea.[9] Graziani requested the change mainly to facilitate military operations against the rebel chief, Haile Kebbede. Also, Lasta did not have any communications with Gondar and was separated from Amhara by the Takaze River. Thus relations were closer with Eritrea.

Amhara, like Shoa, although officially organized into district commissioners and residencies, was really divided into military zones. Residencies were not secure and Patriots dominated the villages. It was impossible to extend Italian administration and establish residencies without adequate military support. Political control in Amhara was non-existent outside the areas occupied by the Italian army. To protect Gondar and the Densa region, which served as a buffer zone around the town, Mezzetti reduced the number of residencies, and closed vice-residencies to eliminate possible weak points, where the Patriots scored military successes to the detriment of Italy's reputation.

Governorship of Oromo-Sidamo

Ethiopian confidence in the Italian government was undermined by the boundary dispute between the Governorships of Harar and Oromo-Sidamo, which divided the territory occupied by the Arussi. The Muslim part of Arussi was attached to Harar, and the remaining "pagan" region was assigned to Oromo-Sidamo. To be consistent with the ethnic principle, Graziani insisted that all Arussi be governed from Harar.[10] The transfer of all Arussi territory to Harar would deprive Oromo-Sidamo of its main communication route, the Wondo-Sashamane-Mojo road, which connected Sidamo with the railway and Addis Ababa. It was difficult to reach an agreement on the basis of ethnic principles because the Arussi were widespread and divided into numerous tribes.

The confusion of authority along the boundary of Harar and Oromo-Sidamo persisted. Incidents took place and the Arussi took advantage of the unsettled situation, playing on it to avoid paying local taxes or submitting to justice. In 1939 both Governorships reached a friendly agreement handling the situation in a spirit of co-operation and political sensitivity.

The Italian administration of Ethiopia was affected by impractical regional boundaries. The ethnic system proved unworkable. The administration was left to incompetent colonial officials which in turn created major political problems, leading to rebellion. This state of affairs showed that basing internal regional boundaries on the ethnic principle did not work.

Notes

1. Mondaini, *Legislazione Coloniale Italiana*, II, p. 426-37; Meregazzi, *Lineamenti della Legislazione*, p. 25; Consociazione Turistica Italiana, *Africa Orientale Italiana*, p.33-115; *Annuario Dell'Africa Italiana*; Lessona, *Memorie*, p. 271; Bertola, *Storia ed Istituzioni dei Paesi Afro-Asiatici*, p. 264; MAI/GAB 204/28 Lessona to Viceroy, 27 April 1937; MAI/AS 181/47-221 Lessona to Viceroy, 5 August 1936; MAI/AS 181/56-272 Nasi: Political report 1937; MAI/AV 2 Duke Aosta to Teruzzi, 18 January 1940.

2. Italy: Ministero degli Esteri, *Governo dei Territori d'Oltremare*, p. 373; ACS/PCM 1937-1939 1/1.27/8313 Italian Central Institute of Statistics to PCM, 21 October 1939; MAI/GAB 72/XI-IX Cocchieri: Observation ... on the population of Ethiopia, 11 September 1940; MAI/AS 181/52-245 Cesareni: Notes on Cullo region, 26 June 1937; MAI/GAB 73/XI-II Duke Aosta: Political report of AOI, August 1939; MAI/AS 181/52-245 Gazzera: Political report of Oromo-Sidamo, March 1939.

3. MAI/AS 181/47-221 Lessona to GGAOI, 5 August 1936 and 27 April 1937; Ibid., Geloso to MAI 10 July 1936; Ibid., Pirzio Biroli to GGAOI, 15 December 1936; MAI/AS 181/53-248 Pirzio Biroli: Political Bulletin of the Governorship of Amhara, May 1937; MAI/AS 181/47-221 Graziani to MAI, 15 June 1937; Ibid., Geloso to Resident of Neghelli, 5 July 1936 and 22 June 1936; MAI/AS 181/56-272 Nasi: Political Report, 1937.

4. MAI/CSC 22/125 Meregazzi to CSC, 14 November 1936; MAI/GAB 218 Lessona: Report to the House of Deputies, Budget 1936-1937; MAI/AS 181/47-221 Lessona to GGAOI, 5 August 1936; MAI/GAB 277 Viceroy to MAI, 28 June 1936; MAI/GAB 46 Political and Administrative Organization of AOI, 1938.

5. MAI/AS 181/47-221 Nasi to MAI, 1 October 1938 and December 1938; Ibid., Mezzetti to MAI, 3 December 1938; MAI/GAB 59 Gazzera to MAI, 12 December 1938; Bongiovanni, *Problemi dell'Etiopia Italiana*, pp. 4-9; MAI/GAB 288/XIII-II Bonaccorsi: Impressions for the Duke of Aosta, 1938; ACS/MAI 13/1 GGAOI to MAI, 27 April 1939; ACS/RG 15 Geloso to GGAOI, 5 November 1937; MAI/GAB 74/XI-V Caroselli to Piccioli, 24 August 1939.

6. ACS/RG 57 Hazon: Memorandum on the functioning of the Government of Amhara, October 1937; MAI/GAB 75/5-C Meregazzi to Teruzzi: Information from *Dejaz* Hosanna Jiotte, 1938; ATR 24/163 Di Revel: Notes on Ethiopia, 1938; ACS/EB 42: 15 December 1937; *Le Matin* (Paris) 31 January 1938.

7. MAI/AS 181/37-176 *Bando*, (Adowa), 14 December 1935; MAI/

GAB 309/26 Lessona to Governor of Harar, 16 September 1937; MAI/AS 181/59-282 Moreno to MAI, 28 November 1938; MAI/AS 181/59-255 Meregazzi to Teruzzi, 25 June 1938.

8. MAI/GAB 32/XI-II-F Graziani to MAI, 15 March 1937; MAI/GAB 298 Teruzzi: Commission for the Supreme Defence: Minutes, 3–9 February 1938; MAI/GAB 253/32 Meregazzi to Teruzzi, 15 January 1939; MAI/GAB 265/169 Teruzzi to Meregazzi, 19 January 1939.

9. MAI/GAB 204/28 Lessona to Graziani 27 April 1937; MAI/GAB 18/XI-2 Lessona to Graziani, 22 June 1936; MAI/GAB 31/XI-II Graziani to MAI, 3 November 1937.

10. MAI/GAB 272/365-Bis Mezzetti: Political report of the Governorship of Amhara, October 1938; MAI/GAB 272/361 Mezzetti to MAI, 4 July 1938; MAI/AS 181/47-221 Graziani to MAI, 21 August 1937; Ibid., Geloso to GGAOI 7 September 1937; MAI/EF R/2Bis Nasi: Political report of the Governorship of Harar; MAI/GAB 261/82 Cerulli to MAI, 27 March 1939.

12. Italian Colonization

Colonization Projects

Italian plans to colonize Ethiopia go back to the 19th century, therefore long before the advent of the Fascist Regime. Mussolini's objectives in colonization was that Italian East Africa should produce enough food to to feed itself and a surplus to feed the Fatherland, in order to reduce the outlay of over 2.5 billion lire per year for food imports. Furthermore, the export to foreign countries of Ethiopia's traditional products (coffee, skins, civet cat, wax, grains) would supply the Italian economy with badly needed foreign currency.

More immediate, however, was the need to provide a place for Italian immigrants in the Empire. Ethiopia, as the new home of many Italians, was supposed to eliminate unemployment at home. Politically and culturally, Ethiopia was also considered a centre for the dissemination of Italian and Fascist civilization in Africa and Asia. Although aimed at meeting Italian needs first, humanitarian, social and political reasons demanded that Italy improve the conditions of life of the Ethiopians and increase agricultural output to turn a subsistence into a surplus economy. Ethiopian crops could be sold to the Italians, thus increasing the average income of the local population.[1]

In the first two years of the Italian presence in Ethiopia, colonization was following an uncharted course. A number of scouting missions were sent to explore the agricultural possibilities of the new Empire and to report on the best localities where Italian settlers could be sent. These missions confirmed that Ethiopia's main riches were based on agriculture, but that not all territories were suitable for Italian colonization. For reasons of safety it was at first advised that Italian agricultural colonies should be established along the Addis Ababa-Debra Berhan and Addis-Jimma roads.[2] Faddis, near Harar, was considered good for the culture of cereals and suitable for immediate colonization. At Chercher, there were about 6,000 hectares belonging to the State Domain. Italian colonization possibilities in Amhara and Oromo-Sidamo were extremely good, but because of poor communications they would have to be developed at a later time. The missions found that in regions where the climate was good and the land was fertile there were no vacant lands; they were intensely cultivated and belonged to private owners. Therefore, in the early stages of Italian colonization the greatest problem was lack of land to be given to Italian farmers.

However, because of the unsettled political situation, the initial Italian colonization of Ethiopia was military. According to Lessona, the first programme of colonization had to be launched around Addis Ababa. The colonization was entrusted at first to two military agricultural legions. The soldier-farmers were housed in two separate military villages, one along the Addis Ababa-Addis Alem road and the other in the direction of the Addis Ababa-Mojo highway. The land to farm was provided from Haile Selassie's expropriated estates and the former Ethiopian government domain.

In view of all these difficulties, the colonial authorities came to the conclusion that the colonization of Ethiopia should proceed slowly and cautiously. Before Italian farmers invested their capital in Ethiopia they wanted assurance of good crops and immediate returns. Experience was needed, which required years; time alone would tell which products were most economically profitable.[3] Italy's agricultural knowledge of Ethiopia during its five years' occupation remained limited and experimental and thus financially uncertain. Another reason for allowing only slow Italian immigration into Ethiopia was lack of roads and public works. It was recommended that they, too, be introduced by degrees lest in the rush to transform Ethiopia other dislocations were produced. Public works required huge sums. Italy had limited capital and, if too much was invested in such projects, money would be taken away from activities like agriculture. Ethiopians attracted by high-paying jobs would leave their fields and agricultural production would fall.

Financial limitations also affected Italian colonization. The establishment of an Italian family on a farm in Ethiopia was estimated to cost 50,000 lire. One thousand families would cost 50 million lire and for 10,000 Italian farmers Italy would have to invest 500 million lire. Hence Italian colonization was contained within modest limits because Italian colonization absorbed large amounts of state capital. Colonization itself was retarded by the inadequate information on land tenure and ownership.[4]

In the end, the Italian government decided to sponsor the colonization of Ethiopia with the help of colonizing agencies, with the aim of providing financial and technical aid to the new Italian farmers until the farmers became financially independent.

The first three agencies were the *Ente Romagna d'Etiopia, Ente Veneto d'Etiopia*, and *Ente Puglia d'Etiopia.* They received, respectively, lands in Woggerat (Amhara), Jimma (Oromo-Sidamo) and Chercher (Harar). All three were created in December 1937 but their initial operations were long delayed. However, until the colonizing agencies were able to contribute towards relieving the demographic pressures in Italy by settling immigrants in Ethiopia or providing Italy's population in Ethiopia with its food needs, Italy continued to be burdened with the high cost of imported foods and other necessities. The long-range plan was that the colonizing agencies would produce all foodstuffs for the Italians in Ethiopia, but that would take years and no one knew exactly how many! In this insecure situation, the colonial authorities resolved that food could be produced in sufficient quantities and at lower cost by using soldier-farmers in Ethiopia. This plan had multiple benefits: it put under cultivation without delay all available land, eliminated the cost of transporting farmers from Italy, afforded easier control of wheat and other staple food production, and solved the colonial government's problems with the defence of agricultural districts from Patriot attack.

Military Colonization

The Italian colonization of Ethiopia was delayed not only by lack of land and limited capital but also by the military opposition of the Ethiopian Patriots. In Amhara the Patriot activities prevented colonization from expanding; at Azozo, where modern Italian quarters were being built, the Patriots burned the nearby woods. In Woggerat, near the *Ente Romagna* several villages openly co-operated with the Patriots. The region of Achefer, with 180,000 hectares of land, was not colonized because of the presence of guerrilla forces, which forced the colonization of Amhara to be postponed. Agricultural concessions were limited around Gondar and Dessie; the *Ente Romagna* was able to cultivate only a few thousand hectares. For reasons of security the new farmer-immigrants were not allowed to bring their families. In areas besieged by the Patriots, the mail was delivered by air. Life at the *Ente* was conducted in a military fashion. At night the agricultural district was guarded by sentries.[5]

In Shoa the politico-military situation was kept turbulent by the presence of *Ras* Abebe Aragai and his Patriots. Italian colonization could not expand because Ethiopian farmers were unwilling to give up their land to the Italians. At Ambo, the farmers were given barbed wire and slept at night in forts to facilitate their defence. To protect Italian farmers and the capital, the military district of Bishoftu was created. In Oromo-Sidamo, the displaced Amhara resorted to armed resistance in an attempt to regain their former positions. In Jimma Italian colonization was of moderate dimensions. Here the demographic colonization suffered little from Ethiopian Patriotic pressure.

However, the problem of security remained the paramount preoccupation of the colonial government. Farm houses were built close together in militarily strategic positions, with surrounding walls and defensive works.[6] At Holetta in Shoa the farm houses were organized in groups of eight. Each group of about 40 farmers, properly armed, was thus able to defend itself. In Amhara at the *Ente Romagna* houses were grouped in fours forming a square to ensure protection and inhibit guerrilla attacks. In Oromo-Sidamo farm houses were grouped in fours not more than 200 metres from one another. Farmers were at all times considered soldiers and formed a military-agricultural colony. Soon after the conquest of Ethiopia the Italian government, for propaganda and political reasons, lured the troops being demobilized with the mirage of a land concession 20 lire per day salary, plus room and board. These conditions appeared advantageous, and in a moment of euphoria soldiers decided to remain in Ethiopia. By the end of 1936, however, of the circa 250,000 demobilized soldiers, only 13,881 had decided to settle in Ethiopia and, in 1937, an additional 1,525.[7] Despite the enticement of land concessions and good salaries, the experiment in military colonization failed. Soldiers were willing to stay in Ethiopia as farmers to escape military service, and after a time of work in the field left agriculture to dedicate themselves to better remunerated commercial activities.

Sporadic attempts were made in the different Governorships to accomodate demobilized troops. In Amhara two experiments were conducted with *Pattuglie del Grano* (Wheat Patrols). Their military colonization was supposed to be financed by an insurance company, the *Instituto Nazionale Fascista Contro gli Infortuni Sul Lavoro*. But since the institute was unwilling to risk its capital, the Amhara Governorship ended up paying for it. The Patrol, besides cultivating the land assigned, was fully armed and responsible for the defence of 250 farming units. Because of the constant guerrilla warfare, the agricultural-military programme was eventually phased out.

In Oromo-Sidamo, however, military colonization at first promised success. The Wheat Patrol stationed in a strategic position around Jimma, provided both food and a defensive line around the capital of Oromo-Sidamo. The Wheat Patrols received financial support amounting to 1,000,000 lire from the Agricultural Office of the Governorship of Oromo-Sidamo and a loan of 250,000 lire from the Bank of Italy to cultivate the 700 hectares. Of the 40 soldiers who received a farm of 50 hectares, only two remained; the others, because of bureaucratic complications and technical deficiencies, failed to make their colonization profitable.

The same form of colonization was attempted in Shoa, around Addis Ababa. To stimulate military men to engage in agricultural production, the Fascist Party gave prizes of 10,000 lire to the best fields and to the highest production of wheat per hectare.[8] In 1939, of 7,000 soldiers applying for land, none had any finances to pay for the expenses of farm tools and housing. As a result only 279 petitions were accepted. The Duke of Aosta proposed helping only those who had some savings to advance toward the construction of farm houses, which was the greatest expense and was, because of its high cost, a limitation on demographic colonization. Since not one of the soldiers had that capital, he suggested that the government give financial help to them in the form of a loan. At first 200 were selected to form the *Centuria Agricola di Pre-Colonizzazione* (Agricultural Centurion of Pre-Colonization). The farmer-soldiers were also organized to perform military tasks. They acted as garrisons around Addis Ababa and other Ethiopian centres. It was estimated that the cost of 18,000 lire per farm house could be reduced to 8,000 lire using military labour and local building materials.

Mussolini enthusiastically endorsed the plan and sent 5 million lire to build 600 houses in a period of four years. The Duke of Aosta anticipated that the sum advanced to the former soldiers could be repaid to the government after five years.

The Agricultural Centurion received 1,800 hectares of land at Guder, 650 hectares at Makanisa near Addis Ababa. The first phase of the military colonization was to be completed by 1940 with 43 farms at Makanisa and 150 at Guder. By 1940, however, 45 had been built at Guder and 24 at Makanisa, at an average cost of 26,000 lire. In one year about 2,000 hectares were under cultivation and 69 farm houses built; about 200 farms were released to soldiers.[9]

The military colonization, as planned and sponsored by the Duke of Aosta, had all the prerequisites of success in its serious intent and well-planned programme. The soldier-farmers were thoroughly and rigidly selected and were not favoured by party affiliation. Moreover, the Agricultural Inspectorate was committed to instruct and aid the soldier-farmers, who were to become the model for future colonization. In other regions military colonization failed because it was sponsored by the Fascist Party, which had no agricultural competence and was at odds with the local agricultural specialists. Demographic plans were politically motivated and not supported by the local authorities. After their first burst of enthusiasm, soldiers realized that colonial life was no assurance of a better future. There was concern over Patriot attacks, land concessions were hard to get, and quick returns were hard to come by. Military colonization (like colonization with the aid of colonizing agencies) faced difficulties which did not encourage the migration of Italians to Ethiopia.

Thus, not even military colonization assured Italy enough food for its immigrants. Ironically, Ethiopia, once self-sufficient in food, instead of improving its food output under Italian rule had to import food, much to the disadvantage of Italy's balance of payments. To counteract this situation the Italian authorities waged a campaign for the cultivation of wheat. The "battle for bread" was intended to produce enough spaghetti to keep the Italians happy!

The Battle for Bread

Optimistic forecasts claimed that Ethiopia would become a granary of Italy. Ironically, the conquest of Ethiopia, instead of relieving Italy's wheat imports, increased them. The estimated 500,000 Italians in Ethiopia had to be provided with wheat from Italy. Ethiopia was never self-sufficient, although progress was made in the five years of Italian occupation of Ethiopia toward an increase in wheat production.

In the second half of 1936 Ethiopia imported about 75,000 tons of wheat from Italy at a cost of 43 million lire. Prospects for 1937 were not better. For that year, imports grew to 128,000 tons at a cost of 132 million lire. In 1938 Italians began to settle on farms and wheat autarky for the whole Italian Empire was anticipated. To everybody's dismay, although wheat imports were reported to be declining, wheat was actually imported into Ethiopia at a cost of 200 million lire for the year. The quantities of wheat imported into Ethiopia in 1939 passed the mark of 100,000 tons.

Italians and Ethiopians were called on to participate in a drive for wheat self-sufficiency with the incentive of a high price paid for their wheat. Self-sufficiency in food in the Empire was a military necessity and essential if there was to be economic development and demographic colonization. The colonial government was anxious to improve the army food stockpiles in case Addis Ababa was besieged, as in July 1936. In April 1937 it had on hand enough pasta for 36 days. Later in the year food stockpiles increased to 175 days. The food supply situation of Ethiopia was so critical for both civilians and military that Graziani formed the Defence Commission to assure food autonomy for the Empire. To meet the need for wheat, all military camps and schools were ordered to cultivate gardens to produce food. Without realizing the difficulties that had to be overcome, Mussolini decreed that by 1 July 1938, the Empire had to become self-sufficient in wheat. In 1940 Mussolini admitted that Ethiopia had reached only 35% self-sufficiency. Of the estimated 100,000 tons of wheat per year needed for bread and spaghetti in Ethiopia, the colony's output was about 38,000-43,000 tons a year between 1937 and 1940.[10]

Wheat production in Ethiopia for 1937-8 totalled about 25,000 to 40,000 tons of which 7,000 tons were contributed by Ethiopians under the *asrat*, tithe to the government. The highest documented yield of wheat in Ethiopia during the Italian occupation was 70,000 tons in 1938-9. In that year Oromo-Sidamo and Harar Governorships reached self-sufficiency for the first and only time. In Amhara the hectarage under wheat cultivation increased by 30%. In 1940 production declined to 20,000 tons,[11] perhaps because of the war preparations which might have diverted government attention from farming priorities in favour of defence.

Whatever the reasons, Italy failed to live up to the promise of food autarky in AOI. Lack of wheat deepened the already existing military apprehension created by Patriot guerrilla warfare and the ever-present fear of an impending international conflict in which Ethiopia would become isolated from Italy. In addition, for a variety of political, technical and material causes, the battle for bread brought no decisive victories.

Italo-Ethiopian Share-Cropping Agreements

The colonial government policy aimed at elevating the Italian farmer's position in the Empire to that of land-owner or manager, supervising Ethiopian peasants. Italians could not work as day-labourers, a job reserved for the Ethiopians alone. For reasons of prestige, political opportunity, and the upholding of Fascist racial policy, Italians were given a high social status in Ethiopia, even though the average Italian farmer was humble enough to work side by side with the local people and did not understand the artificially imposed differentiation between him and the Ethiopian peasant.

In order to maintain a high standard of living, the Italian farmer was given the best farming land and promised high profits, the assistance of cheap Ethiopian labour, and the use of tractors. But even with mechanized agriculture, food autarky was not reached. It was then decided to enter into share-cropping contracts with the Ethiopians. The Italian farmer prepared the land for cultivation with tractors while the Ethiopians were responsible for sowing, weeding, and harvesting. In return, the Ethiopian farmer received only one-third of the crop. In other words, the Ethiopian did all the manual work, while the Italian farmer provided mechanized assistance. This type of co-operation was advantageous to the Italian farmer because he received the necessary help and made the Ethiopian peasant dependent on him.

The Ethiopians, however, did not always keep their part of the contract and were reluctant to engage in any form of agreement with the Italians because they were suspicious of Italian ulterior motives. Perhaps the underlying reason for this lack of trust in the Italians was the peasant belief in the return of Haile Selassie, who would then reverse the political situation, and the peasants would become owners of all crops. This may explain in part why the Ethiopian farmers were reluctant to harvest the crops.

In the Govenorship of Amhara the profit-sharing contracts were not accepted by the Ethiopians because, in addition to sharing the crop with the Italians, the farmers were obliged to pay a tithe, the *asrat*, to the Italian government. Only after Governor Frusci consented to remove the *asrat* were 350 profit-sharing contracts written, but they covered only 95 hectares of land. Only two Italian farmers scored success in the crop-sharing system; in the Bishoftu area, the Boidi brothers, because of their honesty, understanding of local conditions, reciprocal trust and respect for the Ethiopians were able to share crop profits in proportion to the effort and capital invested by both parties. The Boidi brothers concluded 3,000 contracts involving over 2,000 hectares of land.

Land-grabbing

Although Italian scholars studied Ethiopia's landholding systems, they did not realize how complex it would be to convince the Ethiopians to relinquish their property and verify their land titles. The government was faced with the dilemma of wanting to acquire land for the Italians; and at the same time, not wanting to upset the Ethiopians by expropriating their lands.

In the first period of the Italian occupation, 1936-7, over-enthusiastic Italian authorities, ignorant of local landownership traditions, confiscated Ethiopian lands to give to Italian farmers. The landholding system in Ethiopia varied from region to region, it was admitted that, although seen as antiquated compared to European standards, it met the socio-political needs of the Ethiopians. It was a system that had become perfected over many centuries. To facilitate understanding the land problem under Italian occupation an outline of Ethiopian landholding systems is in order.

In the Amharic-speaking territories the land tenure was called *gult*, meaning to give in concession. *Gult* land was part of the Ethiopian government domain which the Emperor conceded to a family or a military colony to cultivate and live on. *Gult* was a temporary, even annual, concession to soldiers and government officials as a means of remuneration instead of wages. *Gult* could also be considered a fief granted by the Ethiopian government, which also included the rights to collect land products, levy taxes, raise troops, and administer justice. On other occasions, the Emperor gave *gult* appointments for political-military reasons to keep watch on the local aristocracy and prevent them from rebelling against the central government. In practice, however, chiefs invested with a *gult* transformed their temporary privileges and concessions into hereditary property. *Gult* given by the Emperor to worthy followers was usually land that the state had acquired when the land was abandoned by a migrating tribe, or the family who possessed it became extinct. The Ethiopian state also had authority to expropriate the land of rebel chiefs and to incorporate the territory of those villagers who did not pay tribute. But the most common way the Ethiopian government formed a *gult* was by conquering other people.

It was not always clear whether *gult* land was a fief only or whether it could be interpreted also as public land domain. As a compromise, the Italians made a distinction between hereditary *gult* (which was recognized as private property) and feudal *gult* (which became public domain). This decision applied to Gojam, Begemder and Lasta only. In the Wollo region *gult* was recognized as hereditary for the most influential families. This arrangement left the Oromo of Wollo with the burden of taxation. To appease the Wollo population, after a ten-year payment of land tax the Oromo farmer would be recognized as the owner of his land.[12]

Rist was private property or hereditary land which was not held by a single person but by a community, village or tribe. Each family of the community shared the plot of land assigned to it by the village council for a period of three to seven years. The family had full authority over these alloted lands so long as it paid tribute. This communal form of wealth-sharing did not allow personal private property. Only around Gondar had the concept of personal private property become prevalent. Thus, regardless of the type of property, *rist* was recognized by the Italian authorities, as communal land and also as private property. It was difficult for untrained colonial officials to differentiate at first between *gult* and *rist* land, especially when Ethiopians claimed hereditary titles but did not have documents to prove it. Therefore, land was often expropriated out of ignorance.

During the Amhara conquest of southern Ethiopia the Ethiopian government assigned one-quarter of the land to the local chiefs' *ballabat* and three-quarters were retained by the government. The division of land did not mean that the *ballabat* and the Ethiopian government became owners of the land, but merely affirmed the concept of eminent domain, leaving the original owners proprietors of their land on condition that they cultivated it.

Rist land in the Governorship of Oromo-Sidamo was a gift of land that could be transmitted to the heir of the family. *Gult* was also hereditary but non-alienable and tax-free; furthermore, the beneficiary could collect tribute for his own benefit. *Gult* was usually reserved for members of the imperial family or the Ethiopian nobility. To lesser nobility the Ethiopian government gave *maderiya*, a type of temporary *gult* concession. *Maderiya* was a form of payment by the government for services performed by a civil or military dependent, in lieu of a stipend, but the recipient was obliged to pay a tax to the government.

Gebbar means he who pays tribute. *Gebbar*, besides being a tax, was associated with peasant-servant relationships between the Oromo and the Amhara conquerors. The system involved the allotment of land and peasants by the Ethiopian government to the soldier-settler. The Oromo were obliged to perform forced labour as payment to those new masters imposed upon them as a result of conquest. *Rases* and *dejazes* received several thousand *gebbars* with their land, a *fitaurari* 300 *gebbars* and soldiers, between 10 and 20 *gebbars*, whose Amhara masters considered them their serfs.

In south-eastern Ethiopia, in the Italian Governorship of Harar, land was possessed by the group; private property was rare, except in the urban centres. In the territories inhabited by Oromo, property was concentrated in the hands of the local chief, called *garad* or *burka*, who was responsible for seeing that the land was cultivated. Hence, it seems that in south-eastern Ethiopia, the farmers did not have collective property claims; they had the right to use the land, rather than the right of property, as in Oromo-Sidamo. The Ethiopian government – in an attempt to assure state revenue – recognized the property of those who cultivated the land with the right of succession to their heirs. Moreover, the Ethiopian government considered as public domain all uncultivated lands, which were expropriated and distributed to Amhara and Shoans, who however were not proprietors, but beneficiaries of crops and tribute; these later became *gult* and *rist* lands.[13]

In principle the Italian, like the Ethiopian, government, recognized the original property of those who effectively cultivated the land. They recognized *rist* and *gult* systems. In ascertaining landownership, the Italians were interested first in obtaining enough free land for Italian farmers and in stimulating Ethiopian farmers to produce food. The Italian government tried to dispel the widespread Ethiopian fear that their land would be given to the Italians. Hence, the colonial government reassured the Ethiopians that their traditions and customary land laws would be respected.[14] Yet at the same time it promised the Oromo and Muslim population that their interests would be foremost in the land resettlement process.

Official Italian land policy was based on using for Italian colonization only estates that had previously belonged to the imperial family, the Ethiopian

Administration and Colonization

government land domain, exiled *rases*, and the Patriots. The Italians also considered public domain lands which were not cultivated; to these they ruled the Ethiopians could have no claim. Moreover, cultivated land could not be expropriated and Ethiopian property was respected *de facto* until ownership and status as *gult* or *rist* was ascertained. But the majority of Italians believed that all Ethiopian territory was public domain!

Nevertheless, for political reasons, colonization could not be slowed down for lack of land. The first expropriation was announced by the military proclamation of General Pietro Maravigna in November 1935 declaring the properties of *Ras* Seyum, *Dejaz* Sahle Araya and other nobles state domain. The lands of *Ras* Kassa of Lasta and his sons, Wonde Wassen and Aberra, followed later.[15] So did Haile Selassie's two main properties of Holetta and Bishoftu. The greatest amount of land came from the Achefer expropriation near Lake Tana of 180,000 hectares of land, part of which was *gult* of *Grazmatch* Babil.

Another 180,000 hectares of *rist* property were obtained in the Woggerat region, 213 hectares of which belonged to *Dejaz* Ayalu Burru. Since Woggerat was one of the most fertile areas, it was decided to install *Ente Romagna* farmers there, but only 6,000 hectares could be secured.

The Governorship of Harar was more successful in obtaining land for Italian colonization. Lands confiscated came from the feudal lands of *Ras* Desta Damtu in Sidamo and from the estates of *Dejaz* Burru, former Minister of War, in Arussi. Haile Selassie's 6,000 hectare estate in Chercher was given to the *Ente Puglia* and his estate at Errer (300 hectares) was kept as an experimental farm. As a whole, Harar was able to form a public domain of some 30,000 hectares. The public domain in the territories of Oromo-Sidamo was more promising. Some 60,000 hectares of *gult* lands in Kaffa given by Menelik II to *Negus* Wolde Giorgis in 1897 were declared state land. The same was done in the Kambatta region and Sidamo, as the heirs of *Dejaz* Ambarber were deprived of their feudal territories. Other lands were expropriated from *Ras* Desta in Neghelli, Borana. In Oromo-Sidamo the public domain was estimated to be more than 200,000 hectares. To increase the availability of land, the Italian government adopted, against the wishes of the Ethiopian farmers, the system of *permute*, that is, agreements with Ethiopian landowners to trade off their land for other lands in the public domain. The exchange of land was necessary because there were not enough contiguous lands in one place to make a farm economic.[16]

Although the Italian government decreed that it would protect Ethiopian private property, in the first years it had to close its eyes to abusive land occupation by Italian speculators. In 1936-7, for political and economic reasons, the colonization began precipitously without real knowledge of the land system. Commissions were sent to Ethiopia to "choose" land for demographic colonization – unaware of Ethiopian land claims. It was part of the attitude of the colonial authorities in Ethiopia that, although the principle of private property was to be recognized, when the interests of the Italian colonization were at stake, the latter had to prevail over the former. The

Director of the Colonizing Office in Gondar issued illegal farming permits in Dessie and other parts of Amhara allowing Italians to occupy land which was really Ethiopian property. The same applied to the process of obtaining land for the *Ente Romagna*, *Veneto* and *Puglia*, in which cases the examination of private property was done superficially.

With the agreement of the resident and commissioners, Italian agricultural concessions were allowed to double their land surface and expand beyond their boundaries only because adjacent fields seemed uncultivated. Seasonal cultivation permits were allowed to become *de facto* concessions. To stop the spread of unlawful practices in obtaining land from Ethiopians without legal permission, the Ministry of Africa at first decided to give one-year cultivation permits[17] and land expropriated from Ethiopian Patriots was temporarily assigned to Italians for the period of forfeiture. In the uncertainty of the landholding system, the government resolved to make all land concessions "temporary" until the study to determine private property was completed.

Thus, arbitrary land distribution and delay in surveying land worked to the detriment of Ethiopians, who saw their land alienated to Italian landlords. To appease the widespread discontent among the Ethiopians, the Italian government attempted to compensate the colonial subjects for the loss of their property by giving new land, building huts, digging wells, and paying for eucalyptus trees and coffee trees. Late in 1939, the Governorship of Amhara began to inquire into unlawful land concessions. By 1940, 400 Ethiopian families had received compensation for the loss of about 5,000 hectares. In Oromo-Sidamo an average of 20 lire per hectare of land were paid to Oromo families.[18] In Shoa, the Governor-Generalship of AOI paid about 40,000 lire to Ethiopians who had been removed from Holetta and Bishoftu. In Addis Ababa, where lands were not only needed for colonization but also for planning a new city, some 10 million lire worth of property were expropriated between 1937 and 1938, of which only 1,127,175 lire was paid to the expropriated owners.

Although the Italian government found it politically advantageous to compensate for land taken from the Ethiopians, payments were slow to reach the owners and they usually received from one-sixth to one-sixteenth of the real value of the land taken. It is difficult to ascertain exactly how much land was grabbed from the Ethiopians and even less clear how much they received in exchange. Nasi mentions that in five years the Italian administration paid the exaggerated sum of 600 million lire to Ethiopian owners for their property.[19] Land expropriation from lawful owners was probably limited in extent and in time (1936-7) but, even so, the early mistakes were damaging enough to become one of the principle reasons for the Ethiopian rebellion.

The cause of these abuses are to be found in the long delay in setting up and sending to Ethiopia the commission to ascertain landownership. Because of the short time they had, the difficulties of languages and traditions and the unstable political-military situation, the Italians made little headway in their study in depth of landholding systems, thus leading to postponement of a full-scale Italian colonization of Ethiopia.

The Policy of Limited Colonization: 1938

The Italian government's new policy of limited emigration was a reversal of previous declarations that millions of Italians would settle in Ethiopia. The decision to go for small colonization was justified by the large amount of money needed to transfer an Italian family, and the lack of specialized and technically-prepared men to cope with the problems of colonization. Furthermore, the limited availability of farm land and the problem of security, influenced the Italian authorities to proceed cautiously.

The first colonizing agency called to Ethiopia was the *Opera Nazionale Combattenti* (ONC) (the Association of Ex-Servicemen) on the basis of its wide experience acquired in colonization programmes in Libya. In order to ensure food supplies for the capital and to protect Addis Ababa, the *ONC* received land concessions at Bishoftu and Holetta.

In the Governorship of Oromo-Sidamo, demographic colonization proceeded at a slower pace; this territory was the last to be occupied militarily and had very few roads. Although Oromo-Sidamo was the most promising territory for Italian colonization, the *Ente Veneto*, never functioned. Instead, a new demographic enterprise was created locally, the *Ente Thesauro De Rege*, named after an Italian captain who died at Neghelli in 1936. Oromo-Sidamo was chosen by another colonizing agency composed of Italians residing abroad: the *Ente di Colonizzazione Italiani all'Estero*. Italy needed the experience and capital of Italians who had worked in tropical areas to help produce raw materials in Ethiopia and thus save Italy a period of crop experimentation and financial investments.[20]

One last colonizing scheme was sponsored by the Duke of Aosta: the *Ente Aosta* on 30,000 hectares of land in the valley between Lake Zwai and Mount Chilalo, near Asella, Harar.

In the first years of the Italian Empire, people went to Ethiopia moved by a spirit of adventure. The Duke of Aosta estimated that 30% of the Italians in Ethiopia were adventurers and unscrupulous men.[21] These speculators entered with the aid of influential Roman politicians. Farmers who went to East Africa did not plan to settle permanently in Ethiopia. They went to Africa only to escape unemployment, accumulate a small fortune and return home; they were disenchanted by the situation in the Empire, where the future was uncertain. They complained of poor housing, insufficient food, lack of agricultural tools, delay in land assignments, absence of spiritual and moral assistance and delays in payment of their salary. In other instances women found it hard to remain in isolated agricultural districts and some of them left the farm to work in Addis Ababa.

Once in Ethiopia, many of the farmer-immigrants proved themselves unsuitable for the tasks assigned. Farmers were badly chosen and even the

ONC, which had a reputation for having better farmers than any of the other colonizing agencies, was compelled to expel a number of them for inefficiency. Of the *Ente Puglia's* 105 farmers, 42 were repatriated for the same reason.[22] At the ONC farmers were sent away for dishonest deals with Ethiopians, fraud and unlawful commercial activities. Farmers found it hard to live together and families quarrelled among themselves. Moreover, Italian demographic colonization, apart from a lack of farmers willing to go to Ethiopia, was faced with a crisis of leadership and a shortage of technical personnel to assist the new farmers. The Directorate of Colonization and Labour created in 1937 did not start work until 1938. In 1941 there were some 60 agricultural offices in Ethiopia but they came into existence late and were chronically short of personnel.[23] Thus, although the agricultural specialists were among the best-liked and respected of the colonial officials in Ethiopia because of their dedication, there were not enough of them to meet the needs of Italian demographic colonization.

Those Italian farmer-immigrants who received a farm house from a colonizing agency complained that their living quarters were too small or not well-built, which added to their disappointment and frustration with colonial life. Although by 1940 the goal of building enough housing for Italian farmers had not been reached, the first two-roomed houses met the most immediate needs. The farms however lacked a stable and a garage for the animals and agricultural machinery. Houses with only two rooms were too small for Italian families of nine.[24] The quality of the buildings was also poor. Even before the farm houses were completed, considerable damage could be seen – mostly walls collapsing and cracking; rain came in the nearly-finished houses. Engineers attributed these problems to excessive use of mud and little cement; when it rained, walls eroded and parts of them collapsed. In other instances, toilet facilities were not provided and the oven in the kitchen blackened the walls for lack of ventilation.[25]

Although the immigrants in Ethiopia were provided with poor housing, the Italian colonial authorities claimed they were better than the quarters farmers had in Italy. However, the immigrant-farmers were unhappy because the promises given them in Italy were not kept in Ethiopia. Farmers' reports to relatives in Italy show their dissatisfaction: they advised them not to come to Ethiopia.

The Investment in Colonization

Following the conquest of Ethiopia, the Italian press, with the blessing of the Fascist Party, had launched a propaganda campaign regarding the great future of Italian colonization in the newly-conquered territory. Between 1936 and 1937, there was an atmosphere of euphoria; everybody was interested in the Empire. Newspaper columns were filled with long articles by journalists who used their best rhetoric to convince the public of the riches of Ethiopia and the great opportunities for farmers. The media beguiled the public by treating the first demographic and agricultural experiments as accomplished facts to give the illusion that, with the conquest of Ethiopia, the problems of emigration, and unemployment were solved. By May 1937, however, Lessona warned the Chamber of Deputies against unwarranted optimism about colonization, which faced serious difficulties.

The early enthusiasm could not be easily silenced. The press continued to argue that there was room for millions of Italians in Ethiopia. Even the Pope believed that within ten years five million Italians would transfer to Ethiopia. These were all guesses; no one knew how many Italians would be able to settle in Ethiopia and in how long a time. Badoglio pointed out that the colonization of Ethiopia would take several generations. It would take 10 to 25 years before a farmer in the tropics could be self-sufficient.[26] Armando Maugini, director of the *Instituto Agronomo Coloniale*, and Francesco Caroselli, Governor of Somalia, declared that relatively few Italian families could be absorbed by Ethiopia in the near future. Thus, the plans of the Italian demographic campaign were curtailed.

By 1941, the *Ente Romagna* found that of the 1,000 anticipated farmers only 350 had come to Ethiopia. Although the *Ente Romagna* carried out only one-third of its colonizing programme, the *Opera Nazionale Combattenti* in Shoa, which reported more success than other colonizing agencies, was faced with similar difficulties. Its original plan to settle 400 farming families came to nothing and only about 100 received farms. The *Ente Puglia*, like the *Ente Romagna*, had programmed the settlement of 1,000 families from the Apulia region in Chercher. Despite the fact that the region where the *Ente Puglia* operated was peaceful, its results were minimal. Only about 100 farmers were present in 1940, which is one-tenth of the number of farms to be created. The *Ente De Rege* at Bonga-Jimma was more successful. The Ente started late; in less than two years it settled 41 farming families.[27] Each colonizing agency planned to settle in Ethiopia an average of 1,000 families (the *Ente Italiani all'Estero* proposed settling 3,000 families and the *Ente Veneto* 1,500), that is at least 6,000 Italian farming families in five years. By the end of 1940 (depending which sources are used), the demographic colonization had brought about 500 farmers to Ethiopia or less than 10% of what had been anticipated, although the press gave the number as 854. A more reliable source estimated that about 400 farmers had settled in Ethiopia.

In addition to demographic colonization a number of small and large private and state-sponsored agricultural enterprises were functioning in Ethiopia with the same goal. The number of Italian farmers used by these concerns was estimated to be between 2,000 and 4,255, — a smaller number than the millions of farmers Italy originally planned to settle in Ethiopia.

In Amhara the *Ente Romagna* planned to give 50,000 hectares of land to Italian immigrants.[28] By 1940, of the promised 50,000 hectares of land, 5,600 had been allotted, but only about 1,000 were cultivated and less than 1,000 actually sown! To compensate for the limited amount of land in Amhara, the *Ente Romagna* received additional land in Shoa but this was of little overall importance. The *ONC* was assured 24,000 hectares of land. How-

Table 12.1
Farmers Settled in Ethiopia 1936-1940

Colonizing Agencies	1937	1938	1939	1940-41	1946
Ente Romagna (Woggerat, upper Awash River basin, Villa Anna-Maria)	–	124-150	181-200	195-350	138
ONC (Holetta-Bishoftu)	120-150	74-100	92	93-105	98
Ente Puglia (Chercher)	50-200	100-105	92	96	20
Ente De Rege (Bonga-Jimma)	–	–	30-35	41-55	41
Centuria Agricola di Pre-Colonizzazione (Guder-Makanisa)	–	–	200	69	80
Totals	*170-350*	*298-355*	*595-619*	*494-675*	*377*

ever, the real problem was that Holetta, Bishoftu and nearby lands were intensively cultivated and land ownership jealously guarded. The war did not allow further expansion and the *ONC* was left with 7,500 hectares of land, of which only 2,300 were cultivated. It was less than 10% of what the *ONC* had once planned to achieve.

The results of the *Ente Puglia*, to which 50,000 hectares were conceded, were no better. Poor leadership and the choice of incompetent farmers doomed the experiment to failure. In 1940, of the 6,000 hectares allotted to the *Ente Puglia*, 1,100 were under cultivation but only 500 sown. The experiment in demographic colonization of the *Ente De Rege* in Oromo-Sidamo started late but gave good results during its short life. In one year, of the 1,600 hectares given, 400 were ploughed and about 200 sown.

Official Italian statistics on the amount of land destined for demographic colonization give a total of 33,000 hectares, of which 13,000 were farmed. We do not have accurate data as to how much land was cultivated by colonizing agencies and by other agricultural enterprises. Figures do not always differentiate between private farming and state-supported concerns. However, the press continued to quote astronomical figures for land concessions to Italians in an effort to keep Italian interest in Ethiopia alive.

The Ministry of Africa had no precise information on the amount of land actually allotted to Italian agricultural companies. Estimates of the total land concessions range from 50,000 to 248,729 hectares but, again, it is hard to ascertain how much of this land was actually under cultivation. The same lack of knowledge of the number of agricultural concerns – both private and state-supported – in Ethiopia is apparent. Estimates vary from 208 to 574.[29] The number of Italian farming enterprises more than doubled

Table 12.2
Hectares of Land Reserved for Demographic Colonization[30]

Colonizing Agencies	Place	Concession (Hectares) Planned	Concession (Hectares) Actual	1938	Hectares Cultivated 1939	1940	Hectares Sown 1937	1938	1939	1940
Ente Romagna	Woggerat	50,000	5,600	380	1013	–	–	105	837	–
	Upper Awash									
	River Basin	50,000	6,000	750	2000	–	–	220	900	–
	Villa Anna									
	Maria	300	300	–	(200)	–	–	10	75	–
	Total	100,300	11,900	1,100	3,213	–	–	335	1812	–
ONC	Holetta	12,000	5,000	2,100	–	–	869	1,405	(2300)	–
	Bishoftu	12,000	2,500	1,935	–	–	1,181	456	–	–
	Total	24,000	7,500	4,035	–	–	2,050	1,961	(2300)	–
Ente Puglia	Chercher	50,000	6,000	1,100	1,100	–	–	700	500	260
Ente De Rege	Bonga-Jimma	2,350	1,600	–	–	400	–	–	–	160
Centuria de Pre-Colonizzazione	Guder-Makanisa	2,450	2,000	–	2,000	–	–	–	–	–
Grand Total Demographic Colonization in Ethiopia		179,100	29,000		10,748			4,972		

in two years, to about 713. The same applies to the capital invested in agricultural businesses which was estimated at 850 million lire[31] – including assets invested in Eritrea and Somalia, which accounted for half of all the agricultural enterprises in Italian East Africa. It can then be fairly assumed that the total capital investment in the agriculture of Ethiopia was 400 million lire.

After five years in Ethiopia, Italy had been able to attract to the colony only 3,200 farmers and about 40 agricultural companies, as compared to 1,436 commercial and 1,225 industrial firms. The numerical disparity between agriculture, commerce and industry shows that the Italians were attracted more toward businesses assuring a quick return for their capital. Private concerns were unwilling to take financial risks, therefore, the Italian government had to encourage investments in the colony by providing investors with state capital insurance. As a result of these economic privileges, industrial, commercial and agricultural complexes monopolized the most lucrative activities and left nothing to independent businesses. Hence, by the time Italian rule ended in Ethiopia, the economic life of the colony was dependent upon government funds and not upon private capital.

Colonization proved very expensive, and investments were sought from Switzerland and the United States of America. But Italian and foreign capital was slow to flow into Ethiopia; the Italian government had to pressure banks and insurance companies to sponsor Italian colonization with their funds. At the end, the Ministry of Africa used part of its budget to meet the needs of Italian farmers in Ethiopia. Furthermore, while the Italian government anticipated that the cost of the colonization of Ethiopia would be 100 million lire over a six-year period, for budgetary reasons, it was divided into twelve annual installments. Since Mussolini wanted his countrymen from Romagna to receive the best financial terms, the *Ente Romagna's* capital of 50 million lire was financed by state participation.[32] The *Ente Romagna* received special treatment: it borrowed 50 million lire without interest, had 50 years in which to repay the loan, and did not have to make the first repayment until after the tenth year. Moreover, the *Ente* received an additional financial contribution of 2 million lire from the region of Romagna. In 1939 the *Ente* invested about 18 million lire in Ethiopia and anticipated an income from its agricultural activities of less than 2 million lire. By 1940 *Ente Romagna* had used 33 million lire of its budgeted 50 million.

The *Opera Nazionale Combattenti* was another state-financed colonizing agency with special provisions. Its budget was 400 million lire. In Ethiopia its average yearly investments were 15 million lire. After the war, the *ONC* claimed to have spent about 55 million lire in Ethiopia, of which at least 25 million lire were spent for public works.[33]

The financial situation of the *Ente Puglia* was more difficult. The *Ente* was financed by the Bank of Naples (25 million lire), the *Instituto Nazionale della Previdenza Sociale* (25 million lire), and the Province of Apulia (5 million lire) – for a total of 55 million lire – but contrary to the two other *enti* had to pay a fixed interest of 5% per year. The loan was repayable over a 20 year period. In 1938 the *Ente* had invested about 3 million lire in Ethiopia and had an income of 700,000 lire from agricultural products. Projections for 1939 estimated a financial investment at Chercher of 18 million lire. The last budget of the *Ente Puglia* in 1940 was 25 million lire of which 20 million was spent in Ethiopia.

The last of the active colonizing agencies, the *Ente De Rege*, was financed by the Agricultural Office of Oromo-Sidamo (450,000 lire) and the General Governorship of AOI (6 million lire).

The *Ente Veneto* never went beyond the paper stage. However, the plan was for the agency to receive a 50 million loan from the *Instituto Nazionale Fascista per l'Assicurazione contro gli Infortuni sul Lavoro* at 5% yearly interest. Also, a 3 million lire contribution was given by the province of Veneto. Although the *Ente Veneto* never cultivated one hectare of land, the paperwork alone cost the Italian tax payer one million lire.[34]

Similarly, the *Ente di Colonizzazione Italiani all'Estero* never defined its aims and was unable to find financial backing. A first draft proposed raising 25 million lire in capital with the aid of several financial concerns; capital repayment was to be assured by the Ministry of Foreign Affairs and the Ministry of Africa. Although the colonizing agency never implemented its plans in Oromo-Sidamo, the expenses involved were of a bureaucratic nature and reached approximately half a million lire.

In conclusion of 578 million lire of investment capital earmarked for the demographic colonization of Ethiopia, only 121 million lire were actually invested in Ethiopia. Most of the expenditures for the colonization were absorbed by the transport of farmers from Italy to Ethiopia, by housing and by putting the land under cultivation.

To support an Italian family, a farm in Ethiopia had to be 50 to 60 hectares. The *ONC* and *Ente Romagna* farmers had 50 to 60 hectares. Each farm of the *Ente Puglia* had 25 hectares because a moderate climate and abundant rainful warranted the possibility of two crops per year. Its farmers could also cultivate a variety of rich cash crops such as cotton and coffee.

Of capital importance to demographic colonization was the cost of bringing one hectare of land into production. The figures vary from the extreme of 3,250 lire to a propaganda cost of 625 lire. Thus an average farm of 60 hectares for cultivation would cost a farmer between 98,220 lire and 109,560 lire, but low crop production did not provide enough income to support a farming family and repay the capital invested.

Further, to these costs the price of the farm house must be added. During the five-year period, Italy built between 279 and 373 farm houses. Farm units were to become Italian districts, assuming the names of the towns from which the farmers came. To create these Italian centres, the Ministry of Africa had set aside in its budget six million lire for each colonizing agency, or a total of 24 million lire, at least half of which was put to use in the building of *Bari d'Etiopia*, – one of the centres of colonization at *Ente di Puglia* – and the centres of Holetta and Bishoftu. The cost of these farming centres and their facilities was so high that the success of colonization would be compromised unless the government took charge of them. But the farmer who received land and a house was responsible for the repayment of the total cost of his holding. The house price was the heaviest financial burden for the farmer. Costs varied from district to district. At first, the price of a farm house was optimistically estimated at 6,000 to 15,000 lire but experience proved that, in some instances, it reached as high as 75,000 lire.

The cost of housing had a great bearing on the colonization of Ethiopia. Farming expenditure could be reduced, but the expenses of the house were fixed and affected the total indebtedness of the farmer. In addition, the cost of relocation and settling a farming family from Italy in Ethiopia was prohibitive. In 1937 it was calculated at 50,000 lire, but in 1939, that estimate doubled, slowing down Italian emigration to Ethiopia.

Table 12.3
Cost for the Settlement of a Farming Family

Colonizing Agency	*Estimated Cost in Lire*
Ente De Rege	90,000 – 140,000
Ente Veneto	120,000 – 200,000
Ente Puglia	80,000 – 110,000
ONC	80,000 – 85,000
Average Cost	*92,500 – 133,750*

Although the land was given to the farmer free, the cost of improvement and housing and interest on capital borrowed by the colonizing agencies made their financial burdens too heavy; it would take from five to 30 years before a family could own its farm. Realistically however, more than one generation would be needed to pay for it. Farmers paid off their indebtedness by selling all crops to the *ente* at a fixed price for a number of years. The *Ente Romagna*, financed by the Ministry of Africa, paid no interest; therefore, it was estimated that in about ten years the settler could become owner of his farm. The farmers of the *ONC* from the very beginning were given their farms on credit. The farmer would be able to pay his debts in about five to seven years.

The *Ente Veneto* and the *Ente Puglia* were financed by state-controlled financial institutions charging 5% interest on the capital, which increased the cost of a farm from an estimated 110,000 lire to about 200,000 lire.[35] The farm could be paid for in 30 years. Thus, the immediate aim of demographic colonization to make the Italian settlers landowners, was not achieved.

By 1940, 40% of the farmers of the *ONC* had established credit toward the payment of their estates. They were exceptional because of the high price they received for their crops and the easy access they had to the Addis Ababa market. Before the start of the Second World War there were plans at the *ONC* to give farm deeds to ten families; at least one farmer, Giovanni Beruzzi, had

Administration and Colonization

discharged his debt to the *ONC*. Although the *Ente Puglia's* financial burden was greater, 14 farmers had also established modest credits with the organization, varying from 315 lire to about 9,000 lire.

Thus Italian colonization was hampered from expanding as rapidly as expected, for psychological reasons, local problems, and financial restrictions. It cannot be said that it failed in its objectives because resolution of its problems required a greater number of years than Italy had in Ethiopia. Yet, on account of unwarranted optimism, the problems of colonization were misrepresented to the Italian people, who grew suspicious and unwilling to take part in the greatest colonial enterprise that, according to Mussolini, the world had ever seen.

Notes

1. Pankhurst, ". . . Italian Settlement Plans", pp. 145–56; MAI/GAB 119/XII-I Lessona to GGAOI, 29 May 1937; *Autarchia Alimentare* (June 1938), p. 14; IAA 1990 Tassinari: Report to the Duce, February 1937; Ibid., Maugini: Memorandum for Lessona, April 1936; Colucci, "La Distribuzione delle Terre", in Reale Accademia D'Italia, *Convegno di Scienze Morali e Storiche*; MAI/GAB 157 Programme of the Ente Veneto d'Etiopia, 1938; MAI/GAB 160 Lessona to Graziani, 5 August 1936; *Espansione Coloniale*, July 1938; Caroselli, *Scritti Politici*, p. 245; Giglio, *La Colonizzazione Demografica*, p. 12; IAA 2056 Maugini: Notes for Lessona, 20 May 1937.

2. *Rassegna Economica* (March 1939), p. 379; IAA 1936 MAI to GGAOI, 4 June 1937.

3. MAI/GAB 160/IX Lessona to Graziani, 13 June 1936; ACS/RG 13 Lessona to Graziani, 2 July 1937; ONCA/1GGAOI Di Crollalanza to Petretti, 15 March 1937.

4. MAI/GAB 183/8 Maugini: Report on the Agriculture of AOI, April 1936; MAI/GAB 256/52 Teruzzi: Notes on the Voyage in AOI, 1940; IAA 1936 De Benedictis to Viceroy, 21 May 1938.

5. MAI/GAB 157 Sebastiani to Teruzzi, 19 May 1940; Ibid., Resident of Dabat: Ente Romagna, 24 January 1939; IAA 1808 Agricultural Office of Amhara: Report on Colonization, 1940; MAI/GAB 31/XI-C Paviriani: The Achefer, 1937; IAA 1921 Fuzzi: Programme of Ente Romagna, 1939; MAI/GAB 272/322 Duke of Aosta to MAI, 21 October 1938; MAI/GAB 157 Ente Romagna, 1938; Ibid., Savini to Molla 9 June 1939.

6. ACS/INT-P 9/B–97/14 Confidential information, 19 September 1936; IAA 1936 Pini: Land Concessions along the Akaki and Jimma Roads, 2 June 1938; MAI/GAB 46/XI-II-F Duke Aosta to MAI, 8 April 1938; MAI/AS 181/47-221 Geloso to MAI 22 March 1937; ONCA/1Capo del Governo, Petretti to Di Crollalanza, 2 December 1932; Bartalozzi *Case Rurali nell'AOI*, p. 7.

7. ONCA 3A/1 ONC Ethiopian Office to ONC Head Office, 27 June 1937; MAI/GAB 157 Graziani to MAI, 9 December 1937; IAA 1922 Fuzzi: Ente Romagna programme for 1939; IAA 2919 Agricultural Office of Oromo-Sidamo, Ente De Rege, 1940; *Italia Oltremare* 20 January 1940;

Italian Colonization

ONCA 1/Teruzzi Lessona to Di Crollalanza, 15 June 1937; MAI/GAB 156/XI Valli to Starace, 1 March 1939; MAI/GAB 13 MAI: Military Personnel Desiring to Remain in AOI, October 1937; ACS/RG 13 Graziani to Mussolini, 26 October 1936.

8. MAI/GAB 157 Maugini to MAI, 22 January 1937; ONCA 1/Teruzzi ONC Ethiopian Office: Conditions of Holetta and Bishoftu, 1936; ONCA 1/Capo del Governo, Di Crollalanza to Duce, 15 March 1940; *Corriere dell'Impero*, 18 June 1939; MAI/GAB 157 Pirzio Biroli to MAI, 22 November 1937; IAA 1933 Maugini, Mission in AOI 1936; MAI/AS 181/68–348 Geloso to MAI, 2 May 1937; IAA 1818 Agricultural Office of Oromo-Sidamo: Activities of the Office ... January 1940; ACS/RG 36 Cortese to Graziani, 8 May 1937.

9. MAI/GAB 7/XI-V Mussolini to Duke Aosta, 4 October 1938; Ibid., Duke Aosta to MAI, 7 October 1938; MAI/GAB 282/XI-2 Nasi: Report of the Governorship of Shoa, 1939; IAA 1097 Agricultural Inspectorate of AOI: Activities ... for 1939; *Corriere dell'Impero*, 10 October 1939; *Gazzetta del Popolo*, 19 June 1939.

10. *Notiziario Coloniale*, 9 March 1938; MAI/GAB 157 Ente Veneto: Programme for 1938; MAI/EF N/18 Mussolini to Graziani, 11 September 1937; IAA Vicinelli: Study for an Agrarian Regulated Economy in AOI, 1940; *Azione Coloniale*, 20 June 1940; MAI/GAB 152/IX MAI:EF Notes on the Question of Foreign Currency, 1939; *Impero Italiano*, 31 October 1939; *Il Popolo d'Italia*, 2 September 1939; ACS/RG 36 Gariboldi to MAI, 13 April 1937; Ibid., Gariboldi to all Governors, 11 August 1937; Ibid., Mussolini to Graziani, 30 July 1937; ACS/MAI 9 Commission for the Supreme Defence, February 1940.

11. MAI/GAB 159/XI Duke Aosta to MAI, 20 January 1938; IAA 1774 Pini: Economic Activities, 15 December 1940; MAI/GAB Teruzzi to Duce, 8 May 1940; Ibid., Duke Aosta to MAI, 7 May 1940; MAI/GAB 276 MAI: Commission for the Supreme Defence, Overseas Territories, February 1941: MAI/GAB 278/483 Teruzzi: Report to the Duce on the Voyage in AOI, 1939; MAI/GAB 292 Gazzera: Minutes of the Meeting of the Commissioners of Oromo-Sidamo 28 December 1939; MAI/AS 181/53–248 P. Biroli: Political Report of the Governorship of Amhara, May 1937; *Corriere Mercantile*, 29 September 1939; IAA 4579 Italconsult: Melka Amibara Proposed Irrigation Project, December 1968; IAA 4299 Rocchetti: Notes on Ethiopian Agriculture, 1966; Ethiopia: Food and Agricultural Council, *Report to FAO, 1947* p. 20.

12. Hoben, *Land Tenure Among the Amhara of Ethiopia*; Mahteme Selassie Wolde Maskal, "The Land System of Ethiopia", pp. 283-301; Markakis, *Ethiopia: Anatomy of a Traditional Polity*, Chs. 4-5; Pankhurst, *Economic History of Ethiopia*, Ch. 4; Gilkes, *The Dying Lion*, pp. 101–36; IAA 794 Ciocca: Elements of Land Holding in Shoa, n.d.; Rossini, "Il Regime Fondiario Indigeno in Etiopia", pp. 46–55; Pollera, *Il Regime della Proprietà Terriera in Etiopia*, pp. 7–43; Ambrosi, *Aspetti del Diritto Agrario nelle Terre dell'AOI*, p. 30; Bologna, "L'Agricoltura degli Indigeni e i Mezzi per Farla Progredire", pp. 63 ff.; MAI/MC 15 Colucci: Memorandum for the Governor of Amhara, 27 September 1939; Ibid., Sarubbi: Land Holding in Wollo, November 1938.

13. M. Moreno, "Il Regime Terriero Abissino nel Galla Sidama", pp. 1496–1508; D. Prinzi, "Il Regime Fondiario e Colonizzazione in AOI",

pp. 1424–1521; IAA 591 Sozio: Agricultural Survey of Sciaradda, Kaffa, 7 February 1939; Brotto, *Il Regime delle Terre nel Governo dell'Harar*; IAA 2813 Prinzi: Aspects of Land Holding in Ogaden, n.d.

14. Colucci, "La Distribuzione delle Terre"; Rivera, *Prospettive di Colonizzazione nell'AOI*, p. 123; MAI/GAB 158/XI Moreno to MAI, 20 September 1938 and 20 August 1938.

15. MAI/GAB 119/XII-1 Teruzzi to GGAOI, 30 March 1939 and 19 May 1939; MAI/GAB 119/XI-1 Teruzzi to GGAOI, 7 January 1939; ACS/RG 30/5 Forese to Duce, December 1937; MAI/EF A/3–6 Graziani to MAI, 26 December 1936; MAI/AS 181/37–176 Maravigna: Proclamation No. 9 to the People of Tigre, Adowa, 29 November 1935; MAI/POL 70/155 Lessona to GGAOI, 20 June 1936.

16. MAI/GAB 31/XI-C Paviriani, Woggerat, April 1937; G. Nasi, "Governo Dell'Harar: Tre anni d'Occupazione" (Harar, 1939) pp. 169–70 (unpublished report); MAI/POL 69/147 Lessona to GGAOI, 1 May 1937; MAI/AS 181/56–272 Nasi: Political Report, 1937; MAI/AS 181/52–244 Geloso to MAI, 18 May 1937; MAI/AS 181/52–245 Gazzera: Political Report of Oromo-Sidamo, February and March 1939; IAA 920 Sozio: Agricultural Observations in the Neghelli Zone, 1936; MAI/GAB 157 Resident of Dabat: Ente Romagna, January 1939; IAA 1921 Fuzzi: Ente Romagna, 1940.

17. MAI/GAB 74/XI-V Mezzetti to Teruzzi, 19 July 1939; MAI/AS 181/67–341 Cerulli to MAI, 25 July 1938; MAI/GAB 309/17 Duke Aosta to MAI, 15 January 1938; IAA 2214 Vicinelli: Italian Colonization, April 1942; ONCA 3/A-1 Di Crollalanza: Meeting with ONC in Addis Ababa, 11 February 1937; MAI/GAB 45 Mezzetti: Political Report of the Governorship of Amhara, 1938; MAI/AS 181/53–247 Gorini: Political Report of Harar, August–September 1939.

18. IAA 1896 Governorship of Harar: Minutes of the III Meeting of the Committee on Colonization, 15 January 1937; IAA 1896 De Rubeis: Memorandum for Teruzzi, 12 May 1938; MAI/GAB 32/XI-II-D Lessona: Notes for the Duce, 19 September 1937; MAI/GAB 322 Di Revel: Diary 1938; IAA 1965 Agricultural Activities in Oromo-Sidamo, 1939; IAA 2919 Agricultural Office of Oromo-Sidamo: Ente De Rege, 1940; ONCA 3/3 Graziani to the Resident of Holetta, 16 April 1937; MAI/EF Misc. 1/100 Frusci: Administrative Report of the Governorship of Amhara, January–March 1940; MAI/GAB 157 Teruzzi to Duke Aosta, 17 August 1938; IAA 1934 Gazzera to MAI, 13 December 1939.

19. MAI/GAB 158/XI Notes for Teruzzi, 19 November 1939; MAI/EF 0/194 De Rubeis to MAI, 10 December 1938; MAI/GAB 73/XI-II Canero Medici: Political Report of the Governorship of Addis Ababa, 1938; ACS/RG 47 Boidi: Activity of the Municipality of Addis Ababa 1939–1940; Nasi, *Noi Italiani in Etiopia*, p. 12.

20. Italy: Ministero degli Affari Esteri, *L'Avvaloramento e la Colonizzazione*, pp. 405–7; IAA 845 Colonizing District Ente De Rege (1939); *Gazetta Del Popolo*, 9 May 1940; IAA 1923 Lessona to MAE (1936); ACS/RG 40-B/100-14 Appelius report to the Duce, 1938; IAA 1768 Laurenti: Colonization plan with the Italian residing abroad, 3 December 1937.

21. *Corriere Dell'Impero*, 3 March 1940; *Azione Coloniale*, 28 March 1940; *Corriere dell'Impero*, 29 February 1940; IAA 1936 Teruzzi to GGAOI,

13 February 1938; MAI/GAB 253/55 Cafiero to Montenapoleone, 3 March 1940; Caroselli, *Scritti Politici*, p. 25; IAA 2056 Maugini: Primi orizzonti sulla valorizzazione dell Impero, April 1937; Duke of Aosta, Diary, in *Gente*, 22 March 1969; MAI/GAB 256/52 Teruzzi: Notes on the voyage in AOI, 1940.

22. R. Trevisani, Report on the Mission in AOI, April-May 1938 (unpublished report); MAI/GAB 152/IX Caroselli to Guarnieri, 1 December 1938; Gennari, *Agricoltura nell'AOI*, p. 43; IAA 1775 Meeting of the Agricultural Council, 16 April 1937; *Autarchia Alimentare*, June 1938, p. 19; MAI/GAB 32/XI-II-D Lessona to Duce, 19 September 1937; ACS/INT-P 9-B/97-12 Confidential information 22 May 1937; Ibid., 4 August 1938; Ibid., 3 December 1938; MAI/GAB 157 Lessona to GGAOI, 10 August 1937; Ibid., Meregazzi to MAI, 15 June 1940 and 31 May 1940; MAI/GAB 256/53 Riccardo to Duce, 15 March 1940; IAA 1922 Fumelli: Situation at Ente Puglia, 31 December 1939; Ibid., Pegutti: Memorandum for Maugini on Bari di Puglia, 1940; Ibid., Maugini to Giannoccaro 27 May 1940; ONCA 3/B-1 Taticchi to ONC, 11 March 1939; Ibid., Fornari to ONC, 18 October 1939; IAA 1992 Parigi to Maugini, 7 October 1940.

23. ONCA 3/B-1 Taticchi to ONC, August 1940; Ibid., 24 July 1938; ONCA 3/B-4 Curti to Marzocchi Alemanni, 19 March 1939; Ibid., Pistone to President ONC, 18 March 1939; *Notiziario Coloniale*, 20 January 1939; Italy: Ministero degli Affari Esteri, *Avvaloramento e Colonizzazione*, p. 264.

24. IAA 1992 Parigi to Maugini, 1 August 1940; MAI/GAB 157 Giannoccaro to Teruzzi, 1939; Bartolozzi, *Case Rurali*, p. 6; MAI/GAB 167 Di Crollalanza: Memorandum for Mussolini, March 1940; ONCA 3/B-1 Fornari to ONC, 25 September 1939; ONCA 1/Teruzzi Duke of. Aosta to MAI, 4 September 1939; Ibid., Di Crollalanza MAI 27 October 1939.

25. ONCA 3/B-1 Di Crollalanza to Taticchi, 19 February 1941; ONCA 3/B-2 Mazzuccato: Report, 31 July 1938; Ibid., Mazzuccato: Building Report, 2 October 1938; Ibid., Todaro: Memorandum, 7 September 1938; ONCA 1/Capo del Governo, Di Crollalanza to Duce, 4 March 1937.

26. Lessona, *L'Africa Italiana nel Primo Anno dell'Impero*, p. 11; Scarin, *Hararino*, p. 175; MAI/POL 72/174 Pignatelli to MAE, 3 July 1936; Badoglio, *L'Italia nella Seconda Guerra Mondiale*, p. 19; IAA 2646 Maugini: General Information on Agricultural Colonization, 23 September 1953; Caroselli, *Scritti Politici*, p. 232; IAA 1793 Tommasini to Instituto Agronomo, 19 May 1944.

27. ONCA 3/B-1 Taticchi to Vice-Governor General, 14 October 1938; MAI/GAB 309/17 Duke Aosta to MAI, 15 January 1938; MAI/AV 110 Gazzera: Political Report of Oromo-Sidamo, December 1939.

28. *Italia Coloniale*, 15 May 1940; *Impero e Autarchia*, 9 May 1940; Istituto Agronomo per l'Africa Italiana, *Main Features of Italy's Action in Ethiopia 1936-1941*, pp. LXXII-LXXVIII; MAI/GAB 322 Di Revel Diary, 1938; IAA 1792 Tommasini to Istituto Agronomo, 19 May 1944; ONCA 3/18 Danni di Guerra, Notes on the Activity of ONC in Ethiopia, 1944; G. Tallarico, "Possibilità Agricole," *Corriere Mercantile*, 22 July 1937; MAI/GAB 157 Giannoccaro to Teruzzi, 1939; Santarelli, *Storia del Regime Fascista*, p. 213; ACS/PCM 1937-1939 14/3/3922/2 MAE to PCM, 12 August 1938.

29. ACS/RG 36 Santini to Petretti, 24 September 1937; MAI/GAB 102/XI-2 MAI-Colonization Office to MAI-EF, 13 April 1943; IAA 1802

Governorship of Harar, Agricultural Office, Agricultural Concessions, 1 August 1939; MAI/GAB 367/X-Trier Corporative Organization in AOI 1943; *Italia Oltremare*, 5 May 1940.

30. ONCA 1/Teruzzi, Di Crollalanza to MAI, 13 May 1938; IAA 1792 Garanelli: Ente Romagna, 10 October 1946; MAI/GAB 52 MAI: Data for Parliamentary Discussions, 1939/1940; ONCA 1/Relazioni Fagotti, Report Activity at Bishoftu, 1937; IAA 1799 Duke of Aosta to MAI 21 October 1938; IAA 1992 Volpi: Report Ente Puglia, 1940; IAA 845 News on Ente De Rege, 1948.

31. MAI/GAB 102/XI-2 MAI-Colonization and Labour Office: Notes for MAI-EF, 13 April 1943.

32. MAI/GAB 265/170 Farinacci to Duce, 25 December 1938; Guarnieri, *Battaglie Economiche*, II, p. 197; MAI/AS 181/63-321 Colombi to MAE, 23 March 1939; MAI/GAB 157 Teruzzi to Starace, 31 March 1938; Ibid., Lessona to Starace, 10 August 1937.

33. MAI/GAB 157 Teruzzi to GGAOI, 18 January 1938; MAI/GAB 101/XI-2 MAI-Colonization and Labour Office to Piccioli, 13 April 1943; Ministry of Italian Africa; *Memorandum on the Economic and Financial Situation of the Italian Territories in Africa*, p. 37; ONCA 2/2 Taticchi: Report on the Activity of Taticchi in AOI, 1939-1946; ONCA 3/18 Danni di Guerra, War Damages Suffered by ONC in Ethiopia, 28 October 1955; Ibid., ONC Investments in Ethiopia to 30 June 1941; Ibid., Di Crollalanza to Duce, 1 August 1941.

34. IAA 1992 Ente Puglia Budgets 1938, 1939 and 1940; IAA 1821 Mariottini: Expenses of the Ente De Rege, 1940; MAI/GAB 157 Cantalupo to Ciano, 26 March 1940; Ibid., Cantalupo to Ciano 13 February 1940; Ibid., Cantalupo to Maugini, 19 February 1940; Ibid., Cantalupo to Teruzzi 26 March 1940.

35. Caroselli, *Scritti Politici*, p. 263; IAA 1990 Tassinari: Report to Mussolini on the Voyage to AOI, 1937; *Corriere Eritreo*, 28 November 1939; *Il Popolo D'Italia*, 31 January 1940; Santagata, *L'Harar*, p. 207; MAI/CSC 27/55 Teruzzi to CSC, 21 April 1938; ONCA 1/Capo del Governo, Marzocchi Alemanni to MAI 22 April 1938; Giglio, *Colonizzazione*, p. 48; IAA 1934 Gazzera to MAI, 13 December 1939.

Part III: Victor and Vanquished

13. Italy and Haile Selassie

The majority of the Ethiopian people opposed Italian rule and prepared themselves for a general uprising to coincide with Haile Selassie's return from exile. It was in Italy's interest therefore to convince the Ethiopians of the impossibility of their Emperor's coming back. In an attempt to discourage and disperse the resisters and make them more willing to accept Italian rule, Italy entered into indirect negotiations with the Ethiopian royal family in England, seeking the formal submission of Haile Selassie or his son, Asfaw Wassen, and the recognition by either of the Italian Empire. In addition to the political advantages, a successful agreement would have had a great psychological bearing on Ethiopia's attitude toward its conquerors. With Haile Selassie on their side, the Italians would have been able to exploit the colonial situation easily, and co-exist with the Ethiopians in peace. Quite possibly, however, the Patriots would have opposed any agreement of this kind.

The events leading to secret talks between emissaries of Haile Selassie and the Italian government are of great importance for the study of Italo-Ethiopian relations. They reveal the uncertainty of the Italian authorities in colonial matters, and the wavering attitude of the Ethiopian royal house toward reaching a compromise with Mussolini.

Secret Negotiations Between Haile Selassie and Italy

In 1937, after a year of occupation, the rebellion had spread to areas of central Ethiopia. Under those uncertain conditions Italy decided to approach Haile Selassie, although opinion differed on whether it was the Italian government through the Vatican or Haile Selassie who actually made the first move.

In London, Haile Selassie was under pressure to abdicate with financial compensation, from a group of financiers and businessmen of the *Société des Salines de Djibouti*, the Bank of Indochina, and his legal adviser Gaston Jeze. These were preoccupied with safeguarding their financial interest in Ethiopia from Italian confiscation. However, although at times Haile Selassie considered renouncing the throne of Ethiopia, he managed to keep his crown. According to Lessona, Haile Selassie's abdication had no judical or political value after 9 May 1936, when the Italian government proclaimed Ethiopia to be part of the Italian Empire with the king of Italy as Emperor; therefore, the only act Italy could recognize was his complete and formal submission.[1]

Publicly, Haile Selassie declared that he would not remain in England forever. He claimed that he wanted to return to Ethiopia as soon as conditions permitted.[2] He was disappointed at the League of Nations' lack of support, even after his personal appearance before the assembly at Geneva, and he was equally disillusioned when the British and French governments ignored his requests for aid. It was reported that he admitted that, if he had known earlier that his allies would desert him, he would have accepted Mussolini's offer of a protectorate.[3] On 23 July 1936 it was revealed that he went so far as to draft a letter promising that he would give up his plans to reconquer Ethiopia. On 5 August Vittorio Cerruti, the Italian Ambassador in Paris, alleged that the letter of abdication had been signed.[4] Jeze also reported the news on 1 August 1936. But when the letter reached the Secretary-General of the League, Sir Joseph Avenol, he refused to accept it because it had been signed not by Haile Selassie but by the Ethiopian representative at the League of Nations. Why Haile Selassie did not sign the letter is not clear. Perhaps he resented the fact that it had been forced on him by his advisers. Possibly he hoped that if the international situation changed in his favour, his abdication could not be upheld without his signature. If Great Britain went to war against Italy, he would claim that he was still the legal Emperor of his country.

The Italians promised that if Haile Selassie signed a declaration he could rely upon Italian generosity to alleviate the rigours of exile. Italy insisted that its role in the negotiations remain secret, and that Haile Selassie surrender all claim to his throne in exchange for monetary compensation rather than have Haile Selassie sign an act of submission which might leave the door open to possible future claims. The British Foreign Office asked Dino Grandi, the Italian Ambassador in London, about the secret negotiations, but Grandi denied the possibility of any compromise. Grandi believed that Dr. Martin, the Ethiopian Minister in London, deliberately wanted to give the Foreign Office the impression that Italy was seeking a settlement with Haile Selassie.[5] At the same time the British Ambassador to Italy, Eric Drummond, reported that in a conversation with the Duce, Mussolini promised Haile Selassie a generous reward in return for his abdication.

Officially, then, Italy denied any compromise, while indirect negotiations continued. During the month of December 1936, an Egyptian prince named Mohammed Ekrem Riza approached the Italian Ministry of Foreign Affairs on behalf of Haile Selassie. He proposed the abdication of Haile Selassie in favour of his eldest son, Asfaw Wassen, to whom Italy would give a small territory in Ethiopia to govern. Haile Selassie would be offered a large sum of money as compensation. Despite Italy's rejection of the proposal, the Italian government apparently was willing to discuss the suggested terms contingent upon Haile Selassie's outright surrender.[6] The Vatican also took part in the negotiations, although on which side is not clear. Ciano denied its participation, but Father Cyril C. Martindale, the Jesuit scholar representing the Pope, confirmed that the secretary of state at the Vatican, Eugenio Cardinal Pacelli (later Pope Pius XII), offered Haile Selassie £1 million on behalf of Italy in return for his abdication.[7] In late 1936, the negotiations failed when the *negus* refused to accept the Italian terms. Six months later, in June 1937, Count L. Sibour told Cardinal Pacelli that Haile Selassie was willing to reopen negotiations. Ciano answered that Italy was not interested but the *negus* should make his proposals clear and precise.[8]

Perhaps the Italians, confident of the sympathy from other nations and in view of the forthcoming recognition of the Italian Empire by Great Britain and France, felt that Haile Selassie was of secondary concern. News of the secret negotiations leaked out, and British newspapers even reported that Mussolini had promised to send Haile Selassie back to Ethiopia to quell the rebellion, once he had abdicated.[9] The Arab press advocated the restoration of Haile Selassie to the throne in Addis Ababa as king under the protection of the House of Savoy. It suggested that he be given a status like that of the Indian princes, but with no rights of future succession for him or his heirs. Members of the League of Nations viewed such a compromise as facilitating *de jure* recognition of the Italian conquest.[10]

Later in December 1937, as his financial situation became precarious, Haile Selassie again opened talks with the Italian government. This time he did not use the Vatican, but proposed the mediatory services of Count Sibour and the Italian Embassy in London. His probings failed however, the Italian government took no immediate action and 1937 ended without any practical conclusion.[11] Both sides were interested in continuing contact, but neither was willing to yield enough to reach an agreement.

As long as Great Britain did not recognize the Italian conquest of Ethiopia, (it did in 1938) Haile Selassie had hopes of regaining his throne. He felt that after the Italian war crimes were made public — he had in mind the use of gas and the massacres that followed the attempted assassination of Rudolfo Graziani — the League of Nations would take a strong stand against Italy. But by the end of 1937 he realized that Great Britain might very well reach a diplomatic accommodation with the Italians, and he prepared contingency plans to retire to Jerusalem, where he had acquired a house. Others reported that Haile Selassie was so discouraged that he planned to retire for life to a Coptic monastery in Palestine.

On the eve of the British-Italian Colonial Pact of Easter 1938, Lord Perth, the British Ambassador in Rome, approached Count Ciano, asking whether Italy would be willing to make political or financial concessions toward Haile Selassie and allow him and his family to return to Ethiopia. The Italians responded that the matter would be taken under consideration only if Haile Selassie assumed the right attitude toward Italy.[12] This could only mean his abdication and recognition of the Italian conquest. Demoralized and on the verge of bankruptcy, Haile Selassie was willing to accept the Italian terms in 1938. To Lord Halifax he expressed his great desire to return to his country and his apparent willingness to submit to Italian demands in exchange for jurisdiction over a small part of Ethiopia. He requested that Lord Halifax inform Italy of his desires, but Halifax refused to interfere in Italo-Ethiopian affairs.[13]

Once Great Britain recognized the Italian Empire, in 1938, personalities such as Lord Lugard advised Italy to make some concessions to Haile Selassie, and allow him to rule over Gojam province in order to suppress Ethiopians opposing Italian rule there. At the same time Italy could rest its weary soldiers and make much-needed economies. Bishop André Marie Elie Jarosseau, Haile Selassie's former tutor and a man who had influence over him, also invited the exiled ruler to recognize Italian sovereignty over Ethiopia. By submitting to Italy he could rule with Italian consent.[14] Yet Haile Selassie still sought an influential intermediary to work out an agreement suitable to both sides.

Mediation on the part of French personalities had failed, and the Vatican had withdrawn its sponsorship. Only the English remained, but for political reasons they would not consent to Haile Selassie's negotiating with the Italians. Haile Selassie therefore contacted a German authority, since at this time Italy enjoyed close relations with Germany.

Ato Wolde-Giorgis, personal secretary to Haile Selassie, made one last effort to mediate. He sent a letter to Major Hans Steffen, former honorary German Consul in Addis Ababa. This letter requested that Steffen try to bring about an agreement between the two parties. The Major may not have been very influential in the Nazi government, but he maintained contacts with highly-placed officials. Was Haile Selassie attempting to enlist the help of Hitler? In 1936 Hitler had supported Haile Selassie's war against Italy for his own political purposes,[15] but by 1938-9 he was clearly interested in Italy's lessening its involvement in Ethiopia. Moreover, the threat of war in Europe relegated Haile Selassie and his problems to a place of secondary importance. He would become valuable to the British again only after Italy had entered the war on the German side.

Negotiations for the Submission of Asfaw Wassen

Although negotiations for the abdication of Haile Selassie never reached a positive conclusion, Italian authorities were hopeful that Asfaw Wassen could be persuaded to subscribe to their cause. Perhaps they wanted to capitalize on the reported disharmony between Haile Selassie and his eldest son. It seemed to intermediaries that the Prince's youth and inexperience, his desire to free himself from his father's authority, and his aversion to the rigid English surroundings of his life in exile made his submission a prospect. Yet Italy failed to offer even this more favourable subject inspiring terms. Government officials treated Asfaw Wassen arrogantly, and their dealings with him lacked common sense. *Ras* Getachew was in contact with Asfaw, reporting to the Italian authorities a number of questions that would determine the submission of Asfaw. Asfaw wanted to know if he could retain his property and that of his father, if he were made Governor of an Ethiopian region. If he should refuse to return to Ethiopia, what kind of financial reward would he be offered. The gist of the negotiations leaked to the British press was that the Italians had suggested that Haile Selassie cease all opposition to Italy, and in return his son could reign under the Italian government in Ethiopia. Although Getachew's contacts were not pursued the negotiations with Asfaw Wassen seemed to reach a conclusion in favour of Italy. Wolde-Giorgis, passing through Bouveret, Switzerland, visted Ferdinand Bientry, an engineer who worked in road planning in Ethiopia before the war. Bientry had rendered important services to Italian intelligence in the country, especially in the logistic information he provided the invading army in the north. Wolde-Giorgis also visted Bientry's wife, Daragonie Beressie, an Ethiopian woman of a noble family who had lived at the imperial court in Addis Ababa and had been a friend of Asfaw Wassen since childhood. Asfaw Wassen wrote to Daragonie saying he hoped to apply for special consideration from the Italian government and wanted to know its terms.[16]

Negotiations were slow; the two ministries involved, the Ministry of Italian Africa and the Ministry of Foreign Affairs, and the Italian consulate in Sion, Switzerland, could reach no clear agreement on how to handle the situation. The exact concessions had not yet been settled. For the agreement to have positive repercussions in Ethiopia Asfaw would have to receive generous treatment. However, the most Italy was willing to concede was a mere stipend of 15,000 lire and a residence in Turin. On 19 June, Ciano ordered the Italian consul at Sion to authorize Daragonie's trip to London, to convince Asfaw Wassen to accept Italian terms.[17] Asfaw counterproposed to sign a letter of submission in exchange for the Italian government document, guaranteeing his rank and prerogatives as a prince in his country. He also asked for £50,000 for his personal use, of which £10,000 to be paid in advance. Asfaw Wassen was concerned that once he had signed his submission he would be discarded.[18] The reaction of the Italian Ministry of Africa to his demands was positive under the circumstances. It found the request for £50,000 exorbitant, but was willing to fix a sum as personal compensation. The Italians categorically refused his demand to title, rank, and rights as a prince of Ethiopia, since all imperial rights had been transferred to the King of Italy on 9 May 1936. Italy might have considered giving Asfaw Wassen a title, as it had done in Libya with Hassun Pasha Caramanli, but such a title would be only honorary. Asfaw Wassen would under no circumstances be allowed to return to Ethiopia.

The unwillingness of the Ministry of Africa to accept Asfaw Wassen's terms produced a snag in the negotiations. One tricky point was the question of a title. Other Ethiopian noble families in exile had been able to retain their titles; some served in Addis Ababa as advisers to the government in matters concerning the Ethiopian people. His residence in Turin might give Asfaw Wassen's followers the idea that he was being kept in splendid exile.

The Italian government thought £10,000 too high a sum and suspected that the Bientrys had padded the request to include a percentage for themselves. The Ministry of Italian Africa then proposed that enough money be forwarded to facilitate Asfaw's leaving England, with a substantial amount as personal compensation to be put at his disposal once he arrived in Italy. The new offer meant that Bientry would have to make another trip to England to deliver the last of the Italian proposals. But for unknown reasons Bientry was denied an entry visa by the British authorities, perhaps because British intelligence had discovered his activities.

With the Italian entry into the war, the Ministry of Italian Africa broke off negotiations with Asfaw Wassen.[19] The talks had cost Italy only 6,377 lire.[20]

An examination of the secret relations between Italy and Haile Selassie and his family raises the difficult problem of ascertaining the intentions of the Ethiopians. On the Italian side, a certain political and military advantage lay in demonstrating to the world that Haile Selassie or Asfaw Wassen could be bought over to the Italian cause. Their submission would have been an important step toward the complete occupation of the country. An agreement would have denied the Patriots their focus, since they saw their role as preparing the way for Haile Selassie's return. Haile Selassie's abdication would have put an end to resistance and guaranteed the support of the population. The Ethiopians on the other hand, may have made overtures to discover Italian interests and pinpoint Italian weaknesses. Perhaps they hoped that lengthy negotiations would distract the Italians from their harassment of the Patriots or would reveal to world opinion that Italy needed a member of the Ethiopian imperial family to solve its military, political, and economic problems in East Africa.

At the same time, as early as September 1938 the Italians were informed through the Ethiopian Makkonen Desta in Cairo, that in case of war between Italy and Great Britain, Haile Selassie would be sent to the Sudan to organize the Ethiopian refugees and the Patriots against the Italians.[21] In less than two years Haile Selassie was in the Sudan. Furthermore this plan assumes credibility in light of the statement of the late Swedish pilot, G. Van Rosen, a personal friend of the Emperor. Van Rosen confirmed the Italian offer of one million pounds to Haile Selassie for his submission, but he adds that he refused the money because he wanted to go to Ethiopia to help with guerrilla warfare, which the British authorities were preventing him from doing.[22]

It is possible that Haile Selassie and Asfaw Wassen were toying with the Italians. Their motives remain a matter of speculation, as neither man nor their close friends and associates have approached the subject. Haile Selassie's biographers do not mention the negotiations. Haile Selassie's autobiography does not consider the period from 1937 onward, least of all his negotiations on abdication.[23] Clearly, however, on several occasions during the period between 1935 and 1943 Haile Selassie considered an agreement with the Italians, an agreement which failed because of Haile Selassie's diffidence and Italy's intransigence.

Notes

1. I wish to acknowledge, with many thanks, the permission of the editor of the *International Journal of African Historical Studies* to include in this study part of my article "Secret Talks for the Submission of Haile Selassie . . ."; MAI/POL 70/157 MAE to MAI, 24 July 1936; Ibid., Lessona to MAE, 1 August 1936.
2. *La Gazette de Liège*, 16 August 1936.
3. MAI/POL 70/157 MAE to MAI, July 1936: Interview of Bertrand De Jouvenel of the *Intransigeant* with Haile Selassie; MAE to MAI, 17 April 1937.
4. MAI/POL 70/157 Cerruti to MAE, 5 August 1936; Ibid., MAE to MAI, 8 August 1936.
5. MAI/POL 70/157 MAE to MAI, 31 August 1936; Ibid., MAE to MAI, 11 September 1936; Ciano, *L'Europa verso la Catastrofe*, p. 124; Ibid., MAE to MAI, 19 December 1936.
6. ACS/INT-P 128/K-7-68 Confidential information, 7 March 1937; MAI/POL 70/157 MAE to MAI, 19 December 1936.
7. FO 401/1937/XXIX/ No. 45.
8. MAI/AS 180 48-142 Grandi to MAE, 13 November 1937 and Ciano to Grandi, 17 November 1937; MAI/POL 70/153 Pignatti to MAE, 2 June 1937 and Ciano to Italian Ambassador at the Vatican, 5 June 1937.
9. *News Chronicle*, 18 August 1937.
10. *La Bourse Egyptienne*, 27 November 1937.
11. MAI/AS 180/42-142 Grandi to MAE, 13 November 1937; and Ciano to Grandi, 17 November 1937.
12. Cecchi, *L'Accordo dei due Imperi*, p. 49.
13. Ciano, *L'Europa*, p. 291; MAI/POL 70/157 MAE to MAI, 12 March 1938.
14. *Times* (London), 29 April 1938; *Le Petit Parisien*, 22 August 1939; *La Garonne*, 22 August 1939; Bernoville, *Monseigneur Jarosseau et la Mission des Gallas*, p. 360.
15. MAI/AS 180/42-142 Wolde-Giorgis to Major Steffen, 7 November 1938. It is possible that this letter was passed to the Italian authorities by the German Ministry of Foreign Affairs; Funke, *Sanzioni e Cannoni*, pp. 39-51.
16. MAI/POL 70/157 MAE to MAI, 19 March 1937; ACS/RG 23 Italian Consulate in Cairo to GGAOI, 26 October 1936; *News Chronicle*, 29 April 1938; MAI/AS 180/42-142 MAE to MAI, 17 March 1939.
17. MAI/AS 180/42-142 MAE to MAI, 6 May 1939; Ibid., Moreno: Memorandum for Mussolini, May 1939; Ibid., Ciano to Consulate in Sion, 19 June 1939.
18. MAI/AS 180/42-142 Ciano to MAI, 3 July 1939; Ibid., MAI to MAE, 17 August 1939.
19. MAI/AS 180/42-142 MAE to MAI, 20 December 1939; Ibid., MAE to MAI, 3 May 1940.
20. MAI/AS 180/42-142 Teruzzi to GGAOI, 29 November 1940.

21. Del Boca, *Gli Italiani in Africa Orientale*, pp. 304–6.
22. Interview with Count G. Van Rosen, Stockholm 20 November 1970.
23. Haile Selassie, *My Life and Ethiopia's Progress*. See also the last chapter in this book "The Return of Haile Selassie".

14. Italy and the Ethiopian Nobility

Only a very few great *rases* defected to the Italians during the Italo-Ethiopian War. Many aristocrats had either been killed in the war, or decided to go in exile with Haile Selassie to England. Those who remained were imprisoned, some in Italy; others in Somalia. A few maintained the flame of rebellion, and one by one they were defeated and executed by the Italians. The remainder meekly submitted to the conquerors, receiving a salary from the state. A handful, considered loyal to Italy, were actually employed by the Italians as military allies in the suppression of the rebellion. The aristocracy was not given the opportunity to come to terms with the victors, and had to endure Fascist racial policy. They were treated as conquered subjects and commanded to follow orders under penalty of death. Ironically, in spite of harsh treatment, the Ethiopian nobles did not join the Patriot resistance. Opposition to Italian rule was conducted by parvenus (see Chapter 18). The position of the aristocracy is difficult to understand because, with the Italian occupation, they were deprived of their feudal, political, and economic privileges and made directly dependent on Italy for their livelihood. Italy gave them hand-outs according to their political relevance. They had no lands but occasionally a small retinue.

It is hard to ascertain whether or not the great *rases* in Ethiopia remained loyal to Haile Selassie. The fact that many of them also claimed the throne of Ethiopia makes it unlikely that they would support him perhaps because secretly they hoped the Italians would one day recognize their royal claims. Nevertheless, when Haile Selassie returned from exile in 1941, not one of the great nobles sent him a note of welcome. Only when the British Army defeated the Italians during the Second World War, did the nobles recognize Haile Selassie as Emperor.

Italian Policy Toward the Ethiopian Aristocracy

Before the conquest of Ethiopia, the Italians had courted Ethiopian chiefs and encouraged their independence from the central government. They had also played on the mutual distrust and jealousies of the great chiefs, finding eager listeners in several Ethiopian nobles who had legitimate claims to the throne of Ethiopia. The Italians watched with interest the power struggle between Haile Selassie and *Lij* Yasu, grandson of Menelik II and former Emperor deposed by Haile Selassie, but when the latter was defeated and imprisoned it became obvious that Haile Selassie would continue to limit the hegemony of the *rases* and centralize all power in his hands.

Limiting the power of the great feudal chiefs had started with Theodore II in the 19th Century. Haile Selassie had successfully completed this process by 1932. The *negus* maintained a check on the *rases* to assure the throne for his family, and to make Ethiopia a united modern country. With intelligence, intrigue, and subtlety he prevented his enemies from forming a coalition against him, and destroyed them one by one. The means Haile Selassie used most skillfully to eliminate his opponents was to call them to Addis Ababa to confer with him. Once in the capital, the *ras* became a guest of the Emperor for months – even for years – if he was not subsequently banished to some remote mountainous district.

After the defeat and death in 1930 of *Ras* Gugsa Wolie (husband of Empress Zauditu), the imprisonment of *Lij* Yasu, and the forced exile of *Ras* Hailu of Gojam, Haile Selassie was better able to control the power of the remaining *rases*. Haile Selassie removed the reactionary nobility from their governmental positions and replaced them with the officials favourable to his regime and his modernizing ideals.[1] Thus, Italy had very favourable ground upon which to cultivate sympathies among the discontented Ethiopian aristocracy prior to 1935-6. Before the war of 1935-6 the Ethiopian aristocracy entertained friendly and sympathetic relations with Italy; some even hoped that Italy would become the colonial ruler of Ethiopia because they were given the hope of improving their position. The Italian dream of occupying Ethiopia had long focused on fostering the sympathies of the most prominent leaders. Counting on the greed of the great chiefs, Italian consular and commercial authorities in Ethiopia gave lavish gifts and, in exchange, obtained concessions in the outlying territories of the Ethiopian Empire. On other occasions, Italian schools and medical and veterinary institutions were used as centres of propaganda and political observation, and Ethiopians appeared to be influenced by their contacts with these Italian institutions.

The most influential feudal lords, *Ras* Gugsa, *Ras* Seyum, *Ras* Hailu, *Dejaz* Ayalu Burru, *Abba* Jifar and the Sultan of Aussa, received special attention from the Italians. They all shared the hope of independence from Addis Ababa and some of them had claim to the throne of Ethiopia. *Ras* Gugsa Araya was the son of *Ras* Araya, elder son of Emperor Yohannes IV, and therefore had a direct claim to the imperial title. Instead, he was only in charge of the southern part of Tigre, while the western part was given to *Ras* Seyum. In hopes of securing his position, *Ras* Gugsa Araya arranged for the marriage of his son, *Dejaz* Haile Selassie Gugsa to Haile Selassie's daughter, Princess Zenebework; when she died in 1933 all hopes for an alliance with Haile Selassie ended. *Ras* Gugsa had a long history of relations with the Italians from whom he received medical care, but he too died in 1933. He was favourable to Italian rule of Ethiopia and anticipated regaining his grandfather's throne with Italian support. The *ras* influenced his son, *Dejaz* Haile Selassie Gugsa to maintain friendship with Italy, from whom he thought his house and his people would benefit. In 1934, aware of the Italophilia of *Dejaz* Gugsa, Haile Selassie made *Ras* Seyum paramount commander of all Tigre and added to his western Tigre fiefdom southern territories taken away from *Dejaz* Haile Selassie Gugsa, among which was the important holy city of Axum. In so doing, Haile Selassie attempted to exploit the differences between *Dejaz* Gugsa and *Ras* Seyum and weaken them both. In an attempt to regain his lost territories, *Dejaz* Haile Selassie Gugsa put his troops at the disposal of Italy.

Gugsa's cousin, *Ras* Seyum Mangasha was also a direct descendent of Emperor Yohannes IV: his father, *Ras* Mangasha, was the second son of Yohannes. Seyum in his youth rebelled against Menelik II and married the daughter of *Negus* Michael of Wollo, a sister of *Lij* Yasu. When Michael rebelled against Haile Selassie, Seyum remained neutral. To come closer to the ruling family of Haile Selassie, Seyum married his daughter, Woletta-Israel, to the heir to the throne of Ethiopia, Asfaw Wassen. As the ruler of western Tigre he was important to the Italians. He maintained friendly and correct relations with them, although he was accused by Ethiopian nationalists of giving in too much to the Italians. To the Italians he appeared a mild person; others interpreted him as timid, fearful and unwarlike. He was preoccupied with retaining his feudal territories. The Ethiopians believed that Seyum had sold Tigre to the Italians, and felt at any moment the *ras* might side with the Italians. Instead when the war came, *Ras* Seyum did fight the Italians, but surrendered to them without too much opposition once he had been defeated.[2]

Another important Ethiopian noble was *Ras* Hailu, the third son of *Negus* Tekle Haymanot of Gojam, who aspired to govern his father's lands without any imperial check. *Ras* Hailu opposed Haile Selassie's rise to power and used the political differences between the Regent, *Ras* Tafari (Haile Selassie's title and name before he became Emperor in 1930) and Empress Zauditu for his own purposes. Haile Selassie, afraid of being overthrown, held an inquest which found Hailu guilty of participating in *Ras* Gugsa's plot against the state. For this reason he was heavily fined and the Agawmeder region was taken away from him in 1932. To take revenge against Haile Selassie, Hailu conspired with *Lij* Yasu, who was held prisoner at Fiche, and cemented their alliance by giving him his daughter, Sable Wangel, as wife.

On 18 May 1932, Yasu escaped from prison with the alleged help of his father-in-law. But Hailu vacillated and failed to give military support to Yasu, who was defeated by the imperial troops. It is not clear what went wrong with the plan and who betrayed *Lij* Yasu. When Haile Selassie found out about Hailu's involvement in the escape of *Lij* Yasu he condemned Hailu to death. The sentence was subsequently commuted to life imprisonment at Dendi, near Addis Ababa, and confiscation of all his wealth. To rule over *Ras* Hailu's territories, *Ras* Imru, cousin of the Emperor, was sent to Gojam.

Ras Hailu's relations with Italy were friendly. He favoured Italian commerce and requested an Italian medical station in 1929 and a school in his capital of Debra Markos. It is alleged that relations became closer when *Ras* Hailu received arms from Rome in pursuit of his independence from Addis Ababa. Perhaps he gave up the plan to support the rebellion of *Lij* Yasu because Italy did not give enough help. When the Italians advanced in Gojam in 1936, they met with hardly any opposition, and after the Italian victory most of the Gojami chiefs retained their positions. In 1936 *Ras* Hailu surrendered to Graziani.

Another dissatisfied and ambitious Ethiopian personality was *Dejaz* Ayalu Burru, a relative and protege of Empress Taitu. He demonstrated his military skills when he captured *Lij* Yasu in 1916. In compensation for his devotion and help to the Empress he received a number of feudal lands such as Wolkait, Tzeggede, Woggerat and part of Semien. In the early 1930s when there were a number of uprisings, he put his military skills at the disposal of the imperial government to put down the rebellions. *Dejaz* Ayalu however, did not feel he had been fully compensated for his help to the central government. He remained discontented, and the Italians used this to draw him to their side with tempting promises of making him *ras*. His intelligence matched his ambitions; he had a strong personality, was a good speaker and possessed great energy. Ayalu maintained close relations with Di Lauro, the Italian Consul at Gondar. He promised to facilitate Italian commercial penetration in Ethiopia and activate communications and trade between Amhara and Eritrea. Senator Jacopo Gasparini won him over to Italy, and he did not oppose the Italian advance toward the south.

A less political figure was *Ras* Kebbede Mangasha, Governor of Agawmeder, Wollo, Pator, Yejju and Wadla. Being the paramount chief of the warlike Oromo people, he tacitly allowed raids by the Yejju against the Danakils. Perhaps because of this, Haile Selassie relegated him to Illubabor (1930) as Governor and, later, to the unimportant regions of Gedem, Emfrata and Antosha. The Italians felt that as former chief of the Wollo Oromo, he could be used against Haile Selassie and, with Italian help, conquer Dankalia, which he knew well. He could easily be brought under Italian influence because he was in disgrace with Haile Selassie.

The same can be said for *Ras* Getachew, whose father, *Ras* Abbate, was instrumental in the opposition to and final defeat of *Lij* Yasu. Getachew, whose mother was related to *Negus* Michael, father of *Lij* Yasu, made a brilliant career capitalizing on his father's friendship with Haile Selassie and his own marriage to the daughter of *Ras* Seyum, *Woizero* Aster. He served as Ethiopian Ambassador to Paris and Minister of Interior. In 1933, he was named Governor of Kaffa, Maji and Gimirra. His surrender to the Italians was used as political propaganda: his name was added to the list of the *rases* who had capitulated.

The leader of the Oromo Muslims, *Abba* Jobir Abdullah, and his uncle *Abba* Jifar had managed to keep his state of Jimma autonomous by paying to Addis Ababa an annual tribute of 100,000 Maria Theresa dollars. Although

Abba Jifar was an old man he was endowed with political ability and had great ascendancy over the Muslim Oromo. It is alleged that in 1879 he sent a declaration to the Italian government by which he accepted Italian sovereignty over his kingdom. *Abba* Jobir, his nephew, opposed the introduction of Amhara soldiers and the payment of new taxes. He therefore was imprisoned in Addis Ababa. Once free, he submitted to Graziani, formed an army of Oromo Muslims, took part in the occupation of Jimma and fought against *Ras* Imru. He greatly contributed to the pacification and submission of Oromo and for his loyalty to Italy, his culture and intelligence, he was regarded as one of the most important Muslim leaders of the Italian Empire.[3]

Italy capitalized on the aspirations, ambitions, traditional hatred and rivalry of the Ethiopian aristocracy and their desire to improve and advance materially. Few were motivated to improve the conditions of the Ethiopian people. Ethiopian chiefs co-operated with Italy because of greed and personal interests. Italy dangled before them a mirage of great honours and material compensation.

No Power-Sharing with the Rases

Before hostilities broke out, the Italians were hopeful of a peaceful accommodation of Italian colonial demands: Ethiopia would be a protectorate in which the *rases* would be used in the administration under Italian supervision. The recognition of the authority of the feudal nobility, however, had to meet the requirements of Italian political interests: Italy would delegate authority to the local chiefs. Thus, in 1935 Italy considered it a good political expedient to reconstruct the traditional Ethiopian provinces, restore their leaders and recognize their authority, thus rendering Italian administration easier. Muslim states destroyed by the Ethiopian conquest would also be resuscitated.

Of the Muslim areas, the most important was Harar, which had a long history as the most outstanding Islamic centre of Ethiopia. Since the French and British had some claims in that area, it was important to set up a political organization favourable to Italy. The form of government in the territories of south-west Ethiopia was to be direct administration solely in the hands of Italian officials, because of the region's backwardness, its lack of important chiefs, and its suitability for Italian settlement.

The Italians were also interested in areas where local rulers were potential enemies of Haile Selassie, such as Tigre, whose chief *Dejaz* Haile Selassie Gugsa's defection to Italy would, they judged, be followed by other chiefs'. He, like other leaders, would be assisted by an Italian colonial official to execute orders. Beside the extension of his rule over Tigre, *Dejaz* Gugsa would be handsomely paid and receive a bodyguard. If *Ras* Seyum found it hard to defect to Italy, the Italian good treatment of his cousin *Dejaz* Gugsa should entice him and other nobles of Semien, Lasta and Amhara to go over to the Italians.

Italy was very fortunate to find in Ethiopia a feudal society which, with little effort, would allow the population to continue to be governed through their own chiefs. The Ministry of Africa, however, had not yet defined its policy toward the *rases*. Badoglio, who favoured keeping and using the great nobility, had made verbal and written promises to *Dejaz* Haile Selassie Gugsa and *Ras* Seyum about retaining their positions and rank. Badoglio had a more individualitic personality: he tended to reject policies suggested by Rome and make his own. Also, he was on much better personal terms with Lessona and the latter gave in more easily to Badoglio's request and suggestions.

Badoglio followed a policy of making use of the local chiefs as intermediary organs. Their use, he argued, would make easier the imposition of Italian rule, and smooth the introduction of Italian administration. Badoglio also favoured maintaining the command of the noble families of the various provinces on account of their prestige and authority. Graziani, also favoured the plan of his predecessor of using the great *rases* in the administration of Ethiopia. Hence at first Italy thought of introducing indirect rule with the collaboration of local chiefs. This idyllic situation did not last long, however, since the preservation of the vestiges of the former Ethiopian government was opposed by the racist and totalitarian Fascist regime.

Exactly why Mussolini reversed the earlier thinking on ruling through the aristocracy is not clear, but several factors may have influenced his change in attitude. First, the territory outside Addis Ababa was proving difficult to subdue. In addition, the Ethiopian people were expressing growing hostility toward the colonialists, and the nobles were said to be behind this feeling. Moreover, Mussolini's military campaign was in part motivated by his desire to avenge Italy's shameful defeat at Adowa in 1896; Ethiopia's royal families had combined with Menelik II to resist the invaders, and as a result were partially responsible for Italy's humiliating loss. Finally, the victory over Ethiopia produced a state of euphoria in Italy. Its army had conquered an Empire, and the defeat of 40 years earlier had been revenged. The economic sanctions imposed by the Western democracies had been challenged and successfully resisted. Militarily, politically, diplomatically dominant, Eternal Rome ruled again on three seas. To share this power with the Ethiopian elite was no longer a tolerable idea, nor did such a civilized and powerful nation feel the need for intermediaries to govern its new subjects. There was also the fear that the nobles, allowed to stand between the government and the Ethiopian people, would delay penetration and threaten sovereignty. For all these reasons, once in power the Italians came to consider the *rases* not as collaborators but as enemies whose power and lives were to be eliminated. Hence Mussolini ordered "No power to the *rases*". Italy he said, would not rule Ethiopia on a *metayer* basis by sharing power with the Ethiopian nobles. This programme flowed directly from the Duce's authoritarian and intransigent temperament.[4]

Graziani, with orders from Mussolini, and against his own convictions, threw himself blindly into the programme to eliminate the *rases* and their power. To compensate the *rases* for the loss of their privileges, Italy resolved to give them salaries, various economic compensations and honours. Some could even have a bodyguard of armed escorts that in some cases reached 300 men. The *Ordinamento Politico Amministrativo* provided that the Viceroy, upon authorization by the Ministry of Africa, could confer or recognize such traditional titles as *ras*, *dejaz*, sultan or emir, but these titles were to be purely honorary and did not entitle those invested to political or military powers.

A number of nobles collaborated with Italy and expected that after the conquest they would receive compensation from Italy for their aid. It was customary in Ethiopia for nobles to receive such compensation after a war; in this case they were hoping to receive wider territorial commands and more power from the Italians. Instead they were pushed aside, not always with full financial compensation and always with incomes far inferior to their previous ones. They were also promised honours by Italy, but these were not always given. Whatever they received was never enough to console them for their lost authority. The Italian occupation of Ethiopia created a social revolution ruining the dominant class overnight by taking away all their authority and concomitant financial resources.

The Italians failed to understand that the Ethiopians could not be loyal to Italy without looking first to their own interests, and that they were too proud to be bought with a bag of Maria Theresa dollars. At the League of Nations, Haile Selassie pointed out that precisely because the Italians had taken the traditions and structure of Ethiopian society into little account, Ethiopia was in rebellion against its Italian rulers.[5]

The Rases

Graziani tried to use the indigenous nobility loyal to Italy to facilitate Italian penetration of Ethiopia, and the defence and organization of the country.

Ras Hailu was Graziani's favoured noble who remained loyal to Italy to the very last. Among other things he took part in the conquest of western Ethiopia. One reason for his collaboration with the Italians was his hope that with Italian help he could fulfill his life's ambition of becoming *negus*. Unfortunately for him, Mussolini gave orders that no promises should be made to restore his power in Gojam. Graziani instead suggested he should represent the Ethiopian people in the Italian government as a reward for his collaboration in the pacification of the Empire. But all that *Ras* Hailu received was the honorary decoration of the Star of Italy.

Another supporter of Italy was *Abba* Jobir of Jimma. He co-operated with the Italians in the conquest of the south-western territories. Although Mussolini had given orders to deprive the Ethiopian nobles of their feudal rights, he promoted *Abba* Jobir sultan in reward for his services to Italy, and paraded him in the Islamic world as an indication of Italy's good disposition toward the Muslims of Ethiopia.

Italy was less generous toward Ayalu Burru. At first Governor Pirzio Biroli used him to influence other *rases* in Amhara to submit to Italy. In exchange for his political services, Pirzio Biroli promised him the title of *ras*, but Graziani refused to consent to it, since Italian colonial policy did not contemplate the making of new *rases*. Instead, the Viceroy gave him an honorary decoration, the Star of Italy. With the exception of *Ras* Hailu and *Abba* Jobir none of the nobility was employed by Italy in military campaigns. Their function was to pressure the undecided chiefs and convince the Ethiopians to accept Italian rule.

Ras Seyum unconditionally submitted to Badoglio on 7 May 1936. Badoglio had promised him treatment according to his royal status, and that he would not be dependent on *Dejaz* Gugsa, his cousin, toward whom Italy was committed to give the leadership of all Tigre, including the western part *Ras* Seyum previously ruled. Badoglio further stipulated a monthly salary for the *ras* and a territorial command which would assure the *ras* and his family a means of livelihood. The *ras* served as an intermediary with his cousins, Aberra and Wonde Wassen Kassa, to convince them to submit to Italy. But his role as mediator was not successful. In any case Graziani kept *Ras* Seyum as a back-up in case *Ras* Hailu failed him.

The treatment reserved for *Dejaz* Haile Selassie Gugsa, the first of the nobles to surrender to the Italians, was no better than that received by those who fought against Italy. It was soon obvious, however, that Italy did not plan to employ him for anything important. In 1936 he was nominated chief of Tigre, but the only activity of the *dejaz* was to look after the repair of his residence at Makalle and enjoy a large salary from the Italian government.

Ras Kebbede, old and ill, retired to Enfrata,[6] where he remained under house surveillance. *Ras* Getachew, in his forties, instead enjoyed the amenities provided by the salary given by Italy. Thus between May 1936, and February 1937, the powers of the *rases* had definitely been curtailed. According to the Ethiopians, they were living in shame.

Differences of amounts paid were also noticed among Ethiopian *rases* themselves. For example, *Ras* Getachew, not trusted by the Italians, had 7,000 lire per month, while *Ras* Seyum collected 22,900 lire. Getachew resented being financially discriminated against. Disparities were also created between Haile Selassie Gugsa, 25,000 lire per month, and *Ras* Seyum, who got 22,900 lire. Although there was possible justification in the case of Haile Selassie Gugsa because he was the first great noble to defect to the Italians, it is hard to reconcile the inequality of salaries between the brothers *Dejaz* Hosanna and Yohannes Jiotte, of Beni Shangul, who each received 15,000 lire per month, and the salaries received by *Abba* Jifar and his nephew, *Abba* Jobir, who were entitled to about half of what the Jiotte brothers received, that is, 8,000 lire per month. Both the Jiottes, *Abba* Jifar and *Abba* Jobir had helped the Italians conquer western Ethiopia. To pay less to *Abba* Jifar (*Dejaz*) chief of all Muslims in western Ethiopia, was a sign of political myopia.

Table 14.1
Ethiopian Nobles Who Received Salaries
From the Italian Colonial Government

Title	Name	Monthly Salary in Lire
Ras	Hailu	40,874
Ras	Seyum	22,900
Ras	Gugsa	25,000
Ras	Getachew	7,000
Sultan of Aussa	Mohammed Jaja Amfari	15,000
Sultan	Abdullah Abba Jifar	8,000
Sultan	Abba Jobir Abdullah	8,000
Dejaz	Hosanna Jiotte	15,000
Dejaz	Yohannes Jiotte	15,000
Sheik	El Hogeli	25,000
Dejaz	Taye	1,000
Ras	Imru	1,000
Dejaz	Ayalu Burru	16,000

Exiled Nobles to Italy

While some *rases* were used to further Italian rule in Ethiopia, others, who were ambivalent toward Italy and hence considered potentially treacherous, were sent to Italy to pay homage to Mussolini. It was hoped that once having seen the marvels of Italy they would be won over. On their return from Italy — while they were at Suez — the attempt on Graziani's life took place on 19 February 1937. Available evidence shows that the Ethiopian nobles, either abroad or in Ethiopia, were not directly involved in the assassination plot; Graziani, however, believed they were. For this reason, they were considered accomplices, for which they were deported to Italy and kept in concentration camps. Mussolini endorsed Graziani's actions and went so far as to suggest that if the *rases* were even vaguely suspected of having participated in the attempt against him, they could be executed without due process of law. *Ras* Seyum, *Ras* Getachew, *Ras* Kebbede and *Dejaz* Asserat, who has just returned from Italy, were put into detention in Asmara, before being sent to Italy.

When these nobles found out that they would be relegated to Asmara they wrote letters of complaint to Graziani. *Ras* Getachew reminded Graziani that in 1936, he was assigned by Haile Selassie to Gore, not yet conquered by the Italians; on receiving Graziani's letter in Egypt with the promise that all his property would be returned and he would be able to live with his family, he accepted submission while he was abroad, free and honoured. Now, for having believed the Italian government, he was interned as a

Victor and Vanquished

traitor.[7] *Ras* Seyum, who wrote on behalf of himself, *Ras* Kebbede and *Dejaz* Asserat, asserted that he had always acted loyally toward Italy. These *rases* had written letters to Ethiopian nobles in exile in Europe and Jerusalem and to Asfaw Wassen in England to persuade them to submit to Italy. Graziani, however, was convinced that the nobles' signature on a document of submission was insufficient proof of their loyalty to Italy. It was alleged that *Ras* Seyum and other nobles and followers aimed at regaining their feudal lands. Graziani insisted that the undesirable guests in Eritrea be sent into exile in Italy. According to the Viceroy, the presence of Seyum and Getachew was against Italian interests. As for old and sick *Ras* Kebbede, Graziani hoped that nature would come to his rescue by a sudden death.

In the summer of 1937, about 400 nobles and their families left Massawa for Italy. On hearing this, Graziani, satisfied, wrote: "May they go to hell!"

Among those sent to Italy were many who had served the Italian government and rendered many favours. Their dishonourable discharge created the belief in Ethiopia that to submit to Italy put at risk one's life and liberty. This reinforced Ethiopian lack of trust in Italian justice.

The return of the Ethiopian aristocracy to Ethiopia* was accelerated by an incident provoked by Zerai Derres, Eritrean interpreter of the confined *rases*. On 13 June 1938, in front of the monument of the fallen heroes of Dogali in Rome, he pronounced words in favour of Haile Selassie in a loud voice. In an attempt to stop him, several persons were wounded. As a result, Mussolini gave orders to send the Ethiopians back to Africa; in the meantime they were forbidden to leave their houses because Mussolini did not want to see any more "niggers" in the streets of Italy.[8]

In 1938, a plan was worked out for the repatriation of Ethiopians. Those Ethiopians who were not politically dangerous could return to their homeland. The others would be sent to Somalia. *Ras* Imru remained on the island of Ponza, while women and children, *Ras* Seyum, *Ras* Getachew, *Ras* Kebbede and *Dejaz* Asserat returned to Ethiopia.[9] *Abuna* Isak and Afework Gebre Yesus (former Ethiopian Minister in Rome) were also repatriated. One hundred and forty-five of those confined at Asinara, Italy, went to Somalia.

---

*In the confused days after the attempted assassination of Graziani in February 1937, Ethiopian nobles were indiscriminately arrested; but it was realized that some of them had served the Italian government and rendered many favours. Their repatriation to Ethiopia was thought to restore their faith in the Italian government and help restore peace and reassure their people. Mussolini agreed that, for political reasons, women, children and individuals unlikely to pose political problems should be repatriated.

The Rases and the Council of the Empire

Another colonial policy error was to prevent Ethiopian participation in a Council of the Empire.[10] The constitution of Italian East Africa, as spelled out in the *Legge Organica* and the *Ordinamento Politico Amministrativo*, provided that a council be called at least once a year. Six members of the assembly were to be leaders, one representing each of the six Governorships into which Italian East Africa was divided. Although the council was to be an advisory body, it could have functioned as a forum for discussing colonial matters with those familiar with the problems of their people, and served as a contact point between the Italian government and its subjects. In 1936, however, Graziani had been unable to make the appointments because he was not familiar enough with the *rases* to know which ones were loyal to Italy. The one individual he felt was trustworthy, *Ras* Hailu, he nominated as adviser for internal affairs.

Eventually Graziani submitted a list of nominees. He thought that *Ras* Hailu could represent Gojam; *Ras* Kebbede, Shoa; *Ras* Gebre Haiwot, Amhara; *Dejaz* Gugsa, Eritrea; Suffian Abdullah, Harar and Somalia; and *Abba* Jobir of Jimma, the Oromo-Sidamo peoples. Graziani also suggested to the Ministry of Africa that, considering the ethnic and linguistic diversity of Ethiopia, their representation in the council was very small. Moreover, limiting membership denied the Viceroy the use of other important personalities in the Empire, such as *Ras* Seyum of Tigre and *Dejaz* Ayalu Burru of Amhara. As a result, instead of encouraging co-operation by allowing the aristocracy a voice in the administration, the establishment of the Council of the Empire was a source of resentment among those traditional leaders not chosen to sit on it. To avoid this, Graziani proposed that the number of Ethiopian councillors be increased.

Mussolini and Lessona rejected this suggestion, although Lessona counter-proposed calling the most important nobles to Addis Ababa and giving them salaries scaled according to their rank. Politically advantageous as their presence in the capital might be, however, it would also give rise to the more immediate danger of gathering all the potential troublemakers in the Empire in one place. Graziani foresaw in Lessona's suggestion the possibility of creating a class of people paid to do nothing but breed dissatisfaction. On the other hand, he was certain that, given constructive employment in which they could take pride, many of the *rases* could prove as useful to the colonial government as was *Ras* Hailu. The Gojami chief had been officially nominated adviser to the Viceroy, and had disarmed the people of Addis Ababa and Shoa in a short time when all Italy's attempts to do so had failed. Another person who could have been very helpful to the Italians was *Ras* Seyum of Tigre, but Mussolini suspected his loyalty, and therefore denied him council membership.

Thwarted in his attempts to exploit the *rases* in administering their people by ministry objections and Mussolini's opposition, Graziani found it expedient to postpone calling the council indefinitely. Other causes contributed to the delay as well, such as the conquest of western Ethiopia, the mass exile of the nobles to concentration camps, and revolts in Amhara and Shoa. By the time Graziani left, no one paid attention to the lack of council meetings, despite the fact that the colonial constitution required that it be convened yearly. The Duke of Aosta inherited this situation but he had little chance to rectify it, since by that time most of the Ethiopian aristocracy was interned away from Addis Ababa.

In a general review of how best to exploit the *rases* after their return in 1939, it was suggested to raise the number of council members. Moreover, it was proposed that each of the Governorships be provided with a consultative body on internal affairs. In this way all Ethiopians above a certain rank would become involved in a colonial government. Participation in these bodies could be made attractive by generous salaries, which was a cheaper proposition than maintaining the large army required to keep order without the *rases'* co-operation. Despite these arguments, by the end of 1939, the colonial Governors expressed the opinion that calling a council would be useless: the Ethiopian representatives, divided by race, religion, language, and understanding of Western culture, and of Fascist policy, shared neither the same interests nor the same opinions on how internal problems should be solved. As a result, the Council of the Empire never met, and in 1940 the Committee for the Reform of the Fundamental Laws of Ethiopia recommended its abolition in the light of the new racial law which prohibited the participation of colonial subjects in the administration of the Empire.

The death of the council, the only approved structure for Ethiopian participation in the colonial administration, had been assured by the policy of *niente potere ai ras* ("no power to the rases"), which prohibited sharing power with the *rases*. Mussolini reminded the Duke to keep the *rases* happy and paid generous salaries: they could be consulted individually on questions concerning Ethiopian matters. Despite Mussolini's strict proscriptions, the condition of the Ethiopian nobility improved under the Duke of Aosta, since the Duke sometimes followed his own judgement rather than the Duce's orders in dealing with his aristocratic subjects. By 1939 his policy had done a great deal to restore the authority and prestige of the more powerful traditional rulers. Some he appointed his personal advisers; others were given judicial posts. Increasingly Ethiopian opinion was heard on conflicts between ethnic groups. Particularly in Amhara and Shoa, where the presence of many notables created the potential for an influential and dissentient class of unemployed, the Viceroy called on these people for help and advice.

The Duke's efforts to involve the *rases* in the colonial structure marked the beginnings of a radical transformation in the traditional system of governing. No longer would a *ras* rule his territory absolutely; instead, he would become a representative of the central government. Elites, especially among the Amhara, would serve as advisers to the Viceroy and to Governors of regions or as regional Governors themselves.

The Rases and the Second World War

The political and military situation of the Empire remained at all times delicate and became more precarious with the European conflict. Too late the Italians realized how little influence they had on the Ethiopians. In an effort to increase Italian control over the people, the Duke of Aosta sought the co-operation of the nobles in exchange for pecuniary compensation.

The Duke's plan to use loyal nobles as high-ranking state functionaries and executives in the colonial government was strongly criticized by the Fascist Party. Nevertheless, it was evident that restoring at least some of the nobles' former power was necessary. In Amhara and Shoa, government control had little impact outside the resident's territorial seat, and, with few well-qualified colonial officials to represent it, Italy elicited only limited co-operation from the people. Moreover, Ethiopians traditionally obeyed only their own Governors, another reason to put them in leadership positions. The Viceroy won his point, and a move was made to restore authority on conditional terms, with the first two to assume their old positions being *Dejaz* (made *ras* by the Italians) Gugsa of Tigre and *Ras* Hailu of Gojam.

The wider political situation made some kind of accommodation crucial. Italy anticipated an international war, in which case a hostile population and an unfriendly elite would prove a disadvantage. In an attempt to inspire trust and eliminate uncertainty, the Duke contacted a number of dissident notables in Amhara and asked for their submission in return for a guarantee of justice. Preliminary discussions were opened in 1939 with nationalist leaders like Asfaw Bogale of Debra Tabor and Dagnau Tessema of Belesa to determine the concessions the Italians would make in return for acceptance by these notables and their followers. The same method was followed in Shoa, with Abebe Aragai. In 1939 as negotiations continued, military incidents diminished. The Viceroy's appeasement policy, however, was too late to be beneficial to Italian rule.

With the outbreak of the Second World War and the entrance of Italy into the conflict on 10 June 1940, it was decided to use the great nobles of Shoa and Amhara to resist the British invasion. *Ras* Seyum was given command of the northern front; *Ras* Gugsa went to Enderta; *Ras* Hailu became Commander of western Ethiopia, and *Ras* Ayalu regained the leadership of Semien. *Ras* Seyum was made chief of Tigre — which previously had been given to his cousin, *Ras* Haile Selassie Gugsa — and nominated chief of all northern Ethiopia with the title of *Ya-Ityopya Semiani Mesfin*, Prince of Northern Ethiopia, including Tigre, Tembien, Lasta, Wag, Yejju, Wolkait, Tzeggede. When the Viceroy gave *Ras* Seyum this title and these territories, they had already partly fallen to the British troops. Therefore, he did not have political-military command over them. With this investiture, it was hoped that the *ras* would be motivated to resist the enemy. The title of *mesfin* given to *Ras* Seyum had a real significance in the territories actually occupied by the enemy, but only honorary value in Italian-held territories.

It was obvious that *Ras* Seyum would remain an honorary holder of his title as *mesfin* and that his prerogative would decrease if the Italians were victorious at the end of the war.

The sudden decision to put *Ras* Seyum in charge of all northern Ethiopia had a contrary effect. The Tigreans perceived the change of colonial policy as Italy's loss of power. The return of *Ras* Seyum to Tigre provoked internal breakdown. Other royal families of the house of Emperor Yohannes IV resented his presence and were unwilling to accept him as overlord, precipitating a rebellion within Tigre, which until then had been orderly and more or less content under *Ras* Haile Selassie Gugsa. In an attempt to correct the imbalance of power in northern Ethiopia, *Ras* Haile Selassie Gugsa was made *mesfin* of eastern Tigre and given an army of 1,000 men. *Ras* Haile Selassie Gugsa, too, had become demoralized and unhappy with the Italians. Although De Bono had promised him the title of *ras* in 1935, it was not given to him until late 1938.[11] He was also promised that he would be treated as an Italian citizen, that his traditional family rights would be recognized, and that he would be addressed as "highness" and given a high salary in place of the tribute he was no longer able to collect from his lands. All these things were pledged, but only partially kept.

The great ambition of *Ras* Hailu was to become *negus*, and his wish came true if only for a very brief time. In 1940, because of the menacing military situation, Teruzzi was willing to give *Ras* Hailu the title of "Delegate of the Viceroy in Gojam" (in Amharic, *Taqlai Endersalassie*), with the power to collect tribute and administer justice. *Ras* Hailu was also put in command of an army of 3,000 men, which enlarged as he advanced into Gojam. But with the military situation worsening every day and *Ras* Hailu's army withdrawing in front of the enemy, the Duke of Aosta promised him the title of *negus* to spur the defensive action of Hailu in the west. Mussolini and Teruzzi, however, would not consent to the title unless Hailu first effectively occupied Gojam in the name of the Italian government and drove out the returning Haile Selassie.[12] Rome requested the impossible. Ethiopian Patriots armed and financed by the British, were advancing with Haile Selassie and British troops into the heartland of Ethiopia.

Ras Ayalu felt he had not received proper compensation for his services to Italy. His rewards were slow in coming because he was suspected of corresponding with the Patriots. In a period of relaxation toward the Ethiopian nobility the Duke of Aosta made Ayalu *ras*. At the outbreak of the Second World War, he was sent to Begemder to attract all Ethiopian dissidents to the Italian side. When the military situation in Ethiopia became more critical, the Viceroy gave *Ras* Ayalu the title of *Teqlai Endersalassie* of Amhara, allowing him to exercise the same full political and military control as Hailu in Gojam.

But these remedies came too late. Italy recognized the authority of the lords over their traditional lands only when Italian ascendancy was lost. The resolutions taken amounted to giving away what Italy no longer controlled; the *rases* were recognized rulers of those areas which they conquered for themselves; and yet they were supposed to be submissive to Italy. The *rases* had no reason to be thankful to Italy: they had lost their titles, reputations and wealth.

Ras Seyum, once installed in his capital city of Adowa and sure of the support of his 20,000 troops, presented himself to the British authorities in April 1941, and communicated to Haile Selassie that he would obey his commands to fight the Italians and help the Emperor regain his throne. With Seyum's forces gone to the British, the military and moral stature of the Italians was lost. When the Duke of Aosta was besieged at Amba Alagi, *Ras* Seyum, perhaps cynically, perhaps humanely, offered his good offices for an honourable compromise between the British and the Italians. He claimed that he wanted to prevent further Christian bloodshed; he also had a grateful memory of what the Duke had done for him and Ethiopia during his Viceroyalty. The Duke refused his good offices. *Ras* Seyum then co-operated with the British in storming Italian positions at Amba Alagi.

Ayalu was no more reliable for the Italians. He sold his support to British Major B. I. Ringrose for 300,000 Maria Theresa dollars. The Italians had sent him with 6,000 men to Dabat to build up reserves in Wolkefit and prevent the infiltration of the Patriots at the *Ente Romagna*, which provided food for Gondar. *Ras* Ayalu, however, proclaimed himself Patriot leader and gathered all Ethiopians to combat the Italians. His main attack was made against the Italian fort of Wolkefit, where he was wounded and captured by Italian troops. He would have been shot had Nasi not intervened.

Nor did *Ras* Hailu of Gojam achieve the success the Italians hoped for. At first *Ras* Hailu received the submission of many Patriot followers of his cousin *Dejaz* Belai Zelleke. Another cousin of *Ras* Hailu, Patriot leader *Dejaz* Hailu Belau, submitted to the *ras,* as did most of eastern Gojam.[13] The majority of the people of Gojam, however, did not help *Ras* Hailu. The Italians did not take into consideration this change of attitude of the Gojami. The Italians beguiled themselves into thinking that the old feudal lord of Gojam would beat the Patriots and would be able to detach them from Haile Selassie's incoming troops. Times had changed; the Italians thought that Gojam was still in the era when the order of *Negus* Tekle Haymanot, father of *Ras* Hailu, was obeyed without objection in all Gojam.

The people of Wolkait, Ermachaho, Enderta, Wag, and Tembien, influenced by the action of the Patriots and sustained by British money and weapons, rebelled too. From his capital at Debra Markos, *Ras* Hailu watched his province elude his grasp. One by one, the *rases*, upon whom Italy had played the last card, surrendered to Haile Selassie. On 6 April 1941, *Ras* Hailu submitted and so did *Ras* Gugsa.

During its short-lived occupation of Ethiopia, Italy was hindered by the chaotic political and military situation from formulating a stable policy on how best to govern its new subjects. The available documentation suggests that Rome was beginning to appreciate the positive results of the Duke of Aosta's attempts to involve the aristocracy in the administration of the country. Despite his short tenure and its experimental nature, the Viceroy's policy was having some effect on anticolonial feeling among Ethiopians. In general, however, the memory of past abuses was strong, particularly among the nobles, for whom the restoration of titles could never compensate for the loss of their revenue, prestige, and authority. Blindly, Italy continued to antagonize its Ethiopian subjects and underestimate their worth. Anticipating the outbreak of war in Europe and Africa, the government in Rome nevertheless refused to consider making friendly overtures toward the aristocracy to secure its co-operation in Ethiopia's defence. Mussolini's ignorance of and lack of interest in colonial affairs partially explains this posture, as does his acceptance of second-rate administrators like Attilio Teruzzi, Minister of Italian Africa. And after 1938 Italy embarked on a policy of racism second in its ferocity only to that of its ally, Nazi Germany, that was to bring about the total destruction of the Mussolini regime.

Notes

1. Bertola, *Storia ed Istituzioni dei Paesi Afro-Asiatici*, p. 270; Rubenson, *The Survival of Ethiopian Independence*; M. Moreno, "Biografie Etiopiche" (Rome, 1935) (unpublished); MAI/GAB 308/8 Franchetti report on Ethiopia, 19 June 1932; Villa Santa, Scaglione et al., *Amedeo Duca D'Aosta*, p. 173; M. Moreno "La Politica indigena dell'Italia," 1942 (speech made at a conference organized by the Ministry of Africa); MAI/GAB 340 Government of Eritrea to De Bono: Ethiopian Chiefs . . . 1934-1935; FO 401/1937/XXIX/18/50–75 Records of Leading Personalities in Abyssinia, 18 March 1937.

2. MAI/AS 181/63-322 Documentary on the Ethiopian War, 1937; Bairu Tafla, "Three Portraits"; Bairu Tafla, "Four Ethiopian Biographies"; MAI/GAB 322 Government of Eritrea to De Bono: Abyssinian Personalities, 1935; Ibid., Government of Eritrea to De Bono: The Abyssinian War Preparations, 1935; MAI/POL 18/139 MAE to MAI: Notes sur l'Ethiopie, 25 November 1935.

3. ACS/RG 23 Hazon: Report on the Events of Debra Markos, 1936; ACS/RG 69 Graziani; Diary, 9 June 1936; ACS/RG 19 Meregazzi to Lessona, 5 May 1936; ACS/RG 12 Mussolini to Badoglio, 26 April 1936; MAI/POL 107/412 Biographical Sketch of Abba Jobir, 1938.

4. MAI/GAB 160 MAI: Ethiopian Protectorate, 18 July 1935; Ibid., MAI: Instructions for a Possible Protectorate in Ethiopia, July 1935; Canevari, *La Guerra Italiana*, I, p. 379; ACS/RG 12 Lessona to Badoglio, 21 May 1936; Pankhurst, "The Secret History . . .", pp. 39–43; Mori *Mussolini e La Conquista dell'Etiopia*, pp. 281-2; Goglia, "Un Aspetto Dell' Azione Politica Italiana"; pp. 791-822.

5. MAI/GAB 160/XI Lessona to Graziani, 5 August 1936; MAI/AS 181/44-210 Graziani to MAI, 10 July 1936; MAI/AS 181/47-222 Lessona to MAI, 16 November 1936; MAI/CSC 22/125 Meregazzi to CSC, 14 November 1936; MAI/AS 181/59-294 Memorandum for Teruzzi, 20 May 1938.

6. ACS/RG 35 Graziani to Teruzzi, 22 December 1937; Ibid., Graziani

to MAI, 28 December 1936; ACS/RG 12 Mussolini to Badoglio, 7 May 1936; ACS/RG 18 Graziani to MAI, 7 November 1936; ACS/RG 40-A/101-5 Graziani to Duke Aosta, 4 January 1938; ACS/RG 23 Bastico to Governor of Eritrea, 31 May 1936; ACS/RG 34/58-A Graziani to MAI, 12 September 1936; Ibid., Graziani to MAI, 30 September 1936.

7. For salaries paid to Ethiopian nobles see: *Bolletino Del Governo dell'Amara; Bolletino del Governo del Galla-Sidama; Bolletino del Governo dell'Harar; Bolletino del Governorato di Addis Abeba*; ACS/RG 34/59 Olivieri to Viceroy, 28 February 1937; ACS/RG 39/59 Graziani to MAI, 28 February 1937; Ibid., Graziani to Mussolini, 1 March 1937; ACS/RG 34/58 Lessona to Graziani, 14 March 1937; ACS/RG 34/58-A Graziani to Guzzoni, 2 March 1937; ACS/RG 23 Ras Getachew to Graziani, 6 March 1937.

8. Sbacchi, "Italy and the Treatment of the Ethiopian Aristocracy", pp. 209-41; MAI/GAB 287/2 Teruzzi to MAI, 23 June 1938; MAI/GAB 251/16 Meregazzi to Teruzzi, 15 June 1938; For a different version see Greenfield, *Ethiopia*, p. 242; MAI/GAB 148/VIII Moreno to Prefects of Avellino, Cozenza, Sassari, Rome, 15 May 1938.

9. ACS/RG 23 C. Starace to Graziani, 8 March 1937; ACS/RG 34/58 Graziani to MAI, 1 June 1937; ACS/RG 23 Graziani to MAI, 28 May 1937; Ibid., De Feo to Graziani, 11 June 1937; MAI/Pol 26/25 Moreno: Memorandum for Teruzzi, December 1938; MAI/GAB 148/VIII Moreno to Teruzzi, 26 April 1938; Ibid., Meregazzi to Teruzzi, 24 May 1938.

10. Sbacchi, "Italy and the Treatment of the Ethiopian Aristocracy", p. 223-30.

11. ACS/RG 23 Ras Seyum to Graziani, 18 May 1937; ACS/MAI 13/6 Duke Aosta to MAI, 15 February 1941; MAI/GAB 294 Duke of Aosta to MAI, 3 February 1941; MAI/GAB 307 Di Lauro: Report on the Events in AOI, 1942; Di Lauro, *Come Abbiamo Difeso l'Impero*, p. 251; ACS/MAI 13/6 Duke of Aosta to MAI, 14 March 1941; MAI/GAB 251/16 Meregazzi to Teruzzi, 20 June 1938.

12. ACS/MAI 107/410 Duke of Aosta to MAI, 25 January 1940; MAI/GAB 115 Duke of Aosta to MAI, 28 January 1941; ACS/MAI 13/6 Teruzzi to GGAOI, 28 January 1941; USNA/ICD T-586/412/005061, MAI to Ministry of Finance, 6 February 1941; ACS/MAI 13/6 Duke of Aosta to MAI, 24 March 1941 and 2 April 1941; Ibid., Teruzzi to Duke of Aosta, 29 April 1941.

13. MAI/GAB 115 Duke of Aosta to MAI, 27 January 1941; ACS/MAI 13/6 Duke of Aosta to MAI, 14 March 1941 also 28 January 1941, 13 January 1941; Di Lauro, *Come Abbiamo Difeso*, pp. 274, 339; MAI/GAB 269 Nasi to MAI, 22 June 1941; MAI/GAB 318 Vecchi: Notes on the Events in AOI, 1942.

15. The Lesser Chiefs

The Local Chief: Italian Government Spokesman

The local notables became essential to Italian rule in Ethiopia, because they were used as a means of communication between the Ethiopian people and the colonial masters. Hence, the latter treated the lesser chiefs, many of whom they created, far more benevolently than they did the great *rases*.

The unexpected Italian conquest upset the social order of Ethiopia. Ethiopians who had enjoyed the privileges of their offices fled before the Italian armies or were deposed by the colonial authorities. Their place was taken by others, whose sole qualification was that they had supported the Italian columns or had served as guides or informants. Recognizing the diversity of ethnic groups, languages and cultures, the Italian government decided to form each ethnic group into one administrative unit with local chiefs nominated by the commissioner in consultation with the resident. Chiefs of urban centres and of large and important ethnic groups were selected by the Governor, upon the recommendation of the commissioner. The selection of chiefs was made known to the people by means of a proclamation after the chief had taken an oath of loyalty to the Italian government. Each chief received a badge which he carried at all times. These chiefs were dependent on Italy for their livelihood, but because of lack of qualifications this created a situation where the Italians had incompetent assistants, but this was not realized immediately because of the precarious condition of the first period of the Italian Empire. Lesser chiefs who had not fought against Italy thus became colonial civil servants.

The use of lesser chiefs had important political consequences, since they could influence their people to accept Italian rule, so the Duke of Aosta outlined the procedure for choosing chiefs. Attention was given to their personality, qualities of leadership, and loyalty to the Italian government. The Ethiopian chief was a means to intensify contacts between government and people. He was the government spokesman among the people. Lesser chiefs replaced the great feudal chiefs. In the Governorship of Oromo-Sidamo, where the Amhara had eliminated all local chiefs of importance, Oromo chiefs appointed by the Italian government without the despotic powers of the Amhara produced a favourable effect among the people.

However, it was observed in 1938 that there was hatred between Oromo and the former Amhara chiefs and that the latter had every intention of regaining their dominance. The antagonism between the Oromo chiefs and the deposed Amhara chiefs was what the Italians wanted. In order to maintain their newly won privileges, the new chiefs needed Italy's support and, therefore, had to be loyal to the Italian government. In this way, they became dependent on the colonial power, without whose help they could not exist.

It is hard to ascertain whether the Ethiopian peoples actually understood Italian colonial policy. To them it was confusing that the majority of their chiefs had been reappointed; yet they were also told that the power of the village or regional chiefs was delegated to them by the Italian resident or commissioner as an expression of the power of the Italian government. It is equally unclear whether the chiefs realized that they were invested with authority and had to consider themselves as fiduciaries who held in trust the powers Italy bestowed on them.[1] Although Italians selected and dismissed the chiefs at will, they failed to inculcate in the minds of the local peoples that all authority belonged to the Italian government. The Ethiopians obeyed their chiefs as they had done for centuries, regardless of the source of their power. The Italians failed to understand this process and deluded themselves into thinking that the people actually recognized the Italian government first, and then their chiefs. In truth the opposite was the case.

Chiefs and people co-operated with the Italians as long as their interests were served. The Italians thought of involving the chiefs in lesser administrative tasks, such as the management of local laws, the observance of Italian decrees, the maintenance of law and order, informing the resident of daily events, communicating the movements of the nomadic population and assuring the equitable sharing of water and pasture land. Chiefs had authority to arrest criminals and report to the government on the economic and social conditions of the people. Assisted by Italian officials, they also exercised their authority in matters of tribute, and assessment of landed property. If found guilty of an illegal act, chiefs and people of an ethnic unit shared the penalty.

Before the Italian occupation, the Ethiopian chiefs performed the essential duties of a judge. Under Italian rule — although his power was curtailed and given to the resident — he still kept vestiges of the original authority. Above all, the Italians needed him to report to the authorities on the mood of the people. When local administration became too difficult a task for one chief, he would select a group of elders and appoint a council of elders whose names had been approved by the commissioner. De Bono assured the people of Tigre that their *chiqa-shum* (chief of a village), would remain in charge of law and order. For example *kagnazmatch* (district chief), Tzahai Bisserat of Adi Abo, was named chief with a council of elders of four. *Fitaurari* (commander of the frontline troops) Kebbede Negussie was named as adviser.

The Chiefs of Amhara

These promises were political expedients to gain the support of the people. But promises to respect their institutions and keep their chiefs in place were disregarded, especially during the period of confusion and uncertainty between 1936 and 1937. In an attempt to quell a revolt in Gojam, Gojami chiefs were replaced whether or not they had co-operated with Italy in the war of occupation. Among them were members of the family of Abebe Aragai, a sworn enemy of Italy. However, his father, Aragai Benere, served as assessor at the courthouse at Debra Berhan and his mother, *Woizero* Askale Gobene, was given the office of *malkagna*, administrator of a small territory of the village of Melein in the residency of Mendila.[2]

In an effort to impose better control over his Governorship, which was overrun by Patriots, Governor Ottavio Mezzetti of Amhara proposed revising the system that had divided his territory into too many small political-administrative units, each with an average of 30 villages. This called for about 1,000 chiefs to supervise the units. Because of the lack of communication and the problem of security, chiefs remained isolated for long periods. If they resided in the residency and had close contact with the Italian authority, they remained out of touch with the people, who disregarded their orders. If the chiefs lived in a local village far away from the resident, they too often assumed an autonomous attitude toward the Italian government, and defected to the Patriots. One remedy for restoring the Italian presence was to eliminate unreliable chiefs by reducing the number of administrative units and concentrating them into larger ones, taking into consideration political and traditional needs and using only those chiefs who had given proof of loyalty to Italy, shown ability to lead and had prestige among the people. Mezzetti restructured the administrative village units and gave them to chiefs such as Kassa Mangasha, Mesfin Gemek and Buzuneh Zallelu. An immediate benefit was that these Ethiopian chiefs successfully coped with Patriotic attacks.

Although the colonial authorities criticized Mezzetti, they agreed that in order to strengthen the Italian authority in Amhara no important chief could be considered merely a "towncrier", and that he should have more power. In the end, Mezzetti's resolution to use fewer but more capable chiefs was accepted.

Nasi and the Lesser Chiefs

Whereas Amhara was not the best Governorship in which to make experiments in the territorial administration, General Guglielmo Nasi, Governor of Harar, was actually able to obtain the support of local chiefs.

Nasi's humane treatment of Ethiopian chiefs won the co-operation of *Fitaurari* Mellion Tedla, of Chercher. Mellion's submission was followed by others, because once the chiefs submitted, Italy would take care of their needs.[3] Strangely enough, Nasi reported that his best collaborators were the Amhara chiefs, the ones who theoretically had the most to lose by Italian rule. Undoubtedly Italy used the venality of the chiefs to acheive its political purpose. Nasi however went further than that. He fought hard to rout the residents' mistrust of the chiefs. The fact that a chief was a civil servant under the Ethiopian government was not a drawback and no reason to reject him. Rather, because of his past experience, Nasi reasoned that properly supervised by Italian colonial officials, the chief would be an asset to Italy.

Nasi also pointed out that accusations reported against chiefs, such as having connections with the Patriots, were not proof of guilt. To incriminate, let alone imprison or execute a chief for mere hearsay, would do Italy a disfavour. Nasi's lenient policy continued when he became Vice-Governor-General of Ethiopia. Nasi nominated Wolde Maskal Tarriew, the former Minister of the Pen and keeper of the Privy Seal under Haile Selassie, who had just returned from confinement, chief of the Ethiopian community of Addis Ababa, which then numbered over 100,000.

The nomination of an Ethiopian to direct Addis Ababa's urban affairs was a significant step in Italian colonial policy. It meant that the example of Italo-Ethiopian co-operation established in the capital could be expanded to other parts of Ethiopia. It showed that Italy had an interest in improving the status of the Ethiopians. It was to give at least the impression that, organized by their own leaders, the people could report their needs to the responsible colonial authority. By the end of 1939, although steps toward the utilization of Ethiopian chiefs were modest, scarce and timid, there was a clear tendency to use more chiefs in the colonial bureaucracy as archivists, book-keepers and newspaper editors. All this occurred in an atmosphere of political detente, and it was hoped that soon the *pour-parlers* between General Nasi and Abebe Aragai, chief of the Ethiopian Patriots of Shoa, would bring the guerrilla warfare to an end.

Honorary Titles

A similar easing of tension could be observed in Oromo-Sidamo and Harar where everything was done to make the people forget their former Amhara-Shoan rulers. In Oromo-Sidamo traditional Oromo titles were widely used. In the Governorship of Harar, titles were assigned according to existing ethnic groups, such as the Arabs, Somalis or Amhara, with the exception that former Ethiopian government titles did not carry the same authority as the title formerly had. In short, a new Ethiopian aristocracy was formed, the old one was allowed to decay, and new designations were created.

To control the proliferation of honorary titles, Oromo-Sidamo recognized six titles. The highest title of *ras*, or sultan was granted only exceptionally to royal families for special military services rendered to Italy. Other titles could be awarded, but chiefs could not be promoted to the next rank for five to ten years after they had received an honorary title.[4] In the regions of Wollega, Kaffa, Gimirra, Borana and Sidamo the Italian government recognized the positions of *ballabat*, chief of a group of districts or regions, and *abbakoro*, chief of a district. In the region of Ometo there were other honorary titles: *waraba*, chief of district and *sangadogna*, chief of a sub-district or village chief. In Beni Shangul, the *ballabat* of that region was traditionally given the title of *sheik-el mashaik*, chief of chiefs.

For the Amhara, the Harar Governorship retained the titles of *abagas*, chief of regions, newly defined as adviser to the commissioner for Ethiopian matters; *meslanie*, chief of district, associated with the resident, as spokesman for the people; *dug*, chief of circuit, collaborated with the vice-resident; and *chiqa-shum*, village chief. Oromo chiefs had had lowly titles in the Ethiopian government. The Italians created new ones for them like *balabat-el kebir*, chief of a region, while the chief of district in Arussi and Bale used the Amhara term of *ballabat*, in Chercher, *abba burka*, and in Harar, *damina*.

It was Italian policy to revive and elevate the other ethnic groups of Ethiopia to set them against the Amhara. However, the Amhara heritage could not be erased. In the Governorship of Amhara, for example, it was impossible to replace traditional titles with new ones. The Italian government gave lip service to *ras*, head of an army, *dejazmatch*, general, *grazmatch*, commander of the left, and *kagnazmatch*, commander of the right, but recognized and exploited the positions of *chiqa-shum*, *meslanie*, and *kantiba*, mayor. Residents, commissioners and governors awarded titles indiscriminately, creating an inflation of honorary titles. The Governor of Eritrea, Alfredo Guzzoni, even gave titles to butchers, tailors, waiters, cooks, drivers, gardeners and launderers. On account of the precarious military situation in Amhara, Mezzetti reported that honorary titles were generously distributed without any numerical limit.

To eliminate title inflation and restore confidence in their value, it was proposed that only three offices with traditional titles should be recognized, that is, chief of a region, chief of a district, and chief of a village or sub-district, who were to be nothing more than Ethiopian advisers to the commissioner, resident and vice-resident. However, long-established titles continued to be used, although devoid of their traditional political authority. The Viceroy retained the power to award the titles of *ras*, *emir*, sultan, *pasha*, *dejazmatch*, *bitwodded* (chancellor); *afegesar* (spokesman for the Emperor); and the highest ecclesiastical titles. All other titles could be given by the Governors. The number of the *rases* for the Empire could not exceed twelve. In order to control the number of titles, their number was limited to 167 per year in each Governorship, amounting to 1,002 per year for Italian East Africa; the number of titles on the level of *meslanie*, *chiqa-shum* and *ballabat*, reached almost 20,000.[5]

The Chief: A State Employee

The Italians took advantage of the greed and covetousness of the chiefs to fulfill their colonial aims. They intended to eliminate the ascendancy of the *rases* over the population and set one chief against another. The subordination of Ethiopian chiefs was widely used by the Italian consuls in Ethiopia before the conquest, and by accepting their "gifts", the chiefs made political concessions and allowed Italian influence to penetrate deeply. Great and lesser chiefs were tied to Italy by money. Several were indebted to the Italian consulates. They borrowed heavily from Italy and never paid back; thus these loans of an unknown amount were really bribes, which Italy gladly paid for political and economic favours. The most important chief bought by the Italians was Haile Selassie Gugsa of Tigre.

Notables and chiefs benefited from Italian generosity, also during the war of conquest. The special political office of the advancing Italian troops received money known as "Black Funds" to distribute to people and lesser chiefs to influence them to be better disposed toward Italian rule. Colonel Luigi Talamonti, in charge of the Political Office of the Second Army Corps, distributed gratuities of about 40,000 Maria Theresa dollars in less than three months. Another branch of the Political Office gave away over 1,200,000 lire. Although these are only partial figures, they give an idea of the intense campaign of funds distributed in the early period of Italian rule in Ethiopia. No doubt many were tempted to expect that better times had come with the Italian presence. Political funds in the ordinary and extraordinary budgets, for 1938-9 amounted to 35 million lire. In 1940 this became 70 million lire.[6]

Thus the Italians used title-giving, public investiture and ceremonies to entice the Ethiopian chiefs to co-operate with the Italian government. But this was not enough. Honours would not assure loyalty to the Italians unless material needs were met. The lesser chiefs were on the state payroll, meaning that they were practically bought to perform the tasks the Italians wanted. Besides a salary, the chief and his family also qualified for other fringe benefits: the families, widows and orphans of chiefs who had fallen fighting for Italy received pensions. But the remuneration the Italians gave was modest compared to what the chiefs had received before the Italians occupied Ethiopia. To supplement their government income they were allowed to engage in commercial activities, even though this would prejudice their administrative duties. In addition they received traditional gifts from the people and a percentage of taxes collected for the government. Besides the salaries, the Governor could give chiefs special allowances for political or religious reasons.

Because the colonial legislation did not fix the actual amount of the salaries, the precise figure was left to local authority without a standard rule. Commissioners, residents, and military commanders temporarily active in some areas issued orders on the amount of salaries to be paid to chiefs. Salaries greatly varied from one governorship to another. Ironically, Ethiopian chiefs were receiving higher income than the chiefs in the older colonies of Eritrea and Somalia.[7] Under the former Ethiopian government the chiefs had received more than the Italians were giving them. Lowering their earnings was not politically expedient because it would produce discontent; yet, if Italy had to pay them what they received before the Italian occupation, the colonial budget would be inadequate.

In an attempt to resolve the question of salaries for lesser Ethiopian chiefs, six categories were devised according to services rendered, the ascendancy they had over their people, and their relationship to some special family. Salaries ranged from 100 to 1,200 lire per month. It was found that 1,200 lire per month was too much and 200 lire too little. Life was too expensive for the average chief to be able to manage with an average salary of 300-400 lire per month. Moreover, he had social obligations to fulfill, like the tradition which called for the chief having a small retinue of faithful servants and giving hospitality. He was also responsible for supporting or giving help, not only to his immediate family, but also to his kinsmen. The only way to resolve the problem was to eliminate inept chiefs, reduce their number, and increase the salary of those chiefs regarded as indispensable.

From a political point of view it was better to have many chiefs — even poorly paid — who by virtue of being on the Italian payroll would be prevented from exercising a negative influence on the people. Although several thousand chiefs were on the Italian payroll, costing the state over 100 million lire a year, chiefs were never satisfied because with the Italian occupation they had lost financial security, prestige, and power. Inequality of treatment led to desertion and resentment toward Italy. Mezzetti rewarded with more money those chiefs who, despite enticements or threats from the Patriots, remained loyal to Italy. The Viceroy suggested increasing the number of chiefs whose salaries reached 1,200 lire per month.[8]

Because of Nasi's vigilant policy and serious screening of his chiefs in the Governorship of Harar, their number was reduced, and his was the only Governorship where the budgeted funds for chiefs' salaries had a surplus. They were not excessively paid. On the average, chiefs received about 330 lire per month but, of course, there were also those who, because of their office, received up to 3,500 lire per month. Among them there were well-paid chiefs. This can be explained in terms of political opportunism: Nasi wanted to keep them content, even though they had lost their lands and prerogatives under Italian rule. They remained on the political payroll, even though they were not called to perform any office.

Oromo-Sidamo too, experienced unequal distribution of salaries which made chiefs resentful. For example, the *kao*, chief, of Dauro, received as much as 4,500 lire per month while his cousin, the *kao* of Konta, had a salary of 500 lire per month. Chiefs of Kaffa received higher wages than chiefs in other regions, although they had the same qualifications and equal duties. In spite of wide inequality in economic remuneration, chiefs in the Governorship of Oromo-Sidamo had the highest salaries of all Italian East African chiefs. Their income averaged 393 lire per month even though this was the most backward of the Ethiopian territories.

Table 15.1
The Best Paid Chiefs of Amhara

Name	Position	Monthly Salary in Lire
Aragai Benari (or Becceri)	Judge	3,000
Askale Gubene (wife of Aragai)	Village chief of Melein	(1,000)
Belai Meshesa	Chief of the region of Mota	1,000
Admasu Burru	Notable of Debra Tabor	3,000
Merid Mangasha	Notable of Debra Tabor	1,100
Jggiju Dereso	Notable of Debra Tabor	1,000
Bezzabe Adal	Notable of Debra Markos	3,000
Amedie Omar	Notable of Debra Markos	1,009
Neghesti Tekleymanot, *woizero*	Notable of Debra Markos	1,000
Mulunesh Hoeli, *woizero*	Notable of Debra Markos	2,000
Dummunesh Hailu, *woizero*	Notable of Debra Markos	2,000
Gabremariam Woldesellasie	Chief of Celga	600
Agage Tzehaiu	Chief of the region of Gondar	400
Ogbagaber Tesfu	Chief of the region of Gondar	400
Mohammed El Alamin	Cadi of Gondar	800
Mohammed Hosman Melchen	Cadi Matemma	1,000
Gebre Mariam	Cadi of Dessie	6,561
Gedeon Yasu	Notable of Dessie	1,100
Mesfin Hailu Kemec	Notable of Gondar	3,280
Kassa Meshesha	Chief of the region of Gondar	3,000
Taferra Bajene	Mayor of Gondar	1,500
Zeudu Ayalu	Notable of Gondar	1,100
Gebre Kidane	Bishop	6,600

Although Nasi asserted that discontented chiefs were in the minority when the time of crisis came during the Second World War, the majority of Oromo and Amhara chiefs deserted the Italians, one of their reasons being their dissatisfaction with their economic circumstances. On the other hand, the nationalism and self-interest of the Ethiopian chiefs who tried to take advantage of the international situation must also be considered. Another cause of resentment on the part of the chiefs was the policy of the Italian authorities to appoint and distribute titles and honours to chiefs, regardless of local traditions. The chiefs' indignation increased because the Italians appointed men of little capacity. Uncritically, Italy put its trust in unpopular Ethiopian leaders who in the past had oppressed their own people and who now, with Italian consent, pursued the same policy of self-interest. Rebellion – especially in Gojam – and resistance to Italian authority were the outcome of this Italian policy of trusting inept chiefs.

Table 15.2
Best Paid Chiefs of Harar[9]

Name	Position	Monthly Salary in Lire
Aleka Desta Negheu	Advisor of Commissioner of Harar	1,087
Sufian *Emir* Abdullah	Chief of Harrari people	1,200
Ghezau Chetama	Chief of Amhara community of Harar	1,200
Jasseim Ben Jusuf	Somali Chief	700
Omar Ali Abdullah	Oromo Chief of Gambolchia	550
Haile Maranu	Amhara Chief of Gambolchia	800
Desta Damtew	Amhara Chief of Graua	866
Demmeche Uberre	Amhara Chief of Mojo	400
Waz Assan Erzi	Chief of Issa people	2,200
Zicheta Woldaja	Amhara Chief: Advisor of the Commissioner of Chercher	1,200
Mellion Tedla	Amhara Chief of Chercher	3,333
Aden Abdi Sabur	Oromo Chief of Deder	1,166
Hamel Gamedda	Arussi Chief of Ticho	550
Turi Tula	Arussi Chief of Cofole	500
Nuh Dadi	Chief of the region of Ghigner	1,639
Said Mohammed	*Imam* of the Sheik Husseim	1,100

Another colonial blunder was committed by the Italian authorities in imposing upon the people Eritrean and Somali chiefs who were chosen only because they could speak Italian and had served bravely in the Italian colonial army; there was no assurance that they would be capable administrators or knowledgeable about local needs and traditions. Meanwhile, dissension between Italian-imposed chiefs and local chiefs assumed catastrophic proportions. The people did not support the *chiqa-shum* or *meslanie* appointed by the Italians; they, and their natural chiefs, secretly decided to oppose the policies of the official *meslanie*. The people of Burie-Damot, Gojam, defied — with arms — the arrival of the Italian-appointed *meslanie*. In Wag-Lasta, the Italians had imposed *Dejaz* Woldeselassie, but the chiefs, who were directly descended from the rulers of that region, continued armed resistance against Woldeselassie, whom they considered a usurper.[10]

In short the Italians failed to make good use of another segment of Ethiopian society: the lesser chiefs whom the Italians specifically selected to replace Ethiopian nobility. The local chief was supposed to represent the Italian government to the Ethiopian people and be an intermediary between the people and the colonial masters. Incomprehension, lack of psychological and political tact, and financial chaos prevented them from keeping the Ethiopians happy under Italian rule. All evidence leads to the conclusion that Italian colonial policies were not clearly thought out.

Notes

1. Meregazzi, *Lineamenti*, pp. 65-6; Mondaini, *Legislazione*, II, pp. 444-6; MAI/AS 181/52-243 Geloso: Political report of Oromo-Sidamo, June 1937; MAI/AS 181/52-245 Gazzera: Political Report of Oromo-Sidamo, September 1938; Colombi, *L'Impero dell'Africa Italiana*, p. 125; Masi, "Ordinamento Politico Amministrativo Militare per l'AOI" (n.d.).

2. Scudieri, "Organizzazione Politico Amministrativa dell'Etiopia in Regime Negussista e in quello Italiano con Speciale Riguardo ai Capi Indigeni, 1939" (unpublished); MAI/CSC 22/125 Meregazzi to CSC, 15 November 1936; Mondaini, *Legislazione*, II, pp. 444-8; MAI/AS 181/37-176 De Bono: Proclamation, Adowa, 14 October 1935; Ibid., Maravigna: Proclamation No. 11 to the people of Tigrai, n.d.; Ibid., Proclamation to the People of Gojam, n.d.; MAI/GAB 75/5-C Duke of Aosta to MAI, 4 February 1939; ACS/RG 24 Tracchia: Report on the administration of Northeastern Shoa to 1937.

3. MAI/GAB 272/365-Bis Mezzetti: Political Report of the Governorship of Amhara, October 1938; MAI/AS 181/53-249 Moreno to Meregazzi, 26 November 1938; MAI/GAB 307/Bis Graziani to MAI, 10 November 1936; MAI/AS 181/56-272 Nasi: Political Report of Harar, 1937.

4. MAI/AV 3 Nasi Circular letter, 11 August 1938; *Il Popolo di Roma*, 3 July 1939; Zervos, *L'Empire d'Ethiopie*, p. 277; Nasi, *Noi Italiani*; MAI/GAB 43 Nasi: Report on the Administration of Harar, November 1937; MAI/POL 107/410 Geloso: Governatorial Decree No. 410, 31 August 1937.

5. MAI/POL 107/410 Graziani to MAI, 2 September 1937; MAI/GAB 272/365 Mezzetti: Political Report of Amhara, September 1938; MAI/POL 107/410 GGAOI: Honorary and Customary Titles Recognized by the Italian Government, July 1939; MAI/AS 181/55-255 Duke of Aosta to MAI, 27 October 1938.

6. MAI/AS 181/63-322 Documentary on the Ethiopian War, 1937; ACS/EB 40: 31 March 1935; MAI/AS 181/10-46 Mussolini to De Bono, 11 October 1935; MAI/AS 181/24-119 Talamonti to Second Army Political Office, 24 March 1936; Ibid., Gratuities to Ethiopian lesser chiefs 1936; Ibid., De Bono to Political Office of the Second Army, 14 October 1935; MAI/GAB 151/IX Moreno to MAI, 4 June 1939 and 24 June 1940.

7. MAI/GAB 46/XI-II-F Duke of Aosta to MAI, 17 February 1938; MAI/AS 181/55-255 Duke of Aosta to MAI 26 October 1938; ACS/RG 34/59 Princivalle to Viceroy, 4 March 1937; MAI/AS 181/48-226; Minutes of the meeting of the Commissioners of Eritrea, 12 February 1936; MAI/GAB 272/321 Duke of Aosta to MAI, 25 October 1938; MAI/AS 181/47-222 Lessona to MAI, 16 November 1936.

8. MAI/POL 103/387 Graziani to MAI 22 September 1936; Ibid., Graziani to all Governors, 13 March 1937; MAI/AS 181/47-222 Duke of Aosta to MAI, 1938; MAI/AS 181/55-255 Duke of Aosta to MAI 25 October 1938; MAI/AS 181/53-249 Mezzetti to MAI, 19 December 1938.

9. MAI/POL 103/384 Governorship of Amhara: Ethiopian Notables and Chiefs on Government Payroll, 28 January 1939; ACS/RG 27 Tracchia: List of Loyal Ethiopian Chiefs Proposed to Receive Government Salaries, n.d. (1937); ACS/RG 24 Tracchia: Report on the Administration of Northeastern Shoa to 1937; MAI/AS 181/53-246 Nasi: Political-Administrative

Victor and Vanquished

Report of the Governorship of Harar, June 1938; MAI/GAB 53 Gazzera: Minutes of the Meeting of the Commissioners of Oromo-Sidamo, 12 June 1939; MAI/GAB 40 Geloso: Political Report of the Governorship of Oromo-Sidamo, 1938; MAI/GAB 292 Governorship of Harar: Ethiopian Notables and Chiefs in Service in the Governorship of Harar, 1 January 1940.

10. Nasi, *Noi Italiani*; MAI/GAB 269 Gazzera to MAI, 16 May 1941; MAI/GAB 279/XI-II Daodiace: Political Report of the Governorship of Eritrea, June 1940; MAI/GAB 295/15 Duke of Aosta to MAI: Minutes of the VI Meeting of the Governors, 12 December 1939; MAI/AS 181/73-376 Salvo: Information on the region of Woggerat, November 1937; MAI/POL 4/5-56 Frusci: Political Report of the Governorship of Amhara, May 1940.

16. Divide and Rule: Italian Policy Toward Amhara, Oromo and Muslims

The Amhara

To facilitate the conquest of Ethiopia the Italians were concerned to foment internal discord and warfare and counted especially on the revolt of the non-Amhara populations such as the Oromo and the Muslims.

By means of bribes and promises, Italy had induced some Ethiopians to co-operate in the conquest of Ethiopia. The Italians anticipated resistance from the Amhara. Their legendary military courage was one reason for Italian apprehension. On the other hand, the colonial rulers secured the good will of the Ethiopians by generous gifts of Maria Theresa dollars. Because the Muslims had been subjected to religious discrimination, they were expected to side with Italy. The Italians counted on the support of the people of Tigre on the basis of their traditional bad relations with Shoan domination. The Italians promised them medical assistance, guarantees of justice, and exemption from tributes. It was anticipated that the Oromo would rebel against Addis Ababa with the help of the Italians. The Italian invasion was a unique opportunity for the Oromo to throw off the Amhara yoke imposed upon them by Menelik II when he conquered south-western Ethiopia at the end of the 19th Century. The Amhara had taken for themselves the best lands, imposed on the people the *gebbar* tax system, and reduced the people to serfdom.

Besides the nationalistic reasons, Amhara hostility against the Italians was in part a reaction to the Italian policy of dismantling their power. Graziani advised his Governors to eliminate the Amhara because, "although they might seem submissive, they in reality lay in ambush ready to act at a favourable moment". For this reason, Nasi's concept of peaceful coexistence, reciprocal help, and use of Amhara as colonial irregular troops was at first opposed. In Oromo-Sidamo all power was taken away from the Amhara and they were concentrated in villages to be better controlled. Those found in possession of arms or accused of propaganda against Italy or of questionable loyalty were executed. It was doubtful whether the elimination of Amhara from the Oromo-Sidamo and Harar Governorships could ensure the Italians a better form of government, nevertheless, residents reported purges of the Amhara in their residencies.

Although the Italians tried to humiliate the Amhara before the Oromo, some of them were politically astute enough to maintain their position of predominance. Oromo animosity toward the Amhara, encouraged by the Italians, became so bad that the Amhara, according to Gazzera, were reduced to the level of slaves. The Amhara at the same time tried to regain their privileges by co-operating with the Italian colonial government.[1] The Amhara could not be ignored: they were a dynamic people and had managed to preserve their influence in the life of the Governorship of Oromo-Sidamo. They could not be totally expelled for fear of creating an economic recession: their exodus would bring about food shortages, since they were capable farmers and owners of sizable farms. The total elimination of Amhara from the non-Amharic-speaking territories was impossible to achieve. It was estimated that in Oromo-Sidamo there were about 300,000 to 400,000 Amhara in a total population of about 4 million to 5 million or about 10 per cent. In Harar their percentage was higher. They were estimated to number 300,000 to 400,000 in a total population of about 1 million, about 35 per cent. In Harar they were mostly landowners. Many had married local Harari women; the same was true in Oromo-Sidamo. They had been away too long from their homeland in Amhara and had lost contact with their relatives. Moreover, mass migration to the Amhara Governorship would not make them welcome to the colonial authorities or to the local people because they would have to be provided with land. Expulsion would accentuate the resentment against Italy. Not even the excuse that the Amhara should be sent away from Oromo-Sidamo for their personal safety — because the Oromo wanted to take revenge against their conquerors — was valid, because the prevalent belief among the Ethiopians was that Italian colonial policy aimed at the despoliation of all Ethiopians in favour of Italian demographic colonization. The deportation of the Amhara from Oromo-Sidamo would confirm this theory.

Although some Oromo still respected the Amhara, the majority had not forgotten the ills of half a century of Amhara dominance which had resulted in the weakening of the social, economic, and political framework of the people. The Oromo regarded the Italians as their liberators from Amhara oppression, but they were suspicious of Italy's real long-range aims. To preserve Oromo confidence, the Italians were careful not to allow the Amhara to regain any political power. Ironically, however, the Amhara became Italy's best collaborators in Oromo-Sidamo; they quickly learned and used Italian legislative principles to recuperate their lands, obtain command positions and go back to regions where once they had exercised authority. It was politically important that the Italians restrain the Amhara from reasserting their former position over the Oromo and that Italy show no signs of compromise or partiality toward the Amhara. If the Oromo felt that the Italians would in any way allow the Amhara to have power over them, Italy would lose their trust.

Faced with these problems, the Italian plan to transfer the Amhara from their formerly-conquered lands remained a colonial dilemma. Concentrating all Amhara in one territory — for example, Shoa — might assure peace in the rest of the empire; but concentration of the dissatisfied Amhara in one place would entail controlling them by means of strong military forces. The main Italian concern was the elimination of the Amhara's claim to superiority over other populations. Lessona framed the division of Ethiopia into Governorships in such a way that the hegemony of the Amhara over other ethnic groups was eliminated. Employing Amhara in government offices and using the Amharic language in non-Amhara territories was prohibited.

With the arrival of the Duke of Aosta in Ethiopia, the plight of the Amhara was seen in more humanitarian terms. In Oromo-Sidamo, those who had ties with families in the Amhara territories were encouraged to relocate, but the majority opted for the alternatives given by the Italian government of cultivating State Domain lands, giving one-fourth of their crop to the government, or enlisting as soldiers. At the same time, the number of Amhara held in concentration camps at Filtu, Oromo-Sidamo, decreased to 193.

More effective was Nasi's policy toward the Amhara in the Harar Governorship where he had the co-operation of trusted Amhara chiefs like *Dejaz* Mellion Tedla of Chercher, *Fitaurari* Zeketa of Garamullata, *Fitaurari* Izazu and *Aleqa* Desta, chief of the Ethiopian Orthodox clergy of Harar. The Amhara of Harar became skillful farmers and competent traders, while others engaged in road building or became colonial soldiers.[2] The Governorship of Harar also organized and supervised resettlement of the Amhara. When several hundred Amhara were freed from the concentration camp at Danane (where they had been interned because they were accused of participation in the 19 February 1937 attempt on the life of Graziani), Nasi provided the destitutes with land, animals and 1,000 lire as capital to build a hut and buy seeds. He also returned State Domain land to the Amhara on a usufruct basis. More important yet was the Amhara development area at Babile, where 60 Amhara families were resettled with government financial and agricultural technical help. Italian agricultural enterprises, such as SIMBA, which operated in the Arussi region, employed 120 Amhara farmers because they were dependable workers. Those Amhara who could not be trusted were used in agricultural penal colonies, like the one at Makanisa, Addis Ababa.

Many Amhara enrolled in the army. The colonial administrators judged the Amhara proud and xenophobic but recognized that they had been the best fighting troops against the Italians, if properly trained, they believed they would fight for Italy too. In fact irregular regiments of Amhara fought against other Amhara in Gojam. The Amhara troops became so reliable that in case of military need against other colonial powers Italy planned to rely on Amhara soldiers; the Ministry of Africa envisioned that the Amhara would constitute the best elements of a black army, which would help Italy to conquer territories bordering Ethiopia.

The fact that the Italians wanted the Amhara out of Harar and Oromo-Sidamo for political reasons did not mean they were not appreciated elsewhere. Rather, they were reputed to be competent office workers and good bureaucrats,[3] and Nasi, who employed them in Addis Ababa, was accused of being partial to them. The most evident change in the Italian attitude toward the Amhara came when the titles of *ras* and *dejaz* were given to Amhara rather than to Oromo. However, titles, employment, money, wages, and honours bestowed by the Italians only partially restored the positions that the Amhara had lost with the arrival of the Italians in Ethiopia. They could not erase the memory of executions, persecution, imprisonment, and expropriation of land. The Italians were aware that among the causes of the rebellion was the persecution of the Amhara. The Patriot Bellelu Tekleab opposed the Italians because of Italian injustice and inconsistency. His father, who had contributed to the occupation of western Ethiopia was executed because he had been found in possession of firearms.

Ultimately, the Italians could not convince the Amhara to co-operate fully with the colonial administration since they feared being put to death or exiled to concentration camps. By antagonizing the Amhara and following an anti-Amhara policy, the Italians were building up resentment against themselves. When, in order to restore faith in the Italian government, Governor Mezzetti of Amhara forbade touching "a hair" of the Amhara population, his policy was highly criticized and he was replaced by General Luigi Frusci.

The Oromo

The Amhara were not the only people resentful of Italian policy. The Oromo, the largest ethnic group, gained more in the long run than the Amhara from the Italian occupation of Ethiopia, but were not always too co-operative and did not live up to Italian expectations. The Oromo had a complex political evolution. They had no written literature but their oral traditions and religious songs were indicative of their keen intellect. The Italians saw in the Oromo a natural ally against the Amhara, and estimated that the 5 million Oromo could more than offset any possible Amhara opposition.

To win over the Oromo people to the government, the Italians gave many of them full rights to the land they had cultivated under Amhara landlords. When the Amhara had conquered the Oromo, the Ethiopian government had given land to Amhara soldiers who helped in the war of conquest. With the land the soldier also received a number of Oromo families to till the land. This system of enserfment, known as *gebbar*, was very harsh on the Oromo, who had to pay a tribute to their master in agricultural goods and a tithe to the emperor. The first thing the Italians did was to eliminate the *gebbar* system.[4]

In 1936 some Oromo sent messages to the Italian troops in the south asking for help against the Amhara. Oromo's oppression under Amhara domination became the central theme of Italian propaganda and of de-Amharization campaigns. Amharic was displaced as the legal language; and Arabic, Oromonya and Kaffinya were taught in schools. In Oromo-Sidoma a number of Amhara place-names were replaced by Oromo or Italian names. Urban centres like Averra became Jiga, Yirgallem was changed to Dalle, Wondo Chella became Sole, and Zena Tafari received the name of Mandera Vittorio. While the Italians made geographical innovations, they were unable to modify the attitude of the Oromo people toward the conquerors. The Duke of Aosta complained that both nobles and ordinary people were perplexed and disoriented by the events of the colonial conquest and Italian colonial policy. The Oromo could be persuaded to co-operate with Italy but the people remained mistrustful. The Resident of Gera and Gomma stated that the Oromo were disheartened, apathetic, tired, and frightened. They mistrusted the Italian government and avoided contact with government officials.

Little progress was made in dissipating the mistrust of the people. From the Oromo point of view, not much had really changed from the time of Haile Selassie. Although changes in the administration under Italian rule had been approved on paper, locally they were implemented slowly and the Oromo received no real benefits. Some, however, were drawn into the guerrilla war of the Patriots against the Italians. Davide Fossa, the General Secretary of the Fascist Party in Ethiopia, admitted that the Shoans and the Amhara were not alone in opposing Italian rule; Italy could not rely too much on the Oromo people either. Oromo's lack of commitment to the colonial rulers was shown during the Second World War, when they gave little support to the Italian army and quickly sided with the invading British troops. The Oromo who gave the impression of co-operating concealed their mistrust from the Italians; their deference lasted only as long as Italy remained militarily strong.[5]

The Muslims

In contrast, the Ethiopian Muslims gave the Italians unconditional help in return for the Italian government's support of their religion and institutions. Of all the peoples of Ethiopia, they perhaps benefited most from Italian rule. Although Italian policy was not always very clear, it consistently tended to be pro-Islamic. Officially, the Italian authorities asserted that all races and religions were treated equally. At the same time, Mussolini gave orders to Graziani to develop a policy to win the Muslims of Ethiopia over to Italy. The Governors were reminded that for political reasons Italian policy had to favour the Muslim subjects. Sometimes the balance had to be redressed. Before the Duke of Aosta left for Ethiopia, Mussolini reminded him that the Muslims were to be treated as equal to the other peoples of Ethiopia. The Duce's remarks were in order because Graziani had been so partial to the Muslims that it had become difficult to claim that Italian policy was that all people should be treated equal.

The policy of Italy toward the Muslims was, of course, moved primarily by political-military interests. Even before the Italo-Ethiopian War, De Bono differentiated between Christian Ethiopian soldiers and Muslim Ethiopians. While he saw the former as good soldiers who could give great support to the Italian armies, he considered the Muslims not simply as good soldiers but as a greater asset because they were more loyal. During the war, the northern Muslims—Azebu Oromo, Araya, Yejju, and Danakil—contributed greatly to the Italian victroy. About 35,000 joined the Italian armies and fought against Haile Selassie at the battles of Amba Aradam, Mai Cew, Lake Ashangi and Saharaito. Other Muslims co-operated as guides, spies and informants. With the Italian victory over the Ethiopian armies, Italian trust and dependence on the Ethiopian Muslims increased.

In the event of an Amhara uprising, the Muslims constituted a precious reserve of men upon whom Italy could always count for support. A battalion of Muslims was stationed in Addis Ababa for the protection of the capital against Amhara attack.[6] Likewise, the defence of the Governorships of Harar and Oromo-Sidamo was entrusted to a Muslim battalion and Muslim troops were used to suppress the rebellion in the Christian province of Amhara. Graziani was convinced that only with Muslim support could the Amhara resistance be broken. Furthermore, the Muslims would constitute the backbone of the Italian colonial force and of the "black army". Others saw in the Muslim forces a moral and military strength which Italy could use against the spread of Communism in Africa. Although the exact number of Ethiopian Muslims was not known, it was estimated at 6 million. Nasi suggested that half the Ethiopian population was Muslim.[7] Italian estimates seem to be accurate and explain their interest in the Muslim subjects as a political and military deterrent against the Amhara.

Muslims felt that the Italo-Ethiopian War was a God-sent opportunity to declare a holy war against Haile Selassie, who had suppressed and persecuted them. The Muslims of Gurage exalted the Italian victory as a Muslim victory over the Amhara. On other occasions, Catholic missionaries reported that the Muslims despised and abused Christian Ethiopians because they were considered defeated foes. Perhaps they were encouraged to do so by public statements in their favour by Mussolini, who, in a speech at Tripoli in 1937, asserted that Italy guaranteed to the Muslim people of Libya and Ethiopia peace, justice, prosperity, and respect of their laws. This active encouragement of Islam was designed to make the Muslims feel that Mussolini was their protector and Graziani, a "man of Islam". Muslims were granted full freedom of religion; the *cadi* (Muslim judge) replaced the Amhara judge. Arabic became the legal language in Harar and was taught in Muslim schools, all newspapers in the Italian Empire had an Arabic section and there were also Arabic radio broadcasts. New Muslim chiefs were selected and given positions of honour in official ceremonies. To reunite all Muslim groups, two new great territories were organized into Governorships — Harar and Oromo-Sidamo — (in addition to Somalia and Eritrea). Administrative divisions, such as districts and residencies, were set up with the aim of perpetuating the ethnic and religious unity of Muslim peoples.

Italy also embarked on a programme of well-drilling among the nomadic people of the Ogaden. Other provisions in favour of the Ethiopian Muslims included a mosque-building schedule. The Italians built, repaired and restored mosques wherever there were Muslims. Special attention was given by Mussolini himself to the erection of a great mosque in Addis Ababa as an act of political reward for the co-operation of the Muslims in the Italo-Ethiopian War.[8] In Harar alone the Muslim religious personnel received state salaries amounting to 100,000 lire for 47 *cadi* and 40 *dagna*. Conservative estimates suggest that during the period of Italian rule in Ethiopia 50 stone mosques were built, 16 restored and numberless mud-hut mosques erected all over the country. In addition, Muslim subjects were less restricted in education. Every mosque had a school. The Italians had high hopes of creating an Islamic University at Harar for Koranic studies. This would become a learning centre for Ethiopia and the Red Sea area where Muslim students from as far away as India might attend. Obviously, Italy aimed to revive Harar as a religious centre, as well as receive the political benefits that such a policy would bring to Italy.

The Koranic school of Harar, which under the Ethiopian government had 60 students, had 450 in 1937–8. In Jimma, an Islamic Institute was planned for the study of Muslim jurisprudence to prepare specialists for the interpretation of Muslim law. Islamic schools aimed to restore relations between Muslims of Ethiopia and train Muslim officials to administer their own people under Italian guidance. They were also regarded as training grounds for the selection of Muslim military leaders and directors of agro-commercial enterprises. There was no doubt that the Italians were investing heavily in the Muslims and were sure of good returns. Muslims were also sent on pilgrimages to Mecca at government expense: in 1939, 3,585 travellers went to Saudi Arabia. Thus Italy's skillful use of religion achieved political and military ends. As a result, Ethiopian Muslims like chiefs *Abba* Jobir of Jimma, *Sheik* Isa ben Hamzah el-Qatbari of Gurage, the Sultan of Aussa, *Iman* Saik Hussein, Mohammed Seid of Bale, and *Iman* Rahitu Nuh Dadi of Arussi co-operated closely with the colonial government.

The Italians trusted the Muslims to the point that they did not interfere with religious matters, while, with the Ethiopian Orthodox Church, Italian intervention was more direct. In Muslim territories the Italians encouraged the gradual decay of the Ethiopian Orthodox Church by limiting the number of Christian churches and priests, restricting the development of ecclesiastical lands, and making it possible for local people to send away clergymen. The Muslims were allowed to proselytize among pagan peoples, converting the Arussi people to Islam. Likewise Islam found fertile ground among Christianized Oromo, who had abandoned Christianity, which they associated with Amhara domination.[9] Amhara Christians and Roman Catholic missionaries alike resented Italy's overt pro-Islamic policy. Some Muslims went so far as to apply pressure and violence on Christians to bring about their conversion to Islam.

In the light of available information it can be asserted that one of the reasons for the Amhara rebellion was the outspoken Italian support of

Islam. The Ethiopian Christians saw not only their political institutions erased by the colonial power, but their own religious beliefs threatened in favour of the Muslims, their traditional foes. Italian preference for Islam led to a misunderstanding of Italian religious policy in East Africa. The Christian people of Ethiopia interpreted Italian policy as hostile and anti-Orthodox. When the Christian troops saw that Italy favoured Muslim soldiers, they came to the conclusion that the Italian government did not trust them.

Italian interests in the Muslims of Ethiopia had international repercussions. Favourable treatment of the Muslims in East Africa made a good impression in the Middle East and in Islamic countries in favour of Italy and it enhanced its claim to be the protector of the Arabic-speaking nations with a view to becoming the leader of the Muslim world. To further these aims, Italy publicized in 1936 the liberation of the nephew of the Sultan of Jimma, who had been imprisoned by Haile Selassie. Close relations with Arab states were maintained by means of cultural activities, health missions, official visits, trade, radio and newspaper propaganda. Besides the yearly pilgrimage of Ethiopian Muslims to Mecca, there were also special visits of Muslim chiefs to Egypt and Arabia to advertise the good treatment of Ethiopian Muslims by the Italians. Sultan *Abba* Jobir of Oromo-Sidamo and *Sheik* Isa ben Hamzah el-Qatbari of the Gurage were sent to tour the Middle East. In 1938, *Abba* Jobir was received by Mussolini, to whom he publicly expressed the devotion of all free Muslim Oromo. To further the Italian presence among the Muslim nations bordering Ethiopia, *Sherifa* el Morgagni was invited to make propaganda trips among the Sudanese people.

Mussolini was anxious to expand trade and commercial relations with the countries across the Red Sea. Although exchange of goods between Ethiopia and the Arabian coast was minimal, Italy enjoyed a flourishing trade in military hardware with Yemen and entertained the hope of establishing a stronger sphere of influence there and helping the Arabs to fight the British forces in the Arabian peninsula and Middle East. Thus, besides trade and political influence in the Red Sea, Italy also peddled obsolescent arms and ammunition to friendly Arab states with the aim of creating a political and military uprising against British domination in the Near East.[10]

To collect commercial and political data, a dhow from Bender Kassim, Somalia, was sent, ostensibly on a commercial tour of the Arabian coast but with instructions to report on the local political situation. To intensify Italian political action on the Arabian coast, plans were made for a centre of Islamic propaganda in Massawa, whose Arab elite had strong family, economic and cultural ties with the other side of the Red Sea. The political courting of the Arab countries paid its dividends during the Second World War when the countries of the Red Sea were able to meet some of the most immediate Italian needs in Ethiopia.

Accounts of the war years in Ethiopia substantiate the fact that most of the Italian strongholds after the British occupation of Ethiopia were in Muslim territory – Harar, the area between Addis Ababa-Quorum-Alomata-

Divide and Rule

Dessie-Adigrat, and Dankalia, all regions with a Muslim population. In Harar and Chercher Italian officers and soldiers were protected by Muslims. The people of Ogaden, led by Sultan Olol Dingle also offered their support to the Italians, as did the Sultan of Aussa, who maintained that the people of Dankalia would fight the British. Among the Muslim Oromo were several Italian officers. The Araya, Azebu and Yejju Oromo, estimated at 230,000, declared themselves rebels against Haile Selassie, like the Danakil, raiding British columns to the point where all traffic between Eritrea and Addis Ababa was severed.[11]

The support given by the Muslims to the Italians from 1935 to 1941 was indeed impressive as the Muslims for the first time enjoyed freedom of worship and liberal financial support for their schools and mosques. While the Italian rule lasted, the Muslims dreamed of making Ethiopia Muslim and the Italians hoped to become a Muslim power.

Notes

1. MAI/POL 18/139 MAE to MAI: Notes sur l'Ethiopie, November 1935; MAI/GAB 160/XI Nasi, *Noi Italiani;* MAI/AS 181/52-243 Geloso; Political Report of the Governorship of Oromo-Sidamo, June 1937; MAI/POL 52/244 Gazzera; Minutes of the II Meeting of the Commissioners, 12 June 1939; MAI/AS 181/52-245 Geloso: Political Report, February 1937; Ibid., Croveto: Report on Ghera, 24 February 1938; Ibid., Cesarini; Notes on the Cullo region, 26 June 1937; Ibid., Gazzera: Political Report on Oromo-Sidamo, October 1938.

2. MAI/POL 181/52-245 Teruzzi to GGAOI, 7 January 1938; Scarin, *L'Hararino*, p. 91-2; MAI/AS 181/52-244 Frangipani, Actual Political Situation in Oromo-Sidamo, February 1940; MAI/GAB 204/28 Lessona to Viceroy, June 1937; ACS/RG 30/5 Petretti to Graziani, 13 May 1937; Ibid., Notes on Ethiopia to Buffarini, 6 April 1937; MAI/AS 181/47-221 Lessona to GGAOI, 8 March 1937; MAI/AS 181/52-244 Gazzera: Political Report, May 1939; MAI/GAB 40 Geloso: Political Report, June 1938; ACS/RG 32/23 Nasi: Political Report of the Governorship of Harar, 1937.

3. MAI/GAB 273/394 Nasi: Political Report, November 1938; MAI/AV 111 Cerulli: Political Report of the Governorship of Harar, November-December 1939; MAI/EF R/2-2Bis Nasi: Political Report of Harar, April 1939; MAI/GAB 273/392 Nasi: Political Report of Harar, January-March 1938; MAI/GAB 160/XI Teruzzi to Duke of Aosta, 28 April 1938; MAI/GAB 148/VII Moreno: Memorandum for Teruzzi, 26 April 1938.

4. MAI/AS 181/52-245 Teruzzi to the Governorship of Oromo-Sidamo, 19 December 1938; ACS/RG 27 Pallavicino to Viceroy, 10 February 1937; MAI/AS 181/52-294 Moreno: Memorandum for Teruzzi, 12 May 1938; Cerulli, *Etiopia Schiavista*, p. 163; See Asmeron Legesse, *Gada*; Huntingford, *The Galla of Ethiopia*; Beckingham and Huntingford, *Some Records of Ethiopia 1593-1648*; Chiurco, *Sanità delle Razze nell'Impero Italiano*; p. 1074; Markakis, *Ethiopia: Anatomy of a Traditional Polity*;

Victor and Vanquished

Marcus, *Life and Times of Menelik II*; MAI/AV 112 Lucchetti: Report on the Submissions of Chercher, 13 November 1953; MAI/GAB 52 MAI: Data for Parliamentary Discussions, Budget 1939-1940.

5. ACS/MA 1937 12/X/II Summary of the book *Under the Cross of Geneva: The Norwegian Red Cross Ambulance in Ethiopia* by G. Ulland (Oslo, 1936); MAI/GAB 18/XI-2 Graziani to MAI, 7 November 1936; ACS/SPD-R 83/W-R Fossa to Lessona, 10 September 1937; USNA/ICD T-582/139/000450 Duke of Aosta: Political Summary, June-November 1940.

6. MAI/GAB 307/Bis Mussolini to Graziani, 13 May 1936; MAI/AS 181/59-291 Graziani to Governor of Harar, 10 July 1937; MAI/POL 6/12-7 De Bono to Governor of Eritrea, 4 January 1933; MAI/POL 59/59 Daodiace to MAI: Report on the Muslim Population in AOI, 11 August 1939; MAI/AS 181/47-221 Lessona to GGAOI, 8 March 1937; MAI/AS 181/55-255 Graziani to MAI, 16 October 1937.

7. MAI/AS 181/55-255 Graziani to MAI, 23 October 1937; MAI/GAB 32/XI-II-D Graziani to MAI, 6 November 1937; MAI/GAB 31/XI-C Martinelli to P. Biroli: Political Activities in Beni Shangul 1937; Colombi, *Impero dell'Africa Italiana*, p. 129; Mondaini, *Legislazione*, II, p. 613 note; Moreno, *La Dottrina Dell' Islam* p. 63; Nasi, *Noi Italiani*; Trimmingham, *Islam in Ethiopia* p. 15.

8. MAI/POL 75/205 Lamelin to Marie Louise 8 September 1936, this is a censored letter; MAI/AS 181/55-255 MAE to MAI, 17 July 1936; Bertola, *Il Regime dei Culti nell'Africa Italiana* p. 162.

9. Toschi, *Il Regime dei Culti*, p.6; MAI/AS 181/53-247 Nasi to MAI, 27 October 1938; MAI/POL 59/59 Governorship of Addis Ababa: Report on Muslim Institutions in AOI, 20 January 1937; MAI/GAB 273/395 Nasi: Administrative Political Report of the Governorship of Harar, October 1938; *Gli Annali Dell'Africa Italiana* 1 (1940), p. 708; Nasi, *Noi Italiani*; MAI/GAB 43 Nasi: Report on the Activities of the Governorship of Harar, January-February 1938; MAI/GAB 272/321 Duke of Aosta to MAI, 25 October 1938; Interview with the late Eric Palm, 5 November 1970; MAI/AS 181/52-245 Gazzera: Report of the Governorship of Oromo-Sidamo, December 1938.

10. MAI/AS 181/55-255 MAE to MAI, 17 July 1936; MAI/AS 181/52-247 Marraffa to MAI, 16 February 1939; MAI/AS 181/55-255 Lessona to Graziani, 20 October 1937; Teruzzi, *L'Africa Italiana*, p. 42; ACS/RG 12 Mussolini to Badoglio, 27 April 1936; ACS/MAI 12/2 Teruzzi to MAE, 5 February 1938: Ibid., Daodiace to MAI, 18 January 1938.

11. MAI/AS 181/46-217 MAI to Governorship of Somalia, 18 November 1937; MAI/POL 59/59 Teruzzi to GGAOI, 3 September 1939; ACS/MAI 12/1-1 Teruzzi to MAE, 19 June 1940; Ibid., Teruzzi to GGAOI, 5 August 1940; Ibid., Maginoli: Commercial Interchange between Massawa and the Arab coast, 18 June 1941; ACS/MAI 23/9 Pastore to Italian Delegation for the Armistice with France, 17 July 1942; MAI/AV 112 Lucchetti to Nasi, 12 April 1953; G. Puglisi, "Impero Clandestino" (Rome: n.d. unpublished), p. 326-7, 382; ACS/MAI 25/22 Nasi to MAI' 15 October 1941.

17. Racism Italian Style

Italian Apartheid Policy

In one of his major policy speeches, Mussolini said "empires are conquered by arms but kept by prestige". By this he meant that the Italians needed to maintain their authority among the Ethiopians so that they would willingly obey the Italians and execute orders. Mussolini also wanted to raise Italian colonial consciousness so that Italians sent to Ethiopia would become leaders and rule over the Ethiopians on the basis of racial superiority. Italian emigrants to Ethiopia were to be educated to think of themselves as superior to, but not dominant over Ethiopian subjects. Ethiopians were not to be held in contempt, but there was to be a clear differentiation and separation between "whites" and "blacks". Nevertheless, the two races, although separated, were to engage in harmonious and profitable collaborations.

Although Italian racial policy was tempered by mild laws in the first years of Italian occupation, it became stricter in 1938, when Italy decided to embark on a full-scale racial policy. It then became clear that the Italians alone were to be the main beneficiaries of the Empire's riches and that Ethiopians were to be kept in a state of subordination. The racial concepts of Italian superiority were enforced with military discipline. When an Ethiopian met an Italian, he had to salute respectfully; otherwise he would be beaten up! Italians found guilty of damaging the white race were punished by equally severe laws. The concept of white superiority was also reflected in Italian colonial legislation: if an Italian was caught red-handed by a *zapatie*, (colonial policeman), he could not be arrested because that would undermine the prestige of the Italian race. According to the Italian interpretation, racial laws penalized the offender for the crime, but also offered a modicum of protection to the Ethiopian subject. But legislation was not enforced against Italian citizens.

Separation of the two races was not achieved, partly because of the housing shortage in Addis Ababa and other urban centres. Italians lived in huts and mud houses in proximity to the Ethiopians. In spite of colonial legislation which laid down that Ethiopians and Italians should live in segregated quarters, the Italians continued to live cheek by jowl with the Ethiopians, their dwellings divided from their Ethiopian neighbours only by a partition. The Italians attempted to make Addis Ababa, Gondar and Harar into modern colonial towns, but Ethiopian huts and corrugated iron shanties stood next to new buildings.

Yet the policy of Italian prestige continued to uphold the necessity for "white" and "black" to be separated, including the Ethiopian aristocracy. Italian places of public entertainment were closed to Ethiopians; those found guilty of not observing this rule were punished with six months imprisonment and a fine of 2,000 lire.[1] In early 1937, the cinema in Addis Ababa admitted both Ethiopians and Italians; the former were assigned the very first line of seats nearest the screen and were admitted by a separate entrance. Later, racial legislation prevented Ethiopians and Italians from attending the same theatre. Films for Ethiopians were censored and most of those passed were of a Fascist propagandistic nature. As an exception, the most important Ethiopian personalities could be granted the privilege of attending a cinema for Italians provided they reserved a box or seats at a proper distance from the Italians. Notables were also allowed to sit in a special area in Italian bars and restaurants.

The principle of complete separation of Ethiopians from Italians was also applied in the professions, arts and trades. No Italian could perform humble jobs such as those of porter or shoe-shine boy because these jobs were held by Ethiopians, while Italians performed the tasks of skilled workers. To boost the prestige of Italian workers the job of labourer was abolished and Italian and Ethiopian unskilled workers could not work in the same building yard. In commercial shops for white people, an Italian could not serve an Ethiopian; instead, special Ethiopian attendants performed the task. In other trades — beauty parlours, barber shops, shoe repairs, tailors and artisans — Italians were forbidden to give service to Ethiopians. Restaurants, bars, bakeries, and boarding houses were forbidden to hire Ethiopians if they had to prepare food and drinks. Race differentiation was also enforced in public and private transport. An Italian taxi could not drive an Ethiopian; neither could an Italian truck driver give a lift to Ethiopian subjects; nor could an Italian be employed as truck driver by Ethiopian owners.

If an Italian were found performing degrading work for an Ethiopian subject, he could be fined up to 5,000 lire. Both Ethiopians and Italians could be granted commercial licences, although Italians had priority. For reasons of political expediency, permission to trade was also granted to Ethiopians on the theory that if they secured economic advantages, they would be less resentful of Italian domination. But Ethiopians were limited to certain commercial enterprises, were not allowed to become white-collar employees or to hold government jobs or become members of permanent staffs or skilled workers. They could not aspire to the best positions, which were reserved solely for Italians. Ethiopians could not join Italian trade unions, but Ethiopian chiefs could organize their own unions.[2]

Italian legislation on segregation covered all aspects of Italo-Ethiopian relations. It was not always possible to enforce the law, and reports of breaches of racial laws were common. Colonial legislation considered the Ethiopians a race of subject people; the Italians were the masters, in whose presence they could not sit and whose hand they could not shake. Ethiopians were compelled to observe curfew ordinances from 11.00 pm until sun-rise. The average Italian was, however, blind to the colour bar, and racial legislation was never fully implemented. Colonial government reports admitted that Italians and Ethiopians went together to a cafe or were seen walking on the street or sharing a taxi. Various *rases* and other high-ranking Ethiopian personalities were deferred to by Italians. It was common to see Ethiopian notables in Italian restaurants and bars being served by Italian waiters. It was not uncommon either for Italian officers on the Addis Ababa-Djibouti railway to exchange their first-class seats for second-class to accommodate Ethiopian *rases*.

Italian racial policy was not imposed to the point of fanaticism. Colonial notables and all Muslim subjects dressed in European clothes were allowed to travel on trains of all classes. The Italians also relaxed their already flexible racial laws for motives of political opportunity. In a paternalistic fashion the Duke of Aosta suggested that Italy should not follow any specific colonial theory, but should rather adapt to specific circumstances. He felt that it was the duty of Italy to guide colonial people toward a gradual elevation according to their own capacities and not force them to accept an advanced civilization and different social forms incompatible with their standards.[3]

Lessona was more racist, asserting that the evolution of the colonial people should be gradual in order not to produce semi-Europeanized Ethiopians: Italy did not intend to extend metropolitan legislation to Ethiopia or equality of civil rights to Ethiopians, who he claimed, neither understood nor appreciated these things.

To gloss over racial discrimination and minimize the horrors committed by Graziani, the Italians made great publicity out of the fact that under their rule, slavery was officially eliminated, and that the colonial constitution ensured justice and respect for Ethiopian traditions and culture. In reality, however, these guarantees for basic human rights were not fulfilled owing to indifference on the part of the colonial power and thus failed to produce major social change.

Fascist officials complained that the racial superiority of the Italian conqueror did not exist in Ethiopia because Italian colonial policy indulged in elevating the Ethiopians, according them clemency, and tolerating equality between Italians and Ethiopians. In Harar, Catholic clergymen protested that too much protection was given to the Ethiopians at the expense of Italian prestige. Nasi was accused of conducting a pro-Ethiopian policy and becoming too soft toward them.[4] There were those who wanted to see Italian prestige upheld by treating the Ethiopians to the stocks and the whip!

Italian political leaders, however, admitted that racial policy laid down in laws was never fully implemented, in part because the tenets of Fascist racial legislation were alien to much of Italian tradition. The average Italian's generosity and kindness did win over the Ethiopians to the Italians. Ethiopian collaboration with the Italians became possible because the common Italian almost instinctively avoided despising or abusing the Ethiopians. Nasi affirmed that, although racial abuses were committed, this was due to ignorance.[5] Italy never translated its racial laws into full practice. Rather than establishing "native reserves", it created areas of Italian demographic colonization, in which the number of Italians was limited. Thus, in assessing Italian racial policy in Ethiopia, all the evidence suggests that the Italian government issued the laws to offset the proclivity to fraternize with the Ethiopians and to give the Italians the colonial consciousness they lacked. In comparison with the prevailing racial policy of other colonial powers, Italian racial policy failed. When in 1942, many Italians were saved, it was because they had treated the Ethiopians humanely and had disregarded the colour bar. They were spared, too, because of the ease with which they fraternized with the Ethiopians.

Madamismo

A problem that Italy could not resolve was *madamismo*: the illegal cohabitation of an Italian man with an Ethiopian woman. In Eritrea and Somalia such arrangements had been common since the 19th Century. With the conquest of Ethiopia the custom became more widespread. For this reason Mussolini ordered all married Italians to take their families to Ethiopia. To impress those living in Ethiopia with the gravity of the crime, some Italians cohabiting with Ethiopian women were repatriated.

These admonishments had no practical results. The Italian government could not stop Italians and high-ranking colonial officials from mixing with Ethiopian women. *Madamismo* was resented by the Ethiopian people because it disturbed the sanctity of their families. Yet residents and Italian civilians continued to live with Ethiopian women; in Asmara, Italians seeking to avoid the Italian authorities lived for months in the Eritrean section of town. The Governorship of Amhara was given the nickname of *allegro governo* (the happy government), because of the liberality with which the Governor and his aids indulged with Amhara women. General Pirzio Biroli had a special weakness for beautiful Ethiopian ladies with whom he often associated in his villa at Gondar. Moreover, during the morning in Gondar the roads near the Italian quarters and the armed forces encampment were swarming with Amhara women, returning to their homes.

The problem of *madamismo* was not limited to outlying territories but even extended to Addis Ababa. A number of influential colonial officials of the Governorship-General of Italian East Africa consorted with local women. Ethiopian women who lived with officials of the Office of Political Affairs gathered highly classified information on the military situation of Ethiopia and passed it on to the leaders of the Ethiopian resistance. One such functionary was Giorgio Pallavicino, whose mistress allegedly was

Woizero Mulatuah Belaineh, ex-wife of the exiled former Ethiopian Minister of Public Works. The wife of the arrested *Grazmatch* Haile Mariam Gessese, once the Inspector of the Djibouti-Addis Ababa Railway and one of the leaders of the Ethiopian resistance, Mulatuah, tried with the help of her Italian friends to have her husband and other Ethiopian chiefs freed. Another similar case involved Gherardo Della Porta, Director of the Governorship of Addis Ababa. He was reportedly living with *Woizero* Sara Gebreyesus, former courtesan of Haile Selassie, accused of conspiring against Graziani's life. Associated with Pallavicino and Della Porta were a Major of the Carabinieri, Quercia, who had a liason with *Woizero* Tessemma Andersaghe, and Captain Marone who was indicted for concubinage with *Woizero* Azalech Gobene.[6]

Although it was difficult to know exactly who practised *madamismo*, indications are that it was widespread in all social ranks, but was most common in areas such as Addis Ababa and Asmara. No one reported what they knew to the authorities because the Italians were bound by *omertà* (a conspiracy of silence); and very few saw anything wrong with it in terms of racial policy. The exact number of Italians who kept Ethiopian women is not known, however, there was the danger of Italians becoming too dependent on Ethiopian females. Some felt that the Italian conquerors were conquered by the Ethiopian "weaker sex".

To counteract *madamismo*, a number of steps, which ultimately proved impractical, were taken by the Italian colonial authorities. Italian bachelors were forbidden to have female servants, and Ethiopian women were not allowed to go to the various government offices in person. Because the problem of *madamismo* did not decrease, Italians found guilty were punished with up to five years of imprisonment. Such illicit unions constituted a crime against the racial laws, and were declared an obstacle to Italian demographic colonization. A far more serious problem faced the Italian colonial authorities in regard to marriage between Italians and Ethiopians. Before the Italian occupation of Ethiopia mixed marriages had been permitted, especially to legitimize the status of the offspring of casual unions. The racial laws of 1937 prohibited legal recognition of mixed unions and assigned the mother's nationality status to half-caste children: they were not considered Italian citizens.

The legislation of June 1939 imposed heavy penalties on any Italian found guilty of undermining the Italian race. The immediate result of these laws was the systematic tracking down in Italy of Italian men and women who were married to Italian colonial subjects, and the breaking-up of families which had been united legally for many years.

Far more difficult to eliminate were the occasional contacts of Italian men and colonial women, a widespread practice approved by the Italian government. The shortage of Italian women in Ethiopia created serious problems. More than 90 per cent of Italian men (estimated to be 300,000) had no families in Ethiopia. Those who could not find sexual outlets became nervous, did not want to work, wished to be repatriated and claimed non-existing illnesses in order to secure leave to Italy. There were cases of homosexuality. Many Italians were living with Ethiopian women or marrying prostitutes. The only places where brothels were well-organized were Addis Ababa and Asmara. Madam Mira was asked to come to Ethiopia with her *filles de joie* to entertain the Italians. To fulfill her patriotic duties, Mira chartered a boat for herself; in a short time she set up several houses in Asmara and other cities. But there were never enough white prostitutes in Ethiopia. The colonial authorities therefore set up brothels with Ethiopian females for use by Italians only. Itinerant companies of females visited forts, and the most isolated Italian outposts.

In spite of government medical inspections, conditions in brothels were primitive and unhygienic. The Italian authorities advocated medical supervision to prevent the spread of venereal disease, but there were never enough doctors and nurses.

Italian officials abused their authority in order to obtain privileges from the local women. High-ranking officials exploited prostitution. Della Porta, and others had financial interests in the bordellos.[7]

The "Half-Caste" Children

Mussolini was concerned about the social complications arising from the illegal unions of Italian men and Ethiopia women. The result of these promiscuous relations was the birth of a large number of mixed-race children. The Italians had dealt with this "problem" in Somalia where in the 1920s they were entrusted with the Consolata Mission Orphanage of Mogadishu. The care of these children of Italian citizens was necessary because they were considered to be Italian. In Eritrea children of an inter-racial union were under the tutelage of the Catholic Church's Saint Joseph Institute.

Fascist racial laws, however, affected them negatively. While previously the government had freely assisted these children, the new legislation did not give specific instructions as to what would become of them. But the colonial government could not remain indifferent to the problem for reasons of morality and political opportunism. Nevertheless, they were prohibited from attending schools and institutions for Italian children; their education was cared for by the Ethiopian schools at the expense of the Ethiopian parent. To limit their social position, they were given an agricultural education. Girls of such unions were brought up in orphanages, taught domestic arts and worked as maids for Italian families. Thus the earlier policy was reversed. In Somalia and Eritrea they had enjoyed Italian citizenship and had been allowed to become members of the Fascist Party and hold posts in the colonial administration. With the new racial laws people of mixed Italian-Ethiopian parentage were set apart and clearly exposed to racial discrimination. Those in possession of Italian citizenship could not become officers in the Italian army; they were prohibited from taking promotion examinations, but could perform their military duties in the colonial corps.[8]

Furthermore, the law declared that all such people were to be considered "native" subjects who assumed the status of the "native" parent and could not be recognized by the Italian parent or carry his family name. This law provided, however, that the 800 who had acquired Italian citizenship before 1936 were recognized as Italians because they had received an Italian education and were of good moral and political standards. The immediate reaction to this legislation was antagonism and resentment. The 1940 racial law left the great majority of Italo-Ethiopians dissatisfied because the law treated them unfairly; some became postively anti-Italian. Perhaps the clearest reaction against Italy came in 1947 when mixed-race Eritreans favoured Eritrean federation with Ethiopia.

How many suffered because of the Italian racial laws is not known because no statistics reliable were kept on the birth of children of mixed unions; although the Governorship of Eritrea did occasionally attempt to collect data on the birth of these children. In 1921 it was reported that there were 1,000 in the total white population of 3,000. Between 1936 and 1938 there were about 2,500 mixed union children in Ethiopia, but most probably this was not an accurate figure; the Italian government estimated 35,000.[9]

Toward a Special Citizenship for Colonial Subjects

Differentiation was also made between Ethiopians, Eritreans and Somalis. Because Italy had conquered Ethiopia, its inhabitants were classified as "colonial subjects". With the formation of Italian East Africa, which included not only Ethiopia but also the two older Italian colonial territories of Somalia and Eritrea, not all colonial peoples were treated in the same way. Eritreans and Somalis were classified not as "subjects" but as "Somalis" and "Eritreans", because of their loyalty to Italy and help in the conquest of Ethiopia.

Although Italian legislation did not provide for the peoples of East Africa to change their status from subjects to citizens, toward the end of the Italian occupation of Ethiopia (1939-41) the question of whether colonial subjects should receive special citizenship status equal to that given to the inhabitants of Libya was under study.

The status granted to "Somalis" and "Eritreans" was, of course, motivated by political considerations. Although they received the privilege of being called only "Eritreans" and "Somalis", this did not change their juridical status. Libyans were considered more evolved than the Ethiopians; Libyans, however, could not become full citizens of Italy because some of their traditions, like polygamy, were not tolerated by Italian law. Thus, special Italian citizenship granted them rights to be respected within Libya. Although political privileges were granted, they were limited to the boundaries of Italian Africa. They could not, for example, compete with Italian citizens to become officers, which would involve command of metropolitan troops. Nor could they be members of the Fascist Party.

Victor and Vanquished

Colonial officials, however, were in favour of granting a change of status not only to Muslim citizens of Libya but also to the people of East Africa. It was felt that after half a century of Italian presence in Eritrea and Somalia, Italian institutions and the Italian way of life had raised their standards and introduced a higher civilization. Eritreans and Somalis were aware of their contributions to the formation of the Italian Empire and of the privileges the Libyans enjoyed. They resented the fact that the Indians resident in Ethiopia were allowed to enter cinemas reserved for Italians, while Ethiopian soldiers decorated for military valour several times were refused admittance. They claimed that they deserved more rights than British subjects!

Ethiopians, and especially Eritreans, were disheartened when the Libyans whose territory they had helped conquer received special citizenship. The Duke of Aosta wanted loyal Eritreans, Somalis and Ethiopians alike to be given special recognition for their service. On the other hand, when *Ras* Haile Selassie Gugsa complained that Badoglio and De Bono had promised that after his submission to Italy he would receive Italian citizenship, it was not granted to him.

Archival evidence indicates that, although there was no plan to give full Italian citizenship to the people of AOI, there were designs to extend to them at least the same special citizenship given to the people of Libya to repair some of the political errors committed in the past. The war did not allow the pursuit of these goals and nothing was done. In 1942 Italian newspapers urged the award of special citizenship to Italian colonial subjects as a reward for their special merits and acts of valour in favour of Italy;[10] by then Italian East Africa had been lost.

Notes

1. Mussolini: speech delivered in Trieste, 18 December 1938; MAI/GAB 160 Lessona to Graziani, 5 August 1936; Pankhurst, "Fascist Racial Policy", pp. 272-88; Ambrosio, *Tre Anni fra I Galla-Sidama*, p. 133; *Rivista Giuridica del Medio ed Estremo Oriente e Giustizia Coloniale*, (January-February 1938), pp. 84-7; Meregazzi, *Lineamenti*, pp. 73-9; MAI/GAB 70/XI-V Duke of Aosta to MAI, 29 March 1940; *Ethiopian Star*, 30 November 1941; USNA/ICD T-586 409/003413-003415, Duke of Aosta to MAI, 22 April 1939.

2. MAI/GAB 32/XI-II Governorship of Addis Ababa: Report, 1937; MAI/GAB 70/XI-V Duke of Aosta to MAI, 25 February 1949; *Impero del Lavoro*, 21 April 1939; *Corriere Dell'Impero*, 21 April 1939; MAI/156/XI Poli to Labour Office of the Governorship of Amhara, 16 June 1939; *Notiziario Coloniale*, 1 March 1938; Meregazzi, *Lineamenti*, p. 76; ACS/RG 33 Graziani to MAI, 2 March 1937; Taeger, *Diritto di Roma*, pp. 35-6.

3. ACS/MAI 13/1 GGAOI to MAI: What the British Intelligence Service Thinks of AOI, 27 April 1939; *Colonie*, 7 September 1939; *Corriere*

Dell'Impero, 22 June 1939; *Notiziario Coloniale*, 1 March 1938; MAI/POL 83/241 Guzzoni to GGAOI, 24 September 1936; MAI/GAB 302 Meregazzi to GGAOI, 16 March 1940; ACS/RG 13 Graziani to Governor of Harar, 20 September 1936; MAI/POL 92/299 Teruzzi to Vidussoni, 30 October 1942; UP/FG 91/1925, Duke of Aosta, "I Concetti Informatori", pp. 3-7, 17, 26.

 4. *Italia Coloniale*, 15 June 1937; *Italiano di Tunisi*, 1 November 1936; M. Moreno, "La Politica Indigena dell'Italia", 1942; Chiurco, *La Sanità delle Razze*, pp. 1074-6; Italy: Ministero Degli Affari Esteri, *Amministrazione della Giustizia in AOI*, pp. 225-36; Jesman, "Ethiopia: Test Case of Racial Integration", pp. 492-3; MAI/GAB 288/XIII-II Bonaccorsi, Impressions for the Duke of Aosta, 30 April 1940; MAI/AS 181/53-247 Maraffa to MAI, 16 February 1939.

 5. Pankhurst, "Economic Verdict. . .", MAI/AS 181/55-255 Report of the Secretary of the Fascist Party on his visit to AOI, 18 July 1936; MAI/AV 3 Nasi: Circular letter, 9 November 1937.

 6. MAI/GAB 160 Lessona to Graziani, 5 August 1936; MAI/GAB 70/XI-V Teruzzi to GGAOI, 24 September 1938; ACS/RG 57 Hazon to Viceroy, October 1937; ACS/RG 32/31 Faedda: Memorandum on *Woizero* Mulatuah Belaineh, 28 March 1937; Ibid., 32/25 Graziani to Vice-Governor-General, 23 March 1937; ACS/RG 32/32 Graziani to Hazon, 25 March 1937.

 7. *Rassegna Italiana* (November 1939), p. 125; *Il Giornale di Addis Abeba*, 8 August 1936; MAI/POL 83/243 Ministry of Interior: List of Colonial Subjects in Italy 1939; MAI/GAB 71/XI-V Bofondi to Starace, 7 December 1937; *Esquire* (June 1936), p. 64; MAI/GAB 204/28 Cortese to Meregazzi, 2 February 1937; ACS/RG 32/25 Graziani to Vice-Governor-General, 23 March 1937.

 8. MAI/AS 89/15-57 De Vecchi to Federzoni, 18 December 1926; MAI/GAB 70/XI-V Political Office to MAI Cabinet, 17 August 1939; Meregazzi, *Lineamenti*, p. 82; MAI/GAB 75/5-C Fascist Party of AOI to MAI, 30 December 1938; Chiurco, *La Sanità*, p. 1028; ACS/PCM 1937-1939 17/1/693 De Bono to PCM, 2 March 1934; ACS/PCM 1937-1939 3/2.2/5441/1 Ministry of Interior to PCM, 22 October 1938; Meregazzi, *Lineamenti*, p. 81; ACS/MAI 1/3 Commander of the PAI to Moreno, 21 February 1940; MAI: Commission for Ethiopian Affairs, Minutes 20 January 1947.

 9. MAI/GAB 70/XI-V Moreno: Memorandum for Teruzzi, 9 March 1939; Perria, *Impero Mod*, p. 303.

 10. UP/FG 91/1925 Duke of Aosta, "I Concetti Informatori", pp. 19-23; Meregazzi, *Lineamenti*, p. 61; MAI/AS 181/46-218 Lessona to GGAOI, 27 October 1937; MAI/GAB 261/84 Notes by Meregazzi, 1940; MAI/AS 181/47-224 Teruzzi to MAE, 19 August 1940; MAI/GAB 70/XI-V Pollera to Duce, 10 December 1938; MAI/GAB 251/16 Meregazzi to Teruzzi, 15 June 1938; MAI/POL 107/410 Teruzzi to GGAOI, 10 March 1940; MAI/AS 181/46-217 Teruzzi to GGAOI, 2 December 1937; MAI/POL 91/288 MAE to MAI, 20 January 1939; *Azione Coloniale*, 1 January 1942.

18. Ethiopia After the Occupation of Addis Ababa

Ethiopia After the Occupation of Addis Ababa

The proclamation of the Italian Empire on 9 May 1936 was a piece of propaganda designed to declare to the world that Ethiopia was conquered, while in reality only a third of the country had been occupied, and Italy merely controlled the route from Eritrea to Addis Ababa and the roadway from Somalia to the capital. In the next five years Italy attempted to conquer the remainder of the country, but large areas of the north and northwest eluded Italian rule.

Evidence of Ethiopian opposition to Italian rule is abundant. The Ethiopians resented being ruled by a foreign power. They resisted Italian rule from the outset and, although not always well-organized, their opposition never ceased. Patriotic fervour was further fuelled by indiscriminate mass executions, raids, thefts, rape and abuse by the colonial troops against defenceless peasants, hut burning, cattle and food stealing and deportations were daily routine. In vain Haile Selassie tried to influence world public opinion by informing the League of Nations of Italian crimes in Ethiopia. The pleas of chiefs like *Dejaz* Negash and Hailu Kebbede who had submitted to the Italians, that the Italians had destroyed traditional authority without making provision for its replacement, were equally of no avail: Ethiopian chiefs and priests had been deprived of their authority and cut off from their source of income and their land.

Furthermore, the people of Ethiopia did not know where Italian authority resided since Italian administrative machinery was not efficient. The Ethiopians turned to their village and regional chiefs, who, for their own personal interests, equally had no desire to serve a dictatorial government which aimed at making a *tabula rasa* of Ethiopian traditions. For all these reasons, and others, the Ethiopians rebelled against the Italians. There is no reliable estimate of the number of Ethiopians who offered armed resistance to the Italians. Published sources refer to 300,000 and a foreign newspaper quoted 200,000 armed men against Italy. The Italian archives give an estimate by region of Ethiopians under arms (see Table 18.1).

Table 18.1
Estimated Ethiopian Rebel Forces 1937-38

	Lasta	Begemder	Gojam	Shoa	Oromo-Sidamo	Total
Sep. 1937	4,000	--	14,000	7,000	400	25,400
Oct. 1937	500	5,000	14,600	2,400	400	22,900
Nov. 1937	150	1,800	14,600	2,500	3,000	22,050
Dec. 1937	--	2,000	20,000	3,000	2,500	27,500
Feb. 1938	--	3,000	20,000	500	1,500	25,000

The Italian estimate of the opposing forces seems to be too low because it considers only those men who were actually armed, and does not take into account the people in the countryside who generally co-operated with the Patriots against the Italians, thus swelling their forces. Conversely the city people apparently sided with the Italians because they were under closer police supervision and the Italian government gave them their means of livelihood. The Italians made several attempts to disarm the Ethiopians, but Ethiopian resistance never ceased. The cases of Morocco and Algeria were taken as examples, in which the Berbers fought the French for several decades. Likewise in southern Italy, after unification in 1870, it took more than 20 years to eradicate outlaws. Badoglio and Mussolini were of the opinion that two decades would be needed to pacify Ethiopia.

The Italians treated the Ethiopian opposition as bandits. Because the rebellion at first did not have a political aim, leadership fell upon personalities unknown nationally but who were ambitious and charismatic leaders. Chiefs and peasants short of funds or food, taking advantage of the lack of government authority, plundered Italian installations and exacted taxes from their fellow Ethiopians.[1] Italian leaders explained that the state of turbulence in the Empire was due to nests of outlaws. There were, it is true, cases when Ethiopian attacks against Italian installations and convoys were motivated by pure economic greed and outlaw tendencies of an endemic nature. Banditry has always been a predominant feature of Ethiopian feudal society, its prevalence at this time was attributable to the inability of the new government to fill the vacuum created by the Italian occupation. Very few government officials admitted that the Ethiopians were fighting the Italians also for political reasons. Lessona and Graziani realized that the rebellion had a specific political intent. In the end, Italian misgovernment provoked the Ethiopians to rebel, and the common struggle developed a sense of identity. Nationalism united the several sections of the country, and thus the Ethiopian rebellion can be referred to as "Patriot resistance".

When the Italians occupied Ethiopia, some Ethiopians welcomed the Italians, and hoped for better times. They soon found out, however, that the new masters did not live up to their expectations. The first historical document on the beginning of the Ethiopian resistance dates from 9 December 1935 when *Ras* Mulugeta, the Minister of War, in a letter to the chiefs of northern Ethiopia ordered them to rebel against Italian rule for taking away the independence of Ethiopia. Again, in January 1936, the Ethiopian Minister in Paris suggested guerrilla warfare. Ethiopian Patriots fought for the independence of their country, but their guerrilla warfare was not co-ordinated. At times they fought among themselves for preponderance over a specific region, power, and a large number of men. The people of Gojam fought the Italians to defend their territory; others continued armed warfare to prepare for the return of Haile Selassie from exile. Eventually, the Ethiopians came to define the aim of their opposition to Italy. They wanted the Italians out of Ethiopia. The Italians resorted to all means to pacify the country, but, because they relied on the use of force and rejected the idea of compromise, the end result was military and political failure. The Italians fielded a large and well equipped army against the Patriots, the reason for which the Italian government was compelled to maintain an army of over 300,000.

Table 18.2
Italian Armed Forces in East Africa 1936-40[2]

	Italian troops	Colonial troops	Total
1936	358,000	108,000	466,000
1937	157,000	60,000	237,000
1938-1939	120,000	160,000	280,000
1940	91,000	200,000	291,000
Average 1936-1940	*181,500*	*132,000*	*313,500*

Actually Italy could not afford to maintain such a large army. Its finances, already bankrupt as a result of the Ethiopian war of occupation and Italy's intervention in the Spanish Civil War, further threatened Italy's financial solvency. The military budgets between 1937 and 1940 show that the average military expenditure was 3,989 million lire. To this must be added the special secret political fund to bribe chiefs and clerics, and buy favours from the people. That additional expense averaged 45 million lire a year for the same period.

Table 18.3
Military and Political Expenditures of Italian East Africa, 1937-40

	Military Budget	Secret Political Funds
1937-38	4,335,000,000	20,000,000
1938-39	2,816,000,000	55,500,000
1939-40	4,816,000,000	70,000,000

Patriot opposition must be seen as the main cause of these huge military expenditures and of the Italian failure to colonize Ethiopia. Funds destined for public works and to bring Italian farmers into Ethiopia had to be used instead to sustain the Italian Army. Because the majority of the Italian troops had served longer than required there was discontent among the metropolitan soldiers. The low morale of the army, and the financial burden were two main elements that made the Italian government decide to reduce the number of metropolitan soldiers in favour of colonial troops. Ethiopians were conscripted, or joined up for the money. Lessona was of the opinion that "if more Ethiopians became soldiers for Italy the pacification would be achieved more quickly and there would be fewer rebels". But was it really as simple as the Minister of Africa described it? Hardly, because the Ethiopians were hastily recruited without proper scrutiny. Many of them were Patriots or had nationalistic feelings. Accordingly, in some instances when they were sent to fight fellow Ethiopians, instead of firing against their countrymen they killed the Italian officers. Furthermore, colonial troops were infiltrated by informants. Therefore, the security and defence of the Empire could not be assured, because the majority of the troops were from newly conquered Ethiopian regions which had no attachment to Italy.

The Ethiopian troops in Italian pay were called *askari*. They must be given more credit than they have received for the cause of the independence of their country. When they deserted from the Italians they brought with them modern weapons and intelligence information, and they passed on the military skills they had acquired to the Patriots. One of the most severe military setbacks for the Italians was the mass desertion of 800 *askaris* of the Fourth Eritrean Division. Throughout the Italian occupation desertion remained one of the most pressing problems. Although statistics are scanty in 1939, an official count revealed that about 2,000 *askaris* had deserted and joined the Amhara and Shoan Patriots.[3]

After the 1936 defeat of the Ethiopian army the majority of the armed men had not been captured or disarmed. The Ethiopians kept their weapons not to oppose the Italians, but rather because they were following a tradition; the possession of a gun lent prestige and social distinction, and it was the pride of every man to be considered a warrior. The owner of a firearm could secure employment as a soldier from a local chief or could sell the weapon. In short it was the best investment an Ethiopian could make. The Italians perceived that a naturally hostile armed population endangered the Italian position in Ethiopia. Only with total disarmament could the Fascists rule, and for this reason the death penalty was imposed on any one caught in possession of arms; relatives of such men were imprisoned, their land confiscated and property destroyed. However, these strong measures produced the opposite effect. 400,000 firearms were collected in Ethiopia between 1935 and 1940. These statistics prove that only about a half of the total number of firearms in Ethiopia before the Italo-Ethiopian conflict were actually surrendered.

While Ethiopia was in a state of political and military unrest it seemed that no peaceful solution was in sight and that there was no one able to bring an end to the war. Assessments of the situation varied from the very hopeful

Table 18.4
Weapons Surrendered by the Ethiopians from 10 October 1935 to 14 April 1940

	Guns	Pistols	Machine Guns	Cannons
1935	25,441	107	348	150
1936	93,401	1,113	263	5
1937	179,856	374	402	14
1938	62,080	419	133	-
1939	18,058	185	72	-
1940	4,723	61	21	-
Total	383,559	2,259	1,238	169

to the extremely dark. In the autumn of 1937, Graziani reported that there was absolute calm in the Governorship of Harar. The only centre of rebellion in the territory of Oromo-Sidamo was between Jimma and Lekept. In western Shoa troops were fighting rebel formations in the Ambo region. In northern Shoa the rebels of Ankober were destroyed. In eastern Shoa there was peace. In Amhara there was a continuous explosion of rebellions. Graziani's appraisal was usually objective, but he was not trusted in Rome where people felt that his accounts were exaggerated in order to obtain more troops. In 1938-9 the situation had not improved. Harar and Oromo-Sidamo were not a military problem, but Shoa and Amhara were in open rebellion.[4] The latter were important regions of Ethiopia where Italian rule was almost non-existent, and yet official reports of the visiting Minister of Africa, Teruzzi, judged the situation rather hopeful as far as peace was concerned.

Because of the unrest, people could not leave their homes after dark; Italians could only hold some strong points, but did not venture into the countryside for fear of being killed; Addis Ababa had been besieged on several occasions; and the number of Italian deaths and casualties was on the increase. Mussolini gave contradictory information on the extent of the rebellion in Ethiopia. In 1936 he ordered that military operations to suppress the rebellion should appear in the Italian press as a continuation of Fascist penetration. In 1937, when the Empire was not pacified or even completely occupied, Mussolini prohibited the Italian press from mentioning the continuing military operations since he had solemnly declared to the Italian senate that the Empire had been pacified! In 1938, at the height of the rebellion in Amhara, Mussolini gave an order to publicize the false information that there was peace in Gojam. To reassure the nervous Italians on the eve of the Second World War, the press reported that pacification of the Amhara and Shoan territories was an accomplished fact.

In spite of press reassurances the Italian public opinion wondered why so many troops were leaving for Africa if the Empire had been conquered. Likewise, the people in Italy were negatively impressed by the long list of dead soldiers published and could not reconcile their deaths with the claims that Ethiopia was pacified. In 1938 the already sceptical Italian public opinion concluded from the accounts of returning soldiers that the war against the Patriots had ruined the Italian economy, and that Ethiopia was of no advantage to the Italian people.

In the end the Italians reported the military victory against the Patriots but did not win them over and failed to come to terms and coexist with the Ethiopians.[5] Perhaps the greatest blunder was the assumption that the Italian armies were invincible after they had eliminated the Senusi rebellion in Libya in 1934 and smashed the Ethiopian army in 1936. But the indiscriminate use of force and mass murder took away even those well-intentioned Ethiopians who sought a compromise with Italy, leaving the Italians in an openly hostile and unfriendly country.

The Massacre of Lekept

The reign of terror was inaugurated following Ethiopian attempts at preventing further Italian expansion in south-western Ethiopia. After the defeat of the Ethiopian army, an Ethiopian government was organized in Gore, south-western Ethiopia, under the nominal leadership of *Bitwodded* Wolde Tzadik. He had little actual power since the Amhara chiefs were divided among themselves on the conduct of war. The Oromo were hostile to them because of the long-standing oppression they had suffered under Amhara domination. In June 1936, Graziani was urged by Mussolini to occupy western Ethiopia at once in order to hasten the international recognition of the Italian Empire and eradicate British influence in western Ethiopia. But Graziani was in no position to respond. Addis Ababa did not have enough troops for its defence, and the arrival of troops in the capital was slowed down by the seasonal rains which made transport extremely difficult. Therefore the conquest of western Ethiopia had to be postponed until the end of the rainy season, in October.

In the meantime, the Italian government had gathered information on the internal situation and on the mood of the Oromo people. Although generally speaking they were well disposed toward the Italians, they hoped for a League of Nations mandate under Great Britain. On the other hand the Amhara garrison at Gore, including Tigrean *askaris*, who had deserted from the Italians, the troops of *Ras* Imru, the cousin of the Emperor and leader of the Ethiopian western army, and the Holetta graduates, could not agree on a course of action. *Ras* Imru was for surrender, while the Ethiopian Youth Party was for fighting. Erskine, the British Consul at Gore, who was favourable to a British mandate, encouraged the Amhara chiefs to remain within the British orbit, even though his government had not officially authorized him to do so, thus increasing Italian fears of the possibility of being deprived of western Ethiopia.

In spite of a lack of men and war material Graziani capitalized on the alleged pro-Italian attitude of *Dejaz* Haptemariam of Lekept, the Catholic

Victor and Vanquished

Oromo and the influence of the Consolata Mission. Without requesting permission from the Ministry of Africa, the Viceroy sent three aeroplanes to Lekept on 26 June 1936 with 13 Italian officers and 3,000 Maria Theresa dollars to organize an Oromo army, and occupy western Ethiopia peacefully. The Italian expedition, however, was massacred on the night of 26 June and their aeroplanes burned at Bonaya, the airport near Lekept, by the Holetta graduates and the ex-Tigrean *askaris*. Eleven men were left dead and one wounded, died later. There was only one survivor, Father M. Borello, of the Missione Consolata, who acted as a guide for the expedition.

Lekept was bombed by the Italian Air Force in retaliation, and when the Holetta graduates were captured Mussolini ordered them to be executed. The massacre at Lekept, by challenging its power, was a setback for Italy's reputation; furthermore it delayed the conquest of western Ethiopia by three months, from June to September 1936. During this time *askari* deserters and the remaining part of the Ethiopian army preferred to go into exile in Kenya and the Sudan since they could not agree on a common policy against Italy. The Holetta graduates moved from place to place inciting the people to unite on a national scale against the invader. The Oromo chose to negotiate a settlement with the Italians.[6]

Addis Ababa: a Beleaguered City

After the defeat of Mai Cew, in the spring of 1936, most of the Ethiopian army found its way south of Addis Ababa. A considerable number of armed men joined chiefs like *Ras* Desta in Sidamo, *Dejaz* Balcha in Gurage, *Blata* Tekle Wolde Haywariat who operated in Limmu, *Ras* Abebe Aragai who controlled Gida, *Ras* Imru who was still in Wallega, *Dejaz* Aberra Kassa in Fiche and his brother Wonde Wassen in Lasta. The leaders of these forces met for five days to decide on what day to attack Addis Ababa with the goal of preventing Italian expansion in south-western Ethiopia and strengthening the wavering Ethiopian government at Gore. The strategy used was to attack the capital during the rainy season from five sides. Before the assault, however, there would be raids designed to draw away as many soldiers as possible from the capital.

Some Ethiopians had given up hoping for the return of Haile Selassie, and they looked to *Dejaz* Aberra Kassa, of royal descent, as the most important leader. It was rumoured he would be named *negus*, after the successful occupation of Addis Ababa. The Ethiopian Orthodox Church gave its blessing to the plan to attack the city with the participation of *Abuna* Petros. The Italians did not know the exact date of the attack, but the earliest recorded mention of it in Italian sources is 20 May 1936. Between May and July Graziani received warnings that an Ethiopian offensive on the capital was planned for some time toward the end of July. However, the plan had to be postponed because of heavy rains. The rivers around Addis Ababa were flooded, thus delaying the arrival of all chiefs on the appointed day.

Dejaz Aberra Kassa advanced to Gulele but not hearing the signal of the firing of a single shot, he withdrew his troops.

Addis Ababa was attacked on 28 July from the north-west and south-east, but the assault was not well co-ordinated because of the mutual suspicions among the chiefs: Ethiopian divisions thus saved the capital and the Italian Empire. Another reason for the failure of the raid on Addis Ababa was the lack of co-operation among the people of Addis Ababa to act within the city against the Italians. Since June 1936 letters had been addressed to the people of the capital by the "Ethiopian Heroes", inciting them to rebel and to be ready to act when they would see fires burning around the city. When the time came, the inhabitants of Addis Ababa did not rise against the Italians. Ethiopian sources report that almost the entire population fought, but archival information does not corroborate this. There were some fires on the outskirts of the capital, but otherwise the people remained indoors, assuming a neutral attitude. Eye witness Patrick Roberts, the British Consul in Addis Ababa, also reported that during the attack on the capital the local population made no attempt to assist the attackers. One explanation for this lack of enthusiasm for the national cause is that the courageous and patriotic-minded citizens had left the city in order not to submit to Italian rule, and that the Italian troops were too numerous, keeping a close check on the people. Furthermore, Ethiopians were concerned with the defence of their families and land and were unwilling to attack Italian forces which were better armed and equipped in open battle. Italian sources say that the people of Addis Ababa did not participate in the rebellion, because they were convinced by *Ras* Hailu to support the Italian government.

Nevertheless the Italians were very nervous. They were spared the humiliation in the eyes of the world of not being able to control Addis Ababa. There is no exact information on the number of Ethiopians who took part in the siege of Addis Ababa. Graziani complained that the capital was besieged by 100,000. More accurate sources put the actual Ethiopian forces attacking Addis Ababa at 6,000-10,000.

Against them the Italians had at their disposal the garrison of Addis Ababa, 2,060 officers, 19,703 metropolitan troops and 4,400 *askaris*, but food for only twenty days and an even shorter supply of fuel and ammunition. The city lacked natural defence positions, but the Italians encircled it with barbed wire and 38 concrete forts. People and traffic entering the city were restricted to using only ten gates. Graziani had learned his lesson from his experience in Benghazi and Tripoli where this type of military fortification lasted for 20 years.[7]

The Attack on the Ministerial Train

The Italian occupation was established around the main urban centres, but near Addis Ababa the Ethiopians continued to harass the Italian life-line, the Addis Ababa-Djibouti railway which was guarded by tanks, over 100 aeroplanes and one soldier per every 50 metres of railway. With the road from Addis Ababa to Dessie cut off by the rains and Ethiopian Patriot forces, the only alternative for supplies was the Djibouti railway. The aim of the Ethiopians was to isolate the capital and starve it to death, compelling the garrison to capitulate. Those attacking the railway were at one time as many as 2,000, armed with automatic weapons and led by *Negradas* Bogale and *Dejaz* Fikre Mariam. The Ethiopians, who swooped down on the line and returned to the hill with their booty, proved hard to smash. The Ethiopians were driven off the railway line, but were never defeated. They managed to sever communications between the capital and Djibouti for a week by tearing up rails, blowing up bridges and cutting the telegraph wire.

The most daring guerrilla action took place when the Minister of Colonies, Alessandro Lessona, and the Minister of Public Works, Cabolli Gigli, were travelling from Djibouti to Addis Ababa. The Ministers were compelled to travel in an armoured train escorted by the air force. The Ethiopian Patriots aimed to capture the Italian Ministers and use them as hostages to exchange for the independence of Ethiopia. The time and date of their journey were kept secret and yet the Ethiopians raided the ministerial train at Akaki on 12 October 1936.[8] The ministerial train was under attack for half a day and although the Ministers were not captured, the exact timing of the assault had political repercussions, since it showed that the Patriots' information service was efficient, demonstrating to world public opinion that the Italians did not control Ethiopia. Under heavy military escort the train eventually reached Addis Ababa. A shaken Lessona was even more determined to use force to eliminate Ethiopian opposition to Italian rule.

The First Ethiopian Martyrs

The repression against the Ethiopians for the attack on Addis Ababa and the disruption of the railway line had its heroes. The first important one was *Abuna* Petros. After a staged public trial for participation in the attack on the capital, the bishop was shot on 30 July 1936 in a public square. The population was shocked, and the action undermined public confidence in the Italian government. The execution was considered an act of folly, and worsened the already poor Italian reputation for indiscriminately killing high-ranking Ethiopian personalities.

The next victims of Italian crimes were the sons of the exiled *Ras* Kassa. *Dejaz* Wonde Wassen Kassa was the influential chief of Lasta. The Italians questioned the sincerity of his submission in May 1936. To prevent possible armed resistance, and to use Wonde Wassen's good offices to convince his brothers Aberra and Asfaw to submit, Graziani requested the chief of Lasta to come to Addis Ababa. According to Ethiopian tradition when a chief was invited to go to the capital it was synonymous with disgrace, since the chief was detained under house arrest and not allowed to return to his domain. There is also the fact that rumours of the return of his father and Haile Selassie from England compelled Wonde Wassen to delay his trip to Addis Ababa. Meanwhile the chief had written to his sister that he expected to be recognized by the Italian government and given the commander of Begemder and Lasta, which indicates Wonde Wassen's less than whole-hearted attitude toward complete submission unless he received due recognition of his rank. Afraid to lose his liberty and position, he delayed his departure for Addis Ababa. Graziani perceived his temporizing tactics as treason and ordered the *dejaz* and his 1500 soldiers to be hunted down. The man-hunt ended with the execution of Wonde Wassen on 11 December 1936 and put off indefinitely the anticipated submission of his brothers.

To facilitate the task of securing the submission of the two remaining Kassa brothers who occupied the strategic position of Fiche in northern Shoa, and commanded the road to Gojam, Graziani also used the services of *Ras* Seyum, *Ras* Hailu and *Dejaz* Amde Ali, Aberra Kassa's brother-in-law. *Abuna* Kirillos also participated in the negotiations with these important Ethiopians. Their surrender was a political necessity for the Italians because it would eliminate a major source of Ethiopian unity. At first it seemed that the Kassa brothers would not submit and that they were procrastinating and bargaining for better terms, but after the capitulation of *Ras* Imru and the desperate situation of *Ras* Desta, *Dejaz* Aberra began to think seriously of submission. Furthermore, neither Haile Selassie nor his father had returned as promised. Discouraged, and deeming the continuous killing of innocent people and destruction of villages meaningless, according to recently published letters, he was willing to submit, realizing that the Ethiopians were not strong enough to fight the Italians. In good faith the Kassa brothers presented themselves to *Ras* Hailu who handed them over to General Ruggero Tracchia. On 21 December 1936, the two brothers were shot and beheaded, but no one knows who gave the order. A few days before, Tracchia had promised the Kassa brothers that their lives would be spared and Graziani had assured Aberra on 11 December that his life would be safe. Neither Tracchia nor Graziani took the responsibility for this disloyal and treacherous murder which was condemned even by *Ras* Hailu. Lessona commented that the shameful act lowered Italian prestige and that the Ethiopians no longer had faith in Graziani. Ethiopian sources confirm that the death of the Kassa brothers was a great blow against Ethiopian opposition to Italian rule.

Graziani destroyed the centre of Ethiopian opposition with brutal force and received the submission of many chiefs who were undecided and waiting on events. These submissions were made more from fear than from conviction, and eventually opposition resurfaced. In the latter part of 1936 and early 1937, although the Ethiopian patriotic cause had been practically undermined by Italian persecutions and destruction, the Ethiopians never forgot the unjust death of their leaders who were sacrificed for love of country. *Abuna* Petros and the Kassa brothers were martyrs, the source of moral strength and patriotism. To inflict a final blow on the Ethiopian opposition and free the Addis Ababa-Dessie road, whose insecurity prevented the steady flow of arms and troops to the capital, Mussolini ordered the area around the capital to be cleared of peasants and Patriots with *"spietate rappresàglie"* (ruthless retaliations).

To carry out the Duce's orders, Graziani began to execute any rebel captured. To give examples of Italian might, General Mariotti killed 100 Ethiopians and destroyed 500 huts in the area of the Termaber Pass. General Gallina reported the execution of those orders, bringing order and peace by use of summary executions. Since the main Patriot bases were located at Mt. Zuquala, Mt. Yerer, Ankober, Debra Berhan and Fiche, they were systematically destroyed. General Mischi was given a free hand and executed 43 rebels and burned many huts at Mt. Yerer. At Ducam General Mariotti killed 321 people including the leader, *Dejaz* Fikre Mariam, executed 100 Ethiopians and burned several hundred huts. General Gallina lay waste six villages between Mojo and Las Addas.[9]

The Italians used the ultimate weapon against which the Ethiopians were powerless. The air force was decisive in the occupation of Ethiopia and the maintenance of Italian superiority. Besides aerial bombing, mustard and yperite gas were used on the rebel formations at Mt. Yerer, Zuquala and Lasta.[10] After intensive military operations in north-west and eastern Shoa against the Patriots in 1936-7, Graziani turned to the south where the remainder of the Ethiopian army had found refuge. Among them there were also the Eritrean *askaris* who had defected to the Ethiopians.

The Defeat and Execution of *Ras* Desta

The last major source of opposition to Italian rule was *Ras* Desta Damtu, son-in-law of Haile Selassie. In January 1936, he was defeated at Dolo. Thereafter he was supported by *Dejaz* Gebre Mariam, former Governor of Harar, and *Dejaz* Beyene Merid, who was married to a daughter of the Emperor, Romanwork. *Ras* Desta averted the Italian conquest of southern Ethiopia by attacking convoys and preventing communications between Somalia and Ethiopia. *Ras* Desta did not, however, have a clear plan of resistance. At one time he planned to concentrate his troops in the lake region and Gurage and from there threaten the capital, and he even reached Mojo. Because his strategy looked indecisive and his action was limited, the Italians underestimated his strength and thought the *ras* would retire to Kenya, while at other times movements by his troops toward Bale confused the Italians who thought that perhaps the *ras* would maintain that area in rebellion and pass into British Somaliland in case of Italian attack.

It is not clear who first took the initiative to negotiate the submission of *Ras* Desta. On 4 December 1936 the *ras* allegedly sent the Belgian coffee grower, Collaris, resident at Adele, to Captain Tancredi Tucci, indicating his willingness to submit. In subsequent correspondence *Ras* Desta denied that he intended to come to terms with the Italian government. Possibly the *ras* was trying to gain time by delaying a military showdown with the Italians, hoping for the return of Haile Selassie. Maybe he hoped that by lengthy negotiations with the Italians he could obtain the best terms or find out the weakest points in Italian defence. In conducting previous negotiations between the Italian authorities and Ethiopians like Haile Selassie, his son Asfaw Wassen, the Kassa brothers, or *Dejaz* Hapte Mariam of Lekept, the Ethiopians had requested more time before accepting Italian terms, and at all times had demanded Italian recognition of the Ethiopian leader's position. To the Italians the submission of *Ras* Desta was of capital political importance. It meant that all the south would fall to the Italians, convincing people that all resistance was meaningless.

Graziani guaranteed *Ras* Desta his life in return for his surrender.[11] The Viceroy was not being magnanimous in sparing the *ras'* life; because the *ras* had fought the Italians in defence of his country, he was not a rebel. To show goodwill and demonstrate the importance he attached to his submission, Graziani planned to fly to Yergallem to meet *Ras* Desta personally. *Ras* Desta reciprocated and in a proclamation ordered his troops to abstain from warfare, "the priests to return to their churches, and the peasants to resume farming". To speed up the submission of the *ras*, Graziani sent Sebastiano Castagna as his personal emissary. He was an elderly man who had participated in the battle of Adowa. In Addis Ababa he had become a favourite of Menelik II and Haile Selassie, because of his technical skills. He had become director of the Ministry of Public Works and was related to *Ras* Desta by marriage. Because Castagna was related to *Ras* Desta and owing to his knowledge of Ethiopian customs, he was chosen for the delicate mission of convincing his nephew to submit to the Italians. The task proved more difficult than anticipated, as the Italian reports were inaccurately suggesting that the *ras* had decided to surrender.

The meeting between *Ras* Desta and Castagna took place at Bulancia, Arbagoma. During the meeting *Ras* Desta expressed his fears to Castagna. He knew of the execution of his cousins, the Kassa brothers, and was informed that Ethiopian nobles who had submitted had been exiled to Italy and Eritrea. Castagna's assessment of the talks was that *Ras* Desta was undecided. He feared the reaction of his subordinate chiefs and particularly the Eritrean deserters who realized that they could expect no mercy from the Italians. *Fitaurari* Berke, the private secretary of *Ras* Desta, and instrumental in the conduct of the negotiations, admitted that it was Gebre Mariam who convinced *Ras* Desta not to submit. In spite of the delays, the Italians continued to press for the *ras*' surrender. Reasons of political expediency dictated a policy of accommodation after the murder of the Kassa brothers. Because *Ras* Desta was the son-in-law of Haile Selassie, the Italians wanted to capture him alive, and parade him as a symbol of the new Ethiopia and of collaboration with the Italian government.

According to Italian records, in December 1936, *Ras* Desta met with his chiefs, including Shimellis, Garramu, Beyene Merid, and Gebre Mariam who were divided among themselves over whether to negotiate a peace settlement with the Italians. The differences became so marked that fighting broke out and six soldiers were killed. Troops deserted because they were tired, disheartened and surrounded by hostile Arussi. There were further armed encounters between *Ras* Desta's generals. *Fitauraris* Shimellis and Bekele Haile fought against *Fitaurari* Woshebet, who wanted to submit to the Italians. *Fitaurari* Garramu left *Ras* Desta's army with his men. The most significant defection from *Ras* Desta's camp was that of *Dejaz* Makkonen who submitted to the Italians in January 1937 with ten *Fitauraris* and twenty lesser chiefs followed by several hundred soldiers. *Dejaz* Beyene Merid is also alleged to have sent a letter to the resident of Ticho expressing his intention to submit.[12]

With so many defections, the Italians expected that *Ras* Desta would submit. They underestimated the qualities of the Ethiopian leader, however, and miscalculated the military strength of the *ras*' army. What was left of the Ethiopian army was still commanded by the prestigious *Ras* Desta and *Dejaz* Gebre Mariam, sustained by the hard core of well-trained Eritreans led by *Fitaurari* Tassemma. Their forces were over 10,000 fighters with modern submachine guns and cannon and abundant ammunition. In addition the *ras* could count on a number of irregular troops which he could summon. Lack of military co-ordination was the main defect of *Ras* Desta's army, otherwise he could have carried on a prolonged war. *Ras* Desta's alleged vacillation allowed him to stall the Italians. To reassure his chiefs perhaps, *Ras* Desta dictated his surrender terms in such a way that Graziani would not accept them.

In his letter to the Viceroy he addressed him as "Italian plenipotentiary", implying that he did not recognize Italian authority in Ethiopia. Before submitting, Desta requested to confer with *Ras* Imru. Furthermore he asked for assurance that he would be recognized as *ras*, and allowed to hold his land and properties – and that the conditions and position of his chiefs in the new administration be agreed before submitting. It can be surmised that *Ras* Desta would have considered the possibility of his submission if his conditions had been met. Diplomatically *Ras* Desta never acknowledged the occupation of Ethiopia. He did not address Graziani as Viceroy and did not deal with him on an equal basis, for his army strongly supported him.

The immediate reaction to the failure of the anticipated submission was to give *Ras* Desta an ultimatum to surrender by 7 January 1937, after when he would be considered an enemy and could expect the same treatment as the Kassa brothers. If Desta submitted, Graziani expected that he too would be sent in exile to Italy, but Mussolini added that after his experiment at negotiating peacefully for the submission of *Ras* Desta, all remaining chiefs were to be executed immediately after their capture. To co-ordinate the final attack, Graziani moved his headquarters to Yergalem.

Three columns with several thousand men attacked *Ras* Desta at Arbagoma-Chevenna. General Navarrini was on the main front, Colonel Zambon proceeded from Aghersalam on Arbagoma and Colonel Pascolini marched to Arbagoma from Malgano. The Italian troops were aided by

50 airplanes. To prevent his encirclement *Ras* Desta tried to escape north toward Chikke. He was prevented from reaching Kenya by Colonel Zambon. On 20 January 1937 Colonel Pascolini captured more than a thousand prisoners, many chiefs, and the family of Gebre Mariam. After this setback *Ras* Desta and Gebre Mariam attempted to join forces with Beyene Merid and *Fitaurari* Shimellis died. The troops of General Nasi and General Mischi barred the remaining Ethiopian troops from advancing toward Maki. At Gojetti, very near Addis Ababa, Beyene Merid and Gebre Mariam were killed in battle. The Ethiopians, defeated on several occasions, reduced to a handful, and disheartened at seeing all their escape routes blocked, disbanded in disorder.

The Italians estimated Ethiopian losses at 4,000 of whom 1,600 were executed by firing-squad. *Ras* Desta, with a few faithful followers, escaped to Eya, near Buttajera. On 24 February the *ras* was captured by the Tigrean *Dejaz* Toklu Mashasha, and handed over to Colonel Tucci. Before *Ras* Desta's execution by firing-squad, Tucci requested an affidavit from him, declaring that the *ras* had been captured by *Dejaz* Toklu. The Tigrean received a 20,000 lire reward for the capture of the Ethiopian chief, a silver medal and the honorary title of *Cavaliere dell'Ordine Coloniale Stella d'Italia*.[13] The success of the Italian troops was due to the co-operation of the Italian airforce which almost daily rained an average of 20 tons of bombs upon the Ethiopians creating terror and destruction. Both airforce and troops were given a free hand with the aim of exterminating the enemy. Those chiefs who submitted with their men were executed, including women and children. The village of Gojetti was burned to the ground and all males above 18 years of age executed.

The Attempt on Graziani's Life

The elimination of *Ras* Desta and his army was a great blow to the Patriotic movement. All the major leaders had been killed or had submitted to the Italian government. It seemed as if Italian rule would suffer no further challenge. The unexpected attempt on Graziani's life on 19 February 1937, however, triggered the spark of guerrilla warfare against Italian rule. The authors of the plot, according to oral sources, were moved by indignation against the heavy-handed Italian rule and Fascist racial discrimination.

On Friday, 19 February 1937, an attempt was made to assassinate Graziani by two Eritreans. Celebrating the birth of the Prince of Naples at the Viceroy's palace, Graziani invited the Ethiopian nobility and 3,000 poor to receive two Maria Theresa dollars each from the Viceroy. At noon the conspirators, who had mingled with the crowd, threw seven hand grenades at the Viceroy who stood on the steps of his palace, but only the third one hit him. Graziani was wounded with some 350 splinters, but General Aurelio Liotta, commander of the Italian Air Force lost his right leg and eye, while 50 other Italians and Ethiopians received minor wounds and three Italian soldiers lost their lives. If it had not been for Danilo Brindelli, a film operator, who took the Viceroy in a car to the Consolata Hospital, Graziani would have died of a haemorrhage. There was immediate and complete confusion following the attempt, and a general stampede. The Carabinieri and soldiers on duty fired into the crowd and rounded up everyone within the precincts of the palace.

Wholesale executions followed at once in the grounds and the adjoining field. A large number of innocent spectators lost their lives. For two and a half days there followed reprisals against the Ethiopians. It was an orgy of murder, robbery and arson on the part of the Italians. No one was spared. Ethiopians were hunted through the streets and into their dwellings all over the town and beaten, shot, bayoneted or clubbed to death; their dwellings were burnt by flame-throwers and petrol, and in some cases people were burnt inside their huts; women, children and priests received the same brutality. Ethiopians were thrown over the parapet of a bridge onto the boulders below, a fifteen metre drop, and those still alive were finished off with rifles. Extensive areas in every quarter were ablaze, and more than 4,000 huts were destroyed. The Italian reaction in burning Ethiopian huts was intensified by the explosions of ammunition hidden in the burning dwellings. The church of St. George was set on fire and twenty mines had been placed to blow it up. As if this barbaric fury was not enough, Graziani planned to destroy Addis Ababa and place its inhabitants in concentration camps. Mussolini forbade this draconian measure for fear of negative world public opinion.

Graziani is accused of having given the orders for retaliation, but eye-witness accounts suggest that Graziani was between life and death, and therefore could not have given the command. The Viceroy was described as in a state of shock and bleeding profusely when he arrived at the hospital. For 48 hours Graziani was too ill to realize the seriousness of the crisis. While he was in hospital all power was in the hands of Petretti, the Vice-Governor-General and General Gariboldi, Commander-in-Chief of the Italian armed forces. During those days the Fascists had a free hand. Several sources suggest that the Secretary of the Fascist Party of Addis Ababa, Guido Cortese, gave the signal for the slaughter of the inhabitants of the capital. He ordered the Black Shirts and the workers to kill anyone on sight, to produce another memorable St Bartholomew's night. From all the forts which surrounded Addis Ababa the militia marched to the centre of the city in full war armament, tanks and heavy machine guns.

Cortese, however, was not the only one responsible for the massacre of Addis Ababa. Fearing a general Ethiopian uprising, Mussolini gave orders for rigorous measures of repression. None of the several thousand imprisoned persons could be released without the Duce's permission. The Amhara were special objects of Mussolini's hatred. Although there was no proof of their guilt, they were thought to be the instigators of the plot, and were therefore to be eliminated. As events proved later, Graziani and his collaborators did not need Mussolini's encouragement to be ruthless. Graziani had learned from

Libya how to handle rebels without pity. In Ethiopia all Amharas who submitted or were captured were executed. Graziani reported that General Tracchia was the most faithful executioner. The repressions and indiscriminate executions did not cease until the third day following the attempt on Graziani's life. By this time the Viceroy had recovered somewhat, and ordered Cortese to stop the killing, but to proceed to the systematic search for and elimination of those who had made the attempt on his life. Eventually, by 12 noon on 21 February all hostilities ceased. The following is the essence of the eyewitness account of what happened in Addis Ababa, by a Hungarian physician, Dr. Ladislas Sava:

In the beginning the Ethiopian people behaved quietly, hiding their outraged feelings as best they could. Then suddenly bombs were thrown towards the table at which Graziani was sitting with his lieutenants. At the moment of the explosion he was hiding under the table, while the other Italian officers had flung themselves to the ground. The assailant was an Eritrean whom the Italians employed as interpreter.

A moment of silence followed, which lasted until the Italians realized that no more bombs were to be feared. Then the shooting was started by Cortese, who fired with his revolver into the group of Ethiopian dignitaries. The Italian Carabinieri followed this example. In a few moments there were more than 300 dead in the courtyard and around the Palace alone. . .

Hardly a single Ethiopian escaped alive from the courtyard. The general massacre there, was particularly senseless and revolting, for the people massed there were a crowd of aged invalids, blind and crippled beggars and poor mothers of little children. The Blackshirts ran through the courtyard, seeking any Ethiopians still alive, and shooting any still breathing. . .

There was blood in the stream, there were dead bodies under and over the Makonnen Bridge. I am not easily moved. A medical man, having dealt with the worst kinds of disease, having gone through the world war with front-line ambulances, should have good nerves; and I have good ones. Yet the things I saw were too much even for my medically-trained and war-hardened nerves. . .

No decent man could tell these things without reluctance, to reveal that they were done by white men like himself. But it is my duty to tell that lorries were covered and dripping with blood, that Blackshirts put a stick from behind between the feet of running black men, in order to throw them to the ground, the more easily to murder them. It is my duty to say that I have seen men's heads split open by truncheons so that their brains gushed out; that murder was accompanied by robbery; that the massacre was so systematic that three places in the town were appointed for the collection of corpses. . .

I have had many Italians in my surgery who told with great pride how many black people they had killed. One of them was very modest, he had killed only two. Others had killed, or pretended to have killed eighty or a hundred. I have heard them praising themselves for having stolen four or five hundred thalers [dollars] in one night. Man-hunting was a much appreciated sport. . .

In a domiciliary search, ostensibly for British hand grenades, a group of Italians entered a humble Ethiopian home near the Makonnen Bridge. Of course they found no hand grenades, but there were thalers, kept for safety in a moneybox, and these were confiscated as a trophy of war, victory and civilization. In the same room they found a picture of the Emperor Haile Selassie. For this symbol the whole family were condemned to death. In a few moments the house was in flames, and with it the members of the family locked inside. Their desperate cries were heard, but the Italians did not move from the place till they had ceased; they were anxious that none should escape the fire.[14]

The indiscriminate firing and butchery aroused complaints from some Italian officials. Although they agreed the criminals had to be punished, they saw no need to transform Addis Ababa into a pyre and submit the defenceless people of the capital to the ire of Italians behaving like barbarians. It is estimated that between 2,000 and 4,000 Ethiopians were imprisoned as a result of the Italian reaction. Of these at least 1,500 were executed on suspicion of connivance with the authors of the attempt, or because they were found in possession of weapons. The number of executions directly related to Graziani's attempt had risen to 5,469 by the end of 1937. About 350 chiefs were sent to Italy and exiled, while between 1,500 to 6,500 Ethiopians found their way to the penal colonies of Danane, Somalia and Nocra in Eritrea, many of them never to return. As for the people in the capital who lost their lives during the Italian reaction, estimates vary from the wild speculation of 30,000 deaths claimed by Ethiopian sources, to a low Italian one of 600. Reputable sources, however, estimate the number of victims of the massacre at about 3,000.

In an attempt to explain the causes of the plot Italian officials tried to gather evidence against foreign nations, and against the Ethiopian Orthodox Church. The authorities investigating the attack suggested that the Anglo-Indian trading company, Mohammed Ali, acting as cover for the British Intelligence Service, had financed the organizers of the scheme, but they could find no evidence. A more serious concern of Fascist officials was the involvement of Great Britain. Graziani was sure, but could not prove, that the attempt was arranged by Patrick Roberts, the British diplomat in Addis Ababa. Not being able to substantiate the involvement of the British Legation either, the Italians tried to connect the plot with the Ethiopian Youth Movement and the Holetta Military School graduates, who, despite the fact that there was no proof of their guilt, were tried Kremlin-style, and quickly executed on charges that they were dangerous and opposed Italian rule.

The Italian authorities were shocked that they had learned nothing of the plot beforehand, and were irritated by the idea that the incident would be exploited by unfriendly nations, to show that the vaunted security in

Ethiopia and the grateful response of the Ethiopians to Italian rule were given the lie in the capital itself. Enrico Cerulli discovered that the main perpetrators of the plot were two Eritreans, Abraham Deboch and Mogas Asgadom. Before the Italian invasion Deboch had studied at the Ras Makkonen Tafari School in Addis Ababa after which he had worked at the Italian Legation, obtaining classified information from the French and British Legations. From the Ethiopian government he passed military secrets to the Italian diplomatic authorities. It is possible that he was a double agent. With the Italian occupation of Ethiopia he was rehired as interpreter by the Italian Political Office. He married Taddesesh Istefanos, related to *Ras* Kassa and *Ras* Desta.[15] Her father and relatives were Patriots, and it is possible that it was her influence that convinced Deboch to plan the assassination of the Viceroy.

Asgadom studied at Menelik Lycee. Described as very intelligent, he was employed as a clerk at the Municipal Land Registry Office. At the time of the Italian occupation he lived at the German Legation and it seems he was supported by Deboch. The two were good friends and often spoke disapprovingly of the Italian apartheid policy, and the cruel treatment meted out to the Ethiopian people. They decided to bring these abuses to an end. Before the attempt Deboch sold his possessions and on 9 February 1937 took his wife to the monastery of Debra Libanos for safety. It is possible that Deboch and Asgadom had a few friends to help them. Reports refer to six persons. The conspirators informed *Bekerod* Let Yebelous Gebre, *Blata* Wolde Emanuel and others of their plan to assassinate Graziani. These chiefs did not trust Asgadom and Deboch because they thought they were Italian spies investigating their opinions. It still remains to be proved if *Abuna* Kirillos received advanced information on the attempt. His decision not to attend the ceremony at the Vice-regal palace was considered incriminating. The excuse for his absence was poor health, but the doctor that Graziani sent him found the *Abuna* in good physical condition. The perpetrators of the attack on the life of Graziani found it easy to leave the Vice-regal palace, using a side door. They escaped first to Debra Lebanos and then joined the Patriot forces of Abebe Aragai and Mesfin Shilleshi. The latter would have nothing to do with them because they were Eritreans and could not be trusted. Deboch and Asgadom made for the Sudan, because a 10,000 Maria Theresa dollar reward on each had been posted. Near Matemma, possibly in error, they were shot by passing Ethiopians.

The attempt on the life of Graziani was made easier by the Italian lack of understanding of Ethiopian customs: the Italians isolated themselves and were unable to penetrate Ethiopian realities because they were bound by prejudices and ignorance. There was also a lack of police service and security, and rampant corruption among the Fascist officials which eventually led to repatriation of 200 high-ranking officials including Guido Cortese. Still unable to justify the large number of casualties, especially when faced with the evidence that the people of Addis Ababa had no part in the plot, the only explanation was to exalt the massacre as a demonstration of Fascist courage! The Ethiopians were reduced to a state of abject terror; to the outside world the idealistic humbug of the Italian civilizing mission had been revealed in all its ruthless materialism and shame. The Italians already had experience in repressing colonial dissidents and Graziani had been one of its main executors. In Cyrenaica alone it is estimated that about 60,000 people perished as a result of ruthless Italian policy. Italian cruelties find historical comparisons in the relentless and pitiless killings durint the German massacres of the Hereros of South-West Africa (Namibia) and of the Matumbi people in the Maji-Maji rebellion in East Africa, and later the horrors committed by the French at Setif in Algeria in 1945, and two years later in Madagascar. The British butchery committed by Lord Kitchener in 1898 on the plains of Ansar left over 1,000 Sudanese dead and 16,000 wounded.[16]

The Massacre of Debra Libanos

Meanwhile the Viceroy directed his wrath on another section of the population, the hermits, wizards, soothsayers and travelling minstrels. In Ethiopia they had an important role in the diffusion of information and in the formation of a national conscience. They therefore represented an obstacle to Italian rule by spreading news about catastrophic events such as the destruction of the Ethiopian people by the Italians, the forthcoming attack on the capital by rebel formations with foreign help, and the return of Haile Selassie with an imposing army. To prevent the people from falling under their spell Graziani ordered all soothsayers to be shot. The result of this needless massacre produced an additional 1,500 victims between March and July 1937. With the new Viceroy, the Duke of Aosta, the soothsayers were left in liberty and the Duke hoped that their predictions would be more optimistic if they received government subsidies. Besides the Addis Ababa mass executions and the suppression of soothsayers, Graziani's vengeance fell on the monks of the monastery of Debra Lebanos for alleged complicity in the attempt to assassinate him. Graziani distrusted the priests from the time when they had first attempted to kill him. On 7 May 1936, while visiting a church in Jijiga, he fell into a six metres-deep well. Graziani almost broke his leg and shoulders and the injury prevented him from occupying Harar personally. The Viceroy never forgot this incident, and although he realized the advantage to be gained from winning the support of the clergy to Italy, he was convinced the Ethiopian Orthodox Church was treacherous and against Italian rule.

Debra Lebanos was the most important monastery in Ethiopia, founded by Tekle Haymanot about 1312. Tekle Haymanot was instrumental in the restoration of the Solomonid dynasty, becoming the *etchege*, or the premier monk of the kingdom, and the counsellor as well as the confessor of the Emperor. Debra Libanos became the recipient of special privileges, and, like the European mediaeval monasteries, was a place of refuge for repentant criminals and the persecuted. Others had always been attracted to the monastery for its reputation as a centre of learning, and the poor and destitute received the benefit of alms and food. To Graziani, the monastery was a centre of hostile propaganda and irredentism. Before it was proved that the actors of the plot had sought refuge at the monastery, Graziani intended to disband the institute of religious studies and prevent the gathering of students.

Meanwhile the Italian authorities were searching for proofs of the participation of monks in the attempt on Graziani's life. It was found that Asgadom had lived in the house of *Abba* Hanna, the confessor of the exiled Emperor, up to September 1936 and that the same house was used by Deboch's wife, Taddesech Istefanos, on 9 February 1937. Other women related to Patriot members lived with Taddesech and also the monk *Abba* Confu, a friend of Asgadom. *Abba* Confu was also a long-standing friend of Tzebatie Takle Georgis, prior of Debra Lebanos, and the confidant of *Ras* Desta. *Abba* Confu, it was alleged, was present on the 9 February when Deboch practised grenade-throwing to ascertain the potential of the bomb. Graziani gave a free hand to the Carabinieri to obtain the information he needed to make it appear that the monks were guilty. Therefore it is hard to assess the objectivity of further accounts that found that *Abba* Confu and *Abba* Tzebatie Takle Georgis, were informed about the massacre of Addis Ababa by Deboch and Asgadom on 22 February 1937, and they allegedly advised the prior and *Abba* Confu to flee. The conclusion, on the basis of prejudiced evidence, was that the monks had participated in the attempt to kill Graziani and that only a few of the 3,000 people at the monastery were aware of the plan to assassinate the Viceroy.

It can be argued that by escaping to safety the monks admitted their involvement. Graziani interpreted the reports of the Carabinieri about the complicity of the monks of Debra Lebanos, as involving the whole religious community. He thus ordered the execution of all monks, including the vice-prior, Gebre Mariam Wolde Ghiorghis. On 21 May, General Pietro Maletti executed 297 monks and 23 other individuals labelled as "suspected accomplices". One hundred and fifty-five deacons and teachers were spared and sent to the churches of Debra Berhan, only to find that on 26 May, many of the deacons were also executed because they were "guilty of complicity". Some 30 school-boys remained alive and were returned to their homes. The other several hundred monks were sent to Danane.

The policy of ruthless repression reached its culmination with the massacre of Debra Lebanos, which represents the last of the great retaliatory measures following the attempt on Graziani's life. It was also meant to destroy the Ethiopian resistance, and compel the Ethiopian Orthodox Church, the chiefs and the intelligentsia to accept their subordinate position vis-à-vis the occupying power.[17] The cruelty and unnecessary bloodshed failed to achieve its objective. Although Graziani and Mussolini believed that the Patriots had been eliminated, by August 1937 the rebellion had spread throughout Amhara and nearby regions, never to cease. This demonstrated how precarious was the method of pacification based only on terror.

The Italian Abuses and Cruelties

The Ethiopians were also subjected to abuses and cruelties at the hands of the very Italian administrators who were supposed to look after the well-being of the people and introduce them to Western civilization. Colonial officials used Ethiopian tribute to construct residences. Political funds assigned for distribution to the people were not used for the purpose intended. The increase in crimes, thefts, plunder and embezzlement demonstrated the lack of moral and ethical standards in the colonial administrator. Captain Corda, Resident of Addis Alem, appropriated to himself funds destined to pay Ethiopians who surrendered their weapons. Captain Furlan, resident of Bako and Colonel Silvio Marengo, commissioner of Ticho did the same. Marengo confiscated five-and-a-half kilogrammes of gold from the Orthodox Church of *Woizero* Shibeshi. His theft caused the population to rebel. In the Governorship of Oromo-Sidamo, the resident of Lekept and the commissioner of Gardulla were found guilty of misuse of state funds. The commissioner of Asosa, Colonel Iacobuzzi, was hoarding gold, while the commissioner of Kaffa appropriated 200,000 lire of military funds for himself. In Amhara, the dishonesty of residents and commissioners reached a level that precipitated rebellion. In the eyes of the Ethiopians greedy colonial officials were no different from their former Ethiopian masters, interested in becoming rich at the expense of the people.

During the campaign against the Patriots, Italian troops and colonial soldiers were allowed to plunder the villages that had helped the Patriots. These raids, instead of winning the local people over to the Italian side, only served to increase the number of the Patriots. It was not until 1940 that the Duke of Aosta officially abolished the principle of war booty and decreed that no authority could seize private property without equivalent compensation.[18]

The most infamous case of cruelty on the part of Italian residents was the mass executions by Captain Corvo, Resident of Bahar Dar. He drowned several Ethiopian chiefs in Lake Tana because they were friends of *Ras* Imru, the former leader of the Ethiopian Army in Gojam. Without any trial these chiefs had a weight tied round their necks and during the night were thrown into the waters of the lake. Corvo was also accused of killing 26 people of the village of Addict after they had surrendered their guns and given food to his soldiers. People of another village at Isora, fearing the same treatment as the people of Addict, refused to surrender their arms. They felt they would die regardless of their co-operation with the Italians and hence it was better to die fighting. They refused to co-operate with Corvo, who withdrew with his troops when outnumbered by the people of Isora. Further, Corvo, was accused of having over-taxed the population, while they had been promised that they would not have to pay tribute.

The rigours of Addict, the cowardly act of Isora, the secret killings by drowning in Lake Tana and the unfair taxation contributed to the state of rebellion in Amhara. Once the flame had started, it became impossible to extinguish. The parents and friends of executed people united together to break the rule of Italy. General Cavallero, in charge of the Italian Armed Forces in AOI, ascribed the uprising to the obedience of armed Ethiopians to dissident chiefs who won the support of the population. The people gave full support to the Patriots, whether from conviction or convenience. Thus, Italian mismanagement produced what the Italians feared most. Because of the incompetence of local administrators, because of their arrogance, because of their abuse of the people, the Ethiopians rebelled. Officials like Farinacci and Teruzzi admitted to Mussolini that the Ethiopians had lost all trust in the Italians.[19]

The Beginning of the Revolt

Up to the summer of 1937 Ethiopian opposition to Italian rule was not co-ordinated. Various groups of Patriots operated on their own. The first attempt to organize guerrilla warfare took place at Gindeberet some time in July 1937. The major opponents of the Italian occupation of Ethiopia were a handful of leaders of various backgrounds and political ideologies. Zaude Asfaw had perhaps the largest following of 100 men. Abebe Aragai could only count on 40 and Mesfin Shilleshi on 30 soldiers. *Dejaz* Auraris was the undisputed leader of the resistance in Menz; he was a Shoan noble and had fought in Amba Aradam with *Ras* Mulugeta, and was by birth, authority, and experience, the natural leader of the Patriots. Abebe Aragai, whom his own men had made *ras*, was well entrenched in Marabatie. Zaude Asfaw, of royal blood, had no political ambitions for himself but wished only to drive the Italians out of Ethiopia. Mesfin Shilleshi, also of royal origin, was very loyal to Haile Selassie. Haile Mariam Mammo was half *shifta* (bandit), and half *ballabat*. He was the only one up to this time to have practiced true guerrilla tactics. *Negga* Haile Selassie swore to fight the Italians to death. *Blata* Tekle Wolde Haewariat was about 40 years old, and was the political theorist, a true Patriot and nationalist. He opposed authority based on birth or tradition. To him the best government for Ethiopia was a republic or a constitutional monarchy.

At the Gindeberet meeting, these resistance chiefs tried to select a commander-in-chief. This proved more difficult than expected. Auraris was given the honorary position as leader although some would have liked Abebe Aragia. Tekle Wolde, the secretary and co-ordinator of the Patriotic resistance, was voted in by full agreement. It seems, however, that when the Patriot leaders left Gindeberet there was no consensus on who the commander was, and thus the attempt to co-ordinate the resistance movement failed. Forced to disband to avoid becoming a target of the Italian Air Force and Italian troops who had heard about their meeting, Tekle, Mesfin, and Zaude went toward Gore to establish contact with the Sudan. Haile Mariam, Abebe and Auraris moved to the mountains of Menz and Ankober. There was no co-ordination among the Patriots except in that they all resorted to guerrilla warfare. The Ethiopians had learned their lessons during the Italo-Ethiopian War when their feudal leaders insisted on pitched battles against the Italian armies equipped with modern weapons. The Patriots instead resorted to the strategy of hit-and-run, and employed war of attrition tactics that proved to be effective.

In August 1937, the Italian positions were attacked in different regions at about the same time to the point that the Italians feared a possible co-ordinated Patriot effort to dislodge them. Debra Tabor, Bahar Dar, Bicenna, Burie, Dembeccia, Debra Markos, Enjebara, and Dangila were under Ethiopian attack. From these locations guerrilla warfare spread to other areas of Gaint, Belesa, Wolkait, Tzeggede, Ermacho, and Quoram. Suddenly, the Governorship of Amhara was the scene of spontaneous rebellion led by little-known local chiefs. One among them was *Dejaz* Mangasha Jamberie, one of the most powerful in Gojam.[20]

Stalemate in Patriotic Activities

The Duke of Aosta insisted on respect for private property and justice, but the military in charge of suppressing the rebellion paid only lip-service to the Viceroy's promises. For the whole of 1938 and part of 1939 the army under the new Commander-in-Chief, General Ugo Cavallero, was engaged in a systematic plan to reconquer the lost provinces, using the "Graziani method". It is still difficult to reconstruct the events of Ethiopian resistance. To impress Mussolini and justify his action in Ethiopia, Cavallero composed a lengthy self-serving report. At about the same time Haile Selassie wrote of the extent of the rebellion and about its leaders. Generally speaking, according to Haile Selassie, north and central Ethiopia were partially lost to Italian rule. In Gojam, the most prominent leaders were *Dejaz* Mangasha Jamberie, *Dejaz* Mesfin Berzabhil, *Dejaz* Belayi Zellecke, and *Ras* Hailu Bellew. In the region of Begemder and Semien the Patriots were under the command of *Dejaz* Negash Wubshet, *Dejaz* Hagos Tessemma, *Fitaurari* Mesfin Redda, *Dejaz* Belaye Makkonen and *Lij* Aberra Berhanu. In Shoa, *Dejaz* Fikre Mariam, *Ras* Mesfin Shilleshi, and *Ras* Gerarsu on several occasions threatened the security of Addis Ababa.

A more detailed account of the rebellion in Ethiopia is given by Cavallero. According to his report Harar, Somalia and Eritrea were peaceful. In Tigre there was some armed opposition, but Shoa and Amhara were in open rebellion. In Oromo-Sidamo a few secondary centres of rebellion were reported, but of little concern. The people were loyal to the rebels, either out of conviction or out of necessity. Those who were in possession of arms could increase the number of the rebels, which in some areas reached several thousands. In the territory of western Shoa the zone between the Addis Ababa-Lekept and Addis Ababa-Jimma roads, and the Nile was controlled by the Patriots who had a couple of thousand rifles and were led by *Fitaurari* Zaude Asfaw, *Dejaz* Desta Iscitie, *Fitaurari* Olana and *Ras* Gerarsu Duki. The various chiefs were not in contact with one another and did not join together to fight the Italians because of territorial rivalries among them. North-eastern Shoa contained an irreducible nest of rebels, mostly concentrated in the zone between Ankober and the River Cassam. There were also other groups in the region of Selale, Menz and Marabatie. This area was of great strategic and political importance. The elimination of the rebels of Ankober was a military necessity because they could cut communications between the capital and Eritrea and Djibouti. The main leaders were Abebe Aragai, Haile Mariam Mammo and *Fitaurari* Auraris, commanding 3–4,000 armed men, but supported by the peasants. In the territory of Amhara, including the regions of Gojam, Begemder and Gaint, the rebellion had reached critical proportions. Since 15 August 1937, Italian troops had been attacked, besieged, destroyed and captured by the various Patriot formations on several occasions. The Italian government, unable to meet the challenge, had withdrawn its residents. The Ethiopian Patriots, encouraged by military success, became bolder.

In the sector north of Lake Tana, including Armacho, and Tzeggede, *Fitaurari* Ubne Tessemma and *Fitaurari* Mesfin had more than 2,000 rifles and successfully cut communications on the highway between Gondar and Asmara. Likewise, the area of Belesa, east of Lake Tana, as well as the Ebbenat-Adarseg-Mechetoa triangle was heavily populated with rebels led by *Dejaz* Gebre. In Gaint and Debra Tabor the rebels were estimated to number 2,000 under the leadership of *Lij* Yohannes, a natural son of former Emperor *Lij* Yasu. In Gojam, the Patriots were well-protected by the Nile and could not be reached for lack of roads. Because the Gojami people were fierce and independent in spirit their region was the most difficult to govern. Meccia and Densa were the areas where *Dejaz* Mangasha had 3,000 men under arms; *Dejaz* Negash operated with his thousand Patriots in Damot, and in eastern Gojam, *Dejaz* Belai Zelleke with his men guarded the Nile, preventing the Italians from crossing the river. In Oromo-Sidamo, the Patriots were mostly concentrated in Guraghe, around Mount Gibotti. Their leader, *Ras* Gerarsu with his thousand or so men harassed the Addis-Ababa-Jimma road. So did *Fitaurari* Taffera along the Addis Ababa-Lekept road. Minor groups also operated in Limmu and Jimma-Guenet. In all there were an estimated 2,000 men armed with rifles.

The military plan proposed by Cavallero to extend Italian rule in Ethiopia called for a full-scale military campaign in Gojam. To penetrate that vast country it was necessary to build roads, the most visible achievement of the Italian presence in Ethiopia. Cavallero built a road connecting Addis Ababa-Nile- (Safarak)-Debra Markos-Enjabara-Bahar Dar-Gondar and another network joining Dessie-Debra Tabor-Gondar. He further built a chain of 73 forts along the boundaries of Gojam to prevent the spread of the rebellion to other territories or Patriots from other regions seeking sanctuary in Gojam. The first full-scale attack against the Patriots of Amhara was launched between mid-March of 1938 and the end of May 1938. Cavallero was reported to have killed 2,500–5,000 Patriots in battle, and claimed to have penetrated and re-established Italian authority in Cafta, Armacho, Welkait, Begemder, Tzeggede, Fagulta, and Densa, and to have seen the people flocking to the forts to submit to Italian authority. He did not realize, however, that this was but a sign of deference, which the people paid to ingratiate themselves with the stronger master, but the moment the Italian troops left the area the local inhabitants joined the Patriots again.

Another region of primary importance was Ankober. Twelve battalions were sent "to clean up" and destroy any armed opposition. The military action had became a real "man-hunt". By the end of June 1938 Cavallero reported that Abebe Aragai had not been captured, but over 2,000 of his followers had died. In the following campaign against Abebe Aragai in the autumn of 1938 in spite of being constantly hunted and encircled, Abebe was able to escape from Ankober to his homeland in Worana-Wain, Marabatie. The Patriots of *Fitaurari* Auraris dispersed only to combine their forces at a later date. By the end of 1938 many of the Patriots of north-eastern Shoa were killed or scattered, but the rebellion was not overcome. Likewise the Patriot forces in Amhara in the second half of 1938 were again hard-pressed by the advancing Italian army which was usually able to inflict losses on the rebels but never to defeat them completely.

By 1939, there was a stalemate in Patriot activities. The Italians had failed to crush the Patriots, who on the other hand found themselves unable to dislodge the invaders from their heavily fortified positions. They had lost their impetus, and ceased to attack Italian forts and communications. They had made the mistake of believing in a nationwide rebellion, and of undertaking offensive operations for which they did not have the armaments, On the other hand the Italians availed themselves of the methods of colonial repression tried out in Libya, and the use of up-to-date military hardware, including radio, airplanes, tanks, and poison gas. They encircled the Patriots, pursued and destroyed them by land and from the air. Patriots wary of Italian reprisals first thought to protect their family and land, becoming reluctant to harass the Italians for fear of reprisals. A more important reason for the Ethiopian relaxation was that after years of warfare, food had become scarce and the peasants were no longer disposed to feed the Patriots. Chiefs were awaiting more favourable times. Owing to their underground communication system with the Emperor and other exiles, they anticipated that Italy would enter the war in Europe and, therefore, be unable to send military reinforcements to Ethiopia. At that time the Ethiopians would resume attacking and besieging Italian fortifications and compel them to surrender. Reasons of logistics and international political awareness forced the Ethiopians to change their tactics. However, up to the Italian entry into the Second World War the Patriotic movement controlled Amhara and was the strongest in Gojam, Armacho, Begemder, and parts of Shoa.[21]

Negotiations for the Submission of Abebe Aragai

During this lull in Patriotic activities, and with the uncertainty of international events, the Duke of Aosta and General Guglielmo Nasi, newly nominated Vice-Governor-General, opened negotiations with a number of Patriot leaders. Abebe Aragai was the most important leader of the Ethiopian rebellion. If he could be convinced to submit, his example would persuade other resistance leaders to come to terms with the Italians. Abebe Aragai, born in 1904, was the son of *Afanegus* Aragai and of Askale Gobene, daughter of *Ras* Gobene, an Oromo general who helped Menelik's conquest of southern Ethiopia. After receiving private education he joined the imperial bodyguard and in 1935 became chief of the police of Addis Ababa. When Haile Selassie left for England in 1936, he was supposed to keep the city calm, but on the approach of the Italian troops he destroyed military supplies and withdrew to Entoto. After hearing of the death of the Kassa brothers he became distrustful of the Italians, realizing that surrender or not would equally mean death. At first, Abebe's aim was not to liberate Ethiopia but avoid capture. He took refuge in Jeru, Waya and Ankober and in spite of pressures from many other dissatisfied Ethiopians to become their leader, he refused. On witnessing the crimes committed against his people following the attempt on Graziani's life in 1937 and the Italian use of Azebu and Araya Oromo against the people of Shoa whom they plundered and physically emasculated, he accepted to lead his people in revolt. He organized his troops in Ankober, Menz, Marabatie and Gindeberet, a territory which extended from the Nile to the Cassam River.

Abebe's following was estimated anywhere from a few dozen to 30,000. His presence in Shoa was a continuous threat to Italian rule and the capital. But a large body of men was also a liability. Abebe could not feed them and could not always prevent harassment by the Italian troops. With time, Abebe's men began to desert him because of poverty and famine. It was easy for the Italians to bribe Abebe's men. In order to give his men respite and new provisions, Abebe agreed to open negotiations with Graziani in mid-1937. These talks were not sincere on either side. Abebe knew he would be killed if he surrendered, but the Italians sent him 4,000 kilos of *teff* (wheat flour), and ammunition to lure him to submit. Furthermore, in the negotiations Abebe's men were able to spy and report on the Italian military situation. On 17 May 1937 Graziani promised Abebe and his followers that their lives would be spared on condition that they surrendered. In order to gain time, Abebe replied to Graziani's letter complaining that in spite of a promise of peace he was harassed by Italian troops and airplanes. In September 1937 Graziani restated to Abebe his previous offer, adding a salary and respect for his property. On 18 September, however, Abebe punished the people of Fiche for submitting to the Italians, thereby breaking the armistice.

In May 1938, Sebastiano Castagna was sent to negotiate between Abebe and the Duke of Aosta. Castagna reported that while originally the Patriots were reacting to Italian misgovernment, with the arrival of the Duke of Aosta there was some inclination toward negotiation. Another opportunity for stipulating peace with Abebe presented itself in August 1938 when Major Domenico Lucchetti was instructed by General Nasi to create a residence at Minjar, a region under the influence of Abebe Aragai. Lucchetti received a letter from Abebe requesting permission for the passage of a number of women and children to go to Addis Ababa, because they were too tired and could no longer follow him. The good treatment of these persons inspired other requests. For example, Abebe Aragai's son, Daniel, was allowed to study at the Catholic mission in Addis Ababa. In November 1938 he was transferred to Minjar to meet his father.[22] On 8 October Lucchetti went to Abebe's camp at Meheber Bekur, Mosabit. At this meeting both sides agreed:

1. To stop military activities in the regions where Abebe had authority;
2. To permit the transit of Aregai's men into eastern Shoa;
3. To encourage Abebe's chiefs to visit Addis Ababa to witness for themselves what the Italians had done for Ethiopia;
4. To disarm Abebe's men gradually and employ the chiefs as advisers to residents.
5. To give food to Abebe's followers.

As a result of these *pour-parlers* there was a truce up to March 1940. The Addis Ababa-Dessie road controlled by the guerrilla forces of Abebe Aragai was open to transit night and day without molestation and 3,000 of Abebe's men were used as irregular colonial troops. Abebe's influential chiefs also decided to give up fighting and surrendered. Among them were *Dejaz* Ghiorghis Mangasha Wassen, the most important personality, representing the traditional chiefs, and his nephew *Lij* Gebre Christos. With them ten subchiefs and 500 men also submitted. Other personalities like *Fitaurari* Kebbede Kassa and *Dejaz* Mondefru Gerbi Bulto took the oath of allegiance before residents in Bulga and Debra Berhan.

On their part the Italians kept the agreements. They were hoping to have the submission of Abebe in early 1940 on the occasion of Teruzzi's visit to Addis Ababa. To convince the *ras* of Italian good intentions the Duke of Aosta requested 50 million lire for the economic reconstruction of Shoa ravaged by three years of continuous warfare. With public works, subsidies and social services, it was hoped to attract the people of Shoa toward Italy and remove mistrust of the Italians because of their past ruthless policy. No progress was made on disarmament, however. Some chiefs suggested spinning out talks for submission until the international situation was clarified with the hope of resuming the fighting.[23] A dispatch from the Italian Consul at Djibouti, Arnò, gave information that French agents had sent letter to convince Abebe not to submit to Italy. The news was alarming enough to create suspicion. Abebe confirmed to Lucchetti that he had received communications from Djibouti. It is possible that Abebe volunteered the information to show his sincerity about reaching a compromise with the Italians or to bargain for better terms. Nevertheless Abebe's contacts with Djibouti kept him well-informed about events in Europe and he received correspondence regularly from Haile Selassie.

Meanwhile the work of pacification was made more difficult by radical Fascists. General Bonaccorsi formed a voluntary army unit to attack Abebe Aragai by surprise. It was also discovered that while the Italian colonial government was negotiating peace terms with Abebe, on the other side a certain De Luca, an arms dealer, had received a mission from high-ranking Italian personalities to kill Abebe. The most serious incident, however, was the massacre of a cousin of Abebe, *Kenazmatch* Admasse together with *Balambarà* Timtime and 40 men at Jeru, near Ankober. The incident was provoked by the lack of common sense of Lieutenant Angelo Sabatini. The Italians paid blood money for the people killed, but once more Italian justice was inadequate. Sabatini was allowed free to roam in the same region. The massacre and other attempts at preventing the submission of Abebe and his followers did not reassure the Ethiopians of the Italians' good intentions, which further delayed the submission of Abebe Aragai. It is difficult to establish whether Abebe ever intended to give up fighting the Italians. According to Lucchetti, Abebe Aragai had agreed to submit. The date for the oath of allegiance was postponed to 12 February 1940 to take place in Ankober. The Juru massacre delayed taking the oath before Nasi until 14 March. Meanwhile, Abebe requested that his authority be recognized over Shoa except for Addis Ababa. Although in principle Abebe's request could have been considered favourably, the Viceroy had no authority to grant the privilege. Because of unacceptable requests the Italians who at first were sure of Abebe's submission became pessimistic and proceeded with suspicion.

To ensure that the Patriots did not escape to other regions, over 20 battalions were sent to eastern Shoa. On 14 March Abebe refused to submit because General Nasi, before whom he would take the oath, was not present. Ethiopian accounts reveal that Abebe never intended to submit, but opened negotiations to gain time, and to capture General Nasi on 14 March. Hostilities did not break out immediately; instead a public proclamation was made to show the people the contrast between crimes committed in the past and what the government had done for Abebe Aragai, and that it respected the life and property of anyone willing to submit.

Abebe Aragai did not submit, but he gained time to rebuild his forces, and become better armed and fed. During the cease-fire period the Italians realized that the Patriotic movement involved all Shoa. It offered an opportunity to assess how the chiefs viewed the Italians, to listen to their grievances to see if they would be for or against the Italians; some of them submitted, thus weakening Abebe's forces. It also afforded an opportunity to the Italians to be better known by the common people. However, after Italy entered the Second World War, the latent resistance suddenly revived with British aid.[24]

The Results of Four Years of Opposition

At first the Ethiopians were divided among themselves on the position to take toward the Italians. The people of southern Ethiopia, exploited by the Amhara, were favourable to European rule, but not necessarily Italian rule. They would have preferred a British mandate, which explains their ambivalence in dealing with the Italians. With the rapid Italian advance and the influence of Catholic missionaries, the people submitted to the new conquerors with reservations. In the north the Tigreans and Gojami resented the centralizing authority of Addis Ababa. Influenced by years of Italian propaganda they had come to believe that the Italian government would bring them prosperity. Otherwise the people were bewildered by the mechanized war material the Italians used, and were astonished at the modern ways the Italians introduced. Conversely, the aristocracy and the church felt threatened by the Italians, and therefore opposed Italian rule. Gradually, however, the great *rases* were either killed, or they submitted or went into exile. A few chiefs of secondary rank remained to offer military leadership to the resistance movement, but their cause was practically hopeless, because they were surrounded by apathetic and opportunistic people who wanted to see what benefits they could get from the Italian government. This may explain the lack of opposition to the Italians at first, and the failure of the attack against Addis Ababa in 1936 led by the Kassa brothers. The Italians committed a political blunder in killing the Kassa brothers. At first the people were stunned at Italian cruelty and lack of honour and felt powerless before colonial power and severity, because they no longer had a noble of stature to lead and inspire them to war for the defence of the fatherland.

The surrender of *Ras* Imru and the execution of *Ras* Desta gave a further blow to Ethiopian patriotism. Resistance was co-ordinated by the young, educated Ethiopians such as the Holetta graduates or the Young Ethiopians, who realized the true meaning of colonial subjection. And yet they would have to come to terms with the colonial rulers if their programme for the progress of Ethiopia was to be accepted by the Italians. They thought of a mandate system in which the traditional authorities and the educated class could be used in the task of administration. Fascist racial policy and ignorance of local conditions by government officials severed the only possible ties of co-operation. The Italians reasoned that a proud and warlike people like the Ethiopians would not accept foreign rule without the display of force and authority. Thus ruthless Italian policy, shown in the retaliations against innocent and defenceless Ethiopians, following the attempt on Graziani's life, united the Ethiopians into a common bond to free the fatherland from foreign usurpation.

The Patriots received help and information from neighbouring British and French colonies. This enabled them to keep abreast of the international situation. The hope of the forthcoming return of Haile Selassie kept their resistance alive. After the Munich conference in 1938, however, when the hopes for a European war had failed, the Ethiopian Patriots were discouraged, short of weapons and the people's support, and they were reducing their attacks on the Italians. This was the time when the new administration of the Empire, under the Duke of Aosta and Nasi, negotiated for the submission of a number of Ethiopian Patriot leaders and of Abebe Aragai, as the Italian authorities in Europe attempted to convince Haile Selassie and Asfaw Wassen to submit to the Italian government. The negotiations have many similiarities, which explain the Ethiopian way of thinking. The Ethiopians found occasion to postpone to the last moment the conclusion of their submission. All this seems to indicate that their strategy was to gain time. Historically, in dealing with Europeans, Ethiopian chiefs were concerned with the maintenance and extension of their own power in obtaining advanced military technology and political support and increasing their own prestige. Some chiefs entertained contacts with the Italians with a view to pursuing these aims. This contention is borne out, in post-Second World War years, by the attitude of the Ethiopian Patriot leaders who became conservative defenders of the old way of political life, in order to preserve their prerogatives, frustrating attempts at modernizing Ethiopia.[25]

In conclusion, opposition to Italy was the result of Graziani's and his collaborators' ruthless attempts at subduing the people, and a lack of appreciation of the Ethiopian heritage and traditions. The Ethiopians reacted by challenging the power of Italy for the second time since Adowa. They shattered Italian plans to make Ethiopia the hope of millions of Italian migrants, solve Italy's chronic food and raw material deficit, make Ethiopia a showcase of Fascist imperialism, and use it as a base for further export into Africa of Fascism. Still to be solved is the problem as to whether those who submitted did so out of deference, for opportunistic reasons, or in order to further the cause of their fatherland. All these possibilities were present, but deep down the Ethiopians like any other people resented being under a foreign yoke. Nonetheless, the Ethiopian antagonism to the Italians sharpened their nationalistic feeling, broke down regional barriers, and made Ethiopia a stronger nation than before. The Italian crimes made good propaganda items, convincing the Ethiopian people to unite and fight the common enemy, although some were actually committing acts of lawlessness, in the name of nationalism which, in the overall programme to weaken the enemy, were considered acts of heroism.

Notes

1. MAI/CAB 287/1 Duke of Aosta to Teruzzi, 4 April 1938; MAI/GAB 278 Teruzzi to Duce, January 1940; Ibid., Lessona to Duce, 20 April 1937; MAI/AS 181/9-42 Badoglio to all Military Commands, 9 January 1936; Pankhurst *Italy's War Crimes in Ethiopia*; FO 401/1936/XXVIII/62 Erskine to Eden, 5 September 1936; ACS/RG 39 Graziani to MAI, 14

November 1937; MAI/GAB 261/83 Lessona to P. Biroli, 10 September 1937; FO 401/1937/XXIX/150 Helm to Eden, 9 October 1937; *La Chronique* (Damascus), 5 April 1939; FO 401/1936/XXVIII Widows to FO, 27 October 1936; *Gli Annali dell'Africa Italiana* 3(1940), p. 141; *Great Britain and the East*, June 1940; MAI/GAB 257/58 MAI: Military Office, Patriot Forces 1937-1938; MAI/GAB 265/70 Farinacci to Duce, 25 December 1938; Augenti and Martino, *Il Dramma di Graziani*, p. 175; Di Lauro, *Le Terre del Lago Tana*, p. 21; Di Lauro, *Come Abbiamo Difeso l'Impero*, p. 301-3.

2. ACS/RG 40/2 Graziani to De Bono, 20 July 1937; ACS/MA AOI/ Relazioni con Graziani, Graziani to MAI, 20 June 1937; MAI/AS 181/59/294 Memo for the Minister of Africa, 20 May 1938; *Paris-Soir*, 15 January 1939; ACS/RG 12 Badoglio to MAI, 29 February 1936; MAI/GAB 11 Mussolini to Badoglio, 16 January 1936; FO 401/1936/XXVIII/38-40-83 Erskine to Eden, 17 July and 1 October 1936; League of Nations: C. 193. M104, 1938. VII *Question de Consequences Decoulant de la Situation Actuelle en Ethiopie*, 13 May 1938; FO 401/1937/XXIX/154 Lambert: Notes on the Situation in Ethiopia, 19 November 1937; Italy: Ministero Della Difesa, Ufficio Storico, *La Guerra in AOI*, p. 26; MAI/GAB 286 Commission for the Supreme Defence: Military Organization of Italian Overseas Territories, February 1940; Gebru Tareke "Peasant Resistance in Ethiopia", p. 87.

3. MAI/GAB 151/XI Moreno to MAI/EF 24 July 1940; Ibid., Duke of Aosta to MAI, 7 September 1939; MAI/GAB 306/III-4 Lessona to Graziani, 2 September 1936; ACS/RG 57 Hazon: Memo for the Viceroy, October 1937; MAI/GAB 151/IX Graziani to MAI, 28 June 1937; Hole, *The Making of the Rhodesia*, pp. 283, 340-53; Sykes, *With Plumer in Matabeleland*, p. 91; Del Boca, *The Ethiopian War*, p. 122; FO 401/1936/ XXVIII Erskine to Eden, October 1936; MAI/AS 181/44-210 Graziani to MAI, 5 July 1936; MAI/GAB 285 Duke of Aosta: Minutes of the IV and V Meetings of the Governors, May-October-December 1939.

4. MAI/GAB 282 MAI: Military Office: Memo for Mussolini on the Military Situation in Ethiopia, March 1940; MAI/AS 181/37-176 Meravigna: Proclamation No. 16 to the people of Axum, 20 December 1935; ACS/RG 40 Graziani to MAI, 7 September 1937; MAI/309/7 Duke of Aosta to MAI, 4 January 1938; MAI/AS 181/43-205 MAI Military Office: Memo for the Minister of Africa, April 1940; ACS/EB Diary 36, 24 September 1930; ACS/ RG 15 Graziani to MAI, 7 November 1937; Canevari, *La Guerra Italiana*, II, p. 375; Duke of Aosta Diary in *Gente*, 12 March 1969; MAI/GAB 73/XI-II Nasi: Semestral Report on AOI, July 1939.

5. *Times of India* (Bombay), 16 January 1937; *St. Faller Tagblatt* (Germany), 13 January 1939; *Il Giornale* (Tunis), 14 March 1939, *L'Ordre* (Paris), 9-15 August 1939; *Manchester Guardian*, 31 December 1938; ACS/ MM 4/9 Press Release, 22 October 1936; ACS/RG 14 Graziani to the Governors, 2 February 1937; MAI/GAB 241/16 Meregazzi to Teruzzi, 29 May 1938; *Corriere dell'Impero*, 16 May 1940; ACS/INT-P 9/B-97/14 Italian Public opinion, 9-11 July 1936; Hargreaves, "West African States and the European Conquest" and Ranger "African Reactions to the Imposition of Colonial Rule in East and Central Africa" in Gann and Duignan, *The History of Politics of Colonialism, 1870-1914*, I, pp. 199-216, 293-324.

6. ACS/RG 27 Graziani to MAI, 10 June 1936; FO 401/1936/XXVI/ 192 Erskine to Eden, 30 May 1936; ACS/RG 20 Erskine: Proclamation to

the People of Ethiopia, 30 May 1936; FO 401/1936/XXVIII/66 Eden to Secretary of the League of Nations, 26 September 1936; Mokler, *Il Mito dell'Impero*, p.187-95; Gilks, *The Dying Lion*, pp. 187-95, 202-5; Wondimneh Tilahun, *Egypt's Imperial Aspirations*; ACS/RG Graziani to Duce, 24 October 1936; ACS/RG 18 *Dejaz* Hapte Mariam to Italian Authorities, 9 July 1936; FO 401/1936/XXVIII/83 Erskine to Eden 5 September and 1 October 1936; MAI/GAB 307/Bis Mussolini to Graziani, 13 May 1936; Ethiopia: Ministry of Justice, *Documents on Italian War Crimes*; Ethiopia: Press and Information Service, *La Civilisation de l'Italie Fasciste en Ethiopie*.

7. Mokler, *Il Mito*, pp. 175-84; Salome Gebre Egziaber "The Ethiopian Patriots 1936-1941", pp. 70 ff; ACS/RG 27 Tracchia: Report on the conquest of Shoa, 5 May 1936; MAI/AS 181/44-210 Graziani to MAI, 19 July 1936; Pankhurst, "The Ethiopian Patriots: The Lone Struggle", p. 42; FO 401/1937/XXIX/2-3 Roberts to Eden, 11 January 1937; ACS/RG 35 Graziani to Teruzzi, 22 December 1937; MAI/AS 181/44-210 Graziani to MAI, 28 July 1936; FO 401/1936/XXVIII/94 Widdows: Military Situation in East Africa, 9 October 1936; Augenti & Martino, *Il Dramma di Graziani*, p. 174; Del Boca, *The Ethiopian War*, pp. 212; FO 401/1937/XXIX/2 Roberts to Eden, 16 December 1936; ACS/RG 56 Italian Armed Forces in Addis Ababa, 7 July 1936; ACS/RG 19 Lerici: Food and Military Supply in Addis Ababa, 6 July 1936; *Natal Advertiser*, 26 September 1936.

8. ACS/RG 13 Graziani to MAI 5 May, 7, 8, 9, 10, 13, 29 July 1936; MAI/GAB 307/Bis Lessona to Duce 10 October 1936; ACS/RG 30/3 Graziani to Lessona, 10 October 1936; Ibid., Mussolini to Graziani, 11 October 1936.

9. Poggiali, *Diario AOI*, p. 74-9; 401/1936/XXVIII/55 Roberts to Eden, 25 August 1936; ACS/RG 35 Graziani to MAI, 29 July 1936; ACS/RG 23 P. Biroli to Graziani, 23 June, 31 July, 14, 30 October and 13 November 1936; Ibid., Graziani to MAI, 7 July 1936; MAI/AS 181/44-210 Graziani to MAI, 7, 14 September 1936; Salome Gebre, "Ethiopian Patriots, pp. 70-2; ACS/RG Graziani to MAI, 30 September 1936; Ibid., Princivalle to Viceroy, 9 September 1936; FO 401/1936/XXVIII/54 Roberts to Eden, 25 August 1936; Lessona, *Memorie*, p. 305; Mokler, *Il Mito*, pp. 210-13; Salome Gebre, "Ethiopian Patriots", p. 72; ACS/RG 12 Mussolini to Badoglio, 5 May, 22 June 1936; ACS/RG 13 Graziani to Lessona, 27 October 1936; Ibid., Graziani to Gallina, 22 October 1936; ACS/RG 14 Graziani to Tracchia, 1 January 1937; MAI/GAB 307/Bis Lessona to Mussolini, 16 October 1936; ACS/RG 13 Graziani to MAI, 19 October 1936.

10. MAI/AS 181/44-210 Graziani to MAI, 16 September 1936; ACS/RG 26 Graziani to Tracchia, 22 December 1936 and 27 January 1937; Sbacchi, "Legacy of Bitterness".

11. FO 401/1937/XXIX/55-58, 66 Records of Leading Personalities in Abyssinia, 18 March 1937; ACS/RG 19 Ras Desta Damtu, n.d; Mokler, *Il Mito*, pp. 200-2, 205-6, 213-15; ACS/14 Graziani to MAI, 25 January 1937; Ibid., Nasi to Graziani, 25 January 1937; Ibid., Graziani to Geloso, 21 January 1937; Ibid., Graziani to MAI, 30 December 1936; ACS/13 Tucci to Geloso, 4 December 1936; ACS/RG 56 Desta Damtu to Graziani, 30 December 1936; ACS/RG 23 Graziani to MAI, 27 December 1936; ACS/RG 26 Graziani to MAI, 4 December 1936.

12. ACS/RG 23 Graziani to Ras Desta, 18 December 1936; ACS/RG

13 Geloso to GGAOI, 15 December 1936; ACS/RG 23 Castagna: Report on the Negotiations for the Submissions of Ras Desta, 16 October 1937; Pegolotti, "Un Italiano alla Corte di Menelik", pp. 79-85; Sbacchi, "Italy and the Treatment of the Ethiopian Aristocracy, 1937-1940", pp. 209-41; FO 401/1937/XXIX/10 Roberts to Eden, 8 January 1937; ACS/RG 14 Geloso to Viceroy, 3 September 1937; ACS/RG 24 Geloso: Report on the Conquest of Borana and Sidamo, 23 April 1939; ACS/RG 13 Geloso to Viceroy, 4, 8 December 1936; ACS/RG 14 Tucci to Geloso, 16 January 1937; ACS/RG 26 Geloso to GGAOI and Tucci to Geloso, 1, 16 January 1937; ACS/RG 21 Gallina to Nasi, 22 December 1936; ACS/RG 26 Geloso to Army Headquarters, 16 January 1937; Geloso to GGAOI, 22 January 1937; Ibid., Nasi to Viceroy 23 January 1937.

   13. FO 401/1936/XXVI/90 Drummond to Eden, 3 February 1936; ACS/RG 26 Castagna to Graziani, n.d. (end of December 1936); MAI/GAB 258/III-4 Graziani to MAI, 31 December 1936; ACS/RG 23 Graziani to Lessona, 31 December 1936; Ibid., Lessona to Graziani, 4 January 1936; MAI/AS 181/45-214 Graziani to Duce, 24 February 1937; ACS/RG 64/215 Geloso: Report on the Campaign Against *Ras* Desta, 1937; ACS/RG 24 Nasi: Report on the Military Campaign Against *Ras* Desta, Bejene Merid and Gabre Mariam, 1937; ACS/CP 94/1 Italian Embassy in Prague: Summary of the Czechoslovakian Press, 27 February 1937; MAI/GAB 72/XI-VIII Gariboldi to MAI, 25 August 1937; ACS/RG 14 Gallina to GGAOI, 25 February 1937.

   14. Salome Gebre, "Ethiopian Patriots", p. 81; ACS/INT-P 9/B 97/14 Intercepted communication from Vatican City, 6 March 1937; Mokler, *Il Mito*, pp. 219-28; ACS/RG 27 Bedei: List of Wounded of, 19 February 1937; FO 401/1937/XXIX/32 Bond to Eden, 1 March 1937. Pegolotti, "L'Attentato a Graziani", pp. 94-101; Rochat, "L'Attentato a Graziani", pp. 18 ff.; ACS/RG 39/59 Graziani to MAI, 28 February 1937; MAI/GAB 258/III Memorandum for the Minister of Africa, n.d. (April 1937); ACS/RG 33 D'Alessandro to GGAOI, 21 February 1937; Ibid., Graziani to MAI, 22 February 1937; Del Boca, *The Ethiopian War*, pp. 221-6; Pankhurst, "The Ethiopian Patriots", pp. 44-6; Ethiopia: *Documents on Italian Crimes*, II, pp. 6-7; Pegolotti, "L'Attentato", p. 100; Weerts, "The Late Mr. Antoinin Besse", p. 176; FO 401/1937/XXIX/25 Drummond to Eden, 12 March 1937; Augenti & Martino, *Il Dramma*, p. 176; Interview with A. Lessona, 27 October 1972; Interview with E. Spada, 5 January 1973; A. Pittalunga to W. T. Amatruda 25 October 1975. The author is indebted to Amatruda for this communication; ACS/INT-P 9/B-97/14 Intercepted letter of a Black Shirt from Gorizia, 30 April 1937; MAI/GAB 258/III-7 Graziani to Duce, 22 February 1937; ACS/RG 33 Lessona to the Governors of AOI, 19 February 1937; Ibid., Graziani to Lessona, 21 February 1937; ACS/EB Diary 35, 21 March 1930; ACS/RG 33 Mussolini to Graziani, 20, 21 February 1937; Ibid., Mazzi to the Secretary of the Fascity Party, 21 February 1937; Pankhurst, *Italy's War Crimes*, pp. 9-21.

   15. ACS/RG 30/5 Farese to Mussolini, December 1937; MAI/GAB 258/III Memo for the Minister of Africa, April 1937; MAI/AS 181/43-205 Statistics of Italian and Rebel Losses Between 6 May 1936 and 10 June 1940; FO 401/1937/XXIX/32-35 Bond to Eden, 1 March 1937; Del Boca, *The Ethiopian War*, p. 223; ACS/RG 32/29 Lessona to Graziani, 20 March

1937; FO 401/1937/XXIX/36 Stonehewer-Bird to Eden, 1 and 9 March 1937; Poggiali, *Diario*, p. 189; ACS/RG 56 Radaelli: Biography of Abraham Deboch and Mogos Asgadom, 18 October 1937; MAI/POL 83/245 Cerulli: Report on a Visit to Asinara, 25 April 1937.

16. Del Boca, *The Ethiopian War*, p. 226; Salome Gebre, "Ethiopian Patriots", p. 81; Poggiali, *Diario*, p. 180; Rochat, "L'attentato", p. 22-3; FO 401/1937/XXIX/35 Bond to Eden, 1 March 1937; Rochat, *Il Colonialismo Italiano*, pp. 99-101, 126-8; Zaghi, *L'Africa nella Coscienza Europea*, p. 415; Mannoni, *Psychologie de la Colonisation*, pp. 90-1; Collins, *The Southern Sudan*, pp. 171-2; *The Contemporary Review*, January 1899.

17. MAI/GAB 258/III-7 Graziani to Lessona, 20 March 1937; Ethiopia, *La Civilisation*, I, pp. 59-62, 72-5, 80-3, 128, 152-3; Rochat, "L'Attentato", pp. 32-6; Pankhurst, "The Ethiopian Patriots", p. 48; ACS/RG 12 Graziani to Meregazzi, 16 May 1936; Ibid., Graziani to Badoglio, 8 May 1936; Ullendorff, *The Ethiopians*, pp. 66-7; ACS/RG 38 Hazon to GGAOI, 22 March 1937; ACS/RG 28 Hazon: Report on the Complicity of the Debra Lebanos Clergy in the Attempt on the Life of the Viceroy, 14 March 1937; Ibid., Maletti to Graziani, 21 April and 26 May 1937; Ibid., Graziani to Tracchia, 7 March 1937; p. 128; MAI/AS 181/59-293 Maletti to Military Headquarters, 22 May 1937; p. 48.

18. MAI/AV 3 Nasi: Circular letter, 26 December 1938 and 17 July 1938; MAI/GAB 67/XI-IV Duke of Aosta: Minutes of the VI meeting of the Governors, 5 November 1939; Abbie Gubegna, *Defiance*; MAI/AS 181/52-245 Meregazzi to MAI, 23 April 1939; MAI/GAB 69/XI-V Cerulli to MAI, 6 August 1938; MAI/GAB 287/2 Teruzzi to Duce, 22 June 1938; MAI/GAB 40 Geloso: Political Report of Oromo-Sidamo, 30 June 1938; MAI/AV 3 Nasi: Military Command of Shoa, 6 March 1940; Duke of Aosta: Circular Letter 19 January 1940 in Ethiopia: *Italian War Crimes*, I, Docs. 26, 42.

19. MAI/AV 112 Lucchetti: Report on the Submission of Chercher, 13 November 1953; Nasi, *Noi Italiani*; ACS/RG 57 Valenti: Confidential Report on the Events Leading to the Rebellion in Bahar Dar, 18 September 1937; MAI/GAB 267/213 P. Biroli: Memorandum to Mussolini 12 March 1939; Ibid., Olivieri: Conclusions of the Investigation on the Activity of the Resident of Bahar Dar, 18 February 1938; Corvo to Ato Guila Giorgis, 20 March 1937 in Ethiopia: *Italian War Crimes*, I, Doc. 33; Cavallero, *Gli Avvenimenti Militari nell Impero dal 12 Gennaio 1938 al 12 Gennaio 1939* p. 9; Teruzzi to GGAOI, 6 July 1939 in Ethiopia: *Italian War Crimes*, I, Doc. 5; ACS/SPD-R 41/242-R/39-D Farinacci to Mussolini, 24 April 1938.

20. Mokler, *Il Mito*, pp. 235-40.

21. Besides the already cited works by Pankhurst, Solome Gebre, very useful are chapters 12, 13, 14, 15 in Greenfield, *Ethiopia*. In Amharic there are two mongraphs by Tadesse Zewalde, *The Years of Torment* and Meleselegn Anlei, *Fascism's Five Years Reign of Terror*. In Italian the already mentioned two volumes by Cavallero and more recently *Il Mito dell'Impero* by Mokler which is the most comprehensive work in a modern European language; Salome Gebre, "Ethiopian Patriots", pp. 86-91; Pankhurst, "The Ethiopian Patriots", pp. 51-4; Cavallero, *Gli Avvenimenti*, I, pp. 9-15, 20, 21-33, 66-75, 87-108, 163-74, 183-92; Rochat, "L'Attentato", p. 11;

MAI/GAB 73/XI-II Nasi: Political Report of Shoa, July 1939; Steer, *Sealed and Delivered*, p. 26.

22. Salome Gebre, "Ethiopian Patriots", pp. 74-5; ACS/RG Graziani to MAI, 18 September 1973; Ibid., Abebe Aragai to *Negradras* Afework, 31 August 1937; Ibid., Graziani to Abebe Aragai, 17 May 1937; MAI/GAB 251/16 Cerulli to MAI, 20 May 1938; Del Boca, *The Ethiopian War*, p. 244;

23. MAI/GAB 73/XI-II Nasi: Political Report of Shoa, December 1939; MAI/GAB 256/53 Teruzzi to Duce, 3 March 1940; MAI/GAB 267/214 Duke of Aosta to Teruzzi, 17, 18, 20, 22, March 1940; MAI/GAB 313/296 Duke of Aosta to Teruzzi, 24 October 1939; MAI/POL 58/57 Nasi: Political Report of Shoa, November-December 1939 and January 1940.

24. MAI/GAB 267/214 Teruzzi to Duce, 10 March 1940; ACS/MAI 13/12 Arnò to MAE, 21 March 1940; MAI/GAB 58/57 Nasi: Political Report of Shoa, November-December 1939; MAI/GAB 267/214 *Fitaurari* Abebe Woldie, *Dejaz* Mangasha et al., to *Ras* Abebe Aragai, 23 February 1940; Salome Gebre, "Ethiopian Patriots", p. 75; Mokler, *Il Mito*, pp. 283-301; Nasi, *Noi Italiani*; MAI/GAB 282/XI-2 Nasi: Political Report of Shoa, March 1940; Allen, *Guerrilla War in Ethiopia*, p. 28.

25. L. Hess, review of *Ethiopia: A New Political History* by R. Greenfield in *African Forum*, I (1966), p. 116; Crummey, "Initiatives and Objectives in Ethio-European Relations 1827-1862", p. 435.

19. The Return of Haile Selassie

The Internal Conditions of Italian East Africa

Italy's colonial efforts in Ethiopia from 1936 to 1941, failed partly for lack of organization, and because of incompetent colonial personnel and high costs; Italy was able neither to achieve food self-sufficiency in Ethiopia, nor to obtain enough land for demographic colonization. Nevertheless, the success of new agricultural methods and modern forms of government in Ethiopia could not be accomplished in a short time. When Italy entered the Second World War on 10 June 1940, the Italians in Ethiopia were in the midst of experimentation.

In the summer of 1940, there were fewer troops in Ethiopia than in 1936. In 1938, for reasons of economy, hundreds of seasoned colonial army officers were repatriated to Italy. Although new officers were appointed on the eve of the war, they had no combat experience and were unable to maintain discipline among the colonial troops. Furthermore, the colonial troops had been continuously under arms for four years, and a great percentage were suffering from malaria and tuberculosis. Even the Italian civilians and troops were dissatisfied with colonial life. Under the pressures of war, they found it easy to collaborate with the Allied powers. Discouraged soldiers, after hearing of the rapid British occupation of Somalia and the quick advance into Ethiopia, offered little resistance as they retreated deeper into the central highlands. To limit the fighting the British played on the psychology of the Italian military commanders and repeatedly offered surrender with the full honours of war; alternatively, they threatened to instigate Ethiopian revenge for Graziani's massacres.

Actual fighting was limited because the idea of quick surrender fascinated the Italian generals. Although the Italians could have defended themselves longer at Marda Pass in Harar, they retreated to Addis Ababa, thus precipitating the beginning of the end of the Italian Empire. In the Governorship of Oromo-Sidamo, the Italian forces offered little resistance. Jimma capitulated to General Bisson without a fight and ten Italian generals were captured. Italian resistance was limited to battles at Keren, Amba Alangi, and Gondar, all of which fell between March and November 1941. The Italians in East Africa did not want war and were unprepared for it. Although initially they were numerically superior, the Allied troops were better armed. Above all, the British troops had the great advantage of a free flow of reinforcements.

The Italian strategy in East Africa was to contain the enemy as long as possible. It was assumed that Great Britain would ask for peace after the Axis powers captured Egypt. Mussolini believed the war would be short, and therefore he needed a few thousand dead to give him the right to sit down at the peace treaty to claim his war-booty. The Duce was also persuaded that the decisive battles for the Axis victory would be fought in Europe. Even if East Africa were lost, Italy would be on the victorious side and would be able to claim a sizeable portion of the African continent.[1] When Haile Selassie returned to Addis Ababa in May 1941, he found that there was still Italian resistance in Ethiopia; the main battle for Africa was being fought in North Africa, and the eastern Mediterranean was under constant Axis attack. The Red Sea and the Indian Ocean were menaced by Axis submarines. Haile Selassie's position was in jeopardy because of a possible German-Italian advance into Egypt and the Sudan, whose troops, it was anticipated, would join the Italo-Ethiopian underground movement. As long as there was fighting in north Africa and Mussolini was in power, the Italians in Ethiopia were optimistic about returning to power. With the defeat of Rommel in Libya, however, and the fall of Mussolini on 25 July 1943, the resistance in Ethiopia ceased.

The Return of Haile Selassie: National Concerns vs. Military Strategy

Haile Selassie and the Patriots played an important role in the defeat of the Italians. They harassed Italian troops and with the help of a few British officers made it possible to hold Italian troops in Gojam, and to liberate that region. Before being recognized as co-belligerent by the British, however, Haile Selassie faced scorn and humiliation. Even before Italy entered the war, Churchill had approved of flying Haile Selassie to the Middle East to play a part in the liberation of his country. On 24 June 1940, the British Prime Minister sent a friendly but non-committal letter to Haile Selassie, encouraging him to stir up the Ethiopians to revolt against Italian rule. By helping Haile Selassie, the British also hoped to prevent an Italian advance toward Khartoum and plans were made for British troops to be assisted by Ethiopian irregular troops. On 28 July Anthony Eden recommended to the cabinet that the rebellion in Ethiopia be generously financed.

Although Haile Selassie was flown to Khartoum with the encouragement of Churchill and Eden, it looked unlikely that he would become a belligerent on the side of the Allies. The Governor of the Sudan, Stewart Symes, the army Commander-in-Chief, Williams Platt, and the officials of the Sudan Civil Service felt his presence to be both premature and embarrassing. The British Sudanese administration estimated that following the Italian offensive of July and the occupation of Gallabat and Kassala the whole of the Sudan would sooner or later be occupied by the Italians. Before the war started, the Duke of Aosta had visited Symes and had made a favourable impression. Since the Italian occupation of Ethiopia, the long-troubled relations between the two countries had become stabilized and the Ethiopians no longer invaded the Sudan to carry out slave raids. Therefore, it was felt that Italy had attempted to bring order and civilization. If the Sudan was conquered by the Italians, the inhabitants could not be in better hands, since the Duke of Aosta had given assurances that the British administration of the Sudan would not be wrecked by the Italians. The presence of Haile Selassie shattered such prospects, along with the unrealistic hope that the war would be fought only in North Africa and that the Sudan and Ethiopia should have a truce.[2]

Haile Selassie arrived in Alexandria on 25 June and on the 28th he was at Wadi Halfa. When Symes and Platt were informed that Haile Selassie was on his way, they were very concerned at the effect the presence of the dethroned Emperor would have on the Italians, and fearful of provoking reprisals against the Sudan. For a week, Haile Selassie was allowed to "rot" at the frontier of the Sudan while the British in the Sudan argued with London and Cairo whether to let him in or not. As far as the Sudanese government was concerned Haile Selassie could return to England. He was allowed to reach Khartoum on 3 July, but it did not take long for him to realize that he was not wanted, when he was relegated to a pink villa outside of town. In an interview with Platt he was not given military information, and nothing had been done to prepare for a revolt in Ethiopia; no army was ready for him to lead to reconquer Ethiopia.

Haile Selassie resented his semi-prisoner status in Khartoum, but at the same time he was cheered by the news that the major leaders of the rebellion, *Dejaz* Mangasha and Negash, were prepared to co-operate with the British, but needed money and arms. Furthermore, Ethiopia's cause received favourable attention from Eden when he met in Khartoum on 29 October 1940, with General Archibald Wavell, Comander-in-Chief of the Middle East, and Field Marshall Smuts of South Africa, to urge Platt to speed up the campaign in East Africa. Platt did not approve of the use of Ethiopian irregular troops to be launched against the Italians. He based his conclusion on the information that there was no known Ethiopian local chief to rely on for support and an uprising.

Although Haile Selassie had received messages of support from the leading Patriot chiefs, he was also concerned with how his people would receive him. Haile Selassie was haunted by the fear of a possible rebellion against him, especially in Gojam, which had a reputation of independence. He also had to neutralize the republican ideals proclaimed by Tekle Wolde Haywariat. There was too the possibility of a resurgence of nationalistic feelings from groups such as the Muslims of Harar, Bale, Ogaden, and Eritrea and the Oromo in general. To convince the Ethiopians to support Haile Selassie his return was prepared by intensive propaganda between July 1940 and January 1941 led by the British journalist George Steer. Eden was confident that once Haile Selassie had crossed the frontier his subjects would rise in his favour. However, the British authorities were not absolutely sure of the type of military support Haile Selassie would receive from the Patriots. In this climate of uncertainty he did not receive a treaty for military co-operation with Great Britain, but an agreement recognizing his leadership in the war of liberation. The appointment of Major Orde Wingate resulted from Eden's policy. He was an idealist and the strongest supporter of Ethiopian independence. He organized the Ethiopian troops and made possible the return of Haile Selassie to Ethiopia.

Meanwhile in November 1940, General Wavell was about to launch his attack against the Italians in the Western Desert and was anxious to settle the strategy in East Africa. He promised additional reinforcements to General Platt to recapture Kassala in an offensive to be launched early in 1941, in connection with a general Ethiopian uprising, and help from the Patriots. Wingate, with irregular Ethiopian troops, and Haile Selassie would enter western Ethiopia at the same time as Platt attacked Kassala and threatened Eritrea. The collaboration of the Patriots and Haile Selassie's presence, however, was looked upon rather sceptically: British military officers doubted that Haile Selassie and the Patriots would contribute much to the Allied cause.

Again, it was the intervention of Churchill that made it possible for Haile Selassie to enter Ethiopia. On 30 December 1940, he wrote to the British Foreign Minister that in view of the Allied success in Egypt in December, Haile Selassie should at once enter his country to inspire the revolt and boost the Allied position in East Africa.[3] Haile Selassie entered Ethiopia on 20 January 1941. With the aid of Wingate and the Patriots he reached Debra Markos in the early days of April. At the same time Addis Ababa fell to the South African troops under General Alan Cunningham. On 31 March British airplanes dropped leaflets with a message from Cunningham requesting an Italian plenipotentiary to discuss the peaceful surrender of the capital. The Duke of Aosta thought it best to make Addis Ababa an open city, retiring to Amba Alagi to offer resistance and give the Italians time to regroup in the main urban centres, since it was feared that the Ethiopians would engage in acts of reprisal to avenge Graziani's atrocities. Following a declaration by Haile Selassie on 20 January 1941 forgiving the Italians and stating there would be no retaliation against them, there was little trouble.

It is difficult to assess the reasons for Haile Selassie's plea in favour of the Italians. Today we know from the Emperor himself that no vendetta was ever contemplated. Besides humanitarian reasons, Haile Selassie might have decided to pardon his enemies for practical political reasons, saving many Ethiopians from Italian hands. He was certainly concerned with the fate of his daughter, Romanwork, three grandchildren, and a nephew in Italy in care of the *Missione della Consolata* in Turin. There was also Haile Selassie's cousin, *Ras* Imru, still a prisoner in Italy. Furthermore, his act of forgiveness won him favourable world public recognition as a humanitarian and the appreciation of the Pope and President Roosevelt who had expressed their concern for the lives of white people to the British government.[4] It seems, however, that it was part of a British war propaganda to inculcate fear of Ethiopian vengeance in the Italians. When General Cunningham arrived on the outskirts of Addis Ababa and negotiated the surrender of the capital with the Italian authorities between 30 March and 6 April, he demanded that all military activities cease in exchange for protection of Italian civilians. Failing to secure an agreement with the Italians and believing that the Ethiopians would go wild and assault the Italians if Haile Selassie should enter Addis Ababa before his troops, he ordered Haile Selassie to delay his entry for three weeks and stay in Debra Markos.

Yet, what violence did occur, took place only during the period of transition from Italian rule to Anglo-Ethiopian government. There was a period of disorder in Addis Ababa for about three months when individuals were assaulted, and robberies took place on public roads in broad daylight. Italians who lived in the capital believed that it was Abebe Aragai's presence more than Haile Selassie's proclamation that saved them. In fact, after Addis Ababa was declared an open city, Abebe Aragai entered with several thousand men, ensuring law and order, although at first, his vengeance was feared. Abebe Aragai saw to it that Italians and their property were respected. He posted guards in every Italian quarter and placed sentries outside the homes of prominent Italian civilians and officers. According to the International Red Cross, by the end of 1942 56 Italians had been murdered. 96 wounded, and 103 the victims of armed robbery, in an Italian population of 30,000. These offences were committed by Ethiopians who had old accounts to settle with the Italians. In Lekept, a Patriot leader, *Fitaurari* Kumsa, also protected Italians citizens, and such forgiving behaviour was repeated throughout Ethiopia.[5] Thus, considering that Ethiopian government authority was scarcely enforced for the first few months after the Fascist defeat, crimes and violence against the "enemy" Italians were relatively few.

The Italian Problem

Although on re-entering Addis Ababa, on 5 May 1941, Haile Selassie declared publicly that all Italians had to be expelled from Ethiopia, he admitted that their presence was necessary to maintain roads, industries and farms, because the country was faced with a food shortage. By remaining and using their mechanized agriculture the Italians could at least meet the immediate need for food supplies.

The British military and political administration was dependent upon Italian technicians and clerks. Life in the capital depended largely upon Italian labour and they were quite happy to work for the Ethiopians and the British. It surprised the British authorities that Italians and Ethiopians, far from hating each other, were getting on well together. Shortly thereafter Haile Selassie indicated that any Italian who wanted to stay could do so, and

Abebe Aragai asked that 15,000 Italians remain. The British, however, opposed these proposals. The concern of the British was how to protect the Italians, feed them, and supply their own troops in Ethiopia. Militarily, it was dangerous to have many thousands of enemy aliens at large in the country. The Italian presence in Ethiopia prevented the reinforcement of British troops in Libya and there was the real problem that a number of Italians might join the dispersed Italian troops in various parts of Ethiopia, giving rise to a possible resistance movement against the British.[6] Thus by 3 April 1942, the evacuation from Ethiopia of some 45,000 persons was decided upon.

With the help of his personal Italian physician, Eugenio Pisano, and Ethiopian Minister of Foreign Affairs, Lorenzo Taezaz (educated by the *Missione della Consolata*), Haile Selassie worked out a system to keep as many as 10,000 Italians. Pisano had access, through Taezaz, to the diplomatic correspondence exchanged between Haile Selassie and London dealing with the fate of the Italians in Ethiopia. Churchill at first assessed the number of Italians who could remain in Ethiopia at 5,000, but the British chief-of-staff in Ethiopia, for strategic and military reasons, opted for 2,000, soon reduced to a mere 500. Eventually, with the help of Haile Selassie, several thousand Italians decided to remain in Ethiopia. It was not only to the advantage of Ethiopia that the Italians remain, but also in the Italian interest. When the Duke of Aosta left Addis Ababa for Amba Alagi, he ensured that the city was organized to meet civilian needs. The same was true of Kassala and Asmara. In Eritrea, the British did not disturb Italian civilian life. In Somalia, the agricultural industry founded by the Duke of Abruzzi, the SAIS (Società Agricola Italo-Somala), continued to operate even after the British occupation. All this had a purpose, for the Italians hoped to return to temporarily abandoned territories and find functioning economic units to meet their immediate needs. Not everybody, however, believed in the re-establishment of Italian rule in Ethiopia. Italians freely co-operated with the occupation forces, especially those who were not of Fascist leanings; they called their party, *Italia Libera.* They published the bi-weekly *Il Gazzettino*, directed by the Anglo-Italian Captain G. L. Strina.

The Italians in Ethiopia fell into several categories. Those who were anti-British, mostly well-known Fascists, were sent to concentration camps outside Ethiopia, because they were considered dangerous. The majority, however, sympathized with the British, and their life remained relatively normal. Several thousand Italians chose to serve under the British, including army officers and state officials, who received up to 220 lire per day and special privileges. The CITAO (Campagnia Italiana Trasporti Africa Orientale), a transport company, co-operated with the occupation authorities to move military material, machinery and industrial plants that the Italians had built in Ethiopia to Kenya. Among the Italians there were also those who were undecided. They were a group of opportunists who lived in obscurity and were unwilling to take sides. Lastly there were the army officers who were organizing an insurrection with the help of high-ranking Ethiopian personalities.[7]

Ironically, the Ethiopians not only showed restraint in their relations with the Italians but many assisted their ex-colonial masters by providing them with shelter, food, money and protection and helped them to escape from jails and concentration camps. Abebe Aragai and important chiefs were in close contact with Italian circles in Addis Ababa, especially Pisano, Gianquinto D'Ignazio, and Di Lauro. Abebe Aragai, who wanted to see a speedy solution to the many land controversies, proposed that Italians be part of a land court. When the British put Colonel Domenico Lucchetti in a concentration camp, Ethiopian figures went to visit him, took care of his family, and helped him to escape to safety.[8] Lucchetti, like other former Italian officials, was hidden and protected by the Governor *Lij* Kebret Astatkie of Dire Dawa, who was a nephew of Haile Selassie. The remarkable behaviour of the Ethiopians toward the Italians can be explained in part because Italy, after being defeated, was perceived as no longer harbouring colonial ambitions, and also because their advice would enable the Ethiopians to negotiate better terms with the British military authorities.

Haile Selassie and the British Authorities

When Haile Selassie entered Addis Ababa on 5 May 1941, the problem of who was the legal ruler of Ethiopia was raised, because Great Britain had legally recognized the Italian Empire in 1938. Haile Selassie had come to no preliminary understanding with the British government. There were no records in London, Cairo or Khartoum of what would be the fate of Ethiopia and the position of Haile Selassie after the Italians were defeated. No official discussions with Haile Selassie had been entertained or arrangements made to deal with the situation which would arise when he re-entered his country. There were, however, a number of non-committal statements regarding Ethiopia which were not diplomatically binding. On 24 June 1940, before Haile Selassie left London for the Sudan, Churchill wrote a friendly letter. It was a personal message rather than a legal document. On 29 October 1940, before the British offensives in Egypt and East Africa, Eden recognized Haile Selassie as the leader of the war of liberation. Although Haile Selassie wanted a treaty of friendship with Great Britain, this was not granted because the issue was how to defeat the Italians, rather than what should happen after their defeat. In December 1940, after the Italian debacle at Sidi Barrani, the British Parliament issued a statement reserving for itself liberty of action regarding any commitment entered into in the past with the Italian government. Thus, although Haile Selassie was considered by the British authorities as a participant in the war against Italy, he was not really acknowledged as the ruler of Ethiopia because of Great Britain's previous bilateral treaty with Italy.

The fortunes of war improved for the British in East Africa. Kassala was reoccupied in January 1941; on 4 February the British Foreign Minister stated in the House of Commons that the British government would welcome the reappearance of an independent Ethiopian state, and would recognize the claims of Haile Selassie to the throne. On 8 February 1941, the Political Branch of the British army acknowledged Haile Selassie as a fellow belligerent fighting side by side with British troops for the independence of Ethiopia. On 19 February 1941, while Haile Selassie was in Gojam with the Patriots, Deputy Chief Political Officer, Brigadier Maurice Lush, allowed Haile Selassie to issue proclamations in keeping with these statements. This was intended as a symbol of authority to the Ethiopian people. Lastly on 9 May 1941, Churchill once more wrote a noncommittal letter: he congratulated Haile Selassie on being the first ruler who had been a victim of Fascist aggression to return with the aid of British troops.

The British authorities were slow and vague in their commitments to Haile Selassie because the result of the war was unknown and because of the secret negotiations between Italian officers in Ethiopia and the British authorities in London which might have led to a separate peace between the Allies and Italian East Africa, which was rejected by the Duke of Aosta. In return for this armistice the Duke of Aosta would be recognized as the ruler of the Italian Empire. It would ensure lenient treatment by the Allies of the Italian monarchy and would have saved the Italian colonies. Furthermore, on account of Great Britain's international treaties of 1936, 1937, and 1938 with Italy, Ethiopia was Italian territory and Italian sovereignty remained until formally terminated by the British government. This meant that when Haile Selassie entered Addis Ababa in May 1941, he did not have status or power as Emperor until a peace treaty was signed with Italy. Until then, the King of Italy remained the legal ruler of Ethiopia. The fact that Great Britain unilaterally contemplated repealing the *de jure* recognition of the Italian Empire on 4 February did not annul other nations' recognition of the Italian Empire, which only legally ceased with the peace treaty of 1947. Hence, when Haile Selassie appointed seven ministers without prior approval from the British authorities, he was advised that he had no authority. Therefore they were to be regarded as "designated" ministers only.[9]

From 5 May 1941 to January 1942, when the first Anglo-Ethiopian Agreement was signed, Ethiopia was under British military rule. There were two British views on how to administer Ethiopia. The Foreign Office was interested in keeping Britain's reputation in the world free from suspicion of imperialism, and believed that Ethiopia could reorganize its administration without foreign tutelage. On the other hand, a group, known as the Cromerites, made up mostly of Sudanese and Kenyan civil servants suggested a temporary British protectorate over Ethiopia and detaching the Oromo territories, which, after a period under British administration, would become an autonomous state. The British officers in charge of the political administration of Ethiopia further argued that Ethiopia was of strategic importance to the British Empire because it controlled the sources of the Blue Nile, and Lake Tana was of great importance to the Sudan. The alleged

British imperialistic aims in Ethiopia delayed the negotiations of the Anglo-Ethiopian Agreement. Before Haile Selassie met the Chief Political Officer, Philip Mitchell, for the first time on 23 May 1941, he told his Italian confidants, Ettore Bayon and Renato Piacentini, former Italian Minister in Addis Ababa, that the British treated him like a vassal. Conditions in Ethiopia in 1941 were similar to those in Egypt in 1882, when the British manipulated Ismail Pasha into submitting to British terms. For this reason, Haile Selassie insisted on a written agreement with the British government and on hiring advisers from more than one country.

While the Anglo-Ethiopian Agreement was being negotiated in Addis Ababa, Haile Selassie was in close contact with the Italians, from whom he received a radio transmitter. Colonel Ugo Livi installed it in the basement of the imperial palace and provided two operators, Sergeants Alessandro Sala and Rolando Franciosi. Their duty was to intercept information to keep Haile Selassie briefed on international issues free of British manipulation. Haile Selassie also preferred Italian doctors in Addis Ababa: it was to Renato Piacentini that Haile Selassie turned to for medicines for Empress Menen.[10] Haile Selassie's preference for the Italians, however, was a political calculation. The Emperor's disagreement with the British authorities became evident when they refused to recognize his sovereignty over Ethiopia, which the British considered as conquered enemy territory and contemplated as a future British mandate. Thus Haile Selassie, facing a possible British imperialistic threat, tried to find a counter-poise in the Italians.

Haile Selassie and the Ethiopian Chiefs

In dealing with the British, Haile Selassie also had to consider the attitude of the Ethiopian people. They were suspicious of the British because it appeared they wanted to make Ethiopia a British-controlled territory. The British requisitioned anything that was valuable in the Ethiopian economy. Haile Selassie was also under constant threat of rebellion, and his prisons were full to capacity. Even his supporters had doubts about the wisdom of his return to Ethiopia, since they feared that the Ethiopian chiefs and the people would not accept him. In fact, Captain Kidane Askale, in order to avenge the deposed heir of Menelik II, *Lij* Yasu, rebelled against Haile Selassie. He was joined by some nobles who had become alienated when Haile Selassie did not immediately recognize Italian-granted titles and offices. Furthermore, the Sultans of Jimma and Aussa, who had enjoyed semi-autonomous administration under the Italian government were made directly responsible to Addis Ababa. For these reasons, Haile Selassie used force several times to quell rebellions and local resistance with the help of his British-officered army.

Moreover, Haile Selassie and his chiefs were in disagreement because he did not seem strong enough to break away from British control. The most powerful of the chiefs was Abebe Aragai, who had fought to liberate Ethiopia from the Italians. In Addis Ababa, Abebe Aragai ostentatiously showed that he ruled. On the return of Haile Selassie he moved without delay to Addis Ababa where, significantly, he took possession of the Ministry of War and put his officers into high positions. *Ras* Kassa, the most influential nobleman in Ethiopia, was also at odds with Haile Selassie. He had avenged the deaths of his sons by killing some ex-*askaris* and Italians. When Haile Selassie criticized his actions, Kassa retired to his fief at Fiche with 10,000 armed men, showing how little regard he had for Haile Selassie.

Another important personality was *Ras* Seyum, of Tigre, who had co-operated with the Italians and then surrendered to the British, disingenuously reporting that secretly he had always opposed the Italians. In Adowa he acted as an independent ruler. Haile Selassie's power was also challenged by the "Imru Party" formed by discontented chiefs who hoped to replace Haile Selassie with *Ras* Imru. Among these chiefs, it was said, were Abebe Aragai, Taezaz, and Tekle Wolde Haywariat. It is possible that they intended to set up a constitutional monarchy.[11]

The Italian Underground Movement

The period between 1941 and 1943 was one of uncertainty for the future of Ethiopia. Nasi, the commander of the besieged Gondar, was able to resist with the help of local chiefs who fought the Italians during the day and sent supplies to the beleaguered city at night. In a visit to Debra Tabor, in the summer of 1941, Nasi received the surrender of 1,000 men and noted that in Begemder there was a favourable tendency toward Italy. In reality, the promises of help that Nasi received from the population and chiefs was a political game, because by assisting the Italians the Ethiopians were only gaining time to see which side would be victorious.

Meanwhile, the Italian underground movement extended into different parts of Ethiopia. Soon after the return of Haile Selassie, the aim of the Italian resistance, although not well-organized, was the prevention of the departure of the Italians. They wanted to remain in Ethiopia because, in spite of the military defeat in East Africa, as long as Nasi resisted in Gondar, and the Italo-German troops held North Africa, there was hope of an Italian comeback in Ethiopia. Sabotage and guerrilla warfare kept British troops engaged in Ethiopia and possibly delayed the Allied reinforcement of the North African theatre. Ironically, encouraged by the fact that the Ethiopians resented the British occupation because of their strong colour bar and imperialistic plans, the Italian underground received support from the Ethiopians. (Other than the Fascists, the Italians were not racist, and the Ethiopians differentiated accordingly.)

The population and chiefs of Geleba offered 4,000 armed men to Colonel Calvi, a leader of the Italian resistance. The chief Olol Dingle of Shabelli, *Dejaz* Tedla of Chercher, the people of Garamullata and Ogaden volunteered their aid to Colonel Di Marco, the representative of the Italian underground in south-eastern Ethiopia. Colonel Rougli was in contact with the Sultan of Aussa and, with the help of Azebu Oromo, controlled Dankalia, fought the British troops, and attacked Anglo-Ethiopian columns at Alomata. At one point Eritrea was isolated from the rest of Ethiopia by 35,000 rebellious Oromo.[12]

The Italian underground movement in parts of Amhara and Wollo was important in view of a possible return of Italian forces. Italo-Ethiopian irregulars could make trouble for Anglo-Ethiopian troops, and encourage Ethiopian uprisings. In retrospect, however, it is difficult to see how the Italians could have maintained their position in Ethiopia. A more objective explanation of Italo-Ethiopian co-operation would be that incidents arose because of the inadequacy of the central government, and the existence of an ample supply of Italian arms available to a disorganized and unemployed population after the war, and the wish of local chiefs to return to the days of personal armies.

Nevertheless, Vice-Governor-General Giuseppe Daodiace ordered the leaders of the Italian underground movement to convince the Ethiopian population that the Italians would return. The Italians also had to remain as long as possible in Addis Ababa and Shoa, and organize cells of resistance. At Dessie a number of Italian officers operated under the direction of Major Gobbi. Three officers were reported to be at Kobbo among the Azebu Oromo. Other officers in Wollo were, it seems, protected by the second son of Haile Selassie, the Duke of Harar. Allegedly three hundred Italians were between Kaffa and Jimma; and a few were in Dembidollo and the Chercher-Mojo area. Apparently Captain Edoardo Bellia had the support of Abebe Aragai and of disillusioned Ethiopian chiefs. Nasi provided Bellia with funds to enlist 250 men.

The most serious opposition front, however, was formed in Addis Ababa and Harar in September 1941 by Major P. Farello and other civil and military officers. Lucchetti was hidden and protected by *Lij* Kebret Astatkie, a nephew of Haile Selassie. As a matter of fact this official went to his uncle to explain Lucchetti's plan to co-ordinate relations in case the Italians returned after the fall of Egypt. Lucchetti met with *Lij* Kebret and Colonel Berhan Maskal Wolde Selassie Makonnen on 1 May 1942, in Dire Dawa to discuss details about Italian representation in Ethiopia. Awaiting the moment to attack, Lucchetti organized troops, and gathered arms and trucks in Harar.[13] Monsignor Ossola, Catholic Bishop of Harar, co-operated, providing all kinds of help, including money. Amhara and Muslim authorities also gave their support. It was estimated that there were over 7,000 Italians at large, some of whom were sheltered and protected by Ethiopian chiefs.

Haile Selassie's Negotiations with Italy

In the meantime, Haile Selassie sought advice from the Italian journalist Giuseppe Fabbri, in working out an agreement with the British government which included the formation of an Ethiopian army, British financial help, and advisers for economic and legal matters, the organization and establishment of an Ethiopian provincial administration, the immediate drafting of a treaty, and an estimate of how much Ethiopia owed Britain for its help in the war. In London, Mitchell attempted to persuade Eden to postpone the drafting of the Anglo-Ethiopian Agreement. The Foreign Minister, however, held his ground. On 24 June 1941, the British counter-proposals, although limiting the power of Haile Selassie, were issued. The British government would accept Haile Selassie's proposal if he would agree to abide by the advice of the British government in all matters relating to the government of Ethiopia, accept the prior approval of the British government in matters of taxation and expenditure, reserve the jurisdiction of foreigners to British courts, and agree not to raise objections if the Commander-in-Chief should find it necessary to resume military control of any part of Ethiopia. Although the Anglo-Ethiopian Agreement of 31 January 1942 recognized Ethiopia's sovereignty and provided for the resumption of diplomatic relations, the independence of Ethiopia was subject to many of the features of a British mandate as Great Britain provided advisers and judges were appointed by Haile Selassie in consultation with Great Britain. The military forces were under British command and the finances for the administration were provided by the British government. It was in many ways similar to the British diplomatic understanding reached with Egypt in 1922, the only difference being that Haile Selassie was aware of the British political game and he skillfully, with Italian advice, prevented Ethiopia from becoming a British protectorate. Haile Selassie, dissatisfied with the results of the Anglo-Ethiopian Agreement, intensified his relations with the leaders of the Italian underground. This was especially true after the Axis powers renewed their threat to occupy Egypt and possibly march on Ethiopia. The Italians were so certain of victory in North Africa that they started to sell the skin of the lion before they had actually killed it. Anticipating peace negotiations, they were claiming Nigeria, Chad, and Ubangi Shari.[14] With the coming of General Erwin Rommel to North Africa, Axis troops reconquered Cyrenaica and advanced onto Egyptian soil. Mabruk was taken and the Italo-German troops were not very far from the Nile Delta. Soon, they anticipated reaching Cairo. They anticipated reconquering Ethiopia with the same speed. With the imminent conquest of Egypt, the Italian return to Ethiopia seemed to be coming true. Haile Selassie too expected an Axis victory and sought a possible understanding with Italy. With the help of the Italians in Ethiopia, a number of confused diplomatic initiatives were started to contact Rome and negotiate terms for possible co-operation. Haile Selassie charged Taezaz and Italian officials with the preparation of a draft Italo-Ethiopian agreement. With Haile Selassie's permission and Pisano's co-operation, it was alleged that Taezaz planned to present himself to the Italian commander in Egypt, after the occupation, in order to be transported to Rome to meet Mussolini and to negotiate an amnesty for all Ethiopians, the employment of educated Ethiopians in the Italian administration of Ethiopia, and Haile Selassie's participation in ruling Ethiopia. The Ethiopians were interested in opening negotiations with Italy and making plans for the future before Mussolini became less conciliatory. Moreover, it was decided that even before the Italian troops reached Egypt, Taezaz should meet Ciano in Switzerland.[15]

In the meantime Haile Selassie let General Nasi know of his conciliatory attitude toward Italy and asked that he be liberated from the British concentration camp to form an interim Italian government in Ethiopia. In July 1942, Kebret Astatkie informed Lucchetti that the "delegated Ethiopian ministers" had met to decide if the Ethiopian revolution against the British, with the help of the Italian underground, should take place before or after the fall of Alexandria. But Attilio Teruzzi gave instructions to cool down enthusiasm for these plans. The Italian underground had to keep the hope of the early return of the Italians alive in the Ethiopians. Moreover, Teruzzi pointed out previous Ethiopian duplicity and their tendency to wait until the right moment came to make a final decision. Therefore, the Italian government would not make any promises for future agreements.

Italians and Ethiopians were not the only ones, however, to consider a possible Axis victory in Egypt. The British authorities concluded that in the event of an Italian victory in North Africa the British troops would remain isolated in Ethiopia. In December 1941, the Italian delegation in Addis Ababa was approached by British Intelligence agents to discuss the formation of an autonomous Italian Empire headed by the Duke of Aosta. The idea reflected London's fears not only of an Italian offensive in Libya, but also the consequences of the Japanese attack on Pearl Harbor and the British loss of Singapore and Hong Kong. Japan had conquered Malacca and New Guinea, menaced India and Australia, and approached the Italian African coast of the Red Sea and the Indian Ocean. At the same time the Oromo of Kobbo had rebelled and cut all British communications between Addis Ababa and Asmara.[16]

When General Rommel reached El Alamein on 3 July 1942, he noted in his diary that the British Fleet was leaving Alexandria and moving east. The British were preparing to evacuate Egypt in case the Italo-German forces invaded the Nile Delta. They planned to go to Palestine and, if necessary, to Iraq. Thus the British High Command, too, foresaw a possible conquest of Egypt, but it was General Montgomery's stand that changed the course of the war in North Africa. De Bono reported that Allied superiority in weaponry and especially in the air checked the progress of the Germans and Italians toward Egypt. The Axis powers were pushed back with great repercussions. When an Allied victory in North Africa was imminent, Haile Selassie severed his relations with the Italians and ordered that the officials he had used to communicate with Rome be handed over to the British authorities. He no longer needed their services because the British government had relaxed its grip on Ethiopia. Gradually his power was restored and more assurances were given of American help to develop and administer the country. The limitations of Ethiopia's independence were gradually eliminated with the Anglo-Ethiopian treaty of 19 December 1944, but in

1948, to safeguard her strategic and commercial interests in the Red Sea, Britain agreed to withdraw from part of the Ogaden, but did not withdraw totally until 1955.[17]

Conclusion

The good Italo-Ethiopian relations, after the Italian defeat in East Africa, are an irony of history. Although the Italians were the enemy and expected to suffer from the Ethiopian reaction on the return of Haile Selassie, they enjoyed his clemency and protection. The average Italian did not demand a higher standard of living than his profession or skill could earn him. On the other hand, a defeated Italy was no longer recognized as a world power and was thought not to have imperialistic designs; therefore, Haile Selassie felt it was safe to use the Italians for the development of Ethiopia and to further his position. The Ethiopians realized that the Italian invasion had broken the crust of their ancient traditions. Italian rule provided a demonstration, however incomplete, of European methods of government, industry, and transport. The words of Haile Mariam Gemsu, adviser of Abebe Aragai about Italian achievements are indeed flattering. He told Lucchetti that in spite of the fact that he had fought the Duke of Aosta and General Nasi, the Italians had brought much well-being to Ethiopia. Significantly the Italians were accepted, even popular, in Ethiopia in the post-war years. Ironically, however, the British who had made possible the liberation of Ethiopia received little gratitude and co-operation in the prosecution of the war.

Internal security problems prevented the Italians from invading the Sudan, and despite Italian claims to the contrary, there was a great spirit of resistance and patriotism in Ethiopia. Although divided, Ethiopian Patriots were generally loyal to Haile Selassie and helped the British troops to neutralize the Italians. The latter, who were poorly informed of all developments, assumed that the British and Ethiopians were invading in force, and retreated. The swift Italian collapse made it impossible for gradual steps to be taken by the British and Ethiopian authorities to cope with the changed situation.

When Haile Selassie returned to Ethiopia he was faced with the extremely grave task of warding off possible British imperialistic aims in Ethiopia and also had to deal with revolts in Tigre, Gojam, and Oromo land. The unrest in Gojam, between 1941 and 1943, represented a serious challenge to Haile Selassie. The uprising was motivated by the desire of the local chiefs such as former Patriot leader Belai Zelleke for more power, and resentment against Shoan rule. In Tigre it was a protest against the prolonged confinement of *Ras* Seyum, the hereditary prince of Tigre, in Addis Ababa, and possibly it was aimed at obtaining more autonomy from the central government.

During the same period, *Grazmatch* Sera, an important Oromo leader, had spoken out for some measure of Oromo local autonomy. He was murdered in Adola, near the camp of a British Political Officer. He might be suspected of having tried to negotiate the independence of southern Ethiopia with British help. During these events Italians became political, economic, and military advisers to Haile Selassie and leading Ethiopian personalities, in order to counteract British imperialistic aims. It is understandable that Haile Selassie should turn to them since he could not even rely entirely upon his followers. His defeat and flight to Europe in 1936 had adversely affected his position in the eyes of the people. Haile Selassie knew that exiled Ethiopians in various parts of Europe and the Sudan had approached the British authorities to try to prevent his return to Ethiopia. In Khartoum, Ethiopians talked about setting up a republican government and wrote letters to France requesting assistance. In Ethiopia, the reason for Haile Selassie's re-entering the country via Gojam was that the Patriot leaders of Begemder were not likely to accept him. They had expressed the opinion that the country belonged to those who had shed their blood for it. In defiance of Haile Selassie the people in Gondar were about to proclaim *Lij* Yohannes, a son of the dead Emperor Yasu, as their leader.[18]

Haile Selassie was aware that not all Ethiopians welcomed the advent of a central government, and that there were plans to assassinate him. In an effort to introduce constitutional reforms and to limit Haile Selassie's personal powers, leading Patriots plotted against him. Nevertheless thanks to Haile Selassie's diplomatic skills and Italian support, political machinations were aborted even before they began. The Italian position in Ethiopia was no longer based on the hope of the return of Italian rule. Gradually they realized that their position in Ethiopia could be maintained if they backed Haile Selassie and his government. Thus they became pawns in Ethiopian politics.

Notes

1. Wingate, "An Appreciation of the Ethiopian Campaign", p. 206; A. Sbacchi, review of *La Fine Dell'Impero* (Milan, 1974) by A. Bongiovanni in *ASA Review of Books* 2 (1976), pp. 72-4; Great Britain, *The Abyssinian Campaign*; Great Britain: "Dispatches of General A. Wavell, General, A. Cunningham and General W. Platt on the Military Operations in Abyssinia, 1940-1941", *The London Gazette* (Supplement to 10 July 1946), pp. 3527-99; Lessona, *Un Ministro di Mussolini Racconta*, pp. 124-8; Mack Smith, *Mussolini's Roman Empire*, p. 216.

2. Mosley, *Gideon Goes to War*, pp. 97-9; Mosley, *Haile Selassie*, pp. 25; 249-51 Steer, *Sealed*, pp. 30-31; Gorham, *The Lion of Judah*, p. 20; Eden, *Memoirs of Anthony Eden*, pp. 144-5, 157, 161; Rodd, *British Military Administration of Occupied Territories in Africa*, p. 327; Waterfield, *Morning Will Come*, p. 14.

3. Mitchell, *African Afterthoughts*, p. 202; Mosley, *Gideon*, pp. 95-113; Mosley, *Haile Selassie*, pp. 249-59; Hess, *Ethiopia: Modernization of Autocracy*, p. 69; Steer, *Sealed*, pp. 52-9, 102-3; Sebhat Egziabheir, "Tekle's Struggle. . ." 3 (1973), pp. 8-11; 4 (1973), pp. 15-24; 5 (1973), pp. 8-12:

the text of these articles in Amharic and the dates are according to the Ethiopian calendar; Churchill, *Their Finest Hour*, pp. 621–2; Wingate, "An Appreciation", pp. 22–5.

4. ACS/MAI 4/1 Ottaviani to MAI, 29 April 1941; MAI/GAB 117/XI-7 Riccardo: Report to the Military Commission on Italian ex-Service Men in AOI Returning from British Concentration Camps, 12 October 1942; Del Boca, *The Ethiopia War*, p. 259; MAI/AS 181/42–143 MAI to MAE, 28 May 1941; Ibid., Attolico to MAE, 22 May 1941; Ibid., Suor Rosa Enulia (of the Consolata Mission) to Moreno, 27 May 1941. Romanwork died of tuberculosis 16 October 1940; MAI/GAB 318 MAE to MAI, 3 April 1941.

5. Churchill, *The Grand Alliance*, p. 87; Mosley, *Gideon*, pp. 137–8; Mosley, *Haile Selassie*, pp. 267, 287; Great Britain: "Dispatches", pp. 3568–70, 3598, 3589, 3578; MAI/GAB 307/A Di Lauro: Report on AOI, 1942; MAI/GAB 318 Vecchi: Notes on Ethiopia 1942; Interview with J. Zambon, 4 May 1972.

6. ACS/MAI 25/22 MAE to MAI, 2 October 1941; Faraci, *Ethiopia: Guerra e Pace*, p. 24; MAI/AV 112 Activity of Lucchetti in Ethiopia, 1953; Churchill, *The Second World War*, pp. 76, 80; Rodd, *British Military*, pp. 440–52; Waterfield, *Morning*, pp. 61–5; 72–3; Steer, *Sealed*, pp. 200–2; Mitchell, *African*, pp. 204–6.

7. ACS/SPD-R 22/224-R Pisano: Secret Report to Mussolini on the Activities of the Health Director, 2 November 1942; MAI/GAB 116/XI-1-A Duke of Aosta to MAI, 23 February 1941; MAI/GAB 318 Vecchi: Notes on Ethiopia, 1942; ACS/INT-CM-A-5-G 101/194 Leto: Notes on Italian Nationals Remaining in Ethiopia, 7 March 1943; Del Boca, *Gli Italiani in Africa*, pp. 533–82.

8. Nasi, *Noi Italiani*; Waterfield, *Morning*, pp. 72–3; Mosley, *Haile Selassie*, p. 279; Mitchell, *African*, p. 206; Rodd, *British Military*, p. 86.

9. Great Britain: War Office, *British Military Administration*, pp. 8–9; Mitchell, *African*, p. 203; G. Puglisi, "Impero Clandestino" (Rome, n.d. unpublished); pp. 350–1; Churchill, *Grand Alliance*, III, pp. 91–5; Steer, *Sealed*, p. 201; Rodd, *British Military*, pp. 41–8, 37–31, 559–81; Mosley, *Haile Selassie*, pp. 255, 273–5; Mokler, *Il Mito Dell'Impero*, pp. 404–5; Del Bocca, *La Caduta dell'Impero*, pp. 392–3; Pesenti, *Il Dramma Dell' Impero*; Bruttini and Puglisi, *L'Impero Tradito*, pp. 215–16; Bandini, *Gli Italiani in Africa*, pp. 458–9; Sandford, *The Lion of Judah*, p. 109; Sarubbi, "Il Trattato di Pace", pp. 28–30.

10. George, *Egypt Since Cromer*, pp. 53, 60, 206; Vatikiotis, *The Modern History of Egypt*, pp. 241, 265, 287; Perham, *The Government of Ethiopia*, pp. xi, 392; Mosley, *Gideon*, pp. 114–15; Mosley, *Haile Selassie*, p. 260; MAI/GAB 318 Vecchi: Notes on Ethiopia, 1942; ACS/MAI 25/22 MAE to MAI, 2 October 1943; Greenfield, "Interpretation of Oromo Nationality", pp. 3–14; ACS/SPD-R 22/224-R Pisano: Secret Report to Mussolini, 2 November 1942.

11. MAI/GAB 318 Vecchi: Notes on Ethiopia, 1942; Rodd, *British Military*, pp. 94, 421, 434, 538–97; Mitchell, *African*, p. 206; Waterfield, *Morning*, pp. 68, 70; Mosley, *Haile Selassie*, pp. 275–7; MAI/GAB 307/A Di Lauro: Report on AOI, 1942; ACS/CP 156/4 Wienbolt to Pankhurst, 25 June 1940; ACS/PCM-B 22/2 Report on the Italian Colonies, 4 July

1944; ACS/MAI 25/22 Nasi to MAI, 5 October 1941; *Newsweek*, 14 April 1942; Salome Gebre Egziber, "The Ethiopian Patriots", pp. 64-7, 73-4.

12. ACS/MAI 25/22 Nasi to MAI, 5 and 11 October 1941; Ibid., Duke of Aosta to MAI, 13 March 1942; Wingate, "An Appreciation", pp. 214, 217-19, reports that half of Begemder was hostile to the British, one-quarter neutral, only the remaining quarter co-operated with the British. Waterfield, *Morning*, p. 71; MAI/GAB 318 Vecchi: Notes on Ethiopia, 1942; Puglisi, "Impero", pp. 282, 326-7, 343.

13 MAI/GAB 307/A Di Lauro: Report on AOI, 1942; ACS/MAI 25/22 Italian Intelligence Service to MAI, 1 December 1941; Rodd, *British Military*, p. 77; ACS/MAI 23/29 Pastore to Italian Commission for the Armistice with France, 17 July 1942; Waterfield, *Morning*, p. 74; Puglisi, "Impero", pp. 278-80, 313; MAI/AV 112 Activity of Lucchetti in Ethiopia, 1953.

14. Mosley, *Haile Selassie*, p. 276, Waterfield, *Morning*, p. 68; Mitchell, *African*, p. 204; Rodd, *British Military*, p. 77; Phelps-Stokes Foundation: Committee on Africa, *The War and Peace Aims*, p. 114; Great Britain, *Agreement: 31 January 1941*; ACS/MAI 23/9-2 Teruzzi to Italian Commission for the Armistice with France, 23 August 1940; Ibid., Braida to Azan, 20 July 1940; The invasion of Egypt had been conceived and planned by General Pintor in 1935, when 300,000 Italian troops were ready to march from Libya to the Suez Canal, if the British closed it. The plan was perfected in 1937-8, involving landing Italian troops at Port Said and Suez to coincide with the presence in the Canal of the Italian navy coming from AOI. The British were afraid of the so-called "phantom column" which would cross the Libyan desert under the leadership of General Pietro Maletti. In 1940 Italo Balbo, the Governor of Libya, and later Graziani, seriously considered assembling a caravan of 6,000 camels which would reach the Sudan and Ethiopia from Cufra and take the British from the rear. The purchase of camels was made, but the caravan was not formed because it would become an easy target for the enemy air force. The plan was scrapped, but the myth remained. Ciano, *Diario*, 14 February 1938; Del Boca, *La Caduta Dell'Impero*, p. 552.

15. ACS/MAI 14/2 Maraffa: Revision of Censored mail: Propaganda leaflets for AOI n.d. (1941); ACS/MAI 12/12 Teruzzi to Duke of Aosta, 11 April 1941; ACS/ED Diary 45, 4 July 1942; Mussolini, *Storia di Un Anno*, p. 145; ACS/SPD-R Pisano, Secret Report to Mussolini, 1941; ACS/MAI 23/9 Pastore to Italian Commission for the Armistice with France, 17 July 1942; Del Boca, *La Caduta Dell'Impero*, pp. 549-55.

16. MAI/AV 112 Activity of Lucchetti in Ethiopia, 1953; ACS/PCM-B MAE to PCM in Salerno, 24 June 1944; Puglisi, "Impero", pp. 261, 297, 503.

17. Seymour, *Fatal Decision*, p. 96; ACS/EB Diary 45, 3 and 9 November 1942; Pankhurst, *British Policy*; Rossi, *L'Africa Italiana*.

18. Greenfield, *Ethiopia*, pp. 245-312; Gilks, *Dying Lion*, pp. 175-203; Hess, *Ethiopia*, Chapters 3 and 4; Perham, *The Government*, p. 374; Rodd, *British Military*, p. 77; Schwab, *Decision Making in Ethiopia*, pp. 29-31.

20. An Epilogue

The Fascist invasion of Ethiopia occurred 50 years ago, and, although the political situation today makes possible the publication of some hitherto unknown facts, much remains to be discovered about the events, personalities and motives that led to Italy's conquest of Ethiopia.

Until 1885 Italy's interest in north-east Africa and the Red Sea was limited to commercial concerns; but after the occupation of Massawa in 1885 it developed a political and military dimension.[1] Despite military disasters in Ethiopia in 1887 and 1896, Italy's contribution to the Allied victory during the First World War rekindled the hope of territorial gains in Africa. In 1913 and 1915 the Ministry of Colonies prepared a series of memoranda anticipating the cession to Italy of Djibouti, parts of British Somaliland and Kenya, and various Ethiopian territories; but only Jubaland was given to Italy, in 1924. Italy's self-delusion at the Paris Peace Conference subsequently contributed to the shift in Italian internal politics that led to the rise of Fascism and its international entanglements.[2]

Mussolini had a number of motives for wanting to conquer Ethiopia, including revenge for the defeat at Adowa in 1896, but one practical objective was to obtain territories to which Italians could emigrate. Another possible reason for Mussolini's decision to annex Ethiopia was Fascism's need for the prestige of a military victory and, to use Grandi's words, Italy's "mission to civilize the black continent".[3] Mussolini also used the pretext that Italy had been cheated at the Peace Treaty of Versailles after the First World War to make demands in Ethiopia and claim Italy's right to be dominant in the Mediterranean and increase its prestige in the Red Sea, thus fulfilling Mussolini's dream of Italy's great imperial destiny and territorial expansion.[4] Mussolini camouflaged the economic motives in his imperialism, in the cry to defend the white race against the barbaric Ethiopians. Hitler's coming to power in Germany, may have speeded up the invasion of Ethiopia, because it both raised the tension in Europe which would give Mussolini greater freedom to act, and suggested that Italy had better conquer Ethiopia soon, if it wanted its troops back on the northern frontier before the Germans were strong enough to attack Austria. The Duce carefully calculated that the German army would be too weak until 1937; therefore he aimed to conquer Ethiopia in the autumn of 1935. Mussolini also assumed that other European nations would not protest so long as the conquest was quick enough, especially as it was intended to arrange matters so that Ethiopia would appear the aggressor.[5]

The diplomatic preparations proved less easy than the military preparations. When Laval was informed about Mussolini's aggressive interest in Ethiopia, he made a vague verbal agreement to leave Italy some kind of free land in Africa. Although he did not agree explicitly to an Italian invasion he probably nevertheless gave an ambiguous approval in exchange for Mussolini's promise of Franco-Italian co-operation against Germany.[6] Mussolini certainly acted as though he had the backing of one of the great powers, which indeed shaped his successful diplomacy and eventually made possible his victory in Africa. While France confirmed that it did not care what happened in Ethiopia, Great Britain failed to stand up against the Italian dictator at the Stresa Conference of April 1935. Although Ethiopia was not officially discussed, British and Italian delegates exchanged views on the Italian invasion in Ethiopia but the Foreign Office refused to acknowledge that Mussolini would indeed occupy Ethiopia, even after it learned of an Italian military build-up in East Africa. Perhaps London thought it could prevent the Duce from occupying Ethiopia with the use of traditional diplomacy. Perhaps, too, Great Britain was prepared to hand Ethiopia over to Mussolini provided that it could be done without impairing the League of Nations. On the other hand, Mussolini mobilized his troops in order to extract territorial concessions from Great Britain and France in Ethiopia and to force European powers to accept his demands in Africa. During the Ethiopian crisis, as foreign statesmen who opposed Mussolini's Ethiopian policy dithered, the Duce gave proof of an efficient and unscrupulous capacity to manipulate people and an acute sense of intuition. But Mussolini did not demonstrate the same positive qualities when he had to deal with the needs of Italy, nor did he realize the international implications of the Ethiopian conquest, or the repercussions of the Fascist occupation among the African people.[7]

Yet Mussolini judged correctly that neither Britain nor France wanted to go to war (or blockade, or close the Suez Canal) to stop an Italian conquest, even though for many in Geneva this was a test case of the League's capacity to enforce its system of collective security. Cautiously, the League imposed limited economic and financial sanctions. These sanctions were meant to wear down Italy's fighting capacity over the two years it was estimated the war would run. But sanctions were limited, slow to work, and only partially supported. The United States never joined the boycott. In the short run, stockpiling and strict regulation of the economy allowed Italy to absorb these irritations without damage to the African campaign. Mussolini played on British and French fears in his threat of a European war should sanctions be extended to oil. He also won time by encouraging hopes that some sort of negotiated settlement was possible. War and diplomacy were thus closely related.[8]

Further evidence that Great Britain was willing to reach a compromise

An Epilogue

with Mussolini at the expense of Ethiopia was the Hoare-Laval Plan of December 1935. One of the main reasons for accommodation was the realization of the deplorable state of British defences in the Mediterranean and Mussolini's threats against British installations. Paris made it clear to London it would not go to war against Italy, which made it possible for Vansittart and Grandi to work out the terms of the Hoare-Laval Plan with a territorial redistribution in favour of Italy. When the plan was submitted to the Fascist Grand Council on 18 December, Mussolini instead of rejecting or accepting it, chose to wait until the following day perhaps hoping that the counter-proposals drawn up by his diplomats, which awarded Italy even more territory than proposed under the Hoare-Laval Plan, would be accepted. On the same day of the Grand Council meeting the House of Commons rejected the Hoare-Laval Plan. The Hoare-Laval Plan precipitated the death of the League of Nations because of its inability to defend a member, and because the Plan exposed the hypocrisy of the League.[9]

After the failure of the Hoare-Laval Plan, Mussolini realized that whether opposition was prolonged or intensified would be decided on the battlefield; if any settlement short of total conquest were necessary, the more Italy held the more Italy could claim. Hence the criticism of De Bono's conduct of the first stage of the northern campaign, his war of slow advance, of position, of subversion. Lessona told him in October: "Either Italy wins the war in a few months or it is lost". De Bono estimated no forward movement was possible for another two months. For Badoglio this was defeatism —the northern armies aimed at a rapid strategic offensive to force the battles that would destroy the Empire. On 12 November, increasingly anxious that his war not bog down, Mussolini gave Badoglio the northern command. If Badoglio succeeded, the burden of sanctions and international opposition would lift; if he failed, it would not be a failure of Mussolini's man but of the army.

Then, in mid-December, Ethiopian forces under *Rases* Kassa, Seyum, and Mulugeta opened a strong counteroffensive against the Italian line. These were anxious and uncertain days in Rome, as pressure for settlement and talk of an oil embargo were increasing. By the end of the month the sense of siege lifted dramatically. Britain and France, pursuing a negotiated settlement ouside the League, contrived a plan to carve up the Empire. Oil was never embargoed. At the beginning of January 1936, it was clear that while the Italian forces were not ready to renew the offensive, the Ethiopians could not break their line. The counteroffensive was turned back decisively — air power and poison gas were used to throw back the Ethiopian troops. Badoglio was emboldened, and by the spring of 1936 there remained only the army of the Emperor himself, waiting fatalistically for a final stand at Mar Cew. On 31 March that battle was joined; the next day it was over, the Emperor's forces in retreat. The crushing victory at Mai Cew proved wrong all European assumptions of a long war. No organized force stood between Badoglio and Addis Ababa.

Haile Selassie knew all was lost. The Empire was disintegrating. He had the choice of withdrawal to the west to mount guerrilla resistance or flight abroad, knowing as he had known throughout the conflict, that Ethiopia's cause would be won or lost by the extent of support it had in Europe. Within Ethiopia he was strongly criticized for not appearing on the battlefield against the Italian invaders until the final stages of the war. Instead, Haile Selassie fled the country, ostensibly to present the Ethiopian case before the League of Nations in Geneva. There, on 30 June 1936, he delivered his widely publicized and just as widely ignored speech warning that only collective security could protect small nations against the growing power of aggressive nations like Fascist Italy. From mid-1936 until mid-1940 Haile Selassie lived in exile in Bath, England.

The Emperor's departure solved the problem of how to deal with his authority: it enabled Mussolini to announce on 9 May 1936 that "Ethiopia is Italian" and made continued international measures against Italy futile. Taking advantage of Western irresolution and division, on 6 March Hitler had remilitarized the Rhineland. Eyes turned now to Germany. No one wanted to worry further about Ethiopia. Sanctions were raised on 4 July 1936. To base a state's security on the League made no sense. There was a general retreat from collective security, moves into neutrality, isolation, regional groupings, or appeasement.[10]

Mussolini's was a pyrrhic victory. In internal Italian terms, Badoglio had become a national hero, potentially a man capable of ousting the Duce in a time of national crisis. At the international level Mussolini had to take account of a more immediate enemy. Instead of accepting honourable retirement, Haile Selassie refused to vacate his throne. To do so would have wholly undermined his position within Ethiopia. Even in exile he remained a standing threat to the Italians, a figure of admonition and admiration to the increasing numbers of people in the democracies who were becoming committed to the idea of resisting Fascism in its various forms.

Whether or not the effort had been worthwhile, Mussolini was pleased with the results. Success had converted a war which was by his own reckoning immoral into something right and good. Not only had he defeated the League of Nations and a coalition of fifty-two powers who applied sanctions against him, but it looked like the rest of the world admired him for it, and far from arousing dismay at home, the war of aggression eventually proved hugely successful with public opinion. What the Duce could not see was that, apart from undoubted gains in prestige and propaganda, the conquest by itself was worth little until he had pacified Ethiopia and found the resources for its reconstruction. He did not yet realize that by increasing Italy's maritime vulnerability, a distant Empire would become a huge financial drain on an already heavily unbalanced budget; nor that it would weaken Italy in relation to both Germany and the Western powers. Many people recognized that what could be superficially portrayed as a great achievement might be in fact a potential disaster, especially when Mussolini began to act as though, just because he had defeated a poorly organized and ill-equipped army of irregulars, he could defeat anyone: it was argued that since the victory was

An Epilogue

a logical consequence of Fascist doctrine and organization, Italy had proved itself to be first among nations. A too easy success tempted Italy to play a much bigger role in Europe, without waiting to provide the resources which that role demanded.

The Ethiopian crisis was a perilous slide down the slope leading to the Second World War. By the time Italy became Germany's co-combatant in June 1940, Britain had made good some of the major deficiencies exposed in 1935. As a result of the Ethiopian crisis, the British gained invaluable experience of active-service conditions in the desert; and the Royal Navy had a much clearer appreciation of the types of ships required in the Mediterranean for modern warfare. Many lessons were learned in analysing the logistical problems of the frequent movement of men and materials. But the Ethiopian War had an even more significant result; Mussolini gave a powerful impetus to resentment against European rule in Africa. Italy's subsequent defeat in the Second World War was to have a profound influence on the form that decolonization was to take in Africa. Mussolini's Ethiopia certainly has to be seen in its African as well as in its European context. It may be argued that, while Mussolini's successful conquest of Ethiopia was shortlived, he contributed — through propaganda, subversion and terrorism —, to bring about the fall of other empires as well as his own.[11]

Mussolini employed all available means to procure himself an Empire: bribery was used to buy off Ethiopian chiefs and to corrupt willing politicians in Europe. He threatened armed intervention and used diplomacy to mollify statesmen. Less known is Mussolini's attempt at conciliation with Ethiopia which began before Italian troops ever set foot on Ethiopian soil and never ceased to operate. Mussolini would have settled for a protectorate over Ethiopia, retaining Haile Selassie in power, in exchange for Italian occupation of territories Menelik II had incorporated into Ethiopia half a century earlier, and economic advantages for Italy. These proposals tempted the Ethiopians. However, international mediation, motivated by political self-interest, interfered with Italian plans, and international negotiations for mutually acceptable terms were prolonged by impracticable discussions.[12]

Too busy conducting his foreign policy, Mussolini gave no thought to the development of a master plan for the organization and administration of Ethiopia after its occupation. *Africa Orientale Italiana* (AOI) was the official governmental designation for the reconstituted colonial possessions of Italy in north-east Africa. AOI consisted of the Red Sea colony of Eritrea, which was a union of the older colony and the former Ethiopian province of Tigre; Somalia, which was a union of that older colony and the Ethiopian Ogaden region; Shoa, the central heartland of Ethiopia; Amhara, the historical Christian areas of north-west Ethiopia; Harar, an eastern Muslim region annexed to Ethiopia half a century earlier; and Oromo-Sidamo, the southern provinces conquered by the Ethiopians between 1890 and 1910. The principle underlying this organization was the partition of the Ethiopian Empire into more or less homogeneous religious, political, and/or ethnic blocs that would transfer their loyalty from Haile Selassie I to Victor Emmanuel III. In the process,

Tigrinya-speaking populations of Eritrea and Tigre province were "reunited", as were the Somali of the Ogaden and their ethnic cousins in Somalia. The policy of reconstitution was intended to favour Muslims like the Oromo, Somali, and Danakil over the former ruling elites of Ethiopia, who were, for the most part, Christian Amhara. Despite the constitution of AOI, real power lay in the metropolitan government and the six regional governorships. The Viceroy or Governor-General in Addis Ababa was advised by a general council and had a wide degree of autonomy in budgetary, judicial, and administrative matters, as well as the right of direct communication with the Colonial Ministry. The first Viceroy of Ethiopia, Marshall Pietro Badoglio, was replaced six weeks after the fall of Addis Ababa by General Rodolfo Graziani who had commanded the Italian Army invading from the south. Graziani was replaced in November 1937 by the Duke of Aosta, Amedeo di Savoia, who governed the colony until its demise in 1941 and attempted a policy of reconciliation.[13]

Of all major colonial powers, Fascist colonial policy has been criticized the most because of its rigour and lack of sympathy for the needs of the people. Fascist colonial policy was the reverse of the colonial policy of the progressive powers. Mussolini had established in 1934 that Italy's historical destiny lay in a large African colonial empire stretching from the Indian Ocean to the Atlantic, which probably contributed not a little to the popularity of the Fascist regime. But once Ethiopia had been conquered, once the propaganda value of imperialism had been tapped, Mussolini lost interest. Probably he had no idea how to develop the colonies which had cost him so much to obtain. Perhaps he realized that there was no way of profitably exploiting the Empire. Although his ministers informed Mussolini personally and every day guided the course of imperial policy, he left these ministers for months on end in ignorance of what he intended, or whether he intended anything.[14]

Italian colonial policy in Ethiopia was not coherent. It tended to be a policy of differentiation, because it was different from the British and French colonial model, but had the specific characteristics of being a policy of submission and of suppression. Mussolini was a man moved by instinct and the irrational; he was dogmatic, not well read, amateur and opportunist. Basically a man of the 19th Century, he approached the colonial problem on the basis of the 18th Century, ignoring that the Africans too had made progress. Like the people of the 18th Century, he believed that the white man was superior to the black. Fascist colonization was racist, nationalistic, authoritarian, sterile, and founded on economic exploitation. The Fascist occupation of Ethiopia was the expression of a late imperialism, improvised and anachronistic. Mussolini's colonial policy was archaic and paternalistic; its power was derived directly from the top, reminiscent of Belgian colonialism which was devoid of cultural and social aspects, and the strict and systematic exploitation of Dutch colonialism; in sum, it adopted the old colonial concept of sacrificing the colony to the interest of the metropolis.

The Fascist occupation of Ethiopia repeated what the European powers

An Epilogue

had done in Africa without scruples in the 18th and 19th Centuries, but the West was now no longer willing to tolerate. The African people had made progress; there was the influence of American anti-colonialism, and an active communism, advocating the liberation of colonies. Colonial conquests were now considered obsolete because Europe had begun a period of evacuation of liberalization and self-government. While Fascist Italy in the 1930s conducted an aggressive and exploitative colonial policy, the other colonial powers had introduced a policy of collaboration and association with the African people. In 1935 the colonial people were awakening, while European hegemony was declining. In Italy, with its limited political outlook and lack of political and cultural cadres because the press was controlled by the regime, there was no dialogue between the country and the government on colonialism. Fascist Italy did not grasp the importance of the repercussions of European colonial changes and crisis; Italy, instead of becoming a full time participant, remained a distant observer. It is hard to believe that Mussolini was not aware of the changing world of colonialism but it is possible that because of his pride and conceit he did not understand the revolutionary and innovative character of the colonial empires, or that he interpreted it in a completely opposite way – that he judged the concessions made by the colonial powers to their colonial people, as a sign of weakness of the democracies due to their decaying civilization.

The awakening of the colonial people and the socio-economic-political concessions made to them were widely known. The anti-colonial revolution had its origin in the human desire for freedom, self-determination, opposition to economic exploitation. The process of colonial evolution toward independence and accommodation between the colonial people and the colonial power was well underway; the only powers who did not see this phenomenon were Spain, Portugal, Belgium, and Italy.

The Fascist aggression against Ethiopia awakened and intensified in the African elites the desire for self-determination and contributed to the slow growth of national consciousness. The Fascist occupation of Ethiopia appeared to the Africans as an attempt to consolidate and strengthen European power in Africa so as to block the push toward decolonization already in action. The elite of Sierra Leone, Ghana, and Kenya were the first to strengthen the Pan-African movement with the help of the International African Service Bureau, which included the names of the future chiefs of state of independent Africa such as Nnamdi Azikiwe, president of Nigeria, Jomo Kenyatta, president of Kenya, Kwame Nkrumah, president of Ghana, and I. T. A. Wallace-Johnson of Sierra Leone. Nkrumah was upset when he heard about the occupation of Ethiopia, not only because Ethiopia among the Africans was considered as the emblem of liberty and independence, but also because he considered the Fascist aggression against Ethiopia as offensive to Africa and to its peoples.

In the United States where 15 million black people lived, in semi-segregation, the Italo-Ethiopian conflict was a trauma. Moved by indignation against the Fascist aggressor, they constituted several committees for mutual aid and the defence of Ethiopia such as the American Aid for Ethiopia Society and the Friends of Ethiopia. They mobilized public opinion in favour of Ethiopia, appealed to the League of Nations to prevent Italian aggression and planned the unsuccessful recruiting of volunteers to send to Ethiopia. The blacks of America perceived the attack on Ethiopia as an attack on the black race, and felt a new sense of identity with Africa. Although the number of black Americans who fought for Ethiopia can be counted on the fingers of one hand, they nevertheless saw in Fascist imperialism a danger to liberty and democracy.

Fascism took upon itself the task of formulating a new type of colonial policy, imposing on the colonial people Fascist principles to demonstrate the efficiency and the superiority of Fascist colonial policy. A regime that had taken the liberty of the Italian people could not bring liberty to Africa. In Fascist colonial administration, the African was a small part of the vast bureaucratic machinery, subordinated to Italian interests. Fascist colonial policy did not provide the political and social opportunity for the colonial subjects and the realism of British colonial policy. Neither did Fascist policy come close to French assimilation that tended to make the African a participant in the civilization of the colonizer. Fascist policy followed obsolete schemes, based on authoritarianism and brute racism. There was no provision for local autonomy, no respect for the people's interests. In the Fascist administration, the concept of indirect rule was never considered. Even though the local traditions and institutions were promised respect, in reality the Fascist administrator paid lip service, always chose and nominated the local chiefs, and controlled their power and authority.[15]

Convinced that they had to deal with an entirely uncivilized community, the Fascist administrators, including Graziani, had instructions to impose the ideals of Fascism, which meant direct rule and a refusal to govern through local headmen, even when over so large an area as Ethiopia this might signify no government at all. Everyone was ordered to use only the Fascist salute, and Graziani lectured the Ethiopians patronizingly, pointing out that Italy had come to impose its highly developed civilization on the brutish traditions of a primitive feudal society. The Italian educational system had no long tradition of training colonial civil servants, so administrators came mainly from the party or the army: yet without a large class of local commissioners the Fascist system of direct rule could not work. Lessona laid down that Fascism as an authoritarian system demanded centralized rule.[16] Mussolini, for imperative reasons of publicity, announced in 1936 that all Ethiopia was conquered when in reality only a small area of the country was under direct Italian control; the proclamation of victory soon looked like a mere propaganda stunt. When the Italian generals reported to Rome that Addis Ababa was surrounded by large enemy forces, they were told to treat any surviving Ethiopian troops as "rebels" and hence all prisoners were to be shot without trial. Mussolini ordered that brute force should be preferred to magnanimity; his instructions were not only to execute prisoners, but to continue using poison gas and "a systematic policy of terror and extermination".

One of Mussolini's most infamous decisions was to kill off young Ethiopian intellectuals on the assumption that without them the country would be more easily governed. Some prominent citizens surrendered on the promise of a pardon, only to be shot out of hand. The worst excesses occurred in February 1937, after an attempt on Graziani's life. The would-be assassins were two Eritreans in the employ of the Italian Political Office in Addis Ababa. They were motivated by nationalistic feelings and the desire to free Ethiopia from Italian rule. Italian soldiers and militiamen ran wild for several days, looting and killing indiscriminately. Obviously it was a panic reaction. Telegrams from Mussolini confirmed that "all suspects must be executed immediately", and in any village where resistance was encountered "all adult males must be shot". Foreign observers were appalled by cruelties which seemed to serve no political purpose whatsoever. Known for his brutality in Libya during the early 1930s (he was popularly called the "hyena of Libya"), the ruthless Graziani came to be known among Ethiopians as "the butcher of Addis Ababa" following the execution of the monks and nuns of the famous monastery of Debra Libanos in retaliation for the attempt on his life. By August Graziani believed he had crushed all resistance. Instead, his brutality provoked general revolt. Despite savage reprisals and massive use of poison gas, rebellion spread. He stepped up his repression, taking advantage of the fact that the Ethiopians were without their leaders, without new supplies of arms, and divided against themselves.[17] These events were symptomatic of the failure of the Italian Army to gain effective control over the countryside. Large sections of Ethiopia never came under direct Italian rule during the five years of the Italian occupation.

By the end of 1937 it was clear that Graziani had failed, so he was brought home. The new Viceroy was the Duke of Aosta, a wiser and more moderate man, but he found it hard to choose a different policy, and harsh police methods did not come to an end. The Duke inherited a rebellious colony from Graziani and received an insufferable superior, Attilio Teruzzi and two disloyal subordinates, Ugo Cavallero and Enrico Cerulli, from Mussolini. Despite frequent illness, he overcame these rivals and other colonial problems, assisted by Nasi. Nasi gained appointment as Vice-Governor-General in May 1939. Agreeing that force had failed, the Duke and Nasi obtained approval for less brutal policies in July 1939, which had nearly pacified the Empire by March 1940.

Because Italian colonial policy was based on the use of force and Ethiopia was in a state of continuous war, Mussolini's propaganda that Ethiopia would help overcome Italy's food and raw material shortages proved false. Mussolini's demographic colonization programme was not ready. It was a re-establishment of the 19th Century theory that history had already rejected. The Fascist authorities had assumed that the agricultural possibilities of the Empire were almost inexhaustible, and that in a few years this fact would create a real economic asset for Italy. Although relevant statistics were confused or concealed, exports from Ethiopia were declining and in some cases ceased altogether. Partly this was because a multiplicity of state controls made economic life difficult. Partly it was the widespread refusal by Ethiopians to accept Italian paper currency instead of the familiar silver Maria Theresa dollar which alone they trusted. Partly it was that labour shortages and heavy government expenditure resulted in everyone earning five times what was normal in Italy, which made the prices of Ethiopian goods uncompetitive. Another obvious reason was the fact that many agricultural labourers were drafted to make roads, so that some plantations closed down altogether.[18]

These uncertain political and military conditions in Ethiopia discouraged Italian farmers from migrating to East Africa. Italy was committed to give land to Italian settlers, but attempts to relocate Italian farming families in Ethiopia failed, with much loss of time and money. Only those who belonged to the Fascist Party and had political connections could go. This had the drawback of sending to Ethiopia farmers who were not always competent. Although the historian Benedetto Croce alleged that Fascism had overcome the traditional indifference of the Italians, after the conquest of Ethiopia the Italian people plunged back into their apathy for colonial matters. Few were interested in making a home in Ethiopia, except those attracted by the lure of making a fortune.

Mussolini decided that his new Empire's exploitation could not be left to free initiative, but should be state planned. As early as 1936 the army confiscated some of the more fertile areas, and eventually the law caught up with practice: the categories of land that could be taken included estates belonging to the ex-Emperor or to the Patriots, or which were uncultivated, or where the government thought the land could be cultivated more efficiently. It was admitted that this was a highly delicate matter, since the Ethiopians felt very strongly about land questions, but the practice was justified on the basis that all land belonged to Italy because of its victory over Ethiopia.

If Fascism planned to make the Italian first a sharecropper and later a landholder, the Ethiopian was transformed from landowner to day labourer. The agricultural exploitation was at the expense of the local people: not only in terms of loss of land and manpower, but also in terms of the disintegration of African society. In the colonization programme with government agricultural agencies (*Ente*) the Italian farmer was interested in obtaining from the land and from farm products the maximum profit with the minimum expenditure. This economic process implied that in order to economize, wages paid to Ethiopians were squeezed. Hence the reason for tense relations between the Italian colonizer and the Ethiopian peasant who was defrauded of his land, cheated and under paid.

Despite the fact that the countryside was never fully pacified and that occasionally Ethiopian guerrilla Patriots came perilously close to disrupting the new public order, the Ministry of Italian Africa was determined to develop the new colony as rapidly as possible. It proved to be a Herculean task, for mountainous Ethiopia lacked a basic telecommunications and transportation infrastructure. The costs of the military campaign and occupation of Ethiopia reached the enormous amount of 38,851 billion lire or US$ 7.2 billion for the period 1934-7, and the costs of development were just as huge. For the first year of colonial administration (1936-7), the government of AOI put together a budget request of 19.136 billion lire while the revenue for all Italy that year amounted to 18.581 billion lire! On the road system alone the Italians eventually spent more than two billion lire. Clearly, the Empire was to be a very costly proposition for autarkic Italy. Although plans for the conquest of Ethiopia had been drafted in great detail, virtually no plans had been formulated for the development of the colonial territory after the projected victory, although Mussolini preferred colonization based on agriculture. Because of the paucity of knowledge of the climate, soil fertility, and system of land tenure, a number of investigations were undertaken. Initially, it was decided to encourage the settlement of Italian peasants first in Shoa (near secure Addis Ababa) and in Harar province along the Addis Ababa-Djibouti railway, and then in Amhara and Oromo-Sidamo provinces after the construction of feeder roads. A number of colonizing agencies were recognized, but by the end of 1940, only about 3,200 farmers had settled in Ethiopia, or less than 10 per cent of the agencies' goals. Non-farming colonists were put at between 2,000 and 4,255 – far fewer than the millions of peasant farmers Mussolini aspired to settle in Ethiopia. The seven *enti di colonizzazione* earmarked 578 million lire for investment capital in agriculture, but only 121 million lire were actually invested in AOI.

In sum, Italy's policies in AOI were neither realistic nor coherent. Sullen colonials, occasional guerrilla incursions, problems of terrain and resources as well as lack of capital, and the uncertainty of political and military conditions hampered the development of AOI and discouraged prospective immigrants. The sequel to the facade of dramatic military triumph in 1936 was the failure to achieve sustained colonial development in the few short years remaining before the Second World War and the loss of Mussolini's Ethiopia.[19]

Besides a reign of terror and exploitation of people, Fascist rule in Ethiopia was marred by corruption. This involved Italians and Ethiopians alike. Ethiopians were bribed before and after the Ethiopian War. Because of greed and political opportunism they sided with the stronger party, like the Azebu Oromo. For political reasons some of the great *rases*, like Gugsa and Hailu, went to the Italians in hope that they might be recognized rulers over their regions or even become *Negus*: others may have gladly received Italian handouts because of their venality and sense of deference but also deep down they were waiting for the right moment to remove the foreign yoke.

Although the Ethiopians during the Fascist occupation gave the impression of collaborating with the new colonial masters they were unable to establish smooth relations with the Fascists or to mitigate the effects of violence and cruelty because Fascist racial policy implied the principle of the subjugation of the conquered people. Furthermore, the Empire was plagued by corrupt practices in the bureaucracy. Not having to bother with normal methods of accounting, De Bono and Graziani had been able to award huge contracts to their own friends and clients without competitive tenders and without any effective supervision from Rome. Mussolini did not mind much about minor speculation among subordinates: his first interest was to see that scandals remained a secret, and his second was to use his private knowledge as a kind of threat so as to compel loyalty and obedience. Since public criticism was not permitted, Fascist *gerarchi* knew that they had a guaranteed immunity from the courts as long as they kept in with the party and with Mussolini himself. Lessona accused De Bono of corruption and of deliberately ignoring cheaper contractors in order to give a virtual monopoly of public works to a concern with which he was financially involved. As a result of this method of contracting, roads and airports in East Africa were costing twenty times what they would in Italy, and a few powerful individuals and companies took over the economic life of the Italian colonies. The existence of different police forces in the Empire, each with a different ministerial allegiance, suggests that the Fascist tendency to bureaucracy and to the creation of private empires got completely out of hand. All manner of parasitical offices were set up, often overlapping, and providing the finance and the "clientelistic" retinue for many a minor Fascist *gerarca*. Among these offices were the capillary ramifications of the party, and the corporative system, which hardly worked in Italy let alone in the completely alien conditions of Africa. All this helped to reduce the effectiveness of administration, slowing decisions and depriving individual officials of responsibility for actions taken.

Italy's administration of the new colony was defective from the start. The Minister of African Affairs found his Italian civil servants to be unruly and disobedient, and police reports informed Mussolini about the misconduct of Fascist adventurers who were mainly concerned with the provision of jobs for their relatives and clients. It was reported that there was in Ethiopia much outright robbery, little control, much monopoly, and vast sums of money getting into the wrong hands; two years in Ethiopia was enough to take an unscrupulous man all the way from pauper to millionaire.[20]

Another drawback in Fascist colonial policy was its racialism. Mussolini did not think of racial matters until the conquest of Ethiopia, yet there were trends of some kind of apartheid. Italy, he proclaimed, had conquered Ethiopia because of its cultural and racial superiority and because the Ethiopians had an irreducible mental inferiority. Before 1935, it was argued Italians lacked racial prejudice partly due to Italy's humanistic traditions as indicated by the practice of *Madamismo*. The attitude changed after 1935 when large numbers of Afro-Italian children were born from those contacts, which in the Fascist ideology was offensive to the white race. Hence Mussolini introduced a racial policy that because of the time, the method and the form it took was provocative.

The 1938 racial legislation did not allow the preparation of an elite in Ethiopia: Ethiopians were to be obedient and submissive, destined to be subordinate and hold secondary or inferior positions. They were condemned to be eternal "little children"! In addition, Mussolini believed that the reason for the decline of former civilization was indiscriminate interracial unions. Possessing this pseudo-scientific knowledge, Mussolini forged ahead with his racial policy. To protect the white race, Mussolini prohibited unions between Italians and Ethiopians; condemned *madamismo*; Italians were to live in separate sections of towns, and Afro-Italian children were considered a crime against God! Mussolini's passage of racial legislation may have been motivated more by ideology than racism. The separation of Ethiopians and Italians was emphasized to justify the domination of one race over another. The confluence of these factors, the racism engendered by a new imperialist consciousness, and Mussolini's desire to be ahead of Hitler for the leadership of international Fascism culminated in the publication of the Manifesto of Fascist Racism in July 1938.

By adopting the myth of Aryan superiority, the Duce hoped to infuse the Italians with the same prideful arrogance that the Germans had and to recapture the early Fascist spirit of *menefreghismo* ("Don't-give-a-damn") in preparation for the conflicts which lay ahead. But the new racial theories were poorly received by most Italians who saw the new policy as an embarrassing emulation of crude Nazi doctrines. Moreover, the Italians never went beyond the initial policy of discrimination, and there was a reassertion of a deep Italian virtue: the triumph of old humanitarian values over new Fascist principles. In spite of these drawbacks the Ethiopians made a distinction between Italian Fascists and individual Italians. In fact with the re-entry of Haile Selassie the Ethiopian people showed restraint in their actions against the defenceless Italians. It would no doubt have been hard for Italians to become popular in Ethiopia, but they would have had more chance if they could have afforded to show magnanimity, instead of cruelty, arrogance, and insistence on make-believe.[21] In the long run, however, regardless of what type of colonial policy was adopted by the Italians, the Ethiopian people would have rejected the rule of foreigners in answer to a higher call of self-determination and the inalienable right to live free and independent.

The Italian entry into the Second World War offered Great Britain the opportunity to invade Ethiopia from the Sudan and Kenya. On 20 January 1941, Haile Selassie returned to Ethiopia with the invading Ethiopian and British troops. On 5 May 1941, he re-entered Addis Ababa, five years to the day after it had fallen to the Italian Army.

Fascism brought the evils of war and colonial interests to Ethiopia, but the Italian occupation of Ethiopia also dramatically shook mediaeval institutions and a traditional way of life. Capitalizing upon the Italian attempts to impose governmental authority throughout Ethiopia, the restored Haile Selassie could then launch in earnest his campaigns to bring the whole country under his own rule, which his subjects ultimately found just as oppressive as Fascist rule. Italy spent a great deal of money for its Empire in the five years before it collapsed, but it got little benefit in return and reaped hatred because the basic aims of Fascism were domination and conquest, not economic growth or social improvement. The only original policy of Fascism managing to put Italy in the avant-garde of Europe was investment in Ethiopia for the building of civilian, administrative structures, and for public works. Italy invested in Ethiopia with largesse and generosity huge sums of money, which were badly needed back home where some regions had among the lowest standard of living in Europe. These expenditures, however, were directed more to political and military purposes than to the benefit of the community or to a working economy.

In the postwar period Haile Selassie was determined to wrest control of the former Italian colony of Eritrea. In 1952 he succeeded in federating Eritrea with Ethiopia under a single crown. Behind the scenes, however, there was increasing disaffection from the newly educated classes that he had helped create. Once known as a modernizer and progressive, he became regarded in Ethiopia as an obstacle to greater progress and development. When disillusion spread to the military, his days were numbered. In the unsuccessful attempt to remove the Emperor during the 13-14 December 1960 coup, the rebel government declared an end to the feudal autocracy perpetrated by Haile Selassie and pledged a socialist programme under a constitutional monarchy. By 1963, however, Haile Selassie again emerged as a major figure by summoning the founding meeting of the Organization of African Unity and devised the charter for the body whose headquarters are in Addis Ababa. Despite reconciliation with Italy and the symbolic restitution to Ethiopia of various items looted by the Fascists, the Emperor could no longer capitalize on his earlier image. Indeed, the memory of the Emperor who fled the country rather than die on the battlefield resurfaced. Adding to the erosion of his prestige was the revelation that the government had attempted to cover up a disastrous famine in Wollo province. Beginning in February 1973 the Emperor yielded to one demand after another from the military, from striking workers, and from students. The "creeping coup" evolved into a full-scale military revolution. On 13 September 1974, Haile Selassie was deposed and placed under house arrest. Less than a year later on 27 August 1975 he died and was buried in an unknown place in an unmarked grave!

Notes

1. Hess, "Italian Imperialism", pp. 95-6.
2. Giglio and Ladolini, *Guida*, p. 77.
3. Mack Smith, *Mussolini Roman Empire*, p. 59.
4. Mack Smith, *Mussolini: A Biography*, p. 33.
5. Mack Smith, *Mussolini Roman Empire*, pp. 60, 65.
6. Ibid, p. 65.
7. Mori, *Mussolini*, p. 305.

8. Canistraro, *Historical Dictionary*, p. 186.
9. Robertson, *Mussolini*, p. 185.
10. Canistraro, *Historical Dictionary*, pp. 184–8.
11. Mack Smith, *Mussolini Roman Empire*, p. 76; Robertson, *Mussolini*, p. 189.
12. Lagardelle, *Mission*, p. 168; ACS/MM 7/18 Political Reports to the Duce: Rinaldini to Morgagni, 19 March 1936.
13. Canistraro, *Historical Dictionary*, pp. 5–6.
14. Mack Smith, *Mussolini Roman Empire*, p. 120.
15. Zaghi, *L'Africa*, Chapter 8; Asante, *Pan-African*, pp. 213–16.
16. Mack Smith, *Mussolini Roman Empire*, pp. 78, 111.
17. Ibid, pp. 77–9.
18. Ibid, p. 108.
19. Ibid, p. 109; Canistraro, *Historical Dictionary*, pp. 5–6.
20. Ibid, pp. 80, 110–11.
21. Mack Smith, *Mussolini Roman Empire*, pp. 77, 81, 108.

Bibliography

1. Unpublished Sources

The bulk of this research was conducted in Rome at the archives of the former *Ministero dell'Africa Italiana*, at the *Archivio Centrale di Stato* and at the archives of the *Opera Nazionale Cobattenti*. In Florence I was able to gain access to the *Archivio Documentario dell'Istituto Agronomo per l'Oltremare*. At the *Fondazione Einaudi* in Turin I used *I Documenti del Conte Paolo Thaon Di Revel*.

Without the use of the documents of the Ministry of Africa it would have been difficult to reconstruct the history of Italy's occupation of Ethiopia from 1936 to 1940. Although each of the five Directorates of the Ministry of Africa had its own archives, the documents of the *Direzione Affari Civili* and of the *Direzione Affari della Colonizzazione e Lavoro* are not available; much of their papers were lost or found their way into other files. Whereas the *Archivio Storico del Ministero dell'Africa Italiana* was created in 1926 as a repository for materials of general historical colonial interest, not all the directorates passed on copies of documents to the *Archivio Storico*. Furthermore, the organization of the *Archivio Storico* did not really begin until 1937 and was interrupted at the outbreak of the Second World War. Unfortunately, during the war years the *Archivio Storico* was moved from place to place with the consequent loss and theft of documents. In the early 1950s when the *Comitato per la Documentazione delle Attività Italiane in Africa* was formed to publish a series of books documenting Italian contributions in Africa, it attempted a reorganization of the remaining documents of the *Archivio Storico*. It is upon this archival material that the *Comitato* bases its publications, which are descriptive rather than analytical and may be regarded as an apologia for Italian colonialism. Authors in charge of preparing volumes for the *Comitato* occasionally removed documents for study. Even when such documents were returned to the Archive they could not be found; they were not replaced in the original archival position because of a shortage of clerical help. Although the *Archivio Storico* documents were of limited help, I was allowed after some delay to consult the remaining files such as the *Archivio Segreto del Gabinetto*, the documents of the *Direzione Affari Politici*, and the *Direzione*

Affari Economici e Finanziari and the less important but nevertheless useful documents of the *Consiglio Superiore Coloniale*, the *Archivio Documentario* and the *Archivio Storico al Nord*.

It must be pointed out that the source material in the above mentioned archives are all *segreto* (secret), *riservato* (confidential), and *riservatissimo* (highly confidential) even though I have not included this information in the notes.

None of the archives are well organized; they are, however, of extreme importance because they contain reports to Mussolini from the Minister of Africa, and correspondence with the various Ministries, Governors and the Viceroy. They include information on individuals, on the state of the economy, on the political situation of the Empire and the minutes of meetings of the Governors, the correspondence of the private secretary of the Minister of Africa and the reports of his visits to Ethiopia. They also deal with religious matters; relations with Ethiopian chiefs and the indigenous population; land policy; the political-military situation; economic administration, budget, deficits, expenditures, trade, explorations, and tributes. Special mention must also be made of the 25,000 newspaper articles on the colonies and of the documents gathered by former colonial officials which I found at the archives of the *Comitato*, such as the papers of Adolfo Vitale, Francesco Caroselli and Massimo Colucci.

Equally important for my research were the archival resources at the *Archivio Centrale di Stato* in Rome. Also of a secret or confidential nature, they are mostly documents on Fascist personalities of the *Segreteria Particolare del Duce* and of documents belonging to several ministries and the *Presidenza del Consiglio dei Ministri*. Of the personal papers, the *Carte Graziani* were the most important. They consist of more than 70 folders and are an indispensable tool for analysing the early period of Italian administration of the Empire. The Graziani papers housed at the Italian States Central Archives in Rome were reorganized in 1982. The pre-1982 file numbers used do not therefore correspond with post-1982 numbers. Also important are the *Diari De Bono*, some 50 pocket-size books in which he recorded his memoirs and criticism of Fascist personalities from 1922 to 1943. The *Carte di Pietro Badoglio* are well organized and deal mostly with the preparations for the war of Ethiopia. I have also used the *Carte Barracu*, Undersecretary of the Ministry of Africa during the Fascist Republic of Northern Italy, and the *Carte Stefani-Morgagni*, important for their secret political reports to Mussolini from Italian news agencies in foreign capitals. Equally valuable are the papers of the *Segreteria Particolare del Duce, Carteggi Ordinario e Riservato* from 1922 to 1943 and for the period of the *Repubblica Sociale* from 1943-1945. They are a mine of information on Fascist personalities and political opponents of the regime. Deposited at the *Archivio Centrale* are also documents from various ministries, including 28 folders of the *Ministero dell'Africa Italiana: Direzione degli Affari Politici* on political and international matters concerning Ethiopia. For the reconstruction of Italy's military involvement in Ethiopia and operation of colonial policy there are the *Fondi del Ministero dell'Aeronautica*, whose documents are extremely well organized although only a part refers to the colonies. The documents of the *Ministero della Cultura Popolare* provide a deep insight into the mood of the Italian people during the war of the conquest of Ethiopia; it contains censored mail, articles of front line press correspondents and Italian news agency reports from foreign countries. There is an abundance of documents from the various directorates of the *Ministero dell'Interno* such as the *Affari Generali Riservati*; *Conflitto Mondiale*; *Conflitto Italo-Etiopico*; *Mobilitazione Classe 1911*; and the *Fondo della Polizia Politica*. These give information on the attitude of the Italian people during the war, the number of people sent to prison for opposing the African campaign and the list of military personnel who had refused to go to Africa. Important also are the folders of Fascist authorities who volunteered in the colonial conquest. The documentation of the *Ministero delle Marina* is unique because it reveals the impact of the League of Nation's sanctions on Italy's economy, trade, and shipping. Of significance are the secret reports of the naval attaché in London during the tense days of November 1935-January 1936, when Italy threatened to use force in case Great Britain closed the Suez Canal to Italian shipping.

Another mine of information is provided by the *Documenti della Presidenza del Consiglio dei Ministri 1935-1942*, the papers of the *Presidenza del Consiglio* during the war years in southern Italy at Brindisi-Salerno, 1943-4 and the *Presidenza del Consiglio della Repubblica Sociale 1943-1945* in northern Italy. The 1935-42 documentation deals with all aspects of Italian involvement in Ethiopia, although the files are not systematic and many documents are missing. The files for 1943-5 provide little information on the colonies.

I have used other archives, especially the *Archivio Documentario dell' Istituto Agronomo per l'Oltremare* in Florence, which holds several thousand reports, memoirs and studies on the agriculture and economy of Ethiopia — indispensable for an understanding of the work and the difficulties of Italian colonization.

For materials on demographic colonization, in Rome there is the *Archivio dell'Opera Nazionale Combattenti*, the most successful colonizing agency; letters, reports and memoirs yield a profound insight into the causes of the slow progress of Italian colonization and the frustrations of its leaders. Also very valuable are the *Documenti del Conte Paolo di Revel*, former Minister of Finance, available at the *Fondazione Einaudi* in Turin. The documents are meticulously preserved and although not complete they are the only available source on the economic conditions of Italy between 1935 and 1940; they also evaluate the cost of the empire.

At the *Archivio dell'Università di Palermo, Facoltà di Giurisprudenza*, there is a priceless thesis by the Duke of Aosta in which the young prince expresses his colonial philosophy. I have also gained much profit from the microfilms of the British Foreign Office, *Correspondence Respecting Abyssinia, 1935-1937*, which contain the records and reports of the British consular representative in Ethiopia; and from *The Italian Captured*

Documents 1922–1943 at the US National Archives in Washington, DC. In Rome the *Biblioteca dell'Istituto Italiano per l'Africa* has the best Africana collection in Italy, including pamphlets, important newspapers and periodicals, and a complete collection of the gubernatorial decrees gathered in the *Bolletino Ufficiale* of each of six Governorships of Italian East Africa. Also important is the *Biblioteca dell'Istituto per la Storia e le Instituzioni dei Paesi Afro-Asiatici* at the University of Pavia, which preserves a select and unique collection of books and periodicals on Africa. At the *Biblioteca Comunale di Milano* there is the 800-page report of General Ugo Cavallero on his military activities as Commander-in-Chief of the Italian Army in AOI: *Gli Avvenimenti Militari nell'Impero dal Gennaio 12, 1938 al Gennaio 12, 1939*. In the United States, at the New York Public Library, Manuscript Division, I found the diary of Florence Colgate Speranza, wife of the American Press Attaché at the Embassy in Rome during 1935-6.

I was also able to consult the papers of Dino Grandi, entrusted to the care of Renzo De Felice, in Rome. Grandi, former Minister of Foreign Affairs and Italian Ambassador in London, was instrumental in directing Italian Fascist foreign policy. Among his papers can be found the documentation that explains Mussolini's decision in 1929 to follow a policy of collaboration with France leading to the Laval-Mussolini Agreement. As a diplomat in Great Britain, Grandi expended great effort to bring about closer Anglo-Italian relations during the Italo-Ethiopian crisis and was instrumental in drafting the Hoare-Lavel Plan. The study of Grandi's documentation has given a new dimension to the diplomatic history of the Italian conquest of Ethiopia.

Although this list of archives is extensive, I have mentioned only the major repositories. However, in Italy there is much more to be discovered; almost all public or government agencies, private companies, and personalities were involved in Ethiopia. Documentation and memories of the Ethiopian adventure are awaiting someone to make good use of them.

At the Archives of the Ethiopian Patriotic Association in Ethiopia I was able to consult the documentation on the activities of the Patriots during the Italian occupation. The association is in the process of gathering information and publishing a number of works documenting the Ethiopian resistance against Italy.

Also in Addis Ababa, the Manuscript Division of the National Library houses a number of letters, correspondence of the Patriots among themselves in the various regions and with Haile Selassie. The main library also has a rather useful collection of periodicals during the 1930s selected by the former Director, Stephen Wright. At the University of Addis Ababa Library, there are a number of college research projects and BA theses on topics for which there is little written information. For example, one may find biographies of *Lij* Yasu, Gerarsu Duki, *Ras* Imru, etc. Likewise, the Manuscript Division of the Institute of Ethiopian Studies is the repository of information relating to the Patriots.

II. Published Official Sources

Ethiopia: Food and Agricultural Council. *Report to FAO, 1947*. Addis Ababa, 1947.
Ethiopia: Ministry of Justice. *Documents on Italian War Crimes*. Addis Ababa, 1950, 2 vols.
Ethiopia: Press and Information Service. *La Civilisation de l'Italie Fascists*. 2 vols. Addis Ababa, 194?.
Great Britain: *Agreement and Military Convention Between the United Kingdom and Ethiopia*. Addis Ababa, 31 January 1941.
Great Britain: War Office. *British Military Administration of Occupied Territories in Africa*. London, 1945.
Great Britain: "Dispatches of General A. Wavell, General A. Cunningham and General W. Platt on the Military Operations in Abyssinia, 1940-1941", *The London Gazette*. (Supplement to 10 July 1946.)
Great Britain: *The Abyssinian Campaign*. London, 1942.
Italy: Camera dei Deputati. *Atti Parlamentari, 1935-1942*.
Italy: Consociazione Turistica Italiana. *Africa Orientale Italiana*. Milan, 1938.
Italy: Governo dell'Amara. *Bollettino Ufficiale del Governo dell'Amara, 1936-1939*.
Italy: Governo del Galla-Sidama. *Bollettino Ufficiale del Governo del Galla-Sidama, 1937-1940*.
Italy: Governo dell'Harar. *Bollettino Ufficiale del Governo dell'Harar, 1936-1940*.
Italy: Governo Generale dell'Africa Orientale Italiana. *Giornale del Governo Generale dell'Africa Orientale Italiana, 1936-1940*.
Italy: Governorato di Addis Abeba. *Bollettino Ufficiale del Governorato di Addis Abeba, 1936-1939*.
Italy: (Ministero dell'Africa Italiana). *Memorandum on the Economic and Financial Situation of Italian Territories in Africa*. Rome, 1946.
Italy: Ministero dell'Africa Italiana. *Progetto d'Ordinamento Fondiario per l'AOI*. Rome, n.d. (1942).
Italy: Ministero degli Affari Esteri, Comitato per la Documentazione delle Attività Italiane in Africa. *L'Amministrazione della Giustizia in AOI*. Rome, 1972.
Italy: Ministero degli Affari Esteri, Comitato per la Documentazione delle Attività Italiane in Africa. *L'Avvaloramento e la Colonizzazione*. Rome, 1970.
Italy: Ministero degli Affari Esteri, Comitato per la Documentazione delle Attività Italiane in Africa. *Il Governo dei Territori Oltremare*. Rome, 1963.
Italy: Ministero degli Affari Esteri. *Utilizzazione degli Italiani all'Estero per i Bisogni del Paese in Guerra*. Rome, 1939.
Italy: Reale Accademia d'Italia. *Atti del Convegno di Scienze Morali e Storiche*. Rome, 4-11 October 1938.
Italy: Reale Accademia d'Italia. *Atti dell'VIII Congresso sul Tema "Africa"*. Rome, 4-8 October 1940.
League of Nations: *Official Journal 1935-1940*.

III. Books

Abbie Gubegna, *Defiance*. Addis Ababa, 1975.
Allen, W.E.D. *Guerrilla War in Ethiopia*. Harmondsworth, 1943.
Aloisi, Pompeo. *Journal 1932-1936*. Paris, 1957.
Ambrosi, L. *Aspetti del Diritto Agrario nelle Terre dell'AOI*. Milan, 1941.
Ambrosini, Gaspare. *L'Impero d'Etiopia*. Turin, 1938.
Ambrosio, Vincenzo. *Tre Anni fra i Galla-Sidama*. Rome, 1942.
Asante, S.K.B. *Pan African Protest: West Africa and the Italo-Ethiopian Crisis*. London, 1977.
Asmeron Legesse. *Gada*. New York, 1973.
Augenti, G., Martino, G., et al. *Il Dramma di Graziani*. Bologna, 1950.
Badoglio, Pietro. *L'Italia nella Seconda Guerra Mondiale*. Milan, 1946.
Baer, G. *Test Case: Italy, Ethiopia and the League of Nations*. Stanford, 1976.
Baer, George. *The Coming of the Italo-Ethiopian War*. Cambridge, 1967.
Bandini, Franco. *Gli Italiani in Africa*. Milan, 1971.
Barker, A.J. *The Rape of Ethiopia*. New York, 1971.
Bartolozzi, Enrico. *Case Rurali dell'AOI*. Florence, 1940.
Beckingham, C.F. and Huntingford, G.W. *Some Records of Ethiopia 1593-1646*. London, 1954.
Bernoville, Gaetan. *Monseigneur Jarosseau et la Mission des Gallas*. Paris, 1950.
Bertola, A. *Il Regime dei Culti nell'Africa Italiana*. Bologna, 1939.
Bertola, Arnaldo. *Storia e Istituzioni dei Paesi Afro-Asiatici*. Turin, 1964.
Bongiovanni, Luigi. *Problemi dell'Etiopia Italiana*. Rome, 1936.
Brotto, E. *Il Regime delle Terre nel Governo dell'Harar*. Harar, 1939.
Bruttini, A. and Puglisi, G. *L'Impero Tradito*. Florence, 1957.
Canevari, Emilio. *La Guerra Italiana: Retroscena della Disfatta*. Rome, 1948.
Canistraro, Philip, (ed). *Historical Dictionary of Fascist Italy*. Westport, 1982.
Caroselli, Francesco S. *Scritti Politici*. Bologna, 1941.
Cavallero Ugo. *Gli Avvenimenti Militari nell'Impero dal 12 Gennaio 1938 al 12 Gennaio 1939*. Addis Ababa, 1939.
Cecchi, D. Bolech. *L'Accordo dei due Imperi*. Milan, 1977.
Cerulli, Enrico. *Etiopia Schiavista*. Rome, 1935.
Chiurco, Giorgio. *La Sanità delle Razze nell'Impero Italiano*. Rome, 1940.
Churchill, W. *The Grand Alliance*. Boston, 1950.
Churchill, W. *Their Finest Hour*. Boston, 1949.
Churchill, W. *The Second World War*. London, 1964.
Ciano, Galeazzo. *Diario 1937-1938*. Bologna, 1948.
Ciano, Galeazzo. *Europa Verso la Catastrofe*. Milan, 1948.
Ciccarone, A. *Il Problema delle Ruggini nei Grani d'Etiopia*. Florence, 1947.
Ciferri, R. *Frumenti e Granicoltura Indigena in Etiopia*. Florence, 1939.
Collins, R. *The Southern Sudan*. New Haven, 1962.
Colombi, Emilio. *L'Impero dell'Africa Italiana*. Genoa, 1939.
Confederazione Fascista degli Agricoltori. *Gli Agricoltori per la Valorizzazione dell'Impero*. Rome, 1937.
Confederazione Fascista degli Agricoltori. *Relazione di Una Missione di Agricoltori in AOI*. Florence, 1937.
Conti, Rossini, Carlo. "Il Regime Fondiario Indigeno in Etiopia", in Sindacato Tecnici Agricoli, *Agricoltura ed Impero*. Rome, 1937.

Cortese, Guido. *Problemi dell'Impero*. Rome, 1938.
Dente Di Pirajno, Alberto. *A Cure for Serpents*. London, 1955.
D'Eramo, Ennio. *L'Amministrazione delle Forze Militari Terrestri dell'AOI*. Rome, 1941.
De Felice, R. *Mussolini il Duce: Gli Anni del Consenso*. Turin, 1974.
De Monfreid, Henry. *Avion Noir*. Paris, 1936.
Del Boca, A. *Gli Italiani in Africa Orientale: La Caduta dell'Impero*. Rome, 1982.
Del Boca, Angelo. *La Guerra d'Abissinia*. Milan, 1965.
Del Boca, A. *The Ethiopian War*. Chicago, 1969.
Di Lauro, Raffaele. *Come Abbiamo Difeso l'Impero*. Rome, 1949.
Di Lauro, Raffaele. *Panorama Politico-Economico dei Galla-Sidama*. Rome, 1939.
Di Lauro, Raffaele. *Le Terre del Lago Tana*. Rome, 1936.
Durerelle, J.B. et al. *Italia e Francia*. Milan, 1981.
Eden, A. *Memoirs of Anthony Eden*. Boston, 1955.
Faraci, Giuseppe. *Etiopia: Guerra e Pace*. Turin, 1965.
Federazione Internazionale Tecnici Agricoli. *Atti dell'VIII Congresso di Agricoltura Tropicale*. Tripoli, 1939. Rome, 1941, 2 vols.
Filesi, Teobaldo. "Morte d'uomini", in Fabio Roversi Monaco, *Africa come un Mattino*. Bologna, 1969.
Flandin, P. *La Politique Française 1919-1940*. Paris, 1947.
Folchi, Alberto. *La Figura del Governatore Generale, Vice-Re d'Etiopia*. Tivoli, 1937.
Funke, Manfred. *Sanzioni e Cannoni*. Milan, 1972.
Gann, L. and Duignan, P. (eds). *History and Politics of Colonialism 1870-1914*, I. Cambridge, 1969.
Gazzera, Pietro. *Guerra Senza Speranza*. Rome, 1952.
Gennari, G. *Agricoltura nell'AOI*. Rome, 1938.
George, L. *Egypt Since Cromer*. New York, 1970.
Giglio, Carlo. *La Colonizzazione Demografica dell'Impero*. Rome, 1939.
Giglio, Carlo and Ladolini, E. *Guida delle Fonti per la Storia dell'Africa a Sud del Sahara Esistenti in Italia*. Zug, 1973.
Gilkes, P. *The Dying Lion*. London, 1975.
Gorham, G. *The Lion of Judah*. New York, n.d.
Greenfield, Richard. *Ethiopia: A New Political History*. London, 1965.
Guariglia, R. *Ricordi 1922-1946*. Naples, 1965.
Guarnieri, Felice. *Battaglie Economiche*. Milan, 1953, 2 vols.
Haile Selassie. *My Life and Ethiopia's Progress*. London, 1976.
Hargreaves, J.D. "West African States and the European Conquest" and T.O. Ranger, "African Reactions to the Imposition of Colonial Rule in East and Central Africa", in Gann L. and Duignan, P. (eds). *The History of Politics of Colonialism 1870-1914*. Cambridge, 1969.
Harris, Brice. *The United States and the Italo-Ethiopian Crisis*. Stanford, 1964.
Hess R. (Book Review), *Ethiopia: A New Political History*, R. Greenfield, (London, 1965) in *Forum*, 7, 1966.
Hess, R. *Ethiopia: The Modernization of Autocracy*. Ithaca, 1970.
Hess, R. *Italian Colonialism in Somalia*. Chicago, 1966.
Hoben, A. *Land Tenure Among the Amhara of Ethiopia*. Chicago, 1973.

Hole, M. *The Making of Rhodesia*. London, 1967.
Huntingford, G.W. *The Galla of Ethiopia*. London, 1953.
Istituto Agronomo per l'Africa Italiana. *Main Features of Italy's Action in Ethiopia 1936–1941*. Florence, 1946.
Istituto Fascista per l'Africa Italiana. *Annuario dell'Africa Italiana*. Rome, 1940.
Jones, A. H. and Monroe, Elizabeth. *A History of Ethiopia*. Oxford, 1962.
Konovaloff, T. *Con le Armate del Negus*. Bologna, 1938.
Lagardelle, Hubert. *Mission à Rome: Mussolini*. Paris, 1955.
Laval, Pierre. *The Diary of Pierre Laval*. New York, 1947.
Lessona, A. *L'Africa Italiana nel Primo Anno dell'Impero*. Rome, 1937.
Lessona, A. *Memorie*. Florence, 1958.
Lessona, A. *Un Ministro di Mussolini Racconta*. Milan, 1973.
Lessona, A. *Verso l'Impero*. Florence, 1939.
Levi, Carlo. *Cristo si è Fermato ad Eboli*. Milan, 1970.
Lloyd George, D. *Memoirs of the Peace Conference*. New Haven, 1939, 2 vols.
Lovato, Armando. *Per Una Associazione delle Famiglie Numerose*. Bologna, 1936.
Mack Smith, D. *Mussolini's Roman Empire*. New York, 1976.
Mack Smith, D. *Mussolini: A Biography*. New York, 1982.
Mannoni, O. *Psychologie de la Colonisation*. Paris, 1950.
Marcus, H. *Life and Times of Menelik II*. Oxford, 1975.
Markakis, J. *Ethiopia: Anatomy of a Traditional Polity*. Addis Ababa, 1975.
Marzocchi Alemanni, Nanni. *Colonizzazione Demografica*. Rome, 1938.
Masotti, Pier Marcello. *Ricordi d'Etiopia...* Milan, 1981.
Maugini, Armando. *Appunti sulle Prospettive Agricole*. Florence, 1941.
Meleselegn Anlei. *Fascism's Five Years Reign of Terror*. Addis Ababa, 1955. (In Amharic).
Meregazzi, Renzo. *Lineamenti della Legislazione per l'Impero*. Milan, 1939.
Miège, J.L. *L'Imperialisme Colonial Italien de 1870 à nos Jours*. Paris, 1968.
Milza, P. "Le Voyage de Pierre Laval à Rome en Janvier 1935", in J. B. Duroselle, *Italia e Francia*. Milan, 1981.
Mitchell, P. *African Afterthoughts*. London, 1954.
Monaco, Fabio Roversi. *Africa come un Mattino*. Bologna, 1969.
Mokler, A. *Il Mito Dell'Impero*. Milan, 1977.
Mondaini, Gennaro. *Legislazione Coloniale Italiana*. Milan, 1941, 2 vols.
Moreno, Mario M. *La Dottrina dell'Islam*. Bologna, 1940.
Mori, R. *Mussolini e La Conquista dell'Etiopia*. Florence, 1978.
Mosley, L. *Gideon Goes to War*. London, 1955.
Mosley, L. *Haile Selassie*. London, 1964.
Mussolini, Benito. *Storia di Un Anno*. Milan, 1944.
Mussolini, Rachele. *La Mia Vita con Benito*. Milan, 1948.
Nasi, Guglielmo. *Noi Italiani in Etiopia*. Rome, 1950.
Niliaticus. *Etiopia d'Oggi*. Rome, 1935.
Orsini, Agostino. *Problemi dell'Impero*. Rome, 1938.
Pankhurst, R. *Economic History of Ethiopia*. Addis Ababa, 1968.
Pankhurst, S. *British Policy in Eastern Ethiopia*. London, 1946.
Pankhurst, S. *Italy's War Crimes in Ethiopia*. London, n.d. [1947?]
Papini, Italo. *La Produzione dell'Etiopia*. Rome, 1938.

Perham, M. *The Government of Ethiopia*. Evanston, 1969.
Perria, Antonio, *Impero Mod. 91*. Milan, 1967.
Pesenti Del Thei, F. *Clima, Acqua, Terreno: Dove e Cosa si Produce e si Coltiva in AOI*. Venice, 1938, 2 vols.
Phelps-Stokes Foundation: Committee on Africa. *The War and Peace Aims, The Atlantic Charter and Africa from an American Standpoint*. New York, 1942.
Pignatelli, Luigi. *Africa Amica*. Caltanissetta, 1961.
Poggiali, C. *Diario AOI*. Milan, 1971.
Pollera, Alberto. *Il Regime della Proprietà Terriera in Etiopia*. Rome, 1913.
Preti, Luigi. *L'Impero Fascista: Africani ed Ebrei*. Milan, 1968.
Puglisi, Giuseppe. *Chi è dell'Eritrea*. Asmara, 1952.
Quartararo, R. *Roma tra Londra e Berlino*. Rome, 1980.
Rava, Massimo. *Nel Cuore dell'Arabia Felice*. Rome, 1927.
Rivera, Vincenzo. *Prospettive di Colonizzazione dell'AOI*. Rome, 1939.
Roatta, Mario. *Processo Roatta*. Rome, 1945.
Robertson, E. *Mussolini as Empire Builder*. New York, 1977.
Rochat, Giorgio. *Militari e Politici nella Preparazione della Campagna d'Etiopia*. Milan, 1971.
Rochat, G. *Il Colonialismo Italiano*. Turin, 1974.
Rodd, F. *British Military Administration of Occupied Territories in Africa*. London, 1948.
Rossi, G. *L'Africa Italiana Verso l'Indipendenza*. Milan, 1980.
Rubenson, S. *The Survival of Ethiopian Independence*. London, 1976.
Salvemini, G. *Preludio alla Seconda Guerra Mondiale*. Milan, 1967.
Sandford, C. *The Lion of Judah*. London, 1955.
Santagata, Ferdinando. *L'Harar*. Milan, 1940.
Santarelli, Enzo. *Storia del Regime Fascista*. Rome, 1967, 2 vols.
Santi, Nava. *Elementi di Dommatica della Colonizzazione*. Florence, 1937.
Santi, Nava. *Governo Coloniale*. Florence, 1938.
Scarin, Emilio. *L'Hararino*. Florence, 1942.
Segrè, C. *Libya: Fourth Shore*. Chicago, 1975.
Simoons, Federick. *Northwestern Ethiopia*. Madison, 1960.
Soulie, M. *La Vie Politique d'Eduard Herriot*. Paris, 1962.
Steer, G.L. *Caesar in Abyssinia*. Boston, 1937.
Steer, G.L. *Sealed and Delivered*. London, 1942.
Sykes, F. *With Plumer in Matabeleland*. Westminster, 1897.
Tadesse Zewalde. *The Years of Torment*. Addis Ababa, 1963. (In Amharic).
Taeger, Nicola. *Diritto di Roma nelle Terre Africane*. Padua, 1938.
Teruzzi, Attilio. *L'Africa Italiana nel Secondo Anno dell'Impero*. Milan, 1938.
Teruzzi, Paolo. *Prospettive di Colonizzazione nell'Impero*. Milan, 1938.
Thompson, G. *Front Line Diplomat*. London, 1959.
Toscano, Mario. *Pagine di Storia Diplomatica*. Milan, 1963.
Toschi, P. *Il Regime dei Culti*. Milan, 1939.
Tracchia, Ruggero. *Coloniali ed Ascari*. Milan, 1939.
Trimingham, Spencer. *Islam in Ethiopia*. New York, 1965.
Ullendorff, E. *The Ethiopians*. London, 1962.
Un Emigrato in AOI. *Lettera Aperta dell'AOI al Duce*. Asmara, January 1942.
Vansittart, R. *The Mist Procession: Autobiography of Lord Vansittart*.

London, 1958.
Vatikiotis, P.J. *The Modern History of Egypt*. New York, 1969.
Vavilov, N.L. *Origins, Variations, Immunity and Breeding of Cultivated Plants*. Waltham, 1951.
Villa Santa, N. and Scaglione, Attilio, et al., *Amedeo Duca D'Aosta*. Rome, 1954.
Villari, Luigi. *Storia Diplomatica del Conflitto Italo-Etiopico*. Bologna, 1943.
Virgin, Eric. *The Abyssinia I Knew*. London, 1936.
Waterfield, G. W. *Morning Will Come*. London, 1944.
Wingate, Orde. *Gideon Goes to War*. London, 1955.
Wondimneh Tilahun. *Egypt's Imperial Aspirations*. Addis Ababa, 1979.
Zaghi, Carlo. *L'Africa nella Coscienza Europea e l'Imperialismo Italiano*. Naples, 1973.
Zervos, Adrien. *L'Empire D'Ethiopie*. Alexandria, 1936.

IV. Periodicals

A. Articles

Askew, W. C. "The Secret Agreement Between France and Italy on Ethiopia", *Journal of Modern History*. (March 1953).
Baer, George. "Haile Selassie's Appeal to Edward VIII", *Cahiers D'Etudes Africaines*. 9 (1969).
Bairu Tafla. "Four Ethiopian Biographies", *Journal of Ethiopian Studies*. 7 (1969).
Bairu Tafla. "Three Portraits: Ato Asme Giorgis, Ras Gobena. . ." *Journal of Ethiopian Studies*. 5 (1967).
Crummey, D. "Initiatives and Objectives in Ethio-European Relations 1827–1862", *Journal of African History*. 15 (1974).
Duca Amedeo D'Aosta. "Diario 1922–1943", *Gente*, (February-September 1969).
Faldella, Emilio. "La Campagna d'Etiopia", *Storia Illustrata*. (May 1963).
Gebru Tareke. "Peasant Resistance in Ethiopia: the Case of Weyane", *Journal of African History*. 25 (1984).
Goglia, L. "Un aspetto dell'Azione Politica Italiana Durante La Campagna d'Etiopia: La Missione di Jacopo Gasparini nell'Amara", *Storia Contemporanea*. 8 (1977).
Goldman, A. "Sir Robert Vansittart's Search for Italian Cooperation Against Hitler", *Journal of Contemporary History*. 9 (1974).
Greenfield, R. "Interpretation of Oromo Nationality", *Horn of Africa*. 3 (1980).
Griaule, Marcel. "Le Probleme Ethiopien", *Bulletin de la Societe de'Etude et Informations Economiques*. (Supplement to September 1935).
Hess, Robert L. "Italian Imperialism in its Ethiopian Context", *International Journal of African Historical Studies*. 1 (1973).
Hess, Robert L. "Italy and Africa: Colonial Ambitions in the First World War", *Journal of African History*. 1 (1963).
Jesman, C. "Ethiopia: Test Case of Racial Integration", *Africa*. 23 (1968).
Mahteme Selassie, Wolde Maskal. "The Land System of Ethiopia", *Ethiopia Observer*. (Oct. 1957).

Moreno, M. "Il Regime Terriero Abissino nel Galla Sidama", *Rassegna Economica* (October 1967).
Mori, R. "Come Mussolini Giustificò l'Azione Armata Contro l'Etiopia", *Nuova Antologia*. 535 (October-December 1978).
Pankhurst, R. "Economic Verdict. . ." *Ethiopia Observer*. 14 (1971).
Pankhurst, R. "Fascist Racial Policy", *Ethiopia Observer*. 12 (1969).
Pankhurst, R. "The Secret History of the Italian Fascist Occupation of Ethiopia", *African Quarterly*. 16 (1977).
Pankhurst, R. "Italian Settlement Plans During the Fascist Occupation", *Ethiopia Observer*. 13 (1970).
Pankhurst, R. "The Ethiopian Patriots: The Lone Struggle", *Ethiopia Observer*, 13 (1970).
Pegolotti, B. "L'Attentato a Graziani", *Storia Illustrata*. 163 (1971).
Pegolotti, B. "Un Italiano alla Corte di Menelik", *Storia Illustrata*. 148 (1970).
Perfetti, F. "Alle Origini degli Accordi Laval-Mussolini. . ." *Storia Contemporanea*. 8 (1977).
Prinzi, D. "Il Regime Fondiazio e Colonizzazione in AOI", *Rassegna Economica*. (October 1937).
Quartararo, R. "Le Origini del Piano Hoare-Laval", *Storia Contemporanea*. 8 (1977).
Rouaud, Alain. "Les Contacts Secrets Italo–Ethiopiens du Printemps 1936. . .", *Africa*. 37 (1982).
Robertson, E. "Hitler and Sanctions: Mussolini and the Rhineland", *European Studies Review*. 9 (1977).
Robertson, J. "The British General Elections of 1935", *Journal of Contemporary History*. 9 (1974).
Robertson, J. "The Hoare-Laval Plan", *Journal of Contemporary History*. 10 (1975).
Rochat, G. "L'Attentato a Graziani", *Italia Contemporanea*. 118 (1975).
Rossini, C. Conti. "Il Regime Fondiario Indigeno in Etiopia", in Sindacato Tecnici Agricoli, *Agricoltura ed Impero*. Rome: 1937.
Salome Gebre Egziaber. "The Ethiopian Patriots 1936–1941", *Ethiopia Observer*. 12 (1969).
Salvemini, Gaetano. "Can Italy Live at Home?" *Foreign Affairs*. (January 1936).
Sarubbi, F.A. "Il Trattato di Pace con L'Italia e le Sorti dei Beni Italiani in Etiopia", *Rivista di Studi Politici Internazionali*. 17 (1950).
Sbacchi, A. "Italy and the Treatment of the Ethiopian Aristocracy", *International Journal of African Historical Studies*. 10 (1977).
Sbacchi, A. "Legacy of Bitterness: Poison Gas and Atrocities in the Italo–Ethiopian War", *Geneva-Africa*. 12 (1974).
Sbacchi, A. "The Price of Empire: Toward an Enumeration of Italian Casualties in Ethiopia", *Ethiopianist Notes*. 2 (1978).
Sebhat G. Egziabheir. "Tekle's Struggle", *Yekatit*. 3 (1973); 4 (1973); 5 (1973). (In Amharic; dates given according to the Ethiopian calendar)
Sereni, Angelo. "La Fine del Conflitto Italo-Etiopico ed il Diritto Internazionale", *Rivista di Diritto Internazionale*. 4 (1936).
Serra, E. "La Questione Italo-Etiopica alla Conferenza di Stresa", *Affari Esteri*. 34 (1977).

Shorrock, W. "The Jouvenel Mission to Rome. . ." Paper presented at the American Historical Association, New York, 1979.

Udina, M. "Il Governorato di Addis Abeba", *Giustizia Amministrativa*. 1 (1937).

Watt, D. C. "The Secret Laval-Mussolini Agreement of 1935 on Ethiopia", *Middle East Journal*. (Winter 1961).

Weerts, M. "The Late Mr. Antoinin Besse", *Journal of Ethiopian Studies*. 8 (1970).

Wingate, O. C. "An Appreciation of the Ethiopian Campaign", *Ethiopia Observer*. 16 (1973).

B. List of Periodicals Used

Afrique Française (Paris), 1939.
Annali Dell'Africa Italiana (Milan), 1937–41.
Autarchia Alimentare (Rome - Milan), 1938–9.
Azione Coloniale (Rome), 1938.
Bollettino (periodical used solely for the internal use of the Ministry of Italian Africa, Rome), 1936–9.
Colonie (Rome: Published and distributed only to newspapers and periodicals by the Istituto Fascista per l'Africa Italiana), 1936–40.
La Conquista della Terra (Rome), 1937–40.
Consulente Coloniale (Rome), 1939–41.
Corriere Imperiale (Rome), 1939–40.
Corriere Mercantile (Genoa); 1938–9.
Difesa Della Razza (Rome), 1938–40.
Eco Della Stampa (Milan), 1939.
Espansione Imperiale (Rome), 1938–40.
Esquire (Chicago), 1936.
Ethiopia Observer (Addis Ababa), 1963–74.
Ethiopian Star (Addis Ababa: Published by the British authorites during 1941)
Famiglia Cristiana (Tripoli), 1934–40.
Gente (Milan), 1969.
Illustrazione Coloniale (Milan), 1937–40.
Impero ed Autarchia (Rome), 1939–40.
Impero Italiano (Milan), 1938–40.
Impero del Lavoro (Addis Ababa), 1938–9.
Italia Coloniale (Rome), 1938–40.
Italia Oltremare (Rome), 1937–40.
Newsweek (Washington, DC), 1941.
Notiziario Coloniale (Rome), 1937–40.
Rassegna Economica dell'Africa Italiana (Rome), 1936–41.
Rassegna Italiana, Politica, Letteraria ed Artistica (Rome), 1939.
Rassegna Sociale Dell'Africa Italiana (Rome), 1939–42.
Rivista Giuridica del Medio ed Estremo Oriente e Giustizia Coloniale (Rome), 1938.

Newspapers

Buenos Aires Herald, 1937.
Corriere Dell'Impero (Addis Ababa), 1937–40.
Corriere Eritreo (Asmara), 1937–40.
Daily Herald (London), 1936.
Daily Mail (London), 1936.
Evening Standard (London), 1936.
Il Falco (Dessie), 1937.
Gazzetta Del Popolo (Rome), 1938.
Gazzetta di Venezia, 1940.
Il Giornale (Tunis), 1937–9.
Il Giornale di Addis Abeba, 1936.
Il Giornale dell'Ascari dell'Amara (Gondar), 1940.
Il Giornale D'Italia (Rome), 1936–40.
Il Giornale di Sicilia (Palermo), 1940.
Il Giorno (Turin), 1968.
Hatikvah (Alexandria), 1936.
L'Italiano di Tusnisi, 1937–9.
Le Matin (Paris), 1938.
Il Messagero (Rome), 1936–40.
La Nazione (Florence), 1939.
New York Times, 1936–9.
Ordre (Paris), 1939.
Osservatore Romano (Vatican City), 1938–9.
La Pattuglia (Jimma), 1937.
Il Popolo D'Italia (Milan), 1939.
Il Popolo di Roma, 1937–40.
Il Resto Del Carlino (Bologna), 1938–9.
La Stampa (Turin), 1937.
Sunday Dispatch (London), 1938.
Times (London), 1936.
Times of India (Bombay), 1937.

Index

Addis Ababa 4-5, 15, 26, 29-30, 33, 85, 91-2, 149, 167-8, 170-1, 182-3, 201, 204, 215, 218
Anglo-Ethiopian Agreements *1942, 1944* 218, 222-3
aristocracy, Ethiopian, and Italy 129-44
    Afework, Gebre Jesus, Ambassador in Rome 28-36
    Araya, *Ras* Gugsa, grandson of Yohannes IV 130-1
    Aussa, Mohammed Jaja Amfari, Sultan of 26, 130, 137, 163, 165, 221
    Burru, *Dejaz* Ayalu 36, 104, 130, 132, 136, 142-3
    Getachew, *Ras* 124-5, 132, 136-7
    Gugsa, *Dejaz* Haile Selassie 14, 130-1, 133-4, 136, 139, 141-2, 151, 174
    Hailu, *Ras* 29, 35-6, 130-2, 135, 139, 141-3, 183, 185
    Jifar, *Abba* 130, 132-3
    Jiotte, *Dejaz* Hosanna 90, 136
    Jiotte, *Dejaz* Yohannes 136
    Jobir Abdullah, *Abba* 36, 132-3, 135, 139, 163-4
    Kassa, *Ras* 5, 25-6, 32, 104, 220, 231
    Kebbede, *Ras* 132, 136-7, 139
    Seyum, *Ras* 25-6, 36, 104, 130-1, 133-4, 136-7, 141-3, 220, 231
    Wassen, Asfaw, heir to throne 29, 32, 36, 122, 124-6, 205
atrocities and repression, Italian
    Addict, slaughter at 196-7
    Admasse, *Kenazmatch*, killing of 203
    Debra Lebanos, Monastery, massacre of 194-5
    Desta, *Ras*, defeat and execution 186-9
    executions after attempt on Graziani 189-93
    hermits, soothsayers, wizards, etc., shooting of 194
    Kassa brothers, shooting of 184-5
    Lekept, massacre of 181-2
    Petros, (Bishop) Abuna, shooting of 184
    poison gas, use of 5, 6, 8, 18, 25-7, 60, 186, 200, 231, 236-7
colonial/colonization, Italian 95-119, 211, 233-8
    Academy 90-1
    Administration 43-4, 66-8
    Agencies 96
        Centuria Agricola di Pre-Colonizzazione 98, 109-10; *Ente Aosta* 106; *Ente Puglia* 96-7, 104-5, 108-12, 113-14; *Ente Romagna* 96-7. 104-5, 108-11, 113; *Ente Thesauro De Rege* 106, 108-10; *Ente Veneto* 96-7, 105-6, 108-10, 112-13; *Opera Nazionale Combattenti* 106-11, 113-14; *Pattuglie del Grano* 98
    civil servants/officers/personnel 55, 78-83, 85-91, 106
        Cortese, Guido 190-1, 193; Daodiace, Giuseppe, Vice-Governor-General 82, 221
    finance and investment 71-6, 107-8, 111-14, 178
    General Council 68-9
    Governors 43, 56, 66-9, 72, 85
        Biroli, Pirzio, of Amhara 50-2, 81, 136, 170; Cerulli, Enrico, of Harar 27-8, 44, 59, 63, 193, 237; De Feo, Vincenzio, of Eritrea 50-1
    immigration, Italian 7, 9, 37, 95-7, 106-14, 205, 211, 229
    land appropriation 101-6
    military agricultural colonization 95-9, 109-10

ministerial-bureaucratic interference 69-70
residency system 85-91, 93, 141, 147, 196-7
share-cropping agreement 100-1
troops, Ethiopian 36-7, 159, 162, 164-5, 179, 181-2, 186-7, 189, 211-2
see also: atrocities and repression; Policy, Italian/Islamic; road construction/network; Viceroys

diplomacy, pre-invasion
British Peace Ballot, effect of 13
Eden's proposals 14
Hoare-Laval plan 17-21
Laval-Mussolini agreement 8-11
League of Nations Council of Five 16-17
Maffey Report 12-13
Stresa Conference 11-12, 26, 230
Tripartite Powers/Treaty 4-5, 8-10, 13-16, 20, 34

East Africa, Italian 12, 24-5, 43-4, 51-2, 55-6, 66-9, 71-3, 76, 78, 85-92, 96, 98, 101, 111-13, 139-40, 176, 178, 211, 232-3, 236, 240
Egypt 12-13, 164, 212, 214, 221-3
Eritrea(ns) 4, 7-9, 13, 15, 19, 66, 85, 92, 173-4, 186, 193, 199, 213
Ethiopia(n)
agricultural potential 95-6, 99-100, 238
cash exports 95, 99-100
census 86
chiefs 14-15, 18-19, 35-6, 61, 71, 83, 87, 121-6, 129-44, 151, 168-9, 176, 204, 217, 219-20, 233 *see also*: aristocracy, Ethiopian
chiefs, lesser 18, 130, 146-54
collaborators 35-7, 148-9, 159, 220
constitution 5
as Italian protectorate/mandate 8, 13-20, 27-9, 33-4, 44, 122, 133, 233
Muslims 5, 35, 157, 161-5, 213 *see also*: policy, Islamic
in nineteenth and early twentieth century 3-6
Orthodox Church 36, 56, 162-4, 182, 194-6, 204
resistance 37, 49, 50, 52, 60, 68, 95-114, 121-9, 135, 141-2, 144, 148, 153, 160, 176-205, 224, 237
see also: opposition, Ethiopian; Patriots
slavery, elimination of 5, 14, 87, 169

State Bank 5, 47
youth 32, 34, 204
see also: peoples/regions of Ethiopia
Ethiopia, invasion of/re-occupation of
League of Nations and sanctions 13, 18, 20, 25-6, 29-30, 32, 34, 35, 122, 134, 230-2
military operations 7-8, 18, 24-6, 33-4
negotiations, Italo-Ethiopian secret 27-30

Fascism 7, 95, 167-74, 205, 229, 232, 236
France 3, 7-9, 11-12, 202, 204, 225, 230-1

Germany 7-10, 18, 20, 26, 124, 230
Great Britain 3, 7-8, 11-12, 17-21, 28, 38, 123, 126, 161, 181, 211-25, 230-1, 233
see also: politicians and diplomats, British

Haile Selassie, Emperor 3, 5, 9, 14-17, 20, 24, 26-30, 32, 34, 101, 104, 121-6, 129-31, 142, 176, 200, 202-3, 205, 212-25, 231-2

Italy/Italian 3-5, 8, 15, 24, 27-30, 33-4, 44, 78, 87
see also: aristocracy, Ethiopian and; atrocities and repression; colonial/colonization; East Africa, Italian; military personnel, Italian; policy, Italian; politicians and diplomats, Italian; Viceroys

Japan 17, 18, 223

Libya 8, 9, 173-4, 190-1, 194, 212, 215, 222-3

military personnel, British
Cunningham, General Alan 214-15
Platt, General William 212-14
Wavell, General Archibald 213-14
Wingate, Major Orde 214
military personnel, Italian
Bonaccorsi, General Arcovaldi 81, 203
Cavallero, General Ugo, C-in-C Italian troops 43, 50, 60, 63, 197-200, 237
Corvo, Captain Salvatore, Resident of Bahar Dar 196-7
Gabba, General Melchiade 29
Mezzetti, General Ottorino 49, 60, 83, 92, 148, 150, 160
Mischi, General Archimede 186, 189-90
Nasi, General Gugliemo 49, 59-61, 143,

169, 201-5, 220, 223, 237
Petretti, General Armando, Vice-
  Governor of Ethiopia 43, 49, 190
Tracchia, General Ruggero 185
military situation, Italian 56, 61, 95-9,
  211-12, 216-17, 220-4, 238
Mussolini, Benito 7, 8, 12-21, 24, 27-30,
  33, 36, 46, 121-6, 134-5, 161-2, 164,
  167, 186, 190, 212, 229-31, 234-5

opposition, Ethiopian, to Italians
  Black Lions 34-5
  Holetta graduates 34-5, 182, 192, 204
  see also: Ethiopian resistance; Patriots

Patriots 34-5, 38, 50, 92, 97, 121, 129,
  135, 141-4, 148, 153, 160, 170-1,
  176-205, 212, 214, 218, 224-6, 238
  Aragai, *Ras* Abebe 33, 57-8, 97, 141,
    148-9, 182, 193, 197, 199-205,
    215-17, 219-20
  Asfaw, Zaude 197-8
  Asgadom, Mogas 193, 195, 237
  Auraris, *Dejaz* 197, 199, 200
  Confu, *Abba* 195
  Domtu, *Ras* Desta 25, 36, 104, 182,
    186-9, 195, 204
  Deboch, Abraham 193, 195, 237
  Duki, *Ras* Gerarsa 198-9
  Garramu, *Fitaurari* 187-8
  Haywariat, *Blata* Tekle Wolde 182,
    197, 213, 220, 225
  Imru, *Ras* 25-6, 34-6, 131, 181-2, 185,
    196, 204, 214, 220
  Kassa, *Dejaz* Aberra 104, 182-5, 201
  Kassa, *Dejaz* Wonde Wassen 104, 182,
    184-5, 201
  Mangasha, *Dejaz* 198-9, 213
  Mariam, *Dejaz* Fikre 184, 186, 198
  Mariam, *Dejaz* Gebre 36, 186-9
  Merid, *Dejaz* Beyenne 186-9
  Mulug(h)eta, *Ras* 25-6, 35, 177, 231
  Petros, *Abuna* 182, 184
  Shilleshi, Mesfin 193, 197
  Wubshet, *Dejaz* Negash 198-9, 213
Peoples/regions of Ethiopia
  Amhara 5, 20, 43-4, 66, 85, 91-2,
    95-6, 101-2, 104-5, 147-9, 150,
    157-63, 180, 190-6, 200, 221
  Arussi 15, 92, 188
  Begemder 3, 29, 199, 225
  Danakil/Dankalia 5, 19, 29, 132, 162,
    164-5
  Gojam 3, 5, 26, 29, 143, 148, 178,
    198-9, 204, 212-14, 218, 224
  Gondar 26, 82, 168, 170, 211, 220
  Harar 4, 10, 14, 19-20, 25, 29, 60-1,
    66, 85, 92-3, 96, 103-5, 133,
    148-9, 158-9, 162, 168, 180,
    198-200
  Massawa 4, 164-5, 229
  Ogaden 5, 12-15, 19, 29, 165, 213
  Oromo 5, 28, 30, 35-7, 132, 160-2,
    165, 181, 201, 204, 213, 218-19,
    221, 223-5
  Oromo-Sidamo 3-4, 43-4, 66, 82, 85,
    92-3, 95-6, 102-6, 146-7, 149-50,
    153, 157-62, 164-5, 180, 198-200
  Shoa 3-5, 29, 34, 35, 66, 85, 91-2,
    180, 198-205
  Tigre 3-4, 18-20, 24, 29, 92, 147,
    198, 204, 224
policy, Italian
  colonial 33, 37-8, 55, 60-1, 71, 85-92,
    100-5, 123, 129-44, 149, 157-60,
    167-74, 176, 181, 184-90, 200,
    202-4, 215, 220-1, 224, 229,
    234-46
  Islamic 14, 36, 56, 135-6, 161-5
  racial 167-74
politicians and diplomats, British
  Baldwin Administration 18
  Barton, Sir Stanley 15-32
  Churchill, Winston 212, 214, 216-18
  Drummond, Eric 122-3
  Eden, Anthony 13-16, 212-14, 217-18,
    222
  Halifax, Lord 124
  Hoare, Samuel 12, 17-21, 25, 34, 231
  Mitchell, Philip 219, 222
  Petersen, Maurice 18-19
  Vansittart, Robert 18-20, 231
politicians and diplomats, Italian
  Castagna, Sebastiano, negotiator with
    Ethiopians 187-9, 201-2
  Ciano, Galeazzo, Minister of Propaganda
    10, 49, 53, 123, 125
  De Bono, Emilio, Minister of Colonies
    8, 18, 24, 46-7, 52, 71, 147, 161,
    223, 231
  Di Revel, Minister of Finance 43, 90
  Grandi, Dino, Minister of Foreign
    Affairs 9, 19, 122, 229, 231
  Lessona, Alessandro, Minister of
    Colonies 29, 46-53, 66-8, 122, 169,
    184-5, 231
  Teruzzi, Attilio, Minister of Africa
    59, 61-3, 202, 223, 237

railways 5, 7, 9, 14-15, 25, 29, 33, 183-4
Red Sea 9, 12-13, 223, 229
road construction/network 15, 37, 199,
  239, 242

Ethiopia Under Mussolini

Somalia, British 66, 85
   French 9, 229
   Italian 7-9, 13, 15, 138, 173-4
Sudan 12, 212-13, 224, 225
Suez Canal 17, 29, 230

United States of America 18, 223, 230, 235-6

Viceroys of Ethiopia, Italian
   Aosta, Amedeo, Duke of 37, 49, 51, 55-64, 67-8, 72, 76, 83, 86, 140, 169, 174, 194, 196, 198, 201-5, 212-13, 216, 220-1, 223
   Badoglio, Marshall Pietro 8, 21, 24-6, 29-30, 46-8, 134, 231-2, 234
   Graziani, General Rodolfo 21, 25, 33, 35-7, 46-52, 56, 66-7, 72-3, 123, 137-9, 161-2, 181, 183, 185-96, 201, 205, 234, 237
Victor Emanuel, King and Emperor 15, 33, 43, 233